The Challenge of Crime

Henry Ruth

Kevin R. Reitz

THE CHALLENGE OF CRIME

Rethinking Our Response

HARVARD UNIVERSITY PRESS

Cambridge, Massachusetts

London, England

Copyright © 2003 by Henry Ruth and Kevin R. Reitz
Printed in the United States of America

First Harvard University Press paperback edition, 2006

Library of Congress Cataloging-in-Publication Data

Ruth, Henry S.
The challenge of crime : rethinking our response / Henry Ruth, Kevin R. Reitz.
p. cm.
Includes bibliographical references and index.
ISBN 0-674-00891-X (cloth)
ISBN 0-674-02106-1 (pbk.)
1. Criminal justice, Administration of—United States.
2. Crime—United States.
3. Crime prevention—United States.
I. Reitz, Kevin R.   II. Title.

HV9950 .R88 2003
364.973—dc21   2002038731

For Deb

For Susi

Contents

Figures

Acknowledgments

We gained many insights from colleagues and experts in the crime response field who kindly agreed to read drafts of our individual chapters or the entire manuscript. We deeply appreciate their friendship and selfless effort. The book is stronger for their input, and perhaps weaker for the advice we chose not to incorporate. Readers of earlier material included David Burnham, Nancy Carlston, John Carnevale, John Eck, Delbert Elliott, Richard Frase, Herman Goldstein, Susan Jones, Benjamin Lerner, Jens Ludwig, Shadd Maruna, Deborah Mathieu, Scott Menard, Norval Morris, Anne Morrison Piehl, Carolyn Ramsey, Curtis Reitz, William Stuntz, Jane Thompson, Michael Tonry, Philip Weiser, Ahmed White, and Frank Zimring. Our editors at Harvard University Press, Kathleen McDermott and Julie Carlson, helped us to craft each page.

We are also grateful for unflagging support received from the University of Colorado Law School, including the work of library technician Manuel Santos and research assistants Levi Brooks, Peryn Harmon, Kristen Miller, Michael Shea, Melissa Shearer, and Naomi Wyatt—all of whom were coordinated and assisted by assistant director of the law library Jane Thompson and faculty assistants Cynthia Carter, Linda Speigler, Diana Stahl, Kay Wilkie, and Cindy Winn. We also extend our appreciation for the timely and expert assistance of the staffs of the many libraries at the various schools of the University of Arizona, particularly Director Michael Chiorazzi and access services librarian Maureen Garmon at the law school library. In the late going, the Institute of Criminology at the University of Cambridge, and its library staff, provided invaluable aid. In addition, we are grateful for the data and information provided to us promptly by the Tucson, Arizona Police Department; the Police Executive Research Forum; the Police Foundation; the Bureau of Alcohol, Tobacco, and Firearms; the

Drug Enforcement Administration; and the White House Office of National Drug Control Policy—as well as for research articles forwarded to us at our request by the National Rifle Association. Finally, we thank our agent, Robin Straus.

Introduction

When a nation abruptly breaks a historical pattern in its public, political, and intellectual reaction to a social problem, that radical change merits close scrutiny—and ultimately demands a considered reexamination. For American crime response policy, exactly such a disjunction occurred in the last three decades of the twentieth century. The stage was perhaps set in the 1960s. During this era, assassinations, public demonstrations, urban riots, the Vietnam conflict, and the restructuring of the rights of women and minorities all occurred just as the postwar baby boomers started to enter their volatile teenage years, giving rise to a dominant (and sometimes threatening) youth culture.

Within this context of social tumult, a sharp rise in crime—particularly violent crime such as willful homicide and armed robbery—provided much reason for alarm. According to the only statistics available at the time, national murder rates doubled between 1957 and 1970, while the rate of robberies and assaults appeared to be rising even faster. In reaction, President Lyndon Johnson convened a national crime commission, which in 1967 reported a comprehensive blueprint for American crime response. In retrospect, this document was one of the last testimonials of a liberal era of crime and social welfare policy. The report embraced ideas such as the decreased use of U.S. prisons, the rehabilitation of offenders, and the increased commitment to building life opportunities for the nation's most disadvantaged citizens. Within several years of the Johnson Commission's report, however, a new conservative revolution in crime response policy began to sweep the country with an entirely different agenda.

This book looks at events since 1967 and what they portend for all Americans, including crime victims, offenders, and those who make a living responding to crime. In casting inquiry back more than three decades, we hope to encourage readers to think prospectively on a similarly long time horizon. We should not be focused exclusively on the headlines of the week, or the next one or two legislative cycles. Now is the time to consider the major elements of crime response that the United States should be assembling through the ensuing three decades.

An endemic weakness of crime policy in the past has been the search for illusory short-term solutions, which has led to many missteps and missed opportunities. One critical deficit in long-term investment has been the failure adequately to learn and assess the results of anticrime initiatives. Severe shortfalls in knowledge and data have plagued every facet of American crime response, starting even with good information about the level of crime. The public perception of the national crime picture has been formed most strongly by the FBI's reports of how much change occurs each year in state and local crime, as reported to the police by residents. According to the FBI, the rate of violent crime tripled between 1967 and 1991 (quadrupling in some categories), and then sank by the year 2000 to a rate that was still more than double that of 1967. These numbers, however, do not square with other crime indicators, such as the willful homicide rate or surveys of victims, which suggest that violent crime at the beginning of the twenty-first century had dropped below its peak positions of the late 1960s and early 1970s. Although all of the separate reports finally began to reflect a downturn of serious crime after 1992, the American public was still informed on separate occasions in 2001 that serious crime had leveled off in 2000 (FBI) and dropped precipitously in 2000 (the national victims survey). Indeed, one source said rape incidents were about the same in 1999 and 2000 (FBI) and the other said rape had dropped by one-third (the victims survey). Imagine designing a policy response to such data.

Although the FBI and victims survey crime statistics often disagree on to what extent rates of offending have been going up and down, they often concur on the general trend. Both sources confirm that crime rates have oscillated in the last three decades. Serious crimes fell off a bit in the mid-1970s, turned upward in the late 1970s, dropped in the first half of the 1980s, headed back up through the early 1990s, and fell through the year 2000. FBI statistics for 2001 showed a small increase in reported serious crime, but the victims survey for the same year showed a continued decrease.

In stark contrast to this up-and-down picture of crime, the nation's response to crime has been uniform for nearly thirty years. Indeed, American crime policy has become progressively more severe and at variance with the pre-1970 response. An abbreviated list of developments offers a sense of the weight of cumulative and formidable change. Since the 1970s, America has:

- increased both the number of statutory criminal offenses and the severity of penalties attached to them;
- increased the numbers of people in short-term and long-term incarceration, on probation, and on parole;
- removed from judges much of their discretionary power in sentencing;
- addressed the drug problem through mandatory minimum sentences, and raised drug possession arrests to 80 percent of total drug arrests, with an increasing share devoted to marijuana use;
- reinstated the death penalty;
- given victims a new range of rights in the criminal courts;
- created the belief that police can control crime by aggressive order maintenance in high-crime neighborhoods—including the creation of new loitering crimes and frequent stops, frisks, and arrests for lower-level crimes—and by reaching out to the community in various ways;
- expanded the private sector's crime prevention and crime detection roles in a wide variety of ways to protect individuals, their families, neighborhoods, and businesses;
- moved away from the treatment of juvenile offenders as children and increasingly processed and punished many of them more like adult criminals;
- brought into public view, as an answer to charges of racial discrimination, detailed arguments that blacks are punished at a far higher rate than whites because much higher percentages of blacks than whites commit violent crimes.

As a consequence of these and other developments, in each of the decades from 1980 to 1990 and 1990 to 2000, America added more inmates to its prisons than the nation had added in the entire hundred-year period from 1880 to 1980. The 1990s alone were the highest prison-growth decade in American history. The United States in 1999 had more state and federal drug prisoners than total prisoners added in the hundred years from 1880 to 1980. And in just thirty years, from 1970 to 2000, the prison population increased more than 500 percent even though the nation's total population rose only about 35 percent. According to the U.S. Justice Department, white males born since 1990 have a 4.4 percent lifetime risk of serving a prison sentence; young black males in this same age group have a 28.5 percent lifetime risk.

The radical changes in incarceration began at the same time that the concept and practices of offender rehabilitation were repudiated. In the rush toward short-term crime reduction through temporary confinement, Americans seemed to forget that virtually all criminals would some day leave their crowded cages. As of the early 2000s, roughly 600,000 prisoners each year are released back to their home communities, most of them with little preparation to rejoin the world of freedom.

The leading proponent of the revolution in American crime response in the 1970s was James Q. Wilson. His remarkable 1975 book, *Thinking about Crime,* preached to the public that a new and more punitive crime policy was morally the right path for the nation. In Wilson's portrayal, adult and juvenile criminals were no longer the deprived have-nots of the rehabilitation era. Poverty did not cause crime; youthful and adult criminals chose crime because it was easier and more profitable than working. Raising punitive costs through long-term prison sentences quickly became the eagerly received Wilsonian message. This message remained dominant into the twenty-first century.

We now face the question of whether America will see the need for important changes in direction now that crime dropped for nearly a decade and all indices of punishment and control have been ratcheting upward. Although policymakers are ever reluctant to champion new directions when results seem to be favorable, budgetary constraints now make change inevitable. But the social and cultural reaction to good news about crime includes a certain resistance, or indifference, to attempts to understand the reasons for the good results.

Those who have searched for the causes of crime, meanwhile, have produced little agreement, particularly on how close a relationship exists, if any, between levels of crime and different forms of socially acceptable activity by police, courts, prisons, and supervised release. Professional researchers, for example, have assigned a dizzying range of reasons for the "crime drop": demographics, social and cultural changes in drug use and drug choices (including alcohol consumption), aggressive policing, incarceration, legalization of abortion, reduced lead poisoning, new forms of gun regulation, the wider availability of guns for defensive use, youth programs, the status of the economy until 2001, and basic cultural changes civilizing the populace and steering us away from violent conduct.

While America has radically changed its thinking about crime and crime response since 1970, it has also taken important steps to expand its knowledge base concerning crime and the criminal justice system. Compared with the information available to policymakers in 1967, certain areas of controversy are now much better illuminated. With a patient and redoubled commitment to continued improvements in the next few decades, there is reason to be optimistic that crime policy can be pushed toward rational, information-driven initiatives and can free itself, bit by bit, from sheer guesswork, political rhetoric, and pervasive emotionalism.

In this book we examine select major areas of American crime response policy that both require, and have the potential for, meaningful change. We seek to provide a useful framework of facts and considerations bearing upon the central issues in crime and the nation's response to crime. We have omitted a number of areas in which tradition is too stubborn to yield, or thinking is too narrow, or conditions are too overcrowded, to allow for the prospect of reform in more than minimal ways. For example, the past thirty-five years of both criminal court processing and the prison caging process have produced none of the thinking or capabilities necessary to introduce significant basic change in either. In addition, the reality and future threat of international terrorist activity on American soil presents an unprecedented challenge for various federal, state, and local agencies, some of which are part of the crime response complex. No one can now predict with any accuracy the form and extent of their long-term roles, particularly at the state and local levels, in responding to terrorist threats.

In comprehending the hodgepodge of priorities, activities and imponderables that now make up American crime policy, we find it useful to deviate from the accepted terminology. First, we avoid the term "criminal justice system" because it limits our view to formal government processes such as police, courts, incarceration, and offender release. It is also misleading because it implies that we now move day to day toward the attainment of justice. In contrast to these connotations, private security efforts, though vastly neglected by the research world, should receive as much policy attention and probably already receive more resources than governmental law enforcement. And a wide array of government departments, social programming, and neighborhood efforts operate independently with their own anticrime objectives.

Further, the use of the term "system" implies a basic compact in which all participants are synchronized and motivated by similar priorities. In fact, the system in criminal justice works in the opposite way. If police make too many misdemeanor arrests, courts or prosecutors dismiss them. If prisons are too crowded, prison administrators try to throw the burden on local jails or arrange for early release of prisoners. The reality is that we have "street enforcement" by police that is mostly unregulated by any formal processing and review, and a crowded assembly line for court processing of those who are formally accused of criminal acts. And we do all of this with approximate rather than perfect accuracy. Coordination and consensus are important goals, just as "justice" is an indispensable aspiration, but we ought not mislead ourselves with labels that suggest the nation currently possesses a satisfactory "justice system."

In describing the reality we must work with, we prefer the alternative phrase "crime response complex." No one debates the social necessity to control violence and other serious crime, or the need to devise a comprehensive response. Everyone agrees that the nation's response to crime already proceeds through a large "complex," that is, a group of kaleidoscopic components bonded together loosely in a crime response mission but not necessarily working together under some coherent plan or uniform organizational direction. It is crucial to recognize that, in a democratic society, tensions and cross-purposes will always exist within a crime response complex.

We identify four substantive goals that the crime response complex should try to achieve, and a fifth goal directed to the proper size and scope of the complex itself. Each objective, interrelated with the others, represents an ultimate ideal that can never be fully achieved, but that may nevertheless serve as a guiding aspiration.

The first goal is to reduce the amount of crime in America. To achieve this objective, crime response must reach beyond such immediate reactions as arrests, prosecutions, and punishments. Adequate responses to guns used to commit crimes, illicit drugs, juvenile offenders, and alcohol abuse all include actions unrelated to traditional criminal processing. Executive branch agencies and private security mechanisms help solve crime problems, as do civil processes, administrative regulation, prevention concepts and programming, physical and mental health professionals, and other treatment specialists. Other possible avenues include the budding restorative justice concept that draws on alternative dispute resolution mechanisms borrowed from the civil law context.

The second goal of crime response is to confront the debilitative presence of fear. A fearful society is divided, distrustful, and distracted. In the late 1990s, mass school shootings caused parents in America to fear for the safety of their children. Such vivid fears persisted every day even though the incidence of juvenile gun violence, violence in schools, and all juvenile violent crime had been dropping for at least five years. Realizing that a wide scope is essential to both the reality and perception of effectiveness in crime response, skilled school administrators called on resources outside the traditional criminal justice system. They invoked school prevention programs, parent education about school crime trends, early problem detection, and crisis response planning.

The achievement of justice is a third goal, and includes justice for the crime victim, potential future victims, and the offender. This goal contemplates the formation of just laws, the creation of fair processes for their enforcement, and the evenhanded administration of those processes. We recognize that people often differ on the meaning of "justice" in any of these applications, and that this goal will be a continual source of dispute. Even as people heatedly debate whether long or short prison sentences are better, whether the death penalty is just or morally wrong, whether drug use should be criminalized or legalized, whether the police should be constantly aggressive, and whether we should spend more on punishment or prevention, everyone shares the starting position that crimes such as robbery, serious assault, burglary, rape, and murder require forceful reactions from a civilized society. The pursuit and achievement of basic justice remains something no society can afford to abdicate, no matter how contested the terrain.

Fourth, the crime response complex must operate in a way that engenders broad faith in its moral legitimacy. It is not enough merely to "do justice" in the abstract. The complex must also earn a broad-based reputation, within all sectors of society, for its good faith and evenhanded operations. From this viewpoint, the discovery that portions of our society—such as many African Americans today—do not trust or respect the police and the criminal courts should be deeply disturbing. Just as the fear of crime is a destructive phenomenon independent of the reality of crime, perceptions of injustice are corrosive social forces in and of themselves. If government power is widely deemed to be illegitimate, resistance to that power is easily seen as justified or even required. At the very least, strong perceptions of illegitimacy cut off cooperative synergies between government, community, and private actions.

A fifth and final goal addresses the proper scope of the crime response complex itself. Criminal law has become society's wastebasket for an enormous range of conduct deemed by groups of people to be "wrong." To our knowledge, no state or federal legislative session in the past fifty years has concluded without the creation of new substantive crimes. Indeed, the nation seems unable to deem something morally wrong without also making it criminal. Politicians must start resisting such impulses. Given the long-term consequences and elaborate machinery of the criminal law, we should avoid using it solely as a rhetorical platform. We believe that conduct should invoke the criminal sanction only if it is severe enough to truly merit condemnation as "criminal"; if society needs the criminal sanction in order to control that conduct; and if society provides the resources and mandate to vigorously enforce the new criminal statute.

Addressing crime and crime response is difficult because almost all aspects of these subjects are laden with extreme emotions, deeply entrenched ideologies, opportunities for political exploitation, and the human craving for simple and forceful solutions. In writing this book, we were determined to compartmentalize and resist these temptations. As a result, we have produced a series of findings and recommendations that fit neither traditional liberal nor conservative frameworks. The book will likely anger, or challenge, people who adhere strongly to either conventional viewpoint. In addition, there is a lack of neatness, or theoretical elegance, that necessarily comes with an approach that attempts to bypass ideological divisiveness with empirically informed policies. Answers are partial because probably no one will ever know why crime waves appear and then disappear in a society as diverse, as free, and as wealthy as ours.

We have endeavored to escape confounding ideology, but we also write in a spirit of humility. The complexity and intractability of America's ever-changing crime problems demand a long-term supply of imagination and flexibility, including the power to acknowledge that past beliefs should periodically be retested with experience. Our discussion challenges many existing beliefs and practices, in the hope that positive change can be realized in both the immediate and the more distant future.

1

Crime and Punishment: A Brief American History

The crime response complex, as we know it in the twenty-first century, is in many ways profoundly anachronistic. All of the formal building blocks of the complex were created and took shape in the nineteenth century, during a remarkable period of institutional fermentation. Ever since, we have been subsisting with the matériel of that earlier time.

If we could go back to the days just before the creative surge got under way, to take a "snapshot" of the institutions of the early 1800s, we would recognize very little about the arrangements for criminal law enforcement and punishment. There were trial courts and juries, to be sure, but little else with which we can identify today. No modern police forces had been formed, there were virtually no public prosecutors and few defense attorneys, and public defender agencies were still far in the future.[1] Even the judges lacked legal training, as often as not.[2] Criminal appeals were not yet authorized in most jurisdictions.[3] In 1800, no state had toyed with the idea of a separate juvenile court for young offenders; the "juvenile justice system" remained to be invented much later in the century.[4] Perhaps most striking, there was nothing that could have been called a correctional industry at the turn of the nineteenth century. When society dispensed criminal penalties, it usually relied on quick and inexpensive measures that often involved public pain and humiliation. Such sanctions included hangings, whippings, brandings, mutilations, the stocks and pillories, and public confessions.[5]

Instead of the sizeable bureaucracies familiar today, staffed with trained employees, crime response in the early 1800s was largely carried out by the private sector. That is, policing, prosecution, and punishment usually included government officials, but emphasized the participation of lay citizens as instigators of criminal proceedings, as law enforcement deputies, as private prosecutors, as decisionmakers in grand juries and trial juries, and as participants in open-air punitive dramas. Much of the time, law enforcement and punishment were wholly private affairs, as when transgressors were held to account by church tribunals, vigilante groups, plantation discipline, violent self-help, or the enforcement of the code of honor at the dueling ground.[6]

Through all periods, there has been some such loosely organized confluence of public and private activities, although the relative contributions of private and public actors have shifted from era to era, sometimes quite dramatically. In the early 1800s, the scales were tilted heavily toward private actors and part-timers, who had little or no formal association with federal, state, or local officialdom. One reason for reliance on private resources was that American governments of the day were underdeveloped, shoestring operations.[7] Given the smallness of government at all levels, and the vastness of the territory to be governed, it was often a challenge to get citizens even to take notice of the criminal law as a meaningful presence in their lives.

Throughout the nineteenth century, governmental undercapacity was a fact of life, made ever more pressing by the nation's explosive population growth across the century and well into the next.[8] Most of its institutions grew up in an environment that demanded continuous expansion, sometimes at a breakneck speed, if for no other reason than to keep pace with the demographic snowball of population change.[9] Such habits of institutional survival, established over the better part of two centuries, are not easy to change.

Lawrence Friedman has written that one "master trend" of the late nineteenth century, moving forward into the twentieth, was the professionalization of the criminal justice system.[10] By 1900, if we were to take a second snapshot of the crime response complex, we would see that uniformed police officers were on patrol in virtually every American city,[11] professional district attorneys now handled most prosecutions, defense lawyers were no longer rarities in the courtroom,[12] large urban criminal courts had adopted the modern "administrative" approach of disposing of most cases through plea bargains rather than trials,[13] full-time probation and parole agencies had been established in many jurisdictions,[14] separate "schools" had been built to house juvenile offenders, the specialized juvenile court had recently been invented,[15] and, for serious adult criminals, the new institution of the penitentiary had taken over as *the definitive* criminal punishment.[16]

Nearly all of these developments diminished the crime-response roles of private actors and decisionmakers. The operative model at the turn of the twentieth century favored expertise and political accountability over common sense and lay impetuosity. Of course, private crime response activities were not obliterated with the rise of the official crime response complex; they were simply marginalized. Private police, private detectives, and vigilante groups never disappeared, but they became less ubiquitous and were seen as increasingly disreputable in the late nineteenth and early twentieth centuries.[17] Instead of private prosecutors and untutored grand jurors deciding which criminal cases would be brought to court and allowed to proceed to trial, such screening functions became concentrated in public prosecutors and magistrates. Decisions about ultimate guilt and innocence, formerly regularly made by community representatives serving as trial jurors, by 1900 were shifted in most cases to lawyers and the back-room negotiations of guilty pleas.[18] Even the public's role as witnesses to, or participants in, criminal punishments largely disappeared as the administration of sanctions moved behind the forbidding walls of the penitentiary and into the newly sequestered chambers of the death penalty.

Jumping ahead to the year 2000 for a third and final snapshot of the American crime response complex, one's immediate observation is how little the roster of public institutions changed between 1900 and 2000, especially when compared with the volcanic activity from 1800 to 1900. Within American governments, the twentieth century saw impressive growth of all the crime-response agencies created in the nineteenth, but few structural innovations. By the last third of the century, the main theme in official crime response was not that the nineteenth century approaches had proven defective, but rather that they needed to be strengthened and intensified to meet problems of rising crime and public anxieties about crime. Regular calls for more police, more prosecutors, more judges, and more prisons were signals of residual faith in the inventions of Republican and Progressive reformers one or two hundred years before.

It is not altogether surprising that the spirit of experimentation of the 1800s should have come to a halt. Once invented, the new bureaucracies of crime response generated their own vested interests and power bases, with networks of interpersonal loyalties sustained by pungent institutional cultures. New professional classes arose and, in some cases, grew to political power.[19] Given the self-perpetuating stamina of large institutions in general, the bureaucrats who work within them, and the industries that depend on them, it is understandable that the twentieth century turned to trying to make the nineteenth century crime-response machinery function as best it could. Barring an unexpected upheaval in public administration, such efforts will likewise remain at the core of the twenty-first-century agenda.

Outside of government, however, the twentieth century produced a number of quiet but important developments in private crime response, especially from 1960 on. There was a mass resurgence of private policing and wide experimentation with private security measures such as alarm systems, gated communities, security cameras, unbreakable cash boxes, and the self-arming of citizens for self-defense.[20] Crime victims reasserted themselves as important claimants in lawmaking and litigation, pressing for statutory provisions targeting certain crimes, greater victims' services in police departments and prosecutors' offices, and increased victim input into charging, bargaining, prosecution, and sentencing decisions.[21] Private interests have likewise reinserted themselves into the administration of criminal punishments, including for-profit and nonprofit corporations that now operate some prisons, juvenile detention facilities, and drug treatment centers.[22] Private individuals have gained new powers to monitor ex-offenders in the community, through sex offender registration and notification laws or broader innovations such as "community justice" or "restorative justice" that recognize community representatives as stakeholders in the postconviction behaviors of criminals.[23]

Such developments herald a new movement toward privatization in American crime response that is in some ways reminiscent of prior historical experience.[24] There are large differences, however. In earlier eras, heavy investments in private crime response were unavoidable necessities, given conditions of severe governmental undercapacity. Today, in sharp contrast to the first half of the nineteenth century, the public crime response complex has grown into a collection of sizeable agencies with great potential power over the lives of citizens. One thing "new" about the new privatization is that it has added significant private resources to what was already a baseline of large-scale government activity.

American crime response in the twenty-first century, by a combined public-private measure, is poised for continuing expansion. Some observers have prognosticated that continued investments in the private marketplace will (or should) eventually cause a shrinkage in the funding for public crime response agencies.[25] As plausible as such predictions may sound, they are flatly ahistorical. If one thing has been proven about governmental crime response institutions over 150 years, it is that they are highly effective at protecting their own turf. They are more likely to hold their ground, or expand, than to allow themselves to shrivel away. In planning for the future of American crime response policy, growth in the private sector must be envisioned side by side with ongoing expansion in the public sector. The new century thus presents the prospect of double-barreled growth in the nation's total anticrime activities.

A Long-Term Overview of Crime in America

Knowledge about the amount of crime in society is the starting point for sensible crime response policy in any historical period. In most eras, however, the nation's crime response policy has been fashioned without such elementary data. Through all of the nineteenth century and well into the twentieth, American citizens and policymakers had no statistical information concerning levels of crime, whether crime was going up or down, whether it was more prevalent in cities than in rural areas, whether law enforcement efforts were having any beneficial effects, and so on.

Worse yet, people often thought they knew quite a bit about the incidence of crime, drawing on personal experience, anecdote, conjecture, sensationalism, gut instinct, class and racial hostility, and natural human insecurity. For instance, many people through the nineteenth century believed that crime was on the upswing, that criminals were getting tougher all the time, and that these were especially serious problems in the nation's growing cities.[26] Abraham Lincoln in 1837 deplored "the increasing disregard for law which pervades the country."[27] Charles Loring Brace, in an 1872 book called *The Dangerous Classes of New York City*, depicted the young criminals of his day as increasingly amoral and remorseless. He wrote, "The murder of an unoffending old man . . . is nothing to them. They are ready for any offense or crime, however degraded or bloody."[28] In Brace's account and others, there was an overarching concern among the well-off and well-educated that the nation's social fabric was unraveling—and many were willing to blame the Irish, Italians, Germans, Chinese, and, later, emancipated African Americans for this perceived disintegration of values.[29]

In the South during the 1880s and 1890s, most whites thought they knew that the rape of white women by black men had become a terrifying crime problem. Although historians have been unable to find any evidence that this crime wave really occurred, many Southerners believed it with enough fear and conviction to mount regular lynching expeditions against supposed black offenders.[30] It may sound naive to suggest that "better crime statistics" could have deflected the enormous racial hostilities of the postwar South, but it is equally naive to ignore the overwhelming power of disastrously inaccurate perceptions about crime.

In the 1920s and 1930s, nationally prominent figures warned the country that a dangerous crime wave was swelling, and that there was an urgent need to build up government's resources in response. In the early 1930s a profusion of colorful gangsters became media favorites, including John Dillinger, Bonnie Parker and Clyde Barrow, George "Machine Gun" Kelly, "Ma" Barker, and Charles "Pretty Boy" Floyd. In his 1934 annual message to Congress, President Roosevelt described their exploits as a threat to national security. He called on "the strong arm of Government for their immediate suppression," and on "the country for an aroused public opinion." FDR's attorney general, Homer S. Cummings, made a widely reported speech declaring, "We are now engaged in a war that threatens the safety of our country . . . a war with the organized forces of crime."[31] Such proclamations may have been based on honest belief, or political expediency, but they were not founded on hard information.

Indeed, such statistics as existed for 1931 through 1936, newly compiled by the FBI, suggested that the incidence of serious crimes in all categories was decreasing. That did not prevent J. Edgar Hoover, the FBI's publicity-minded director, from pumping up the scope of the problem, as captured in the following contemporary account:

The Director of the Bureau of Investigation referred in March 1936 to the "armed forces of crime which number more than 3 million active participants." Three months later he stated that "the criminal standing army of America" numbered 500,000, "a whole half-million of armed thugs, murderers, thieves, firebugs, assassins, robbers, and hold-up men." About six months afterward he gave the total criminal population as 3,500,000 and the number of crimes as 1,500,000. Five months later he stated that 4,300,000 persons were engaged *by day and by night* in the commission of felonies . . . In the same address he declared that "there are today in America 150,000 murderers roaming at large"; but it appears from *Uniform Crime Reports* that in 987 cities with a total population of 35,450,666, the police were cognizant of only 3,582 cases of criminal homicide.[32]

Hoover even sponsored a comic strip called *War on Crime*, which was syndicated in forty-five newspapers nationwide through most of 1936, featuring himself as the hero.[33] Samuel Walker writes that such "publicity blitzes" contributed to "rising public fear of crime" in the 1920s and 1930s, and "a new sense that crime was a national problem."[34] Nor did the fear subside. In the 1950s, Arthur Vanderbilt reportedly pronounced that "major crime in the United States has reached an all-time high."[35]

Across much of the nineteenth and twentieth centuries, the reality of crime in America was generally far different from alarmist statements and perceptions. Through painstaking effort, modern scholars have pieced together historical data about U.S. crime rates. There is now a consensus that crime, including serious violent crime, was dropping from the early 1800s throughout the remainder of the nineteenth century and for roughly the first half of the twentieth century. This conclusion applies with greatest confidence to the major cities, where historians have been able to collate police records, court data, prison and jail information, and health and morbidity statistics. Contrary to the beliefs of the time, urban crime rates were falling even as the major cities grew and became more industrialized. Across the nineteenth century, crime was lower in the cities than in small towns and rural areas, and crime was falling faster in the big cities as well.[36]

The long downslope in crime was an epochal story that Americans failed to appreciate while it was happening. There were no national celebrations of greater safety and security unfolding decade after decade. Self-interested public officials, who might have used the crime recession to their political advantage, were mute. Even the most informed researchers who lived through the period were agnostic about crime trends, and busied themselves discrediting those who claimed hard knowledge on the subject.[37]

The sustained crime recession in fact ended long before its existence was known, and at just about the same time that the United States was beginning to cobble together rudimentary year-by-year crime statistics (see Chapter 2). As Americans were first struggling with imperfect "crime reports," in other words, the new statistical machinery was gearing up to deliver bad news. This was a critical juncture. There is no episode more central in American crime response history than the stunning reversal of the long crime drop that occurred in the middle of the twentieth century, including the fact that its broad outlines were perceived by the public. With alarming suddenness in the 1950s and 1960s, U.S. crime rates, especially those for serious violent offenses, broke from their long-established slide as if they had acquired a perverse will of their own.

These trends will be discussed in detail later, but a summary is needed here—especially concerning the most serious categories of violent crime, or "grave violence," which may be defined as offenses that cause death or life-threatening physical injury, as well as forcible sexual assault.[38]

The clearest historical picture of grave violence in the twentieth-century United States can be drawn from homicide data, which became available through nationwide health statistics starting in 1933 (fig. 1.1). As opposed to all other crimes, homicide was measured relatively accurately across the entire period shown on the figure. (This is because homicide is especially likely to be reported to the authorities, and it is in any case difficult to conceal a dead body or the fact of a person's disappearance.)[39] Apart from their unique credibility, homicide data also tell us something inferentially about the number of grave woundings that must have occurred in a given year. Completed homicides, probabilistically, bear rough relation to a larger number of very serious attacks that fell short of causing death.

The first quarter century of data in Figure 1.1 show the tail end of the long crime recession that reached well back into the nineteenth century. Aside from a blip in the 1940s, the nation's homicide rates descended

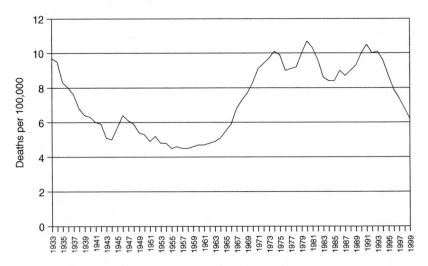

FIGURE 1.1 U.S. homicide rate, 1933–1999. Data from National Center for Health Statistics, *Vital Statistics (www.ojp.usdoj.gov/bjs/glance/tables/hmrttab.htm)* (updated Oct. 10, 2001).

throughout the 1930s, 1940s, and most of the 1950s.[40] Then, in a remarkably short period of ten to fifteen years, spanning the late 1950s through
the early 1970s, the U.S. murder victimization rate shot skyward to surpass
the highest recorded levels of the early 1930s. During this same period, all
crimes of grave violence became most heavily concentrated in the nation's
deteriorating inner cities, especially among African Americans living in
conditions of extreme poverty.[41] The long trend of declining urban crime
was at an end.

Through the late 1980s and early 1990s, the nation suffered through homicide levels that oscillated year to year, but remained on a high plateau of
roughly twice the victimization lows of the 1940s and 1950s. Transnational
victimization information became available in the late twentieth century,
and these data delivered further bad news. By all measures, the United
States was the most dangerous of first-world countries.[42] In a 1993 tabula-
tion, the American homicide death rate was more than double that in
Northern Ireland, more than four times the Canadian and Australian rates,
nine times the rates in Spain, France, and Germany, and fifteen to twenty
times the death rates in England and Japan.[43] For other categories of grave
violence, such as armed robbery, rape, and assaults with life-threatening
injuries, the United States was similarly an outlier among developed nations.[44] With respect to less serious offenses, however, such as property
crimes, or violent crimes without serious injury, America's crime rates
were not noticeably elevated above those of other Western democracies.
The distinctive American crime problem of the late twentieth century was
one of grave violence, not "crime in general."[45]

The introductory sketch of U.S. crime rates cannot end here, however.
Beginning in the early 1990s, and continuing at least into the early 2000s,
the scourge of grave violence that gripped the nation for thirty years at last
began to ease. In every year after 1993, homicide rates dropped until, at the
turn of the new century, they had fallen back to the death tolls of the mid-
1960s. Other categories of gravely violent offenses declined in the same
time period, and the United States enjoyed drop-offs even among many
less serious offenses.

As of this writing, no one knows how long the crime drop of the 1990s
will extend. We do know from history that a long crime recession is possible. Guesswork about the future is greatly complicated, however, by the
fact that no one fully understands the reasons for the contemporary crime
drop—although some have tried.[46] Moreover, homicide rates in some large
U.S. cities have begun to jump again. Violent crimes reported to the police

also rose slightly for the nation as a whole between 2000 and 2001, but the victims survey showed a continued drop.[47] These are paradoxical signals.

Even without the ability to tell the future, the present relaxation in grave violence provides mental freedom, unclouded by perceptions of a crime-wave in progress, to reassess the nation's priorities in the operation of the crime response complex. If so, it is the first such moment in nearly forty years. From an entirely different direction, the attacks of September 11, 2001 and their aftermath also force domestic crime response into new perspective. Here again, the focal point has lifted away from street crime itself. With the new exigencies of a war on terrorism, at home and abroad, including military action, massive investments in terrorism prevention, changing budgetary allocations, and the end of the economic boom of the 1990s, America has little choice but to face the question of what is most (and least) worth doing in conventional crime response.

Punishment from a Citizen's Perspective

Historically, the total quantum of penalties dispensed by the U.S. crime response complex has not borne an obvious relationship to the extent of crime in one era or another.[48] This elusive correlation is not our present subject, however. We address instead the more prosaic question of what historical changes in the nation's punishment capabilities have meant to American citizens.

Prisons and Jails

America's prisons, like all other building blocks of the crime response complex, began on a small scale. As late as 1850, the Census Bureau counted only 6,737 inmates among the thirty-one states.[49] (This yields an average state prison population of 217 inmates in 1850—a trivial number by today's standards.)[50] By 1880, again according to census data, prison populations had more than quadrupled, to 30,659 prisoners nationwide. In 1904, the prisoner count had nearly doubled once again, to 57,070.[51] Although at least half of the prison expansion in the late nineteenth century can be accounted for by population growth, the change in absolute size remains striking: What had begun as a cottage industry in the first decades of the nineteenth century had massed into a visible and important function of state governments across the country by the early 1900s.

If we widen the camera angle to look at the nineteenth and twentieth centuries together, we gain a more sweeping picture of changes in the scale of the American prison industry from its inception through the present. By midyear 2000, the nation's prisons housed nearly 1.4 million inmates.[52] Recalling the census figures for 1850, U.S. prison populations have grown 206 times over from 1850 through 2000. During the same period, the nation's total population expanded about twelvefold.[53] If we make a similar calculation dating back to 1880, we still find the total size of America's prisons have grown by more than a factor of 45 from 1880 to 2000, during a period in which the general population grew by a factor of 5.6.[54] As impressive as American population growth has been in the last 150 years, the expansion of imprisonment has been far more spectacular.

We find it revealing to break down this history decade by decade. Figure 1.2 depicts the raw amount of prison growth that has occurred in each decade since 1880. It shows a nearly unbroken pattern of institutional

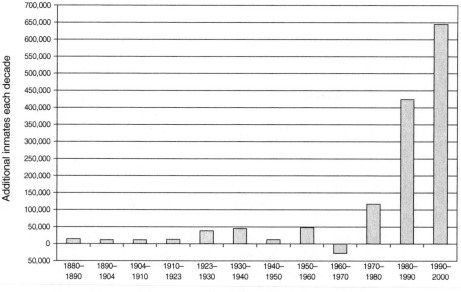

FIGURE 1.2 Prison growth by decade, 1880–2000. Data from Margaret Werner Cahalan, *Historical Corrections Statistics in the United States, 1850–1984* (Washington, D.C.: GPO, 1986), p. 29, table 3-2; p. 32, table 3-4; U.S. Department of Justice, Bureau of Justice Statistics, *Sourcebook of Criminal Justice Statistics, 1999* (Washington, D.C.: GPO, 2000), p. 503, table 6.26; U.S. Department of Justice, Bureau of Justice Statistics, *Prison and Jail Inmates at Midyear 2000* (Washington, D.C.: Bureau of Justice Statistics, 2001), p. 1.

growth over twelve decades. Except for the anomalous 1960s, when U.S. prison populations actually shrunk by 27,513 inmates, the nation added prison beds fairly steadily from 1880 to 1960,[55] very rapidly in the 1970s, and explosively in the 1980s and 1990s.[56] To grasp the full extent of "explosive" change in the last twenty years, we note that the total prison growth over the course *of an entire century* from 1880 to 1980 (a total of 285,315 inmates) was far less than the prison growth for a single decade in the 1980s (424,006 new prisoners) *or* for the single decade of the 1990s (645,512 new prisoners). If we use the period from 1880 to 1980 as a one-hundred-year yardstick, the nation compressed more than three centuries' worth of prison expansion into the next twenty years, from 1980 to 2000.

Historical statistics about jail populations are far less complete than prisoner statistics.[57] Although the numbers are spread out a bit (like measuring the height of your child every three years, not annually), two fairly consistent facts emerge: First, jail populations over the long haul have grown at approximately the same rate as prison populations, at least since 1880 when statistics first became available. Second, the number of inmates in jail has consistently hovered somewhere around one-third of the total number of citizens incarcerated in the United States (plus or minus several percentage points), with people in prison making up the remaining two-thirds.[58] For example, in 1880 the Census Bureau found 30,659 persons in prisons across the country and another 18,686 persons in the jails.[59] For 2000 the numbers were much larger, but in similar proportion to one another: There were 1,385,492 prison inmates and 687,033 in local jails.[60] The story of jail populations over time has closely paralleled the trajectory of prison expansion, including the unprecedented growth of the last two decades. By the 1990s, the average likelihood that an American male citizen would spend time in a prison or jail cell during his lifetime was about 8 or 9 percent.[61]

By the late twentieth century, the United States was reputed to be the world leader in the use of incarceration.[62] On a single day in 2000, the American crime response complex held 702 persons in custody for every 100,000 in the national population—a figure approaching 1 percent of all men, women, and children in the country.[63] Russia, our nearest competitor, had a confinement rate of 675 per 100,000 in 2000.[64] When compared with other first-world nations, however, American incarceration policy has been in a league of its own. In the late 1990s, the U.S. incarceration rate was roughly five-and-one-half times the rate in Australia, seven-and-one-half times the rates in France, Italy, and Germany, and eighteen times the rate in Japan.[65] In 2000, the British Home Office assembled comparative data from 1996 to 1999 indicating that U.S. incarceration per capita exceeded that in the United Kingdom by more than a factor of five, was more than six times the Canadian rate, and was more than eleven times the rates in Sweden and Norway.[66]

Punishment statistics are almost always reported in one-day counts of how many inmates (or probationers, or parolees, as the case may be) were present in the system at a single moment in time. This freeze-frame approach, however, supplies no sense of the passage of time—that is, an understanding of how many people are spending *how many years* behind bars. Thoreau wrote that "the cost of a thing is the amount of . . . life which is required to be exchanged for it."[67] We recommend that confinement policy be scrutinized in relation to how many "person-years" of incarceration it subtracts from our national life.

The durational measure of the person-year is especially helpful for grasping the cumulative human effects of changing incarceration policy. For example, the U.S. prison and jail population grew from 1,148,702 in 1990 to 1,931,859 in 2000.[68] At first glance, a freeze-frame comparison indicates that the size of the American incarceration enterprise grew by 786,559 inmates. This is a sizeable number of human beings, to be sure, but it falls short of describing the cumulative consequences of the expansionist trend. If 1990 incarceration populations had remained stable through the 1990s, the prisons and jails would have dispensed 11,487,020 person-years of incarceration over the full decade. Adding in the cumulative effects of annual expansion, however, the actual total was 15,959,208 person-years. Over the 1990s, roughly 4.5 million person-years of confinement were dispensed by American governments *over and above* the punishments that would have been meted out if prison and jail populations had remained unchanged after 1990.[69]

Just as startling, the carceral expansion of the 1990s will exert powerful continuing effects on the future. Even if prison and jail growth were to halt at 2000 levels, the built-in effects of past growth would generate extraordinary punitive tolls. Figure 1.3 depicts this possible future. From 2000 to 2009, there would be a prodigious 19.4 million person-years of confinement *without* further incarceration growth after 2000. During the 2000s, there would be roughly three million more person-years of confinement than in the 1990s. In other words, a decade of "stagnation" in incarceration

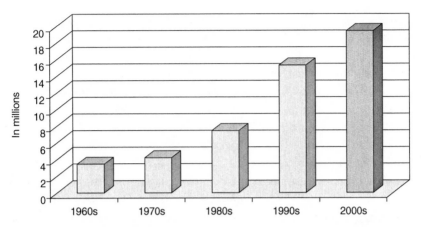

FIGURE 1.3 Person-years of incarceration, 1960s through 2000s (projected). Data from U.S. Department of Justice, Bureau of Justice Statistics, *Prison and Jail Inmates at Midyear 2001* (Washington, D.C.: GPO, 2002), p. 2, table 1; U.S. Department of Justice, Bureau of Justice Statistics, *Sourcebook of Criminal Justice Statistics, 2000* (Washington, D.C.: GPO, 2001), p. 502, table 6.21; p. 507, table 6.27; Margaret Werner Cahalan, *Historical Corrections Statistics in the United States, 1850–1984* (Washington, D.C.: GPO, 1986), p. 76, table 4-1. Person-years for 2000–2009 were estimated on the assumption that U.S. prison and jail populations would stabilize throughout the decade at the number of inmates present in 2000.

growth, if such were to occur from 2000 to 2009, would actually be far more punitive in its total effects on offenders than the "high-growth" decade of the 1990s. In order for the period 2000 to 2009 to be no more severe in its use of confinement than the 1990s, prison and jail populations would have to decline across the decade at the same average pace that they expanded in the 1990s. So far, although there are signs in the early 2000s that twenty-eight years of incarceration growth may be slowing to a rate of slight growth or slight decline, there are no indications of a scaleback in confinement that would significantly unwind the vigorous expansion of the recent past.[70]

Probation and Parole

Incarceration is hardly the only type of punishment imposed on citizens as a response to crime. Midway through the nineteenth century, some American jurisdictions began to experiment with probation (supervision of offenders in the community) as a new form of government-managed penalty.[71] A bit later, parole (early release from prison, often combined with community supervision) also took root.[72] Both probation and parole required the formation of new bureaucracies to monitor offenders in their home communities. This build-up started decades later than the first wave of investment in prisons and prison staff. But in time, probation and parole agencies nationwide were handling very large numbers of convicted offenders, well in excess of those held in carceral institutions.

We lack historical data until well into the twentieth century concerning the numbers of persons on probation or parole.[73] It is clear, however, that from the embryonic programs of the nineteenth century, community penalties have become gargantuan in scale. In 2001 there were more than 3.9 million men and women on probation in the United States and an additional 732,351 on parole. Adding together all individuals in prison or jail, or on probation or parole, the U.S. Justice Department calculated that 6.5 million Americans (more than 3 percent of the nation's population) were serving criminal sentences on any single day in 2001.[74] The average lifetime chances of a U.S. citizen ever serving a sentence on probation were as high as 17 percent.[75]

Like incarceration in prisons and jails, the use of probation and parole exploded in the late twentieth century (fig. 1.4). In 1965, the first-ever national count revealed 431,853 adults on probation and 102,036 on parole.[76] By 1976, a second national count found 923,064 adults on probation and 156,194 on parole.[77] The combined total had more than doubled in eleven years—but the most rapid acceleration was still to come. In the 1980s alone, an astonishing 1.9 million additional probation and parole slots were added to the national total. The upward trend continued, a bit less dramatically, in the 1990s. From 1990 to 1999, an additional 1.3 million slots were created.

The total durational effect of probation and parole on the freedom of citizens can best be quantified using the concept of the person-year. In the 1970s, the American crime response complex meted out roughly 10 million person-years of probation or parole. In the 1980s, the person-year total expanded to 21 million, and to 38 million in the 1990s.[78] From 2000 to 2009, we can forecast that there will be at least 45 million person-years of probation and parole administered by U.S. governments, even if we indulge the unlikely assumption that growth in these sanctions will come to a sudden halt early in the twenty-first century.[79]

From most citizens' perspective, the experience of serving a sentence of

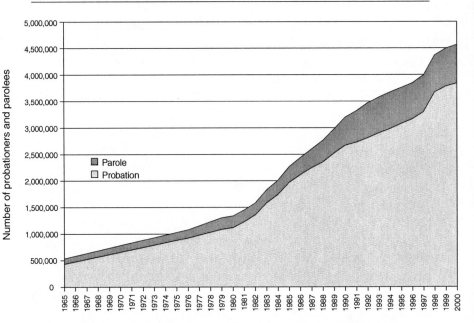

FIGURE 1.4 Probation and parole, 1965–2000. Data from U.S. Department of Justice, Press Release, "National Correctional Population Reaches New High: Grows by 126,400 during 2000 to Total 6.5 Million Adults," Aug. 26, 2001, p. 3, table 1; U.S. Department of Justice, Bureau of Justice Statistics, *Sourcebook of Criminal Justice Statistics 2000* (Washington, D.C.: GPO, 2001), p. 488, table 6.1; Law Enforcement Assistance Administration, *State and Local Probation and Parole Systems* (Washington, D.C.: GPO, 1978), p. 3; Margaret Werner Cahalan, *Historical Corrections Statistics in the United States, 1850–1984* (Washington, D.C.: GPO, 1986), p. 181, table 7-9A.

probation or parole is far less intrusive than any penalty involving round-the-clock confinement. Even so, a person-year under community supervision can be more than a paltry indignity. In the 1980s and 1990s, many American jurisdictions experimented with more intensive forms of community sanctions. Compared with traditional probation, for example, the new "intermediate punishments" have featured a greater number of regular contacts between offenders and their probation officers, more legal conditions imposed upon offenders, frequent and random drug testing, unannounced home searches, and the use of new monitoring technologies such as unremoveable ankle bracelets that emit an electronic signal revealing the whereabouts of offenders.[80]

One consequence of the stepped-up practices of offender monitoring in the 1980s and 1990s was a big increase in the numbers of probationers and parolees who were caught violating the conditions of their sentences. In 1997, for example, nearly one-third of all admissions to America's prisons were due to probation or parole revocations, up from only 18 percent in 1980.[81] In a few states, the backflow into the prisons due to revocations had gotten out of hand in the late 1990s. In 1997, an incredible 64 percent of admissions to the California prison system were probation or parole violators, as were 54 percent of admittees to the Louisiana prisons, and 51 percent in Utah.[82]

Community penalties are important resources within the crime response complex. Some people think of probation and parole as "soft" punishments, probably on the theory that their clientele would otherwise have landed in prison or jail. This perception misses a central historical point: Community punishments in our society have seldom served as *substitutes* for incarceration, but have functioned over time as an *additional* store of penalties, growing side by side with the enlarging institutions of confinement. Long U.S. experience contradicts the hypothesis that increasing the use of probation and parole has any important tendency to subtract from the use of confinement.

The Death Penalty

The death penalty in America currently affects a miniscule percentage of all persons convicted of crime, and is used frequently in only one region of the country. In the recent peak year of 1999, a total of ninety-eight persons were executed in the United States. Seventy-four of the ninety-eight were put to death in Southern states, half in Texas and Virginia alone.[83] Even among all persons found guilty of homicide, the numbers who reach execution make up less than one-half of 1 percent.[84] In the big statistical picture of criminal punishment, the death penalty is barely visible.

Despite the fact that it is a small-numbers phenomenon, capital punishment remains worthy of policy attention because of its moral and symbolic significance—both to its proponents and to abolitionists. Death penalty cases, problems in death penalty administration, and the debate concerning the morality of having such a punishment are often raised high in public consciousness.

The history of capital punishment in America reflects the intermixture of private and public actions noted earlier in the chapter. To the contemporary reader, it may seem inappropriate to classify private executions as a form of crime response. In its day, however, "lynch law" was regarded as an expression of law enforcement at the grassroots community level. From the 1880s to the 1960s, the most common reason for private lynchings (to the extent a reason can be reconstructed) was the belief that the lynching victim had committed a serious criminal offense, usually a homicide, rape, or attempted rape.[85] Lynch mobs, more often than not, regarded themselves as upholding the law, not breaking it.[86]

Through much of the nineteenth century, private executions greatly outnumbered the governmental. There were 1,540 lynchings in the 1890s, 895 in the 1900s, 621 in the 1910s, 315 in the 1930s, 33 in the 1940s, and 8 in the 1950s. Offsetting this trend, however, the number of government-sponsored executions was on the rise for much of the same period. There were 155 legal executions in the 1890s, 289 in the 1900s, 636 in the 1910s, 1,038 in the 1920s, and 1,523 in the 1930s. Thus the total number of executions in the 1930s—public and private—remained virtually unchanged from the 1890s. As with private lynchings, moreover, the most common offenses leading to state-sponsored executions remained murder and rape—with rape becoming an especially important component of the total in the 1930s and 1940s, just as private executions were dwindling toward zero.[87] From 1882 to 1962, 83 percent of all private lynchings in the United States occurred in the South, including 95 percent of all lynchings of black victims.[88]

Unlike all other mainstream forms of criminal sanctions discussed here, capital punishment has not grown steadily across the last two centuries. From the mid-1800s through most of the twentieth century, America seemed on a long-term course (with other first-world nations) toward decreasing its use of the death penalty. A small number of states, beginning with Michigan in 1847, abolished capital punishment entirely in the nineteenth century, with more states following suit through the first half of the twentieth century. Even those jurisdictions that retained the death penalty were using it less often. From 1935 to 1975 there occurred a more or less steady drop in governmental killings as a form of crime response.[89]

In 1972, the U.S. Supreme Court appeared to give strong imprimatur to the abolitionist trend. The Court issued a lengthy set of opinions in *Furman v. Georgia,* with a bare majority of the Justices holding that capital punishment as administered in American court systems was so arbitrary and unpredictable as to be unconstitutional.[90] The stunning effect of *Fur-*

man was to invalidate every pending death sentence nationwide, and the decision raised the possibility that executions would never again be carried out legally in the United States.

Within a few years of the *Furman* case, however, capital punishment in America made a decisive comeback. Thirty-five state legislatures stirred themselves to enact amended death penalty laws in the three years following the Court's 1972 ruling. Seldom has there been such a nationwide rebuke of a judicial decision. The new statutes incorporated legislative standards and procedures for imposition of the death penalty, in the hope that this would address the Court's reasoning that prior laws had been inexplicably arbitrary.[91] The attempt was successful. In 1976, in *Gregg v. Georgia,* the Court declared that Georgia's newly designed capital punishment law was constitutional, giving a green light to similar schemes elsewhere.[92] Ever since *Gregg,* a majority of the Supreme Court has steadfastly adhered to the view that capital punishment is a constitutionally permissible sanction for most forms of murder.

The present course in the nation's use of the death penalty is of a piece with the growth curve in the use of prisons, jails, probation, and parole. Since 1972, when death row populations were temporarily swept clean by *Furman,* they have been replenished, from 134 in 1973, to 691 in 1980, to 1,591 in 1985, to 2,356 in 1990, to 3,527 in 1999.[93] The numbers of executions carried out have also generally been on the upswing, from zero in 1968 through 1976, to one in 1977, to five in 1983, to sixteen in 1989, to fifty-six in 1995, to ninety-eight in 1999.[94]

In the early 2000s, death row populations continued to grow in the United States, but the actual number of executions fell off from the 1999 high point to 85 in 2000 and 66 in 2001. These totals were still higher than for any year in the 1960s through the late 1990s, but suggested that the continuous growth in executions, like annual increases in incarcerations, might be leveling off or entering a period of decline.[95] The State of Illinois even instituted an indefinite moratorium on executions in March 2000, following revelations that thirteen inmates under sentence of death in that state were in fact innocent of the charges against them. The State of Maryland followed suit in May 2002.[96]

Race, Ethnicity, Punishment, and Crime

It is impossible to discuss any aspect of American crime response without confronting, almost immediately, noxious issues of racial and ethnic disproportionalities. Such concerns long predate recent decades of racial tension and interest-group politics. Over centuries, the nation's punishment practices have always affected certain minority groups more heavily than the mainstream population.

Without doubt, the most notorious and racially divisive sanction in the nineteenth and twentieth centuries was the death penalty, in both its private and public manifestations. To the modern mind, the stereotypical lynching involved a white mob and a black victim, although this was not the exclusive paradigm. In the 1880s, only 44 percent of 1,203 known lynchings nationwide were of African Americans. By the 1890s, however, 72 percent of 1,540 lynching victims for the country as a whole were black, and, from 1900 through the 1940s, the percentages of black lynching victims were always 90 percent or higher.[97]

In the changeover from private lynch law to the official death penalty, African Americans became the subjects of death sentences somewhat less often. Seventy-three percent of state-authorized death sentences in the South were carried out against black defendants from 1890 to 1960. Nationwide, from the 1890s through the 1960s, "only" 51 percent of all government executions were carried out against black defendants.[98] This is more than four times the number of executions one would expect, given the percentage of African Americans in the U.S. population as a whole, but it was a little better than the racial demographics of private lynchings in the late nineteenth and early twentieth centuries. Public executions for rape, however, maintained a close resemblance to their private antecedents: From 1930 to 1964, 89 percent of all death sentences for rape were carried out against black defendants.[99]

In the post-*Gregg v. Georgia* era, racial disparities on death row have fallen again from their levels during the first two-thirds of the twentieth century. From 1977 to 2000, the black share of all persons sentenced to death in the United States was 41 percent; 36 percent of all persons executed over the same period were black.[100] Throughout these years, African Americans made up only 12 to 13 percent of the national population.

In the late twentieth century, increasing evidence came to light that the racially slanted administration of the death penalty did not rest solely or even predominately on the racial identity of criminal offenders. A famous study by David Baldus and others based on two thousand Georgia cases in the 1970s, found that murderers who killed white victims were far more likely to receive the death penalty than those who killed black victims—by more than a factor of four.[101] This conclusion coincided with a great deal of historical and anecdotal evidence indicating that American crime response institutions have not been as vigorous in addressing the victimizations of blacks as of whites.[102]

The long and ongoing history of racial and ethnic disparities in incarceration is less widely known than the raw facts of the death penalty. Although confinement is a subject less emotionally charged than lynchings or official executions, the prisons and jails have affected far more lives— and their effects have likewise been focused disproportionately on minority groups. Historians have found that the people most likely to be incarcerated, in any time period, have been young men from the lowest rungs of society's social and economic ladder. Through much of the nineteenth century, up and down the East Coast, prison populations were largely comprised of European immigrants who met this description.[103] Margaret Cahalan has observed that, since 1850, incarceration patterns have always included 40 to 50 percent foreign-born persons, blacks, or other minorities.[104] Before the Civil War, 8 to 37 percent of the prison populations in Southern states were made up of the foreign born, even though those groups made up only about 3 percent of the general population.[105]

Following the Civil War, the demographics of imprisonment began a century-long progression toward ever-increasing emphasis on the confinement of African Americans. The shift began immediately and forcefully in the South, where most of the black population then resided. Before the war, it was virtually unheard of that a black person should be found in a Southern penitentiary, especially in the lower South. In the slavery era, criminal justice for blacks was a private activity administered on plantations.[106] (The incarceration of slaves by the government would have deprived owners of valuable workers.) After the war, however, in the words of Edward Ayers, the racial mix of prison inmates in the South "changed radically overnight."[107] The white immigrants who had formerly been confined in large numbers suddenly disappeared as a noticeable group. The racial composition of the prison and jail populations in the South switched from 90 percent white to 90 percent black and, from the decades of 1865 through 1900, black prison populations increased eight times over.[108] Before long, the perceived need to punish freed slaves in the South outran the available prison facilities. Innovations such as chain gangs, convict leasing, and state farms appeared as low-cost means to control the multiplying numbers of blacks sentenced to criminal punishment. Far from draining the states' treasuries, many such operations became profit centers. Nearly all of the convict workers were African Americans, and often the conditions of labor were considerably worse than in the old days of slavery.[109]

The long-term trend toward increasing criminal punishment of blacks spread more slowly to other regions of the country, but it eventually took root with black migration out of the South, and has continued unbroken from the late nineteenth century throughout the twentieth century. Periodic inmate censuses allow us to trace the black share of national prison populations from 1880 to the present. Over this 120-year period, blacks have made up 10 to 13 percent of the total U.S. population. Yet, already by 1880, 29 percent of state and federal prisoners nationwide were African American. The "black share" of imprisonment since then increased to 31 percent in 1923, 41 percent in 1970, 44 percent in 1980, 48.6 percent in 1990, and 48.8 percent in 1997.[110] The long-term data concerning the growing black share of jail populations, which date back to 1923, are roughly similar. African Americans made up 32 percent of U.S. jail populations in 1923, a figure that has risen over time to exceed 41 percent in 2000.[111]

As striking as these long-term progressions are, the growing presence of incarceration as a factor in African American lives is grossly understated by the slowly increasing percentages. Not only has the black share of the imprisonment pie been growing but, as noted earlier, the entire pie has been growing even faster. Thus, from the perspective of the average black male citizen, the chances of spending time in a prison cell have increased steadily, and at times exponentially, since the close of the Civil War.

Figure 1.5 brings the point home graphically, comparing white male and black male imprisonment rates from 1880 to 2000. In general, confinement rates have risen for both groups over the long term, but the segment of the white male population in prison even at the turn of the twenty-first century had still not reached half of 1 percent—the same as the black male imprisonment rate one hundred years earlier.

In 1997, the U.S. Department of Justice published a report on the probabilities that American males would spend time in prison during their lifetimes. The report was based on 1991 incarceration rates and the assumption that they would remain unchanged in the future. (The statistics have in fact worsened since 1991.) Based on the report, white males born in the 1980s and 1990s faced an overall lifetime risk of 4.4 percent that they would at some point serve a prison sentence. In other words, 95.6 percent of these young white males will never be imprisoned, if the projection holds. For young black males in the same age groups, however, the lifetime risk of imprisonment was 28.5 percent according to the same calculation—or six and one-half times the white risk.[112] Here again, the raw statistics understate the grim realities for many African Americans. While it cannot be calculated, the lifetime risk of imprisonment in America's poorest black neighborhoods is considerably greater than the nationwide black average.

African Americans are not the only group overrepresented in U.S. prisons and jails in the late twentieth century. The same Justice Department study also estimated that for young Hispanic American males the lifetime chances of going to prison were 16.6 percent, or nearly four times the

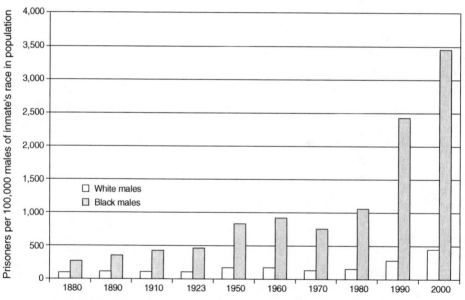

FIGURE 1.5 Male imprisonment rates by race, 1880–2000. Data from U.S. Department of Justice, Bureau of Justice Statistics, *Prisoners in 2000* (Washington, D.C.: Bureau of Justice Statistics, 2001), p. 11, table 15; Margaret Werner Cahalan, *Historical Corrections Statistics in the United States, 1850–1984* (Washington, D.C.: GPO, 1986), p. 34, table 3-6; p. 65, table 3-31; Margaret Cahalan, "Trends in Incarceration in the United States since 1880: A Summary of Reported Rates and the Distribution of Offenses," *Crime and Delinquency* 25 (1979): 40, table 11; U.S. Census Bureau, *Census of Population* (various years).

probability for white males. This is not quite as shocking as the black-white differential, but it is alarming nonetheless. It shows that Hispanics have emerged as a second sizeable target group of criminal punishment, even as the African American share of incarceration has continued to expand. From 1980 to 1996, the number of Hispanic prisoners surged upward by 554 percent, compared to 185 percent growth among whites and 261 percent growth among blacks.[113] Demographers believe that Hispanic Americans will be the fastest growing ethnic group in the U.S. over the next five decades, and will make up one-third of the national population by the year 2050.[114] If these two trends continue, America will hurtle further in the direction of racial and ethnic disparities in punishment.

Finally, although national data are not regularly reported, the punishment rates for American Indians are also disturbingly high. A study of 1997 correctional statistics revealed that the confinement rate of American Indians over age eighteen in American prisons was 2.6 times the equivalent white rate, and in the nation's jails the disparity was more than six to one.[115] American Indians account for roughly 1 percent of the U.S. population, so less attention is focused on them than on other disadvantaged groups. The slender information we possess, however, should give rise to serious concern—and suggests the need to develop better information concerning the punishment of racial and ethnic minorities other than those that are most sizable.

Racial Disparities in Crime and Victimization

It is tempting to view racial and ethnic disparities in punishment as conclusive evidence of past and present bias in the administration of criminal law, and as good indicators of the extent of that bias. But the situation is more complicated than the raw statistics of punishment make it appear.

In the first place, the number of crimes committed by African Americans per capita is considerably higher than among whites, and this has been true as far back into the twentieth century as crime statistics have been gathered.[116] Figure 1.6 illustrates the black-white crime differentials for seven offenses, using arrest data for 1990.[117] The white arrest rate for each crime category is standardized at a value of 100 in Figure 1.6, so that the magnitudes of the racial disparities can be compared from offense to offense.[118]

For the most feared offenses—murder, rape, and robbery—black arrest rates were more than five times the white rates. For murder, the black arrest rate was greater by more than a factor of eight; for robbery, the black rate was slightly more than twelve times the white rate. For property offenses such as burglary, larceny, and motor vehicle theft, black arrest rates were roughly three to four times those of whites, with the smallest disparities existing for larceny and burglary.

The crime of aggravated assault presents a complicated problem in arrest statistics because the offense is relatively commonplace compared with other violent crimes like homicide, rape, and robbery, and because the definition of aggravated assault includes a wide range of guilty conduct, including episodes of near-fatal woundings, episodes of mutual combat, and episodes where no injuries at all were inflicted. As Franklin Zimring has put it, "aggravated assaults range in seriousness from menacing gestures to attempted murder."[119]

As shown in Figure 1.6, the aggravated assault arrest rate among blacks

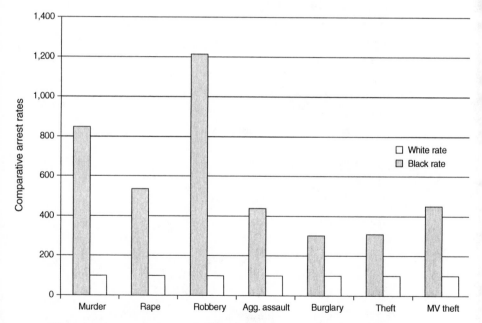

FIGURE 1.6 Black and white arrest ratios, 1990 (white rates standardized to 100). Based on data and rate calculations presented in Gary LaFree, *Losing Legitimacy: Street Crime and the Decline of Social Institutions in America* (Boulder, Colo.: Westview, 1998), p. 50, table 3.1.

was more than four times the white rate in 1990, but there is evidence that the black rate of committing the most serious aggravated assaults was higher than this. In 1990 there was one homicide arrest for every 14.4 aggravated assault arrests among blacks, and one homicide arrest for every 28.2 aggravated assault arrests among whites.[120] These data suggest that aggravated assaults were almost twice as likely to turn deadly when committed by blacks as when committed by whites.[121] Consistent with this evidence, there is a more recent finding that black victims of violent crime from 1993 to 1998 (who were usually the victims of black offenders, in 76 percent of violent episodes) were twice as likely to receive serious bodily injuries than white victims (who were usually the victims of white offenders, in 66 percent of violent episodes).[122] The evidence suggests that blacks commit gravely violent attacks at much higher rates than whites, perhaps approaching a ratio of eight-to-one in the 1990s for the most serious assaults.

At times in the 1990s, the black-white crime differentials were even larger than those shown on Figure 1.6. For instance, in 1993, the black homicide rate hit a peak at nine-and-one-half times the white rate. In that year, for the age group of eighteen to twenty-four, the black homicide arrest rate was more than eleven times the white rate.[123] In the later 1990s, however, the black-white differentials moderated for some offenses, as crime in America dropped across the board. By 1999, the black homicide rate was a bit less than seven times that of whites, and black robbery rates were 7.6 times the white rate. For property crimes like burglary and larceny, however, the black-white differentials did not show an equivalent drop. They remained in 1999 at close to three to one, much as they had been in 1990.[124]

Like so much else in crime response history, racial disparities in offending are not new developments. Gary LaFree examined black-white crime differentials based on arrest statistics for the entire fifty-year period of 1946 to 1996. He found that the essential patterns of the 1990s have been in place throughout. Black rates of grave violence have been dramatically higher than white rates for at least fifty years, and black rates of less-serious offending have been substantially higher.[125] Roger Lane has traced murder statistics back still further. He found that black homicide rates eight-to-ten times the white rates are "no novelty, dating from the earliest trustworthy records in the 1920s and 1930s."[126]

The stable ratios between black and white rates of gravely violent criminality lend themselves to intensified public concern when such crime is on the rise, or is persisting at very high levels. For example, a black-white homicide ratio of eight-to-one is deeply disturbing when murder is at a century-long low point, as it was in the 1950s. If murder rates then double (as they did in the 1960s), the same eight-to-one ratio can become intolerably stark. After such a doubling, the new white homicide rate would be twice the former white rate, but the new black rate would be sixteen times the old white rate. This magnification effect helps explain why racial tension in American crime response reached crisis dimensions during the high-violence years of the 1960s, 1970s, 1980s, and early 1990s.

High rates of black crime in the twentieth century also help explain high rates of black punishment. We saw earlier that imprisonment rates for black males in the 1980s and 1990s had risen to seven to nine times the comparable white rates. Counting prisons and jails together, the black male incarceration rate in 2000 was seven times that for whites.[127] Shocking as the punishment disparities are, they are not wildly out of line with black-white differentials for gravely violent offenses, ranging between a factor of five and a factor of twelve during the 1990s. On the other hand, the black-white differentials for crimes less fearsome than homicide, rape, robbery, and the most serious assaults have not been sizable enough to match the large disparities in incarceration.

Sophisticated attempts have been made by researchers to estimate the amount of racial bias in the American criminal courts, recognizing that a significant share of the imbalances in punishment derives from imbalances in crime.[128] In two famous studies using data from 1991 and 1979, Alfred Blumstein found that 75 to 80 percent of racial disparities in prison populations mirrored racial differences in crime commission based on arrests.[129] Blumstein's methodology could not account for the possibility that blacks on average might commit more serious variants of certain crimes than whites, such as the aggravated assault example discussed earlier. Nor could he correct for the possibility that black defendants on average might come to court with more serious records of prior offending. In either case, racial disparities in imprisonment might be explained by racial differences in crime commission to an even higher degree than 75 to 80 percent. On the other hand, Blumstein could not determine whether penalties for black-on-black crime were sometimes disproportionately low.[130] As suggested in the Baldus study of capital punishment, it is possible that black offenders who victimize whites are treated more harshly than blacks who victimize blacks.[131] Such twin effects, both stemming from indefensible biases, could offset each other and make sanctions imposed on blacks look more justifiable in the aggregate than they actually are in particular cases.[132]

Even assuming that roughly three-quarters of racial disparities in incarceration can be traced back to crime commission, that still leaves a very significant 25 percent that cannot be explained. With total black incarceration now approaching the one million mark on any given day, this would place 250,000 African Americans per day in the suspicious status of "unexplained" confinement. Blumstein's analyses have further suggested that racial disproportionalities in imprisonment are largest, and least justifiable, for crimes at the low end of the seriousness scale—especially for drug offenses. Police, prosecutors, and judges almost always treat violent crime such as homicides and armed robberies as events that require serious repercussions, regardless of whether the perpetrators are black or white. Lower down on the crime gravity scale, however, such officials do not automatically follow the letter of the law in all cases. Frequently, arrests are not made, cases are not filed (or the maximum available charges are not pursued), and the punishment consequences in the long run are often much lighter than legally permitted. Where such discretionary latitude is at its widest, Blumstein posited that there is more room for the personal and racial biases of decisionmakers to enter the process.[133]

In drug enforcement the effects of official discretion are especially worrisome, because no victim calls the police to initiate each case. Instead, law enforcement agencies decide for themselves where to concentrate their antidrug resources. Blumstein found in both of his studies that drug prosecutions led to the greatest prison racial disproportionalities of all offenses, when measured against arrest statistics.[134] In addition to this troubling finding, the rate of drug arrests of black suspects skyrocketed in the 1980s from about two times the white drug arrest rate to a peak nearly five times the white rate.[135] In sum, the drug arrest baseline has lacked the historical stability, and the close connection to victim reports, that lends credibility to the arrest statistics for other crimes. Measured by the racial effects left unexplained, Blumstein's data are every bit as disturbing in the area of drug enforcement and sentencing as they are reassuring in the domain of punishment for serious violent crime.

Racial disproportionalities in punishment are a national tragedy, but so are racial disproportionalities in crime commission, especially at the high end of the violence spectrum. It has for some time been politically correct to avert one's eyes from the facts of black-white crime differentials, but it is not clear that such avoidance tactics do a good service to anyone. If it is true that the bulk of punitive disparity originates in differential crime rates, then anyone who cares about racial justice in America should be focusing major effort on understanding and combating the causes of higher levels of crime in our poor, urban, minority communities. Urban sociologists such as William Julius Wilson and Robert Sampson have long maintained that disorganized communities and concentrated poverty and segregation have produced extraordinarily high levels of crime, especially violent crime, in our poorest minority neighborhoods.[136] A much greater percentage of black than white children are raised in conditions of intense poverty and family disruption.[137] Ethnographies such as Elijah Anderson's *Code of the Street* suggest that, for many black children in the inner cities of the late twentieth century, involvement in gangs, the drug market, and violent interaction was both rational and very hard to avoid.[138]

The risk of serious victimization is also intolerably high among many minority communities in the contemporary United States. African Americans nationwide in the late 1990s faced homicide victimization risks that were six to seven times those experienced by white Americans. (For Hispanics, according to available data, the homicide risk in some communities has been four to five times the white rate.)[139] Ninety-four percent of black homicide victims in 1998 were killed by black offenders, and 76 percent of all blacks who were the victims of any violent crime in the 1990s were victimized by black offenders.[140] In our poorest and most disorganized communities, these daily risks are still greater than the averaged-out figures portray.

Such grim realities should be seen as civil rights issues that coexist with inequalities inflicted by the police, the courts, and our institutions of punishment.[141] Yet if our attention is diverted from the hard issues of criminogenesis and victimization, and if we instead scapegoat our legal institutions for an entire pathology that is only fractionally theirs, we risk consigning the very groups we purport to be helping to a continuing future of community dysfunction, high levels of crime commission, and intolerable levels of victimization.

All of the subjects in this chapter have shown deep roots in the past. Significant changes in crime and punishment have always unfolded over decades and even centuries. In order to apprehend our current circumstances, and to understand how we got where we are, we must look back at least thirty or forty years. When considering what actions to take today to shape the crime response complex, we should likewise cast our eyes several decades to the future, to ask what form of government and society we wish to be building, step by step and brick by brick.

2

Knowledge and Assessment

It is in society's interest that the crime response complex be well managed. This requires that people within the complex gather the best information reasonably available about crime and the effects of responses to crime on individuals and communities. It also requires that those responsible for responding to crime nurture a robust self-critical capacity and be able to see how their roles relate to those of other actors.[1]

The need for good management within the complex increases with time, and the task becomes more difficult with time. Government crime response agencies have grown into massive bureaucracies, each one uncoordinated with the others. Private crime response activities also intensified in the late twentieth century, adding new measures of surveillance, coercion, and control to those supplied by the governmental sector. The larger and more loosely organized the complex becomes, the less subject it is to deliberate coordination and reform.

Principles of good management have seldom been applied to crime response in America. Many observers doubt that the idea is feasible, and some academics have derided the "managerialist" instincts of the research-and-evaluation community as lacking in humanity or artistry.[2] Contrary to such views, we suggest that the knowledge and oversight capabilities within the crime response complex are so abysmally low that the urgent need for more, not less, "managerialism" is obvious. There is no doubt that data and empirical research supply only some of the inputs that influence the making of policy, and that they can be overridden by contrary moral sentiments, the tides of cultural change, the vagaries of politics, emotionalism, sensationalism, residual ignorance, and the inertial forces of laziness, habit, and vested interests.[3] All of the messiness of real-world decision making, even when fully acknowledged and experienced, does not diminish the importance of striving for an improved knowledge base.

The Mismeasurement of Crime

In Chapter 1, we observed that Americans knew virtually nothing about the amount of crime in society through most of the nation's history, and were often misinformed about whether crime was increasing or decreasing. We now consider the imperfect and sluggish efforts that were made during the twentieth century to redress such glaring deficits in information.

In the 1920s, the International Association of Chiefs of Police and the Bureau of Investigation (later renamed the FBI) put together a plan to ask police departments nationwide to track the number of crimes reported to them by citizens and the number of arrests made by each department.[4] A bit later in the same decade, a competing approach was advocated by scholars Samuel Bass Warner and Roscoe Pound, under which state statistical bureaus instead of the police would assemble crime statistics.[5] The contest between the two plans was more than an academic debate. Warner argued that police departments' self-interest would conflict with the mission of tabulating objective information, and that the police would often not have their hearts in the job.[6] Of the two options, the Warner-Pound proposal would have produced the more professional and objective scheme of data collection, but the police plan had momentum in its favor, not to mention the political clout of the IACP and J. Edgar Hoover's Bureau.[7] Beginning in 1930, police-gathered statistics were collated annually and forwarded to the FBI for compilation into a national summary called the Uniform Crime Reports, or the "UCR." The UCR has been the nation's most frequently consulted source of information about crime ever since.[8]

Reflecting on the first seventy years of the Uniform Crime Reports, the question could be posed whether incomplete and misleading information about crime was really better than having no information at all. A fundamental problem was that the UCR never attempted to measure actual crime rates. Instead, it has always tracked only indirect indicators of offending. The UCR tells us how often citizens have reported certain crimes to the police—that have then been recorded by a police officer, sent to the department's recordkeeping department, and finally forwarded to the FBI at the end of each year. The UCR might thus be called an indicator of "reported-recorded-transmitted" crimes—something many steps removed from the actual number of crimes.

The data collected in the UCR have borne an uncertain and inconstant relationship to actual rates of crime commission. For one thing, most offenses are never reported to the police. Even if the UCR data were compiled with perfect accuracy each year, they could tell us only how often citizens sought police assistance. Changes in the behavior of crime victims, however, do not necessarily reflect changes in crime. Indeed, for a number of offenses such as rape, assault, and domestic violence, it is quite possible that victim reporting rates have increased during some time periods—or that the police have changed the amount of effort expended to record each report—but the UCR cannot distinguish among shifts in rates of reporting, recording, and actual offending.[9] Under the right circumstances, the UCR can even indicate that offenses are being committed more frequently when the reverse is true.[10]

An additional problem with the UCR has been its spotty, and changing, coverage. The transmittal of crime data from police agencies to the FBI has always been voluntary under federal law, with quality assurance concentrated at the state and local levels.[11] During the early decades of UCR data, so few rural police departments reported to the FBI that no credible estimates of national reported crime rates were possible. As late as the mid-1960s, national arrest figures were still cobbled together from reports of police departments representing less than one-half of the total U.S. population.[12] Worse still, many large police forces were supplying statistics of flimsy reliability. There were fantastic differences in reported crime rates from city to city, with little apparent explanation except that different police departments had distinct recordkeeping and transmission practices.[13]

The FBI was not overly fastidious about the accuracy of the tabulations it received in the early years of the UCR.[14] Even so, in 1949, the FBI refused to incorporate the data supplied by the New York Police Department because the information was patently unbelievable. The NYPD changed its records system the next year, and the city's reported-recorded-transmitted robbery rate instantly rose by an astonishing 400 percent. Reported-recorded-transmitted burglaries rose by an even more astounding 1,300 percent. Clearly, the previous New York reports had not been worth the paper they were written on. Evidently, however, the new NYPD procedures were still far from satisfactory. In 1966, another revision of the department's recordkeeping system produced further apparent leaps in crime.[15]

This New York tale was hardly unusual. In the early 1960s, at least eleven major cities reported sharp crime spikes over single-year periods, yet all were artifacts of changing police recordkeeping policies, not real crime waves.[16] The FBI, however, dutifully included such numbers in the UCR counts. Continuing into the 1970s and 1980s, the introduction of computerized recordkeeping and steady improvements in the internal administration of some police departments ensured that fewer crime reports were lost or misfiled.[17] Although one cannot fault the departments for tightening their procedures, the new statistics, when matched against the old, exaggerated the impression that crime was on the rise.

The skewing of UCR data has not always been in the direction of inflating the apparent growth of crime, however. Through the 1990s, numerous police departments, large and small, continued to supply the FBI with inaccurate information, unusable data, or no crime reports at all. During that decade, there were also numerous scandals in which local law enforcement agencies were shown to be "cooking the books" to make crime rates appear lower, or in quicker decline, than the facts would bear.[18]

In the late 1990s alone, government audits and media exposés uncovered serious problems of police underrecording of crimes reported by citizens in Philadelphia, Baltimore, Atlanta, Boca Raton, New York, and Ventura County, California.[19] The underrecording was achieved in some cases by ignoring or "unfounding" victims' reports, which made crime events disappear entirely from statistical memory. More commonly, police officials downgraded serious reported offenses into less serious categories for recording purposes. Investigative journalists in Philadelphia, for example, found that the city's police had diminished numerous aggravated assaults into simple assaults, and stabbings and beatings were sometimes classified as "hospital cases." Some robberies were recorded as "disturbances," while burglaries were transmuted into "lost property" or "can't find purse." Hundreds of rape complaints were placed in such generic classifications as "service call" or "investigate person"—and were never investigated further.[20] Eventually the city comptroller conducted an internal audit of the police department's crime records for 1998 and found that the department had failed to record as many as 37,000 major crimes in that year, or 26 percent of all such crimes reported by citizens.[21]

Much of the doctoring of crime statistics in the 1990s appears to have been motivated by the desire to make precinct commanders, the department, and the city look good in each cycle of crime reporting. Philadelphia for years had claimed the distinction of being one of the safest big cities in

America, but the corrected figures for 1998 catapulted it into ignominy as the second most dangerous of the ten largest cities, right behind Detroit.[22] An underrecording scandal in Ventura County, California, was likewise linked to that county's efforts to market itself as "the safest urban area in the West."[23] As Samuel Warner had recognized in the 1920s, police agencies have many incentives other than the compilation of pure and unbiased information.

The shabbiness of police crime statistics would be of limited concern if the errors in counting remained similar over the years and were always slanted in the same direction. If the UCR consistently reflected only 40 percent of violent crimes, for instance, then year-by-year changes in reported-recorded-transmitted rates would bear a steady correlation to the underlying reality of offending patterns. Unfortunately, the twentieth-century experience with the UCR demonstrated that shifts in police behavior, exacerbated by political pressures and the uncertainties of victim reporting, have distorted apparent changes in offending in alternately upward and downward directions. The methodological deficiencies of the UCR are compound, complex (at the level of each police department), and endlessly mutating.

In the last three decades, however, the nation's knowledge about crime has been advancing in other quarters. Starting in 1973, the U.S. Justice Department began a yearly household survey of crime victims. Unlike the FBI's count of reported-recorded-transmitted events, the National Crime Victims Survey (or NCVS) sought for the first time a measure of actual crime rates through interviews of a representative sample of the U.S. population. Surveys are not perfect factfinding instruments, to be sure, and the NCVS is no exception. Survey respondents have fallible memories, they are not always truthful or trustful when answering questions, and their answers can be swayed by how inquiries are framed. In addition, national surveys such as the NCVS rely on samples, which do not perfectly represent the country as a whole. Some groups of victims are underrepresented and some (like the homeless, or business organizations) are not represented at all. Finally, the nationwide scope of the NCVS means that its results have limited bearing on the crime rates of specific states, cities, or counties. If crime is going down in the Southeast but up in the Pacific Northwest, or is following radically different paths in different metropolitan areas, the NCVS has no means to detect or report such geographic irregularities.[24]

Despite its defects, however, the NCVS remains the only tool the nation has ever possessed that even *purports* to estimate true rates of crime. It is the first source that should be consulted for nationwide crime patterns since 1973, and it has served since that date as an essential cross-check on questionable UCR numbers.

Not surprisingly, the victims survey in its earliest days confirmed that UCR figures were badly incomplete. Far more crimes were taking place than the police ever got wind of, and citizens' reporting rates were found to vary enormously depending on the type of offense.[25] The NCVS also proved that the UCR trend lines, showing whether crime was going up or down, and by how much, could not be trusted. From the early 1970s through the early 1990s, the data obtained directly from crime victims produced trend lines that nearly always slanted in a more downward direction than the UCR numbers for the same crimes.[26] (This will be discussed in greater detail in Chapter 3.) Only in the later 1990s, when political pressures made it desirable to report that crime rates were in decline, did the UCR and NCVS come into relative agreement that the nation was experiencing a sustained "crime drop."

The future of crime measurement in the United States should be guided by two priorities: (1) an abandonment of the UCR as a "crime" measure, to be recharacterized as only a form of "police statistics"; and (2) significant increased investments in the NCVS to address its methodological weaknesses and expand its coverage. The first recommendation flows directly from the earlier discussion. The UCR is *not* a crime measure, and has always flown under false colors when claiming to be such a thing. No amount of shoring up police statistics can ever bridge the gap between actual crime rates and reported-recorded-transmitted crime counts, even if it were possible to enforce meaningful quality controls on thousands of police departments nationwide. That is not to say that police statistics are unimportant sources of information within the crime response complex, or that they should not be maintained and improved where possible. It is a good thing, for example, that the federal government is experimenting with a new approach called the National Incident-Based Reporting System (or NIBRS), designed to encode more detailed information about more categories of offenses than ever before reported by the police.[27] The major disservice to public understanding and policy development comes not in the gathering and dissemination of such information, but in its mislabeling. Someone should think of a new name for the Uniform Crime Reports, such as "Uniform Police Statistics." And perhaps the best way to avoid the cognitive dissonance that results from separate publication of UCR and

NCVS data would be to consolidate their findings into a single report issued by a politically insulated government agency outside the FBI and Department of Justice. Such an independent forum could highlight the strengths and weaknesses of each data source, while clarifying the relationship between police statistics and more direct avenues for the tracking of crime.

Meanwhile, the victims survey remains an authentic crime measure that could greatly be improved through technologically unsophisticated adjustments that present-day researchers know how to make. The main obstacle to a more powerful series of victimization data is money. Better information about crime could be generated almost immediately if its importance were sufficiently appreciated when budgetary allocations are made. Larger survey samples and the increased use of in-person interviews (as opposed to perfunctory telephone interviews) would be valuable steps. Perhaps most important of all, the survey must be expanded and disaggregated so that freestanding crime measures for individual states and major cities can be supported from survey data. This is a matter of special urgency because the facts of crime differ from place to place, and because so much of crime response unfolds on the state and local levels. If we want to study the effects of new policing tactics in New York City, for example, or new firearms laws in several states, it is essential to have credible crime data that is specific to the affected areas. At present, however, evaluators of local initiatives must depend on police data for designated geographic areas—and no responsible policymaker should want to rest important decisions on such infirm foundations. The tragedy of America's knowledge gap about crime is that we know how to collect the information we most need, but have been dissuaded by surmountable costs and the availability of a misbranded substitute.

The Slow Growth of an Assessment Mentality

While achieving a better understanding of crime rates is a fundamental need, it is hardly the only knowledge deficit in the crime response complex that matters. It is just as important to ask how well the various agencies within the complex are performing, and whether the parts of the complex are interacting well with one another. Such inquiries, if made regularly and seriously, add up to a self-critical capacity in crime response that we call "the assessment mentality."

It is central to the argument of this book that it is possible to generate and use information about crime response in ways that are far more successful than current practice. We know that such improvements are possible because they began to occur in the late twentieth century. Although the process was excruciatingly slow, and was nearly always placed too low on the list of governmental priorities, over recent decades there have been undeniable advances in our understanding of what the crime response complex is doing, to whom, and to what effect.

There have also been examples of improved knowledge about crime response leading to better policies. Yet we do not wish to exaggerate this point. Any informed observer of American crime response must concede that there has often been a large gap between what we know about crime, crime prevention, law enforcement, and punishment and what we actually do. Our arrangements for official decision making too often choke off the use of policy-relevant knowledge, and the research community has not done all that it can to address the questions that are most salient to responsible officials and the public.

Why has it been so difficult to develop and make use of good information about crime response policy? A large part of the explanation is geographic and intergovernmental balkanization. A defining feature of the American crime response complex is its utter disconnectedness, including the concentration of power at the lowest levels of bureaucracies, where there is little monitoring or higher supervision.[28] Most of our present-day crime response institutions grew up at the state, county, and municipal levels in the eighteenth and nineteenth centuries, following still older English traditions of localized governance.[29]

Balkanization creates two fundamental difficulties for management within the crime response complex: First, relevant information about how the complex operates is scattered across thousands of agencies at the local level. American governments have not been good at creating responsible auditors to require that all of this operational data be collected and collated.[30] And second, the strong tradition of local control in crime response militates against top-down reform initiatives. When ambitious new approaches in criminal law are created at the legislative level, for example, they are often (perhaps typically) circumvented or evaded by officials at the ground level.[31]

Much of the chronicle of American crime response in the last century involved the dawning awareness that the many thousands of micro-units of law enforcement, prosecution, case processing, and punishment nationwide were doing jobs that should be monitored, evaluated, and coordinated in a rational way. In the 1920s, a handful of states and cities formed commissions to conduct "surveys" of how the criminal law was operating through its many institutions. Some of the surveys were led by accomplished and worldly scholars, including Roscoe Pound (dean of Harvard Law School) and Felix Frankfurter (who later became a Justice of the U.S. Supreme Court).[32] For the first time, the surveys advocated that the varied operations of criminal law enforcement, prosecution, and punishment should be examined as a "system."[33]

The new awareness of the need for information and assessment on a systemic level filtered up to the national government in the late 1920s with President Hoover's National Commission on Law Observance and Enforcement, commonly called the "Wickersham Commission." By the time the Wickersham Commission had completed its work in 1931, it had published fourteen separate reports on such subjects as the police, courts, penal institutions, child offenders, "crime and the foreign born," the national costs of crime, the causes of crime, and juvenile delinquency.[34]

In groping toward an information-based approach to crime response, the Wickersham Commission underscored the great complexity of criminal-law-related institutions in the United States and the severe shortage of information about their performance:

> Accurate data are the beginning of wisdom in such a subject, and no such data can be had for the country as a whole, nor have they even been available hitherto with respect to many of the activities of the Federal Government in the enforcement of Federal laws. A proper system of gathering, compiling, and reporting of statistics of crime, of criminals, of criminal justice, and of penal treatment is one of the first steps in the direction of improvement.[35]

Nearly forty years later, a second presidential crime commission found that the extreme knowledge gaps identified by the Wickersham Commission, for the most part, had gone unaddressed. The 1967 President's Commission on Law Enforcement and Administration of Justice (or "the Johnson Commission") reiterated its predecessor's sentiment that "the greatest need is the need to know."[36]

> In some respects the present system [of knowledge and information] is not as good as that used in some European countries 100 years ago. There

are no national and almost no State or local statistics at all in a number of important areas: the courts, probation, sentencing, and the jails. There are important deficiencies in those statistics which are collected. There is . . . no satisfactory test for police performance. In short the United States is today, in the era of the high speed computer, trying to keep track of crime and criminals with a system that was less than adequate in the days of the horse and buggy.[37]

Why had so little progress been made between the Wickersham Commission in the 1920s and the Johnson Commission in the 1960s? Timing had a great deal to do with it. The first preliminary report of the Wickersham Commission was delivered to President Hoover's desk one day before the October stock market crash of 1929.[38] For the next sixteen years, the American people were buffeted by the Great Depression followed by a world war. Virtually none of the commission's recommendations was adopted, and the reports themselves were largely forgotten for decades.[39]

The final report of the Johnson Commission, issued in 1967, was to enjoy more lasting effects than Wickersham. In a number of areas, discussed in Chapter 3, the 1967 report failed to have much effect on subsequent events.[40] In the areas of research, data collection, and systemic evaluation, however, the Johnson Commission provided a distinct push forward. Here it is useful to consider the thirty-five years (or so) between the Wickersham Commission and the Johnson Commission, and the thirty-five years between the Johnson Commission and the writing of this book. If we compare the advances that occurred in knowledge and assessment from 1967 to 2002 with those (conspicuous for their absence) between 1931 and 1967, we see that the final third of the twentieth century was a time of slow, belated, but potentially transformative change. This yields some sense of the possibilities for the next several decades.

As Michael Tonry said at a thirty-year retrospective of the Johnson Commission:

When the Commission reported [in 1967], there were no ongoing national statistical systems on victimization, jails, pretrial detention, prosecution, criminal court operations, sentencing, [probation], parole, or recidivism. New systems were created on all these topics. The Commission proposed changes and improvements in the existing police, juvenile, and prison systems, and many of those were also made.[41]

The current National Institute of Justice and Bureau of Justice Statistics owe their existence to the Johnson Commission. Although the performance of both agencies can be criticized, there is no question that they have generated mountains of information that have provided essential raw material for policy debate over the last three decades. It is rare to find any concerned observer of American crime response who does not make frequent use of data and research emanating from these national centers.

Despite such advances, however, it would be a mistake to conclude that the Johnson Commission shoved the American assessment mentality into high gear, and that the crime response complex is now adequately self-critical and devoted to improvement. It would be more accurate to say that the nation's commitment to such tasks has been half-hearted and at times half-baked. One window into the matter is to look at budget appropriations for crime-related research. In 1967 the Johnson Commission found that "the expenditure for the kinds of descriptive, operational, and evaluative research that are the obvious prerequisites for a rational program of crime control is negligible." The commission observed that 15 percent of the budget of the Defense Department was set aside for research, compared with "only a small fraction of 1 percent of the total expenditure for crime control." Overall, the commission concluded, "There is probably no subject of comparable concern to which the Nation is devoting so many resources and so much effort with so little knowledge of what it is doing."[42]

These findings remained disturbingly intact at the close of the twentieth century. By the end of the 1990s, annual expenditures on criminal justice nationwide had reached $147 billion.[43] Yet in 1995, two leaders in American criminology noted:

> It is striking to contrast criminal justice research budgets, which aggregate to well under $50 million dollars, with the resources used for various other research and operational activities. The total [National Institutes of Health] budget of $13 billion is almost 1,000 times as large as the [National Institute of Justice] budget. It is clear that the research expenditures in this area are profoundly inconsistent with the magnitude of the problem, with the resources being expended to address the problem, and with the resources committed to other comparably important national issues.[44]

Working with these figures, the federal government in the mid-1990s was still providing research spending equal to far less than 1 percent of total national criminal justice expenditures. If we were to imagine a footrace between the raw growth of the crime response complex and the accompanying growth of the assessment mentality, we would see the expansion of the entire complex running well ahead of society's limping efforts to develop rational, information-based controls.

Knowledge Matters

The case for redoubled public investment in research and development in crime response is even stronger today than it was thirty-five years ago. In the late twentieth century the assessment mentality began to demonstrate its potential to contribute to a more thoughtful and effective use of the tools available to combat crime, and to help avoid wasteful or destructive efforts.

Perhaps the best example of a body of research that has made such a difference was the accumulation of studies, collected into a critical mass of persuasive evidence in the 1970s, that ended the hegemony of rehabilitation theory as the overarching rationale for criminal sanctions.[45] Here the scientific community contributed dramatically to policy debate by demonstrating that most well-intentioned treatment programs had little positive effect on their subjects, and some even did harm.[46] The reverberations of these findings have reached throughout the crime response complex ever since (as we shall see in later chapters).

More recently, a growing body of research has found that some crime prevention activities, inside and outside the formal legal system, are demonstrably effective at reducing rates of offending, including a minority of those that still sail under the flag of rehabilitation. A central problem is separating the wheat from the chaff in programmatic options, because there are so many interventions that look good on paper, or succeed in winning political support, only to fail in operation. An impressive sorting of the most useful research findings, commissioned by the National Institute of Justice, was completed by the University of Maryland Department of Criminology and Criminal Justice in 1997. Their report, *Preventing Crime: What Works, What Doesn't, What's Promising,* canvassed crime prevention efforts within communities, families, schools, and workplaces, as well as others mobilized by the police, criminal courts, and corrections agencies.[47]

The Maryland Report found that, for the vast majority of crime prevention measures, we lack sufficient knowledge to judge their effectiveness. But it also found that good evidence already exists to support the efficacy of some interventions, compiled from well-designed studies that sometimes had been replicated in more than one location. These included crime prevention measures as diverse as:

home visitation of young children at special risk of future delinquent and criminal behavior;

increased police patrol in "hot spot" neighborhoods;

some zero-tolerance policing techniques, including proactive arrests of known serious offenders;

some in-prison drug treatment programs; and

the incapacitation of high-rate offenders through extended terms of incarceration.[48]

The Maryland Report also identified a number of crime prevention programs that have been demonstrated not to work, including some high-profile offerings such as DARE, a popular school-based antidrug program, and the ubiquitous boot camps that sprang up across the country to immerse youthful offenders in military-style discipline.[49] The policy message of such findings, if heeded, could save state and local governments hundreds of millions of dollars in misdirected spending in the coming years.

At a further extreme of futility, the Maryland Report and a later follow-up study also highlighted a number of well-meaning interventions that actually backfire, or produce increased levels of crime among their clientele. Such measures included the mandatory arrest of some misdemeanor domestic violence offenders, the arrest of juveniles for minor infractions, and the popular "Scared Straight" programs housed in many American prisons, where juvenile offenders are exposed to an uncensored preview of adult prison life.[50] In the case of Scared Straight, seven of nine controlled studies documented a criminogenic effect rather than a crime-suppressive effect. Such startling results go beyond the question of whether programmatic dollars are being squandered, to raise the specter of a crime response complex that is in fact *creating* crime.[51] Elementary precepts of public accountability demand that we test for such disastrous possibilities even among the most well-intentioned responses to crime.

Before leaving the subject of why more and better assessment is needed in American crime response, we pause to note one large area of political awkwardness entailed by any such proposal: Quite often, rigorous empirical study defeats the hopes, expectations, or beliefs of persons with strong political viewpoints about what the shape of crime response should be, or of persons with vested interests in specific programs—or whole fields of activity—that are vulnerable to adverse research findings.

For example, we might expect criminal justice liberals to applaud greater efforts in early childhood intervention and drug treatment, whereas archetypical conservatives could be expected to support renewed efforts of aggressive policing and lengthened incarceration for dangerous offenders. But may we likewise anticipate that conservatives will ultimately embrace drug treatment while large numbers of liberals will be won over to selective incapacitation? There are few examples of such openmindedness on display. Evaluation results can likewise line up uncomfortably with people's professional affiliations. Police departments might predictably be enthusiastic about the positive results from studies of hot-spot policing, yet be unswayed by the strong evidence that police-sponsored DARE programs in the schools are a waste of time.

Altogether, these are serious handicaps to anyone trying to assemble a constituency to support a comprehensive assessment mentality that will be apolitically executed. Consequently, the largest overall improvement that might be envisioned for the policy formation process would be a new nonpartisan commitment to empirical research, together with a new sense in public ethics and debate that credible research findings should be given a place of importance regardless of their "fit" within a preordained liberal or conservative perspective.

Enriching the Assessment Agenda

Even if the nation were so fortunate as to expand the assessment of crime response to an appropriate level, it would still be important to ask how assessments could be made more relevant to the concerns of policymakers and the public. We think the answer is a *multivalent* assessment agenda that explicitly addresses the five major goals of the crime response complex, as set out in the book's introduction. If these are the objectives that matter most, they must likewise become the performance measures used to hold crime response actors accountable for their efforts.

The argument over what counts as success in crime response is a matter of longstanding contention. Indeed, there is real danger that people, when pushed to evaluate programs, will focus on outcomes that matter little. If left unattended, many crime response professionals will prefer to rate their own performance according to criteria that are easily measured, within their control, and likely to make their work appear useful. This natural human tendency becomes a large problem if credulous outsiders are quick to believe in internally generated reports of triumph. Wherever possible, a sophisticated consumer of crime response assessments should prefer the scrutiny of independent auditors, working with sound scientific methodologies and widely agreed-on evaluation criteria.

The practice of self-monitoring, by agency participants or program advocates, has led to the promulgation of some strange measures of success. Police departments, for example, have in the not-so-distant past assessed their own operations by counting the sheer numbers of arrests made by officers, or by calculating the amount of time it takes the average patrol car to respond to an emergency call.[52] More recently, some victims groups have reconstituted these performance measures and treated increased arrests of domestic violence offenders, or increased instances of reporting of suspected child abuse, as ends in themselves.[53] Such indicators are at best imperfectly related to any of the major goals of crime response. Indeed, empirical studies have shown that overly prolific arrests can increase crime instead of suppressing it—in the domestic violence realm and other settings—and that shortened response times to 911 calls adds almost nothing to the investigation or reduction of crime.[54]

The existence of spurious assessment measures has been propped up by the failure of criminologists to achieve wide agreement on what ought to count as success. Within the research community some believe that crime reduction should be the primary yardstick, and many studies focus exclusively on the recidivism of individual offenders who have been exposed to a particular intervention, or on crime rates in communities where new policing or crime prevention initiatives have been at work. Other researchers have argued that a broader range of outcome variables ought to matter as well, including such things as whether offenders exposed to a given program seem to have changed their attitudes, or whether specific problems or needs of offenders have been addressed, such as active drug addiction or the lack of job or parenting skills. For some evaluators, the tendency of a crime response intervention to reduce reliance on incarceration, either through prevention, diversion, or alternative punishments, is a central assessment concern. For others, the success of a program can be demonstrated if its economic costs are lower than the estimated (usually poorly estimated) economic costs of crimes thought to have been prevented.[55]

Adding to these disagreements, some philosophers of punishment maintain that crime response should aim solely to do justice. Under this perspective, utilitarian concerns such as crime avoidance are not necessary goals—they are either beside the point or icing on the cake. Accordingly, crime response should be evaluated in terms of whether it disposes of criminals in ways they "deserve." Desert can mean that the seriousness of the crime, including the harm done to a victim and the blameworthiness of the offender, should be fully reflected in the amount of punishment. From defendants' perspective, it can mean that the punishment should not exceed what is proportionate to the crime.[56]

We do not think that the American public, or any sensible polity, can ever be concerned only with a single theory or goal as the end product of crime response. Nor should good policy turn on whether the objectives of crime response are rarefied to a level of intellectual coherency that would satisfy an academic philosopher. What is important is to achieve broad statements of the multiple objectives that should count. A realistic goal-directed approach should not seek to settle all controversies in advance, but rather should place contestable aspirations on the table, thus ensuring that they cannot be ignored or assumed away.

The assessment project we envision is one that constantly asks, debates, and seeks the best available answers to the following questions:

Does the crime response program under examination reduce future criminal offending?

Does it ameliorate the fear of crime in the community?

Does it promote justice for victims, offenders, and communities?

Does it foster greater community respect for the legitimacy of law and the crime response complex within all relevant communities?

Does it avoid extending criminal law further than necessary to address serious harms faced by society?

No program will ever score perfectly on these demanding performance measures, and it will frequently be impossible to further all five at the same time. More often than is comfortable, one objective will conflict with another, making it necessary to face difficult tradeoffs. One rule of application must be to seek goals only where they might be found—and only to a degree that is realistic. In this spirit, the multivalent framework is especially powerful when used as a means for choosing among imperfect alternatives in the real world.

Let us assume, for example, that two crime response strategies are equally effective at reducing crime in communities. Perhaps this is true of the alternatives of long-term incarceration of some drug offenders as opposed to long-term drug treatment for the same offenders. If the crime-avoidance benefits of both choices are comparably impressive—or comparably paltry—then we should debate the selection on other grounds. Justice and legitimacy concerns might prove persuasive in "breaking the tie" in such a case. When present in sufficient measure, justice or legitimacy concerns might even outweigh the advantages of crime suppression that flow from a given set of responses—provided that real efforts are taken to find out how affected community members feel. For instance, William Stuntz has argued that serious harms to law's legitimacy in black communities warrant a rethinking of American drug enforcement policies—even if those policies were created in good faith and have been effective at reducing crime.[57]

An assessment mentality will never be successful unless it is realistic about what is humanly possible in research, funding, and the debate between sometimes irreconcilable points of view. Our ability to adduce precise scores or rankings of crime response programs on any or all of the five major evaluation criteria will often be lacking. For example, it can take years to complete a single study of one program, and still longer to wait for convincing replications at multiple sites. New crime response experiments must of course be allowed to proceed before definitive assessment results come in. Otherwise, innovation would be shut down by the requirement that programs be proven before they are ever tried. What must be avoided is the unconscionable negligence of allowing programs to flourish and multiply for indefinite periods of time, affecting thousands or millions of lives, with no scrutiny of evaluation attempted on a feasible timetable.

Difficult questions also surround those crime response efforts that defy empirical study, especially where randomized experiments are impossible or unethical, or where successful interventions cannot be reproduced because they rely on the presence of a charismatic leader or an unusually committed staff. When applying the five-part multivalent scale, therefore, the realistic policymaker will often be working with scoresheets that include entries like "don't know" or "best guess" or "depends on the eye of the beholder" in some of the blank spaces. This need not be paralyzing. Instead, a realistic assessment process must weigh alternative crime response options based on what is known, and what is a matter of speculation, when comparing one program to another.

Realism also demands that the five goals of crime response be pursued with an eye toward cost effectiveness. Neither government nor the private marketplace is likely to fund programs when their costs are astronomical, no matter how successful they are shown to be. There is no formula for determining when an expensive program is nonetheless worthwhile. The issue of cost effectiveness is dependent on nonmonetary value judgments and the total amount of resources available within the crime response complex at any given time. Certainly, America has never committed more dollars to crime response than in the early twenty-first century, largely because of the enduring effects of past investments in the expensive sanction of confinement. Perhaps the same dollar commitment, or a smaller overall budget, could be spent more wisely and to greater purpose. Whatever the overall level of resources a society is willing to dedicate to crime response, however, excessive cost will preclude some good programs regardless of their advantages and, all else being equal, cheaper programs will and should have an edge over more expensive ones.

Illustration of an Enriched Assessment Agenda

An illustration of the multivalent assessment approach can be drawn from ongoing work in the restorative justice field—or at least from one corner of the field occupied by the writings of John Braithwaite. Restorative justice, considered as a whole, is a new and still amorphous collection of crime response theories and practices. All of them purport to elevate the goal of restoring victims and communities over the goal of inflicting punishment on offenders.[58] It is not always self-evident what "restoration" should mean following a criminal act, even to some advocates of the theory. (What if a victim believes her restoration requires harsh punishment of the offender?)[59] One may also question the wisdom and workability of some restorative justice proposals, particularly when the theory is put forward as the new paradigm for all of crime response.[60]

The ambitions of restorative justice can sound attractive, even seductive. A reader of the current literature of restorative justice might usefully be reminded of the romantic claims that were advanced for the newly created juvenile courts in the early twentieth century, such as the inspirational (and widely influential) article published in the 1909 *Harvard Law Review* by Chicago juvenile court judge Julian Mack.[61] It is no insult to Braithwaite to observe that, as a moral entrepreneur, he possesses much of the fervor and talent of Judge Mack. As Braithwaite himself recognizes, the ability to communicate ideas with persuasiveness and conviction does not guarantee that they are correct.[62] In the cold light of experience over many decades, Mack's charismatic advocacy for the new juvenile courts has acquired an impossibly optimistic ring.

Enthusiasm about a new idea or program should be tempered by a cautious commitment to investigate its actual effects. A useful model is the assessment agenda recently compiled by Braithwaite for testing the restorative justice program known as the family group conference.[63] Family group conferences are a prominent form of restorative justice used extensively in New Zealand and now being experimented with in a number of Western countries, especially for juvenile offenders.[64] The conferences are designed to serve as full substitutes for traditional criminal court or juvenile court proceedings. Typically, the offenses brought to a conference are property crimes and violent crimes without serious physical injuries. The restorative approach can be used with more serious crimes, however, if offender and victim are willing, and it has been applied in small numbers of cases with serious victim injuries.[65] The prerequisites for a conference include an accommodating legal framework, the consent of both offender and victim, and a case in which the offender is willing to admit guilt.

Both offender and victim choose supporters from among their families and friends to participate in the conference. Representatives of the legal system are likely also to attend, such as a defense lawyer, a prosecutor, perhaps a judge, and sometimes a police officer. Conferences can be led by a legal professional, but often a social worker or other facilitator (such as a respected person from the community) is used instead. Part of the theory of restorative justice is to place decisionmaking responsibility among those closest to and most affected by the criminal behavior, so the model tries to avoid conferences dominated by government officers or formal legal processes.[66] The average size of the group, once assembled, is eight to twelve persons. Typically, the proceedings last an hour or ninety minutes.[67]

Most conferences begin by asking the offender to tell his or her story about the offense, with later opportunities provided for the victim and all of the supportive participants to do the same. The initial focus of discussion is on the consequences of the crime. Offenders are encouraged to recognize the full effects of their actions on victims, and are confronted with the fact that many other people have been hurt as well, including the victim's broader "community of care," the offender's family and friends, and the offender him- or herself. After consideration of these consequences, discussion turns to what can be done to repair them. An apology from offender to victim is a frequent starting place. In formal terms, however, the conference aims toward a plan of action to which every participant agrees, which may include promises on the part of the offender to compensate the victim, to work in a community service project, or to engage seriously in a needed treatment program.[68] If consensus among the group cannot be reached on a restorative plan, the legal framework often provides for the case to be routed back to the standard procedures of the criminal courtroom and a judge-imposed sentence. In practice, once a conference has convened, such breakdowns in negotiation seem rarely to occur.

In the months following a conference, the offender is expected to discharge the agreed-on obligations of the restorative plan. The theory of restorative justice posits that the execution of the plan will have good consequences for the offender and the community. More importantly, however, advocates say that the conference itself is a restorative process with an emotional effect greater than its brief duration would suggest. Braithwaite believes that a properly conducted conference can produce psychological effects that are inclusive and constructive for all participants. An offender is pushed to better understand the gravity of the crime, but is also shown a path toward earning back a position in the affected communities. The victim and other conference participants are given ownership of a serious problem that has occurred in their lives. In Braithwaite's telling, this can help produce support for those offenders who are committed to positive change.

So much for what family group conferences are *supposed* to do. How well has the innovation actually worked, and how does its performance compare with available alternatives? Braithwaite has devoted serious attention to these questions in his writings since 1999—although his analyses have not been organized into the five-goal agenda that we recommend. Indeed, some critics have chastised Braithwaite for espousing a much longer list of goals (including fifteen in one publication),[69] and for using jargon and shifting, expansive terminology.[70] Still, the comprehensive assessment project Braithwaite has endorsed is an intellectually serious one, and can be mapped onto the more straightforward five-part inquiry that we have suggested.

Crime reduction. At times, Braithwaite speaks of crime reduction in mystifying terms, classifying it as an aspect of "offender restoration" in one publication and seeming to include it under the heading of "community reassurance" in another.[71] When it comes to stating what is to be tested, however, it is clear that Braithwaite is thinking of things like offender change through psychological processes, incapacitation effects, and specific deterrence. He would probably add that crime prevention can be facilitated by changes in the offender's family and community environments, such as when a parent or mentor becomes more attentive to the offender's behavior.[72] Fair enough. How does one evaluate these hypotheses?

The answer for Braithwaite has been to help set up controlled experiments testing offender recidivism for three years following 1,300 restorative justice conferences in Canberra, Australia. The methodology of the recidivism study applies the "gold standard" for research design as enunciated in the Maryland Report (mentioned earlier in this chapter).[73] Indeed, Lawrence Sherman, the lead author of the Maryland Report, was recruited as primary investigator for the Canberra evaluation.

As of this writing, Sherman's research team has published preliminary recidivism findings for the first year of the three-year follow-up period. The early results suggest that the family group conferences can bring about substantial reductions in reoffending by youths who have committed violent offenses when compared with youths who committed similar crimes under similar circumstances, but whose cases were resolved in traditional courts. Oddly enough, the conferences seem to have produced no comparable positive effects for the other categories of crimes in the study, including youth property offenses, shoplifting, and drunk driving by various age groups.[74]

The Canberra results are preliminary and somewhat confounding, but that is not the issue here. The important point is that proponents of the family group conferences, including Braithwaite, have endorsed the premise that crime reduction should not simply be asserted by program advocates, but should be studied under rigorous conditions, with no guarantees in advance that positive results will be found. Whenever large human consequences are at issue in crime response programming, such methodologically sound research should be undertaken—unless a good reason can be cited to explain its absence.[75]

Fear of crime. In his compendium of evaluation research, Braithwaite includes studies of the effect of family group conferences on the fear of crime by victims and other conference participants. The usual testing method is to ask victims and others whether the conference and the outcome of the case have affected their fears of the future behavior of the offender, or their fear of criminal victimization in general. Such questions have been asked immediately following restorative justice conferences, and sometimes in follow-up questioning months later. In the better studies, the same questions are also asked of victims and participants in similar court cases.

The results of such studies have been almost uniformly positive. In particular, victims often report greater empathy for, less aversion toward, and greater optimism about the futures of offenders following conferences, and (where studied) these effects are much more pronounced in conferenced cases than in those that end up in court.[76] These findings are important in themselves, even if limited to small groups of people. Ideally we would want to know the effects of a program on the fear of crime in whole communities, not just among a handful of direct participants in individual cases. Certain types of crime response initiatives, such as community policing experiments that are accompanied by publicity and wide interaction with the public in affected neighborhoods, can aspire to have general effects on the fear of crime (not to mention improved community opinions of the good intentions and legitimacy of local law enforcement efforts).[77] But absent broad community awareness of the process and results of family group conferences, it is not realistic to think that such programs can influence public sensibilities.

One of the most effective means to reduce the fear of crime, however, is to reduce actual levels of criminal behavior. The two are not linked in a lockstep fashion, as much of American history attests, but connections exist. If the Canberra conferences, for example, succeed in cutting back crime rates among youths with a history of violent offending, people in the community will eventually reap the benefits. To some degree the experience of daily life will change for the better as fewer people experience, or hear about a neighbor's experience of, criminal victimization. Also, to the extent that crime statistics make the news, or are disseminated in community forums, the reality of crime reduction can gain leverage on public perceptions.

Justice. A proposal for the "assessment" of justice values can seem an oxymoron. Justice will always be a supremely contested commodity, and its center of gravity can shift markedly across different places, times, and cultures. Of all the concerns included in the multivalent analysis, justice is the hardest to access through concrete empirical methodology. When placing justice high on the list of evaluation criteria, we do not envision that its meaning can ever be settled, or that it will ever be fully reducible to quantitative data. Rather, we think it important that evaluators and policymakers be required to talk explicitly about justice concerns, placing their value judgments on the table for open inspection.[78]

Justice should not be considered narrowly from the perspective of any one person, such as an offender or victim, yet such perspectives should be included within a larger inquiry. In the restorative justice literature, Braithwaite has collected evidence and arguments that speak to justice for victims, justice for offenders, and justice for whole communities.[79] This is the right constellation of questions to be asking.

One way to attempt to measure justice from victims' point of view is to ask them whether they are satisfied with the outcome of their cases. When such questions are posed, studies have found repeatedly that victims express high approval ratings for the restorative justice format. In the small number of studies that compare victim satisfaction in conferenced cases with similar court cases, victims regularly prefer the restorative alternative.[80] A society should not rely on a definition of justice that depends entirely on the sentiments of individual victims, which can sometimes be whimsical or draconian. But levels of victim satisfaction across the board are surely worth investigating. Justice for victims might also be thought to turn on whether offenders make good on providing restitution, community service, or other obligations arising from a conference plan or a judge's order. Here again, numerous studies in Braithwaite's survey indicate that offenders are far more likely to follow through on their obligations in conferenced cases than in court cases.[81]

Researchers have also asked offenders about their feelings of whether justice was done in conferences. Even more than victims, offenders tend to favor the restorative approach and, when comparisons can be made, offenders usually prefer it over the courtroom alternative.[82] Such findings need to be analyzed with care, of course. Offenders have so much self-interest at stake that we can expect them to favor strongly the lightest possible penalties in their own cases. It nonetheless makes sense to ask offenders about their perceptions of justice, even if we are not entirely constrained to believe them. If the courtroom process is somewhat more likely to leave offenders feeling mistreated and resentful than a comparable conferencing process, for example, then that is at least one datum that ought to be considered in light of other information.[83]

Because family group conferences are designed to accommodate the needs and perspectives of their participants, some critics have worried that justice values will be sacrificed to idiosyncratic settlements among the private parties. In response, Braithwaite, and some other proponents of restorative justice, have suggested that proportionate justice might be protected by holding the criminal courts in reserve, as a backup or check on conferences that go awry. If, for example, an intransigent victim insists upon an outsized sanction during a conference, the offender ought to have the right to opt out and move his case back to a criminal courtroom. Similarly, if an offender proves unwilling to agree to a reasonable restorative plan, the victim or a community representative might be given the power to suspend proceedings in favor of a more traditional remedy. In all cases, even when conferences run smoothly and reach consensus resolutions, it may be sound to require a judge to review the outcome to ensure that it is neither too harsh nor too trivial given the seriousness of the crime.[84]

Preserving justice in a courtroom sense is only a small segment of Braithwaite's total ambitions, however, and much of his moral analysis in favor of family group conferences unfolds on an admittedly abstract plane.[85] He offers assertions—which the reader is free to find convincing or not—about the effects of conferences on all participants and their communities, and the relationship between government and affected individuals in the crime response setting. Braithwaite claims that restorative justice conferences enhance the dignity of both victim and offender in comparison with criminal courtroom procedures, and that the conferences extend respect and power to those people most intimately affected by crimes to be closely involved in the fashioning of an appropriate response. In his more heady passages, he raises the possibility that the restorative approach can better equalize the criminal sanctions meted out to poor and rich offenders. Braithwaite even believes that citizens who have participated in conferences may gain new feelings of self-participation in government, resulting in new feelings of dignity, public responsibility, and a diminished sense of the impersonal and uncaring face of government itself.[86]

Regardless of whether these claims hold water, one must admire Braithwaite for posing justice questions alongside other evaluation inquiries, and for showing the courage to argue his moral point of view in some detail. It is now open for persons who believe that justice can better be served by traditional criminal court processes, or by some other means, to join the debate. A number of articulate critics, including Andrew Ashworth and

Andrew von Hirsch, have already done so.[87] In our scheme of multivalent assessment, such explicit contestation of moral values would always be placed in close proximity with more traditional evaluation measures.

Legitimacy. Unlike concerns about justice, people's attitudes toward the legitimacy of law and crime response institutions are testable facts. If we discover that a certain percentage of the American public does not believe that the crime response complex is morally defensible, that is an objective reality that should greatly concern policymakers.

With respect to restorative justice conferences, most research on legitimacy is conducted by asking victims, offenders, and other participants whether they felt that the processes and outcomes were fair and conducted in good faith. The studies to date show that, in the majority of cases, both victims and offenders rate conferences more highly for their overall fairness, and for the dignity bestowed upon participants, than respondents in similar courtroom cases. Conference participants emerge with greater respect for the law, the legal system, and the police than they had prior to the conference.[88] Self-reports of this kind must be treated warily, but it is striking that both victims and offenders tend to agree that there is an added increment of procedural fairness in conferences as opposed to court proceedings.

Legitimacy concerns are most urgent when extended across whole communities rather than a few people here or there. Ultimately, the legitimacy of law is a macrosocial phenomenon with effects upon entire cultures or subcultures. It is unrealistic at this stage to ask evaluators to measure the effects on mass opinion of little-known innovations like restorative justice conferences. In the longer run, it may become fair to ask whether well-entrenched restorative practices, once known and understood in affected communities, have had positive effects on people's attitude toward the legitimacy of law.

Proper limits on criminal law. The first four goals discussed earlier are all *substantive* in the sense that they are things the crime response complex should be trying to achieve. The fifth goal is different, and addresses instead the scope of the crime response enterprise. It encourages us to ask whether the criminal law is in danger of being stretched beyond justifiable boundaries.

In many settings the fifth goal is not at issue. There can be no doubt, for example, that acts such as homicide, rape, armed robbery, and child abuse call for a firm criminal law response. This confidence is based in the seriousness of the conduct, the belief that noncriminal sanctions will not be fully effective, and society's demonstrable willingness to follow through on its criminal prohibitions with meaningful enforcement. But for many categories of human conduct, such as alcohol use, drug use, firearms ownership and use, the performance of abortions, or the violation of federal environmental regulations, there have been unstable and inconsistent views over the years about whether the criminal sanction is truly needed or morally justified. In such ambiguous areas, the fifth goal insists that a comprehensive assessment of crime response interventions should ask whether a criminal law is warranted in the first place.

Braithwaite's assessment discussion touches upon this question in a number of ways, although he asserts that most cases that enter restorative justice processes involve behavior that is unambiguously wrong and ought to be classified as criminal. Nonetheless, he argues that family group conferences may work best only with "crimes that ought to be crimes": "If a group of citizens cannot agree in an undominated conference that an act of obscenity is wrong, then the obscenity should not be a crime; and the conference will fail in controlling obscenity."[89]

According to this theory, the conference might be seen as playing the same role at sentencing that juries are sometimes thought to play when exercising the nullification power at trial. If we accept Braithwaite's argument, the conference imposes yet another group of community representatives with the power to decide that government agencies of law enforcement have overstepped justifiable bounds.

Braithwaite further argues that police officers can be deterred from mistreating criminal suspects by the knowledge that, in due course, they will be obliged to appear at a restorative justice conference that will include not just the offender, but also the offender's family members and other supporters. If an officer has used excessive force or coercion in dealing with the defendant, for example, the officer can anticipate an unpleasant encounter in the formal conference setting: "Mothers in particular do sometimes speak up with critical voices about the way their child has been singled out, has been subject to excessive force, and the like. Police accountability to the community is enhanced by the conference process."[90] In contrast, in the traditional courtroom procedure following a guilty plea, a police officer will rarely be called to court to participate in legal proceedings. Any unwarranted use of criminal enforcement authority against the offender is technically irrelevant.

Finally, although Braithwaite did not explicitly make this argument, a restorative justice experiment like the family group conference might be viewed as a way of diverting cases out of the traditional criminal law docket and into a dispute resolution setting that is not wholly criminal and is somewhat private. Some critics of restorative justice see the move toward privatization as a mistake.[91] But from the point of view of the fifth goal, this would be a great advantage—provided that the first four substantive goals of crime response are not sacrificed. If restorative justice programming dilutes the kind of coercive behavior associated with traditional criminal law enforcement and punishment, and otherwise promotes goals of crime reduction, fear reduction, justice, and legitimacy, we would be hard-pressed to disfavor it.

We have included an extended discussion of the evaluation of family group conferences not because the restorative justice framework can be recommended to policymakers with any confidence, but rather to illustrate the enriched assessment mentality that should be applied to all crime response programs that have the potential to affect many lives. The conscientious assessment of important programs does not require an increased budget for the crime response complex as a whole, but a smarter use of funds that are now allocated. Every recommendation in this chapter would cost money, it is true, but all could be achieved through set-asides within current levels of spending. A research and assessment set-aside of 5 percent of current spending on law enforcement, courts, and corrections would yield enormous advances in our ability to make sound decisions. It would help guarantee that the remaining 95 percent of funds were spent more wisely, humanely, and effectively.

We leave this discussion with considerable hope for the future. Efforts at assessing and managing America's crime response are very new, and the nation's commitment to them has been shallow. Rather than view this track record as proof that crime policy is inherently irrational, culturally determined, and forever insulated from the findings and recommendations of social scientists and other researchers, we would emphasize the unexploited potential of an assessment mentality over the coming decades. The historical record of the last thirty-five years demonstrates that real gains in knowledge-informed policy are possible, even when support for assessment is half-hearted. Such progress unfolds slowly, to be sure, and will inevitably be hampered by vested political interests. The glacial pace is guaranteed to try the patience of many who want to see immediate results, and the ideal of good management is much too plodding and straightforward to remain in good standing with the latest academic fashions. Such vulnerabilities provide all the more reason for policymakers and the public to insist on continued investments in the fragile assessment and management ethic.

3

The Current Era
of Crime Response
Policy

The present era of American crime response policy began in the mid-1970s. Since then, the major initiatives of crime response, and the overall direction of policy change, have followed what might be called, for lack of a better term, a conservative agenda. The basic elements of the conservative program coalesced in the 1970s, achieved growing political popularity, and were embraced by both political parties by the century's end. In almost all of its important features, the conservative program was a stark rejection of the values of the more liberal American crime response policy of the 1960s and earlier.

In the annals of crime response, the conservative era has shown remarkable staying power. Yet the current era cannot possibly continue, full steam ahead, as it has for the past quarter century. In the near or intermediate future, significant changes in direction are all but inevitable.

Rejection of Liberalism in Crime Response

The manifestations of the current conservative era have been impressive indeed.[1] They include:

The enactment by Congress and by state legislatures nationwide of numerous laws increasing the severity of criminal punishments. These have included mandatory penalties, new and expanded death penalty provisions, "three strikes" laws for repeat offenders, laws increasing maximum prison sentences across the board, forfeiture laws for the seizure of assets, and civil commitment laws for the prolonged detention of persons convicted of sex offenses. Overall, there has been a trend toward the curtailment of judicial authority in determining criminal punishments, and toward the abolition or limitation of parole release of prisoners.[2]

Massive and unprecedented growth in incarceration and other forms of criminal punishment. (See Chapter 1.)

Racial and ethnic disproportionalities in incarceration that have become more magnified than ever before. (See Chapter 1.)

Deliberate policies to make the conditions of life within prisons harder on inmates. These have included bans on prison weight rooms, television viewing, soft-core pornography, and cigarette smoking, the reintroduction of chain gangs in some jurisdictions, and, in approximately forty states, the increasing use of "supermax" round-the-clock solitary confinement of selected inmates. There has been sentiment in many quarters that the state and federal prisons have operated as "country clubs," in which conditions of life and recreational opportunities were altogether too favorable to inmates.[3] Also, in the 1990s, Congressional legislation cut back on the legal rights of inmates to challenge the conditions of their confinement in federal court, and limited the power of federal judges to make remedial orders in such cases.[4]

A relaxing of the legal regulation of policing, which has allowed police more latitude in stopping and searching citizens, in conducting car stops, in making formal arrests, in interrogating suspects, and in using advanced surveillance and undercover investigation techniques. Since the early 1970s, the U.S. Supreme Court has issued a steady stream of decisions on the constitutional law governing police behavior toward citizens, the vast majority of which have expanded police authority or diluted preexisting regulations of that authority.[5] These rulings have overlapped with a period of rapid advancement in law enforcement technology and surveillance tactics, including electronic and video monitoring, undercover operations, drug testing, gun and drug detection machines, and DNA databanks.[6]

A general expansion of the powers of the prosecution and a withholding or limiting of procedural safeguards enjoyed by defendants. In parallel with the U.S. Supreme Court's conservative decisions on policing issues, there has been a long line of opinions in the last twenty-five to thirty years that have affected criminal case processing, usually in a progovernment direction, including decisions authorizing preventive detention of defendants before trial,[7] acknowledging that defendants who insist upon their right to trial may be penalized with a heavier sentence than if they had pled guilty to the same charges,[8] limiting the scope of the right to counsel on appeal and in other postconviction proceedings,[9] laying down a relaxed definition of the minimal "effectiveness" (skill and effort) required of defense lawyers,[10] holding that prosecutors have no duty to present exculpatory evidence to grand juries,[11] limiting the rights of state court defendants to challenge their convictions in federal court,[12] finding that jurors with personal qualms about the death penalty may be stricken from jury panels in capital cases,[13] ruling that statistical evidence of race-based disparities in the administration of a state's death penalty was insufficient to invalidate the state's process,[14] and pronouncing that sentences may be calculated in part based on crimes of which defendants have not been convicted—including charges that have resulted in acquittals.[15]

An escalation of enforcement efforts directed toward nonviolent crimes and public order offenses. (See Chapters 4, 5, and 6.)

A somewhat more punitive crime response to juvenile offenses, with increasing racial and ethnic disparities in juvenile punishment. (See Chapter 8.)

Enhanced recognition at every stage of the crime response process of the rights and interests of crime victims. All states have passed laws guaranteeing the rights of crime victims to participate in the criminal process and twenty-nine states have amended their constitutions to include victim protections. Various victims' rights organizations have become active and effective players on the political scene, including Mothers against Drunk Driving (MADD), women's advocacy groups against rape and domestic violence, and hate-crime constituencies. Legislation that is responsive to particular crimes, and is sometimes named for particular victims (such as "Megan's Law") has become increasingly commonplace.[16]

A reversal of the historical trend away from private participation in crime response, toward heavy government activity supplemented by escalating expenditures by private individuals, community groups, and businesses. (See Chapter 1.)

In reviewing the major developments of the current conservative era of American crime response, one can only be impressed with how forceful the overall direction of change has been. This stands in contrast with most of the nation's prior history, when crime response policy had been pursued half-heartedly and intermittently, usually with inadequate funding and in-stitutional support. The current era has been marked by sustained in-creases in law enforcement and punishment. These developments have re-quired and received large investments of time, effort, and money from numerous public and private decisionmakers. They have also required a constancy of political will across nearly three decades from all levels of government: federal, state, and local. No matter what else one may think of the current era, one must give it its due as a period in which a coherent set of programs has been pressed forward with determination.

The observable highlights of the current conservative era are striking for yet another reason. Almost all of the phenomena listed earlier can be seen as diametric *reversals* of events during the liberal period, which reached its peak in the 1960s. Consider the following list of some of the objective markers of crime response in the 1960s and early 1970s:

The 1960s was one of the rare periods in the recorded history of American incarceration in which the nation's prison populations shrank. (See Chapter 1.) This development—over a decade of healthy population growth in the United States—is nearly as remarkable as the massive prison construction that was to follow in the 1970s, 1980s, and 1990s.

The 1960s and early 1970s were marked by expressed enthusiasm among policymakers and criminological experts for programs aimed at rehabilitating criminal offenders, in and out of prisons; programs for the treatment of drug abuse; and social welfare programs aimed at poor and crime-ridden communities. Many have criticized the liberal era for failing to invest sufficiently in rehabilitative programming, or in failing to deliver on its promises to change criminals for the better. Nevertheless, it is clear that the philosophy and aspiration of rehabilitation was the ideal around which punishment institutions and corrections professionals organized their tasks and justi-fied their actions to the outside world.[17] At least some of this belief system was reflected in the actual operations of the crime response complex. For example, in the early 1970s, drug treatment programs briefly became the centerpiece of federal antidrug policy.[18]

The liberal era featured a hands-off approach to criminal punishment by legislators and most elected officials, in favor of laws designed to give judges and parole boards discretion over punishment. Through the 1960s, the dom-inant model of criminal sentencing gave enormous discretion to trial judges to tailor penalties to the needs of individual offenders. For those sentenced to prison, parole boards then enjoyed even greater latitude to determine inmates' actual lengths of stay, depending on their apparent progress toward rehabilitation. Some states, like California and Washington, instituted imprisonment laws under which the length of stay was virtually entirely determined by parole boards or equivalent agencies.[19]

The use of capital punishment in the United States dwindled through the 1960s, with no executions occurring from 1968 to 1976. (See Chapter 1.) By the early 1970s, it appeared to some observers that executions had become a thing of the past in the United States.

The enforcement of laws against drug possession, public drunkenness, and public order offenses was deemphasized in the 1960s and early 1970s. Law enforcement policy in the 1960s was increasingly targeted at serious crime and away from low-level offending such as intoxication, loitering and vagrancy, and other disorderly conduct in public places. With the appearance of a visible middle-class drug culture, drug enforcement efforts were eased, especially with respect to marijuana use.[20]

Through much of the 1960s, the U.S. Supreme Court issued a series of decisions placing new federal limits upon police activities, the operation of state criminal court systems, and juvenile courts nationwide. Under Chief Justice Earl Warren, the Supreme Court carried forward a broad-based program of judicial activism in favor of the rights of criminal suspects, defendants, and those convicted of crimes. Major decisions of the Warren Court era instituted the exclusionary rule for evidence seized illegally by the police,[21] created the controversial *Miranda* warnings for suspects during custodial interrogation,[22] required all states to provide free defense counsel to criminal defendants who could not afford to hire a lawyer,[23] mandated a series of procedural protections for youths brought before juvenile courts on criminal charges,[24] and cleared the way for federal court oversight of convictions obtained in state courts through the federal writ of habeas corpus.[25]

Legal changes in case processing and courtroom procedure during the 1960s focused almost exclusively on the rights of criminal defendants, and either ignored or worked against the direct interests of crime victims. The due process jurisprudence focused on state criminal court systems, particularly in the South, as sources of problems to be solved, and the decisions typically cast defendants as the victims of unfair procedures. For example, the conduct of rape trials, again with a focus on the Southern courts, was viewed as slanted against black defendants—and the punishments inflicted against blacks convicted of rape were indeed notoriously harsh.[26] There was no comparable concern, at the time, for victims of rape offenses. The courts, legislators, and academic commentators promulgated few if any important procedural or substantive innovations to advance the interests of crime victims through the 1960s and early 1970s.

In the early 1970s, the federal courts became active in regulating incarceration conditions at the federal, state, and local levels, working to improve problems of overcrowding and the abuse and neglect of inmates. Beginning in the Southern states, but spreading across the nation, the lower federal courts and some state courts entertained claims brought by inmates that the conditions of their confinement were so poor as to violate the federal constitution. In many cases, trial judges became intimately involved in the internal workings of prisons and jails over the course of years, issuing orders and obtaining consent decrees that affected all aspects of prison operations.[27]

A comparison of the major events of the current conservative era and the earlier liberal era points to a jarringly sudden 180-degree change in direction, along multiple policy dimensions, occurring in the mid-1970s.[28] The great policy shift unfolded on an accelerated time frame, taking firm root in a matter of several years.[29] Just as impressively, the revolution survived to become an established orthodoxy, exiling the liberal agenda to the margins of policy debate for the next three decades. By the 1990s, it was rare for a politician of national or even statewide stature, from either major party, to adopt views that could be identified with the liberal crime response agenda.[30]

What accounts for this stunning reversal of events, and the solidification of the conservative orientation? We will explore two explanations close to the heart of American crime response policy since 1960. First, the liberal program suffered a devastating blow when real and apparent crime rates, especially rates of serious violent crime, shot up throughout the 1960s, and then remained at very high levels for the next twenty years. Second, the liberal program proved to have numerous internal weaknesses that made it vulnerable to the sharp intellectual criticism of conservative thinkers.

The discussion that follows will not attempt a larger sociocultural theory of the decisive transition from liberalism to conservatism in America's crime responses. Certainly, the liberal approach fell out of step with large-scale changes occurring in the nation as a whole following the 1960s, including mutations in popular attitudes about social welfare policy, the effectiveness of government programming, race relations, and the personal responsibility of citizens.[31] The ambitions of the present work, however, are focused on events and attitudes that have been most proximate to crime policy. Unlike some theorists, we suggest that policy-relevant factors have had a great deal to do with the revolutionary shift in American crime response policy in the last thirty years—and that such concerns remain relevant to policymaking in the future.

The High Crime Plateau

It has long been characteristic of liberal observers to downplay the significance of crime rates as a major factor in the demise of liberal crime response policies. Instead, the liberal version of events emphasizes ideological arguments, "cynical" politicians, the media's fascination with crime stories, or covert race / class warfare as the primary supports of various "get tough" features of the conservative program.[32] We differ from such views to emphasize the reality and importance of crime in the formation of American crime response policy.

Americans could be forgiven during the 1960s for thinking that crime was spiraling out of control, and it is understandable throughout the 1970s and 1980s that many people believed serious crime rates, although no longer spiking as they had in the late 1960s and early 1970s, remained at intolerably high levels. Such perceptions were understandable even though they were based in large part on the questionable statistics produced annually by the FBI in the Uniform Crime Reports. The general public could not have been expected to understand, and correct for, the shortcomings of the UCR as a crime measurement system. To the extent that fear of crime exists in a society, whether based on bad or good information, it exerts genuine force on policy formation.

A reanalysis of American crime trends in the late twentieth century with the benefit of hindsight suggests that there was some truth in the UCR numbers. There is little doubt that the nation experienced a shift in serious criminal behavior, from comparatively low levels of crime in the 1940s and 1950s, to a new plateau of higher crime rates in the 1970s and 1980s, with the 1960s as the transitional decade between the low plateau and the high plateau.[33] The reality of crime during these time periods was worthy of concern and attention. In order to reconstruct these patterns, it is necessary to test skepticism for the UCR with other available sources of information.

According to the UCR, reporting rates for most of the major "index" crimes (homicide, robbery, aggravated assault, rape, burglary, larceny, and motor vehicle theft) declined through the 1930s, began to increase somewhat during the 1940s or 1950s, and then exploded to astonishingly high levels across the 1960s and the early 1970s.[34] A good example of the dramatic trend lines since 1960 can be seen in Figure 3.1, which reproduces the UCR's estimates of national reported-recorded-transmitted robbery rates from 1960 to 2001. From 1940 to 1960 (not shown on the figure), FBI data had indicated that reported robbery rates did not change very much, perhaps drifting up slightly over twenty years. Then, from 1960 to 1975, in almost unbroken ascent, the police statistics for robberies soared upward by a factor of 3.7 times. Robbery is a greatly feared crime, involving the use or the threat of force in a face-to-face confrontation between robber and victim. If one put blind faith in the FBI reports, in only fifteen years the nation had become roughly four times as dangerous a place to live where robbery victimization was concerned.

Following this sharp rise, rates of reported robberies remained very high for the next fifteen or twenty years according to the UCR, going up a lit-

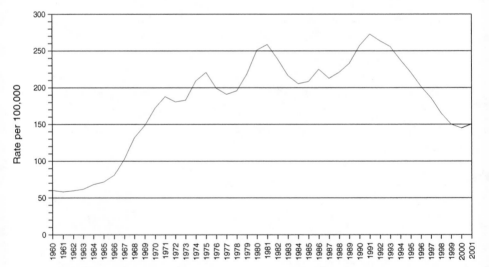

FIGURE 3.1 UCR robbery rates, 1960–2001. Data from U.S. Department of Justice, Bureau of Justice Statistics, *Sourcebook of Criminal Justice Statistics, 2000* (Washington, D.C.: GPO, 2001), pp. 278–279, table 3.120; Federal Bureau of Investigation, *Crime in the United States, 2000: Uniform Crime Reports* (Washington, D.C.: FBI, 2000), p. 29; Federal Bureau of Investigation, *Uniform Crime Reports: January–December 2001* (Washington, D.C.: FBI, 2002), p. 1.

tle in some years, and going down a little in others. The overall drift was upward. By 1991, reported robberies peaked briefly at four-and-one-half times the 1960 rate. It was not until the 1990s that a sustained drop away from the high crime plateau finally occurred in the UCR robbery statistics from 1991 to 2000. Even so, at the low point in 2000, reported robbery rates were nowhere near their low position of the early 1960s, but had relaxed only to 1968–1969 levels.

Similar apparent jumps, based on FBI data, occurred in the reporting of other serious index crimes. Between 1960 and 1975, reported forcible rapes increased by a factor of 2.74—and, by 1992, the rape reporting rates stood at four-and-one-half times the 1960 rate. Aggravated assault reports in 1975 were 2.68 times as frequent as in 1960, according to the UCR, and reached an all-time pinnacle in 1992 at more than five times the 1960 rate. Even reports of nonviolent crimes, which often show trends different from violent offenses, seemed to grow with uncommon rapidity through the 1960s and into the 1970s. Burglary reports tripled from 1960 to 1975 and larceny reports nearly tripled in the same time span.[35]

What were crime rates really doing in these periods? We do not for a minute believe that aggravated assault and robbery rates in the early 1990s were really four-to-five times the 1960 rates. Instead, our best educated guess is that rates of offending for serious violent crimes roughly doubled from 1960 to 1975, and remained somewhere in that 200 percent ballpark for the next fifteen to twenty years.[36]

Our estimate is founded on statistical sources external to the Uniform Crime Reports. First, we look to homicide rates, which are far more reliable than the UCR statistics for all other reported crimes, going back as far as the 1930s. It is possible to cross-check some of the weaker violent crime data against the higher-quality homicide data. Every homicide begins as a somewhat less serious violent crime—usually an aggravated assault—except that the assault achieves the most extreme possible result. Thus, if the FBI numbers suggest that the rate of aggravated assault has quadrupled in a given time period, a critical observer should look for echoes of this four-fold increase in the homicide statistics.[37] Such echoes, however, do not exist. In 1960, the FBI counted 9,110 homicides and 154,320 aggravated assaults—about one homicide for every seventeen reported assaults. In 1992, however, the FBI counted 23,760 homicides and 1,126,970 aggravated assaults—one homicide for every forty-seven assaults. Is it plausible that serious assaults became so much more numerous, but also *so much safer on average*, between 1960 and 1992? Safer by almost a factor of three?

We think not. The truth is that the FBI figures for reported aggravated assaults in 1960 were a severe undercounting of the actual number of assaults nationwide. By 1992, for a variety of reasons, the FBI count of reported aggravated assaults was still lower than the number of actual assaults, but had edged closer to the true total. This slippage in the FBI data creates the appearance of a much bigger jump in assaults than the country really experienced. While the UCR was correct in indicating a profound change in criminality, the UCR added to the nation's sense of crisis by making things look considerably worse than they were. An apparent quintupling of assault rates from 1960 to 1992 was probably really only a doubling, perhaps a bit more, if we assume that even a crude relationship between assault and homicide was maintained.

We also base our educated guess about "actual" changes in crime rates upon the National Crime Victimization Surveys (the NCVS), performed by the Justice Department in every year since 1973. Much like the homicide data, the victimization surveys tend to confirm that, after a sharp rise in crime in the 1960s, rates of offending for the most serious violent offenses stabilized at consistently high levels through the 1970s and 1980s—finally turning downward in the 1990s.[38] Figure 3.2 illustrates the different signals given by the UCR and the NCVS. Using a standardized rate of 100 for the year 1973, and applying this to both UCR and NCVS measures of robbery rates, Figure 3.2 shows a general tendency, from the early 1970s until the early 1990s, for the UCR to drift upward and away from the more reliable NCVS estimates. The NCVS indicates that robbery rates after 1973 held their position at 80 to 90 percent of their 1973 starting point until the impressive crime drop commencing in the 1990s. This was bad news for the country; persistently high levels of robbery are no cause for celebration. But, as with the cross-check of homicide data, the NCVS numbers show that the UCR was making a bad situation look even worse.

We can draw two important conclusions from these reanalyses of crime data. For violent crimes, at least, the high crime plateau was a real phenomenon—and Americans were right to be fearful, outraged, and frustrated at the stubborn persistence of senseless violence. On the other hand, the UCR both overstated the "altitude" of the plateau and indicated misleadingly that serious violent crime continued to drift upward from the mid-1970s to the early 1990s.

These observations expose points of weakness in traditional liberal and conservative priorities on crime policy. Conservatives often cite UCR crime figures going back to the 1960s, or even earlier, as gospel truth.[39] The

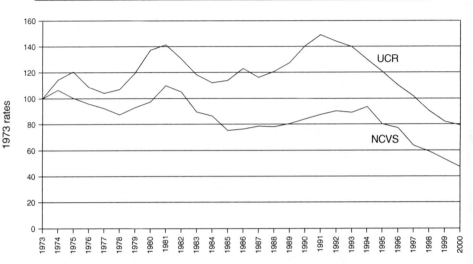

FIGURE 3.2 UCR and NCVS trends in robbery rates, 1973–2000 (1973 rates standardized to 100). Data from U.S. Department of Justice, Bureau of Justice Statistics, *Sourcebook of Criminal Justice Statistics, 2000* (Washington, DC: GPO, 2001), pp. 278–279, table 3.120; Federal Bureau of Investigation, *Crime in the United States, 2000: Uniform Crime Reports* (Washington, D.C.: FBI, 2001), p. 29; U.S. Department of Justice, Bureau of Justice Statistics, *National Crime Victimization Survey Violent Crime Trends, 1973–2000,* displayed at *www.ojp.usdoj.gov/bjs/glance/tables/viortrdtab.htm* (visited Sept. 5, 2002).

further back one reaches with FBI data, however, the more treacherous this practice becomes. It can foster the illusion that there was once a golden age of minimal crime, in the 1940s or 1950s, and that the country has been going to hell in a handbasket ever since. The facts are troubling enough without the exaggeration that faulty statistics make possible.

Yet a cool-headed reanalysis of crime in the late twentieth century renders unmistakable a reality that is often downplayed by liberals: The crime response program of the current conservative era was grounded in fact. Beginning in the 1960s, and certainly by the 1970s, conservatives could make defensible good-faith claims that something had driven actual crime rates upward at a fearsome pace and, once up, they were not coming down.

The Scissors Effect and the Plateau Effect

The crime wave of the 1960s and early 1970s overlapped with an extraordinary period in which punishments for crime were lightening, compassion for offenders as persons of disadvantaged background was temporarily in vogue, and numerous laws and court decisions were reining in the authority of police officers, creating new rights for criminal suspects, and overturning convictions of the guilty on grounds of constitutional principle. If one juxtaposes the list of major developments in crime response during the 1960s and early 1970s with the stark facts of skyrocketing crime, one can visualize what might be called a "scissors effect." As society was becoming more lenient in its attitudes, serious criminality was escalating disturbingly.

Figure 3.3 portrays the scissors effect along two of its dimensions. One line on the graph (the one going up) traces homicide rates from 1960 to 1972. The other line (going down) charts nationwide rates of imprisonment. During the same period, but not shown on the figure, the nation's use of the death penalty was also dwindling, to zero executions in the late 1960s and early 1970s. The major Warren Court decisions, which multiplied the federal constitutional rights enjoyed by criminal suspects and

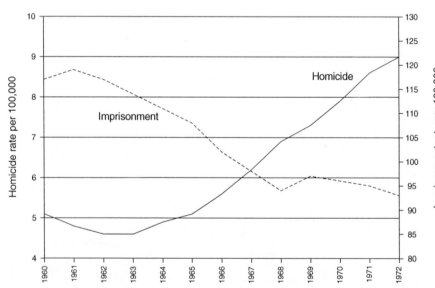

FIGURE 3.3 Imprisonment rates and homicide rates, 1960–1972. Data from U.S. Department of Justice, Bureau of Justice Statistics, *Sourcebook of Criminal Justice Statistics, 1999* (Washington, D.C.: GPO, 2000), p. 266, table 3.120; p. 503, table 6.26.

defendants, were clustered between 1961 and 1968. In 1967, the prestigious President's Crime Commission issued a report on crime policy that marked a high point of acceptance for many tenets of the liberal philosophy, including further deemphasis on incarceration, renewed energy toward offender reintegration programs, and expanded social welfare programs in the inner cities. Such events and proposals can mentally be added to the scissors graph in Figure 3.3 to dramatize the following historical convergence: Just as the liberal program seemed to be reaching full strength and influence, and was starting to look like the launching pad for a redoubled commitment to nonpunitive policy, uncooperative crime rates were jutting upward to suggest serious problems with the plan.

The scissors effect goes a long way toward explaining why the conservative view of appropriate crime response gained such swift ascendancy in the mid-1970s. Conservatives took the position that liberal "soft on crime" policies had helped produce the crime spike (along with liberal social welfare policies), and drew the conclusion that there should be a decisive reversal of direction. It is important to understand how persuasive the conservative argument sounded at the time, at least to most people. For a new set of policy recommendations to be maximally effective, as the conservative revolution was, it helps enormously if the new package appears to have a solid basis in fact, resonates with the experiences of voters and decisionmakers, adopts a plausible problem-solving approach, and reflects the good-faith beliefs of the opinion leaders who are propounding the policy shift. All of these advantages were firmly in place at the onset of the conservative revolution in crime response, and more. The conservative agenda gained further strength from the fact that it had not been tried and thus could not be saddled with evidence of apparent failure.

Following the period from 1960 to the early 1970s, and for the next twenty years, the conservative crime response agenda drew sustenance not so much from the fact that real and apparent crime rates continued to rise, but from the fact that they showed no hints of descending back to mid-century levels. The scissors effect that had catalyzed the initial revolt against liberal policies gave way to a new dynamic that might be called the "plateau effect." Crime was no longer going up as quickly, or as reliably from year to year and, starting in the early 1970s, the overall level of punitiveness in American crime response was no longer going down. Instead, the plateau effect drew on rational and fact-based horror that U.S. rates of serious violent criminality were persisting at their highest levels since crime measurement had begun in the early twentieth century. The plateau effect extended through the 1970s, 1980s, and early 1990s to help ensure that the conservative crime response program solidified into a nearly unchallenged orthodoxy.

Liberal critics of the current conservative program sometimes attack it as irrational on the ground that punishments have inexorably increased since the early 1970s, while crime, year by year, has sometimes gone up and sometimes gone down. The claim is sometimes made that conservative partisanship has driven public outrage about crime, augmented by media salaciousness, and that the public has been hoodwinked.[40] We think that such criticisms are unfair. Through the 1970s and 1980s, public fears about violent crime, and vigorous political responses to the crime problem, no longer required the year-by-year justification that crime was *going up*. They were easily justified by the fact that crime was *staying up*. For example, citizens and policymakers could sensibly take the view in 1984 that U.S. homicide rates were a terrifying problem even though they had dropped 23 percent in steady increments since 1980. Despite this four-year decline (and without knowing that homicide rates would turn back up again in the late 1980s and early 1990s), the "low" homicide rate of 1984 was still twice the rate in 1957. Indeed, even in 2000, seven years into the greatest "crime drop" of the late twentieth century, U.S. homicide rates were still 37 percent higher than the 1957 standard.[41] To the extent that conservative crime response attitudes and reflexes have been based on a sense of profound alarm prompted by the scissors and plateau effects, until the mid-1990s there was very little news good *enough* to call into question that sense of continuing urgency.

The Intellectual Attack from the Right

The success of the conservative revolution in the 1970s also owed much to its cogent criticisms of the liberal framework, and to its creation of an intellectually respectable alternative to the status quo of rehabilitation theory and social welfarism. The ascendancy of the conservative viewpoint was made easier by internal weaknesses in the liberal camp. These included genuine divisions over whether rehabilitation was worth defending, and the self-defeating tendency among liberals to adopt unrealistic or intolerant positions when faced with a strong conservative challenge.[42]

The most articulate spokesperson for the conservative crime response program, and perhaps the most influential over the past three decades, has been James Q. Wilson, a professor at Harvard and later at UCLA. A 1998 encomium in the *New York Times* called Wilson "one of the most important political scientists of the past 40 years."[43] Wilson's brilliant book, *Thinking about Crime,* published in 1975 (with a revised second edition in 1983), became something of an intellectual blueprint for the current conservative era of crime response.[44] Looking back, there is no other contemporary work in the middle 1970s that better captures the fundamental shift in policy that was about to occur. No one can say for certain whether Wilson's writings propelled events forward, or whether he merely gave verbal shape to forces that were already in the air. The truth likely lies somewhere in between. One thing cannot be doubted, however: Wilson has been, and continues to be, the most sophisticated intellectual proponent of the conservative crime response program for more than a generation. If there are respectable rationales for the many changes that have occurred in policing, punishment, and attitudes toward crime prevention, it is likely that Wilson has propounded or championed them.

When *Thinking about Crime* first appeared in 1975, it was boldly original. It also seemed to enjoy little chance of success. Only eight years before, in 1967, the President's Crime Commission had given the liberal outlook a resounding and official endorsement, declaring, among other things, that "Warring on poverty, inadequate housing and unemployment, is warring on crime." The Johnson Commission advocated reduced reliance upon incarceration for juveniles and adults, and increased investments in rehabilitative programming.[45] Wilson himself had served the commission, working on one of its task forces, but had bridled against the direction the project was taking. Despite the imprimatur of a national, presidential report, prepared by the largest collection of criminal justice experts ever assembled, Wilson's involvement convinced him that the country was moving in exactly the wrong direction.[46]

By 1975, Wilson's *Thinking about Crime* mounted a headlong attack on the Johnson Commission and the great verities of crime response in 1960s America: Wilson attacked the supposition that criminals were the products of distressed social environments who could be rehabilitated through correctional treatment. He denied that judges, correctional officials, and parole boards needed maximum discretion to tailor their actions to the perceived uniqueness of each individual offender. He accused liberal criminologists of disseminating their personal ideologies about crime and rehabilitation under the false cloak of "scientific" knowledge. He made the charge, and helped make it stick in the public mind, that liberal crime policy was irresponsibly softheaded.[47]

In contrast to his portrait of the muddled liberal, Wilson wrote in the style of a hard-boiled realist whose judgment was unclouded by sentimentality. Compassion for offenders served as neither a starting point nor an end goal of his analysis. Instead, Wilson applied economic principles to the crime problem and posited that criminals, adult and juvenile, made *rational choices* to engage in crime because, to them, the benefits of criminal activity exceeded the costs. Wilson believed that increased punishments for crime, primarily through incarceration, could in many cases tilt these calculations back toward law-abiding behavior. Faced with stiffer penalties, rational offenders would be forced to rethink their cost-benefit assessment before committing the next robbery, burglary, or assault. Wilson's theory also allowed for hardened criminals who could not be deterred by increased penalties. Such persons were conceived as truly evil, and society had little choice but to separate them from the community through long-term prison sentences—extended even longer than those already lengthened for enhanced deterrence.[48]

Wilson did much to redefine America's image of the typical criminal. Instead of being seen as a casualty of society's neglect and in need of society's help, the offender was now a fully capable person who had chosen willfully to follow an antisocial path. On moral grounds, all law-abiding citizens had good cause to hate the criminal, and to support programs of harsher crime response. Wilson's conclusion to his 1975 edition was a stirring peroration to this revised imagery:

> Wicked people exist. Nothing avails except to set them apart from innocent people. And many people, neither wicked nor innocent, but watchful, dissembling, and calculating of their opportunities, ponder our reaction to wickedness as a cue to what they might profitably do. We have trifled with the wicked, made sport of the innocent, and encouraged the calculators. Justice suffers, and so do we all.[49]

Wilson's clear-cut reformulation of the motivation of criminals, and his recommendations for greater punishment in service of deterrence, incapacitation, and moral firmness, came at the right time to serve as the starting gun for the American incarceration race of the next twenty-five years. Few people in the mid-1970s could have predicted the massive growth in prison and jail populations that was about to occur. Wilson's, however, was the strongest and most clear-headed voice affirmatively calling for it to happen.

To a remarkable degree, the intellectual strengths and weaknesses of *Thinking about Crime* remain the strong and weak points that underlie the current era of crime response policy. For that reason, they are worth considering in closer detail. Wilson's blueprint was compelling and enduring because it was based (in part) on hard evidence, and because it drew on moral arguments that exposed blind spots in the liberal worldview. Strangely, however, Wilson's formulations dissolved intermittently into speculation, ideological assumptions, and blind spots of his own.

Wilson's most forceful arguments depended on the apparent crime wave that had overtaken the country from 1960 through the mid-1970s. He drew confidence from the fact that this was one indisputable reason for people to rethink the dominant strategies of crime response in America. Wilson expressed amazement, with considerable justification, that liberal intellectuals and policymakers of the 1960s had been wont to deny the reality of rising serious crime. Some liberals tried to explain away the crime wave; others saw it as a bump in the road toward enlightened reform. There was no strand of liberal thought, however, treating the crime jump or the scissors effect as pivotal events that called for comprehensive reassessment of American crime response. This field of debate was left entirely to the conservatives.[50]

To dramatize the reality of soaring crime rates, Wilson relied heavily on the UCR and its exaggerated statistical picture of crime's upward slope. Wilson, of course, was sophisticated enough to understand and acknowledge the doubts that infected the UCR data. He recited some of the relevant caveats in the 1975 edition *Thinking about Crime,* but gave them little emphasis. Overall, he plowed ahead as though the uncertainties did not exist.[51] As it turns out, this method of building an argument occurs more than once throughout the book: Wilson proved a master of the art of noting possible qualifications, then leaping past them once they had been presented.

Wilson joined other voices in the mid-1970s to declare that social science research had discredited rehabilitation as an omnibus correctional policy. *Thinking about Crime* made intelligent use of a growing literature on the subject. Robert Martinson, for example, had written a paper in 1974 titled "What Works?" that had collected the evaluation results of hundreds of such programs. Martinson found that most purported rehabilitation programs either made no change in the behaviors of their clients, or very little. Some programs even seemed to make criminals worse. Other scholars, working on a smaller scale, had produced similar conclusions. Martinson did not purport to show that *nothing works* in the domain of rehabilitative efforts (although many readers interpreted his argument in this way). Instead, his evidence might be said to prove that "some rehabilitative programs work, but not as easily or as often as we hoped."[52] Ever since, conservatives like Wilson have stood on the empirical high ground when asserting, not necessarily a nihilistic view of reformist possibilities, but a pessimistic view that rehabilitation is difficult, uncertain, expensive, and can at best reach a minority of all offenders.

The intellectual collapse of optimistic rehabilitation theory occurred at the exact historical moment when the high crime spike of the 1960s, and the scissors effect of rising crime and declining punishment, had reached their most dramatic juncture. The nation's recent experience of crime and punishment seemed to confirm the theory failure of rehabilitation. Heavy investments in rehabilitation programs, and in collateral institutions such as judicial sentencing discretion and parole release, no longer seemed well considered once their raison d'être had been cut down to size.[53]

Again, many liberals seemed unreasonably to resist the empirical evidence. Some argued that rehabilitation had never been given a fair try, with sufficient funding and commitment to realize its promise. Others said that more and better research was needed—which has come to be the standard caricature of the social scientist making a recommendation.[54] If one did not share liberal intuitions about the eventual payoffs of reformism, such responses could seem to spring from a reckless willingness to throw good money after bad.[55]

Elsewhere within the liberal camp, however, intellectual leaders were jumping ship from the "rehabilitative ideal." Francis Allen, who coined this phrase, argued that government's efforts were doomed to failure because of expense, inefficacy, and their tendency to trample the personal freedoms of those being changed (ostensibly) for their own good.[56] Other liberal theorists, including Andrew von Hirsch and Herbert Packer, thought that reformative sentencing could lead to excessive state intervention, and believed that a shift in emphasis toward punishment for moral purposes would actually restrain the use of heavy penalties.[57] And many prominent liberals, like federal judge Marvin Frankel and law professor Albert Alschuler, were simply won over by the mounting scientific evidence. Frankel took the view that rehabilitative sentencing should be pursued only when there was sound reason to think that an offender suffered from a deficit that the correctional system knew how to fix.[58] For a variety of reasons, then, liberal intellectuals lacked the solidarity to mount a determined defense against the assault being waged by conservatives.[59]

All of Wilson's arguments about effective crime response (or its lack of effectiveness) were overlaid with his strong and persuasive views of public morality. Wilson exuded confidence that a new and tougher crime response policy, with less emphasis on making excuses for offenders, was the morally right path for the nation to pursue. He unashamedly portrayed criminals as "wicked" or "calculating" and helped build the case that true concern with justice required harsh penalties to adequately reflect the wrongfulness of criminal acts. Here, Wilson challenged heartfelt liberal beliefs that the liberal framework was clearly superior to punitive measures in furthering the goals of justice and legitimacy. Wilson's challenge was especially threatening to liberals because it tracked the opinion of the average person on the street. To most people, "justice" in the wake of a serious crime has always meant apprehending the right person, prosecuting him successfully, and imposing a condign punishment. In this sense, liberal policy often seemed an impediment to justice.

But Wilson was working with more than popular sentiment. The liberals were in fact wrong in thinking that they had cornered the market on justice and legitimacy. They had focused their justice concerns too narrowly on the backgrounds, needs, and rights of criminal offenders, whose life histories were often thought to relieve them of personal responsibility for their criminal actions. This had evolved into a form of tunnel vision that excluded compassion for victims of past crimes, prospective victims, not yet identified, who would suffer if preventable crimes were not headed off, and whole communities that experienced the fear of crime as detrimental to the quality of everyday life.[60] When considering encounters between police and citizens, liberals reproduced this tunnel-vision effect by generating concern only for the plight of the citizen-suspect, and expressing no empathy for the inherent difficulty and bravery of good police work from the officer's perspective. In terms of human inclusiveness, the liberal viewpoint had come to value the moral claims of offenders and suspects almost exclusively, and had inexplicably hardened to the moral claims of others who had a direct and urgent stake in crime response policies.

Making matters worse, some liberals misbehaved when confronted with the moral critique from the right. Instead of genuine acknowledgment of a profound blind spot, liberals have often resorted to counterarguments that amount to little more than name-calling. Good-faith proponents of retributive justice, or of increased solicitude to crime victims, have been decried as lustful for vengeance, as thinly veiled racists, or as desirous of turning the clock back to some darker time in premodern history.[61] Such ad hominem tactics, when launched at people who believe in what they are saying, tend to be self-defeating. They win few converts, and are especially ill-conceived when the general public sympathizes with the viewpoint being castigated. Above all, the liberal determination to counterattack sacrificed any opportunity to formulate a new and broadly inclusive vision of justice and legitimacy that would embrace the interests of offenders, victims, and communities alike.

Wilson's most audacious claims in *Thinking about Crime,* which have survived the intervening decades in many quarters, concerned the connection between poverty and crime. On one level, Wilson hoped to establish that the liberal belief in poverty-crime causation, treated as an article of faith by the President's Crime Commission in 1967, had never been proven convincingly by sociologists or criminologists. This was true enough, and was a legitimate line of intellectual attack. Wilson, however, wanted to push the envelope even further to suggest that the poverty-crime link could be shown to be false. Indeed, by the end of *Thinking about Crime,* Wilson was willing to leave readers with the impression that prosperity and high levels of public welfare spending in poor communities actually caused *more* crime rather than less.[62]

These arguments were startling, especially when matched against Wilson's criticisms of liberals for their sloppiness of thought and their willingness to jump to conclusions that neatly fit their personal ideologies. Wilson's denial of a causal link between poverty and crime has survived well in public debate, however, and has fitted itself comfortably within the arguments of other conservatives who have charged that social welfare spending has created more negative (albeit unintended) effects than positive improvements in impoverished communities.[63]

Let us examine Wilson's proof. He opened *Thinking about Crime* with a chapter called "Crime amidst Plenty: The Paradox of the Sixties." The main thrust of the chapter began with the observations that general conditions of economic prosperity prevailed in the 1960s, and that the federal government had embarked on energetic programs of public welfare spending over the decade. The chapter then turned to the paradoxical observation that, despite these developments, which might have been expected to reduce crime, crime rates had soared to some of their highest levels in the twentieth century. Based on these correlations, Wilson was willing to venture that "affluence had seemingly increased" crime rates.[64]

The word "seemingly" is important in this quoted passage. Throughout chapter 1 of *Thinking about Crime,* and when referring to the lack of a poverty-crime nexus later in the book, Wilson was always careful to hedge his bets with words like "seemingly" or "apparently," or a prefatory phrase like "if the experience of the 1960s is any guide."[65] Wilson was aware that his argument had not been nailed down. In chapter 1, he catalogued numerous factors that might have contributed to the crime rise of the 1960s and early 1970s, but had nothing to do with the economic boom or increased welfare spending. (These included the large demographic bulge of young males in the U.S. population, the failure of national prosperity to reach the most distressed urban neighborhoods, increasing unemployment rates among minority youths, the breakdown of inner-city educational systems, political dislocations surrounding the civil rights movement and the Vietnam War, and the emergence of a powerful and rebellious youth culture.) Wilson acknowledged the inherent complexity of the forces that determined changing crime rates, and the many reasons for caution in reaching firm conclusions about them.[66] Nowhere in the book did he assert anything beyond a tentative and carefully qualified belief that the poverty-crime connection had been definitively refuted. By such means, he insulated himself from criticism that he had failed to take all the evidence into account, had not bent over backward to be evenhanded, or had overstated his case. And yet, the overstatements that Wilson never made explicit became, at the end of the day, the bedrock of his entire program. Nearly all of *Thinking about Crime*'s large policy recommendations rested on the conclusion that the nation was wasting its time in "warring on poverty" as a strategy for "warring on crime."

Wilson's attack on the poverty-crime connection was rhetorically brilliant in that he succeeded in advancing an aggressive position without ever committing himself to it. But there were other factors that added to the appeal of the argument. For one thing, liberals had weakened their own stature by seeming to argue that the *only* way to address the crime problem effectively was to remake society from the ground up. This remains the core of much liberal argumentation to this day.[67] Conservatives like Wilson, and much of the audience that was receptive to Wilson, had good grounds to ask what liberals meant to do in the meantime, before a renaissance in social and economic relations could be brought about. Or more pointedly, what was the liberal program for crime reduction if, realistically, the nation was not about to embark on massive societal reform? To the extent that liberals were short on responses to these queries, they had placed themselves at a severe disadvantage when matched against an interlocutor like Wilson, who was offering concrete and immediate plans of action.

Finally, we should not underestimate the fact that Wilson's message about the absence of a poverty-crime connection was emotionally congenial to many Americans. Buffeted by fear and guilt through the 1960s, the average citizen was challenged daily to assume new attitudes of social responsibility toward the underprivileged and minority groups—even toward criminals. The psychic penalty for failure to move forward quickly enough with the new program was to be labeled a member of the sinister "establishment," to be called a pig or a racist, to be identified with vague repressive conspiracies, or to be lampooned as an Archie Bunker–like figure. Against this contentious background, Wilson's *Thinking about Crime* granted intellectual permission to middle-of-the-road Americans to return to more familiar and comfortable values, to sleep with clear consciences after all, to distance themselves psychologically from the deterioration of the inner cities, to blame the criminal rather than the social conditions in which that criminal has lived, and to feel good about expressing punitive outrage over a wide range of criminal acts—even if the targets of that outrage were predominately poor and black. The appeal of these formulations to the emotional self-interest of many Americans has remained powerful ever since the 1970s.

Wilson had identified, and had even demolished, a number of points of vulnerability in the liberal crime response agenda of the 1960s. As so often happens in intellectual life, however, it is easier to tear down a set of ideas than to build a satisfactory alternative. Much like the former liberal approach he had criticized, Wilson's new conservative crime control program was beset by intellectual carelessness and a willingness to assume certain truths about human behavior. Most strangely of all, Wilson's "scientific" case in favor of his deterrence-incapacitation package for criminal punishment was flimsy in many of the same ways that the liberal case for rehabilitation had been.

Wilson's recommendations for heavier punishments in pursuit of deterrence and incapacitation were supported largely by the argument that these theories had not been tried or tested during the liberal era. Wilson claimed, with some justification, that liberals had evinced almost no interest in deterrence research, and he could have made exactly the same charge with respect to incapacitation. Until the late 1970s, such inquiries had not been accorded great priority because they ran against the grain of the dominant reformist ideology. If rehabilitation was the be-all and end-all of crime response policy, why waste scarce research dollars chasing down blind alleys?[68]

Wilson's charge was enormously influential, sparking waves of research effort over the next twenty years. But saying that certain theories had gone untried was a far cry from making an airtight case that U.S. punishment policy should be retooled in their image. Here, Wilson took a leap of faith. Prison policy, as outlined in *Thinking about Crime,* was to be based on the expected results of research that no one had yet performed. Wilson's instincts, and his economic suppositions, told him that the new initiatives would work.

Wilson's analysis of incapacitation theory in *Thinking about Crime* is a good example of conservative optimism at work, rivaling anything in the annals of rehabilitative optimism.[69] In his key chapter on "Courts and Corrections," Wilson suggested (again, without committing himself) that "The gains from merely incapacitating criminals may be very large."[70] Aside from commonsense arguments in support of this conjecture, Wilson promised to discuss some "tentative estimates" of the magnitude of incapacitative effects in the last chapter of the book.[71] Given the centrality of incapacitation theory to Wilson's prison-building recommendations, the reader cannot be blamed for turning immediately to the book's end, in search of the deferred "tentative estimates."

The relevant discussion occupies little more than a single page, in a final chapter called "Some Concluding Thoughts."[72] Here, Wilson cited a then-unpublished study by Shlomo and Reuel Shinnar, which contained the bombshell assertion (based on a hypothetical economic model) that serious crime rates in New York City could be reduced by two-thirds "if every person convicted of a serious offense were imprisoned for three years." Wilson's handling of this eye-catching projection is instructive, and characteristic. He praised the study but carefully drew short of endorsing it, noting, "The Shinnar estimates are based on uncertain data and involve assumptions that can be challenged." Despite this caveat, Wilson needed to get mileage out of the study, both for the "Concluding Thoughts" chapter, and to fill in the empirical blank that he had left in the "Courts and Corrections" chapter many pages earlier. He went on to write: "But even assuming they [the Shinnars] are overly optimistic by two, a sizable reduction in crime would still ensue." This worked to firm up the reader's confidence in the policy implications of the Shinnar study, but Wilson still had avoided investing any of his own credibility in it. The very next paragraph cashed in on the smoke-and-mirrors act, beginning with the words, "That these gains are possible . . ." For anyone not reading with a hypercritical eye, the crime reduction effects projected by the Shinnars had been declared within our grasp, but Wilson remained well defended against any charge that he had literally come out and said so.

Within ten years of the publication of *Thinking about Crime,* the idea that large incapacitation effects could be realized from the plan outlined by the Shinnars—or from any similar plan—had been resoundingly discredited by later research. Many attempts have been made to quantify the crime reduction benefits that attend increasing rates of incarceration. And although the methodologies of the studies have differed significantly, the basic findings have not: Crime rates can be brought down with the heavier use of prisons and jails, but the total amount of crime reduction tends to be disappointingly small, and most of the crimes that are avoided are property crimes as opposed to the serious violent offenses that everyone wants most to address.[73] The results, in other words, are not radically different from the social science assessment of rehabilitation policy: "Increased incarceration works to deter and incapacitate criminals, but only some of the time, and not as easily or as often as we would hope."

In his later writings, and much to his credit, Wilson has joined this empirical consensus. In 1995, for example, he acknowledged, "Very large increases in the prison population can produce only modest reductions in crime rates." He wrote that a doubling of the prison population could probably account for "only a 10 to 20 percent reduction in the crime rate." He even went on to elucidate, with considerable elegance, the various explanations of why the optimistic version of pro-prison theory had not been borne out by experience.[74] There is a certain irony here, however. Even as the contemporary James Q. Wilson has become less of a hawk on incarceration policy, his writings from the 1970s have exerted more continuing influence than his later views.

Our review of Wilson's seminal *Thinking about Crime,* as a case study of the intellectual attack on the liberal crime response program and the theoretical underpinnings of the conservative alternative program that has gathered force since the 1970s, yields certain important conclusions. First, it is important for everyone, especially criminal justice liberals, to acknowledge that the conservative framework found traction because it was based upon substantially factual claims, and upon moral claims that resonated persuasively with many Americans. It is unhelpful and self-impeaching for liberals to argue that the conservative shift over the past twenty-five years was based purely on demagoguery, the political desire to find divisive "wedge" issues, or other motivations awash in bad faith. In order to orient ourselves toward the future, it is essential to credit the conservative revolution with a great deal of substantive content, and to acknowledge that the liberal regime, which collapsed so decisively in the 1970s, had made itself vulnerable to such a catastrophe. It is unwise, for the same reasons, to suppose that future policy should merely restore the unfinished efforts of the 1960s.

Yet our sympathetic tour through the theoretical foundations of the current era's conservative crime response policy, as represented by its best and brightest apologist, leaves the unsettling impression that the conservative structure is itself infirm in many of its key elements. Much as the liberal program had been, the conservative agenda is infected with empirical optimism, ideological predispositions, and a selective view of the moral claims of human beings directly affected by the crime response complex. Conservative crime policy is no more infallible a guide to the future than was its liberal precursor.

In the chapters that follow, we will examine a selection of high-priority subjects within the American crime response complex through a critical lens that is neither liberal nor conservative in predisposition. We will advance arguments that might be expected to challenge—and even to anger—readers affixed strongly to both liberal and conservative orthodoxies. The approach we take, however, is badly needed if America is to break free of the frustrations of a polarized debate that is unsound at both extremes.

4

Prisons and Jails

Incarceration is now the major investment our society has made to combat unacceptably high rates of serious criminality. The human stakes are vast. Every person in America should want to know whether the nation's prisons and jails are being used as effectively as possible to prevent crime.

The goals of crime reduction, and justice for crime victims, must be weighed alongside other human consequences of incarceration policy. On any given day in the early 2000s, roughly two million people are confined in some form of prison, jail, or detention facility.[1] Research shows that large-scale incarceration can have harsh effects upon inmates' children and other dependents, the economies of their home communities, and the social attitudes within those communities.[2] To give just one example, the U.S. Justice Department estimated that state and federal prisoners in 1999 were parents of approximately 1.5 million minor children.[3] Many millions are affected, sometimes profoundly, by the ripple effects of incarceration.

Even in terms of cost, incarceration policy is a pressing issue. A recent estimate of the average cost of housing one inmate for one year (including both an amortization of prison construction costs and annual operating expenses) was $36,000.[4] The total dollars have added up quickly since the 1970s as the nation's incarcerated populations have nearly sextupled in size. Across the states in the 1990s, correctional spending grew more quickly than all other line items in statewide budgets except healthcare.[5] At the turn of the new century, correctional expenditures nationwide had swollen to more than 50 billion dollars each year.[6] While money is less important than the core values of justice and crime reduction, the huge sums spent on incarceration in the United States subtract from resources available to other important government services. Spending on education and social welfare programs, perhaps most visibly, has suffered during the thirty years of punitive expansionism.[7]

Whether one is a conservative, a liberal, or a nonpartisan, it is increasingly apparent that the current era of geometric expansion in criminal punishment cannot continue much longer. Since 1970, the raw numbers of persons incarcerated across the nation have grown nearly six times over, with probation and parole populations keeping a similar pace. It is physically and politically unthinkable that, in the next thirty years, such growth curves will continue unabated. Another sixfold expansion would yield an impossible figure of 12 million incarcerees before the year 2030. Would it even be possible, in the next three decades, for the country "merely" to double current punishment rates—resulting in four to five million people in prison and jail by the 2030s—and an additional eight to ten million on probation and parole? (This would entail continued punitive growth of, at most, a couple of percentage points each year.) Given the high monetary costs of corrections, a taxpayers' rebellion would become likely at some point. More fundamentally, such continued "modest" expansion of our punitive machinery would visit ever more devastating effects on America's minority communities. At the end of the twentieth century, on any given day, nearly one of every three African American males in the young adult age group was under the supervision of the crime response complex, either in prison, in jail, on probation, or on parole.[8] A mere doubling of current punishment values, assuming no drastic changes in their demographics, would transform the present-day racial effects to levels that no one could overlook. African Americans would not be the only minority group at risk. Punishment levels for Hispanic Americans and Native Americans, if they were to press further upward, would create multiple additional sources of moral and political backlash.

There are already signs, early in the twenty-first century, that the long and uninterrupted period of incarceration expansion is on the wane. Several large states, including some past leaders in prison growth such as Texas and California, have recently reported small drops in the numbers of prisoners added to their systems each year. Nationwide, incarceration growth from June 2000 to June 2001 was a relatively small 1.6 percent. That still adds up to many additional human beings in confinement, however. The number of new prison and jail bed spaces needed each week in the 2000–2001 period was 587—a significant number but considerably less than the

1,490 beds added each week through the 1990s.[9] In some states, public officials are beginning to tout the budgetary advantages of an incarceration slowdown.[10] This may hint at an emerging political rhetoric of deincarceration.

How Much Is "Enough"?

John DiIulio, who has held academic appointments at Harvard, Princeton, and the University of Pennsylvania, was perhaps the most outspoken intellectual proponent of get-tough prison policies in the 1990s. In the mid-1990s DiIulio blasted the U.S. system of "revolving door" justice. He stated that "virtually all prisoners are violent or repeat criminals" who deserved their incarceration, and that many others who should have been incarcerated were instead given soft probationary sentences, or were released from prison too soon. He proclaimed in 1994 that "America has not been on an imprisonment binge," but has been "gradually recovering from [a] starvation diet" in the use of confinement.[11]

During the same period, DiIulio authored provocative editorials in the *Wall Street Journal* calling for sharp increases in the use of incarceration, and criticizing the "anti-incarceration elite" for opposing popular opinion on this score.[12] In the 1996 book *Body Count,* co-authored with William Bennett and John Walters, DiIulio renewed his calls for the greater use of confinement. The three authors even asserted that "government's failure to restrain convicted violent or repeat criminals has done as much as any other policy failure of the last thirty years to bring about the loss of public trust and confidence in our political institutions."[13] As this quotation suggests, the authors of *Body Count* were more than aggressive advocates for a get-tough prison policy; they were supremely confident in their program: "In the end, the task we face is not an intellectually complicated one. We know what it takes to become a more civilized and decent nation . . . But the hour is growing late. Very late. Many among us have heard the chimes at midnight. It is time to set to work."[14]

DiIulio and his collaborators never set forth a precise number of prison and jail inmates that, in their view, would constitute an appropriately vigorous response to crime in the United States. But it was clear that, even after twenty-four unbroken years of expansion of confinement, DiIulio was arguing for much more.

Then something changed. In a 1999 *Wall Street Journal* editorial, DiIulio declared that "Two Million Prisoners Are Enough."[15] In a 1999 report co-authored with Anne Morrison Piehl and Bert Useem, DiIulio studied the prisons in New York, New Mexico, and Arizona. The authors concluded that, in all three states, approximately one-half of all current inmates were not worth imprisoning based on the crimes those inmates would be expected to commit if released.[16] The authors' conclusion was most emphatic for inmates who had been convicted only of drug sale or use. DiIulio and his collaborators found that society to date has gained precious little crime reduction from the mass confinement of drug offenders.[17] In a separate article, DiIulio advocated the release of drug-only offenders into intensive probation and community treatment programs, and proposed an end to the use of imprisonment for new, incoming drug offenders.[18]

DiIulio's conversion, if we may call it that, illustrates that sooner or later all policymakers, and all concerned citizens, must reach a personal judgment that "enough is enough" in the three-decade growth of our prisons and jails. DiIulio's two-million mark is one man's stopping point. Michael Tonry, in a recent work, recommended an incarceration rollback to 1980 rates, or roughly one million prison and jail inmates.[19]

Such policy judgments cannot spring forth solely from crime and punishment statistics, although these are indispensable starting points for thinking about the problem. Ultimately, the question of the appropriate scale of U.S. punishment institutions is approachable only by applying moral intuitions to the facts as we know them.[20]

The Incarceration Build-Up and Grave Violence

How effective have prisons and jails been in fighting those crimes that worry and hurt people the most? In choosing crime-fighting priorities, most of us care deeply about reducing the numbers of gravely violent offenses—defined as those that cause death, serious physical injuries, or forcible sexual victimizations. The avoidance of such grave violence should take priority over the prevention of other categories of criminal events, such as: (1) more commonplace violent offenses that produce or threaten relatively minor harms, (2) most economic crimes, and (3) the bulk of crimes that lack readily identifiable victims, such as drug offenses, gambling, other vice crimes, and morals offenses.[21] In evaluating incarceration policy, citizens and policymakers should want to know exactly what crime types our prisons and jails have been used to attack, and with what degrees of success.

Franklin Zimring, a long-time student of imprisonment, has broken down the prison build-up since 1972 into three distinct periods.[22] From the early 1970s until the mid-1980s, the U.S. prisons expanded because the courts were sending more "marginal" felons to prison than they had in the past. Many burglars or auto thieves who might have been put on probation in the 1950s or 1960s were instead sentenced to incarceration. Prison sentences on average were not getting longer during this period. The root of incarceration expansion was more human beings entering confinement, not more time served per criminal.

Then, from the mid-1980s to the early 1990s, prison growth was driven most forcefully by the war on drugs. Incarceration for violent and property crimes was also on the upswing during this period, but the single most powerful contributor to the prison boom was drug incarceration. In California alone, the number of drug offenders in prison increased by a factor of fifteen from the early 1980s to the early 1990s. Nationwide, from 1980 to 1996, the imprisonment rate for drug crimes shot up by a factor of ten, accounting for one-third of all U.S. prison growth for the whole sixteen-year span.[23] In the federal prisons, the drug incarceration rate increased elevenfold.[24] The "high tide" of the drug war, in Zimring's words, came during Ronald Reagan's second term and George H. W. Bush's succeeding term of office. The war continued to escalate during the Clinton years, but was outpaced by other factors as the primary driving force of the prison build-up. From 1990 to 1997, drug offender imprisonment accounted for 19 percent of the total growth among state prisoners nationwide—a considerable share of the continuing expansion, but less than in the late 1980s.[25]

In the 1990s, the primary cause of prison growth changed again. For the first time in the expansionist era, the chief engine of the prison build-up became longer sentences rather than more prison admissions.[26] This trend had been unfolding for some time for the crime of murder. Reaching back into the 1980s, the average prison sentence actually served by murderers (as opposed to the sentence "pronounced" in court) was just under five years. By 1996, time served for murder had more than doubled, to more than eleven years for the typical murderer.[27] Other major crime categories also saw substantial increases in confinement length, but not as spectacular as for homicide—and the elongations came mostly in the 1990s. Sexual assault offenders served an average of 3.2 years in prison in the late 1980s, but this had stretched to 5.1 years by 1996. From 1992 to 1996, average burglary prison terms edged upward from roughly eighteen months to two years. Drug law violators served an average of 1.3 years in 1987; this increased 77 percent to 2.3 years by 1996.[28]

Has America's recent incarceration policy, then, reflected an appropriate concentration on crimes of grave violence? The answer is less definitive than one would like. In the last two decades, a meaningful share of the nation's prison growth has been allocated to the incarceration of more violent offenders, and many of these offenders have been imprisoned for longer terms than in the past. U.S. Justice Department statistician Allen Beck calculated that 36 percent of all prison growth during the 1980s was attributable to the more extensive incarceration of violent offenders.[29]

Yet the data do not permit us to say how many of these putative violent offenders committed acts of grave violence (those causing death, serious physical injuries, or forcible sexual assaults), and how many were imprisoned for less fearsome acts. As we noted earlier, "aggravated assaults," as serious as the label sounds, can range in seriousness from a near-murder with serious wounding to an ill-considered threat. Without better information, we can only wonder which fraction of offenders had been imprisoned for less grave acts. Moving past this uncertainty, however, we also know that 64 percent of the prison expansion in the 1980s was built on the incarceration of increasing numbers of nonviolent criminals, with the largest share being drug offenders. As the prisons grew during that decade, the crime response complex was moving away from a determined focus on violent crimes, especially those involving grave violence.

In the 1990s, there was a shift back toward incarceration for violent acts—but here again we may consult only the broad definition of violence used in official statistics. Beck found that nearly 50 percent of all growth in the state prisons from 1990 to 1997 was due to tougher sentences for violent criminals. If one believes that a concentration on grave violence is a good thing in incarceration policy, this suggests that the 1990s were an improvement over the 1980s. But slightly more than half of the total prison growth in the 1990s still occurred in the nonviolent offense categories, including property crimes, drug offenses, and the quickly growing domain of public order violations.[30] These developments fit less comfortably into a rational scheme of priorities.

Further, we once again lack the information necessary to know whether the violent criminals who were selected for more and longer incarceration in the 1990s were the most-serious offenders, or a mixed bag of grave offenders and petty criminals. The overall national trends do not give much confidence that a sensible policy of prioritization was in place.

Incarceration Growth and Crime Reduction

Without question, rates of gravely violent crime have been falling steadily, and at times dramatically, for the last eight years. Writer Charles Murray and Nobel laureate economist Gary Becker have, for their parts, proclaimed that America's recent victories over crime have been due largely to punishment policy.[31] They are hardly alone in their views.

But a full accounting of the incarceration build-up, reaching back over more than twenty-five years, elicits a far more perplexing picture than the last eight years considered alone. Any punishment enthusiast wishing to take credit for the crime drop of the 1990s must be careful to avoid attracting blame for the very meager results of the 1970s and 1980s. Figure 4.1 gives visual emphasis to this point. The figure overlays imprisonment rates against homicide rates for the full span of the conservative era, from 1972

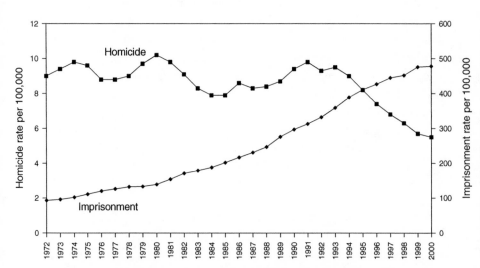

FIGURE 4.1 Homicide and imprisonment rates, 1972–2000. Data from U.S. Department of Justice, Bureau of Justice Statistics, *Sourcebook of Criminal Justice Statistics, 2000* (Washington, D.C.: GPO, 2001), pp. 278–79, table 3.120; p. 507, table 6.27; Federal Bureau of Investigation, *Crime in the United States, 2000* (Washington D.C.: GPO, 2001), p. 14.

(the year when national prison populations began to grow) until 2000. For the first two decades of the expansion period, from 1972 to 1992, homicide increased in some years and decreased in others—about half one way, half the other. By 1992, the death rate was higher than twenty years earlier, and it had hit a twentieth-century peak in the early 1980s (on the conservative watch). For twenty years, in other words, imprisonment advocates had little to boast about when contemplating the most reliable statistic of our most feared violent crime.

The record of incarceration policies in combating other crime categories that include acts of grave violence, such as rape, robbery, and aggravated assault, looks much the same as the analysis for homicide. If one credits the National Crime Victims Survey as our best gauge of such crimes, prison construction and violent crime fought to a relative stalemate from 1973 through 1992 or 1993, before the crime drop finally set in. If conservatives adhered to their fondness for the Uniform Crime Reports' statistics when assessing the crime-reductive effects of pro-punishment policy during this period, the report card would be much poorer still. As we saw in Chapter 3, for example, the UCR showed a marked upward drift in robbery rates from 1972 to 1991, for an increase of more than 50 percent during the first nineteen years of the prison boom. Even greater upward-inclining trends existed in the UCR figures for rape and aggravated assault.[32] These were hardly clear beacons of a successful crime-fighting strategy.

Informed by two decades of experience from 1972 to 1992, we must be suspicious of theories that incarceration suddenly (sometime around 1992) acquired definitive powers of crime suppression that it had lacked beforehand. It is reasonable to suppose that prison growth has always exerted an incremental effect on serious crimes like homicide, robbery, and rape—but this is a long way from saying that punishment policy can be the sole or major reason for large swings in crime rates.

A recent national study of murder and incarceration by Richard Rosenfeld illustrates the point. Rosenfeld estimated that the growth in U.S. prison populations from 1990 to 1995 (an average of 67,032 additional prisoners each year) averted one hundred homicides each year through incapacitation alone—which amounted to slightly more than 27 percent of the total decline in homicide victimization during those years.[33] Extrapolating from Rosenfeld's figures, there would have been a cumulative total of 1,500 additional deaths by homicide in the five years from 1990 to 1995 if the nation's prison growth had stayed flat after 1990. These precious benefits were won, however, at the expense of more than one million person-years of additional incarceration served by hundreds of thousands of inmates, at a financial cost exceeding $25 billion—or roughly 670 person-years of incarceration and more than $17 million for each murder avoided.[34]

Whenever such punishment and victimization statistics are displayed side by side, they raise bedrock issues of moral judgment. Rosenfeld's calculations are only estimates, but they can be used as ballpark figures to help visualize the moral tradeoffs policymakers are forced to consider. This is far more than an interesting conundrum; it is a veritable Sophie's Choice among horrific alternatives. By what rational process can decisionmakers weigh the precious good of (roughly) 1,500 innocent lives saved against the compound costs of one million person-years of incarceration? For some, the preservation of innocent lives will seem the natural priority, even if this comes at the expense of many others who, after all, have been adjudged guilty of crimes. For others, it will appear wrong to confine hundreds of thousands of human beings, some for many years, because we know that a fraction among them will commit horrendous acts if released.

Any moral evaluation of these wrenching choices is aided by more information. For one thing, homicide is hardly the only crime that is prevented by incarceration growth. The crime-reductive benefits of confinement extend to numerous offense categories, further offsetting its human and financial costs. In a 1995 study, for example, Franklin Zimring and Gordon Hawkins prepared estimates of how much crime the state of California had avoided in the 1980s by a single-decade tripling of the state's prison population. By one of Zimring and Hawkins' calculations, each additional person-year of imprisonment had yielded a payoff of 3.5 crimes avoided.[35] Breaking these results down crime by crime, the authors found that nearly all of the crimes avoided were nonviolent offenses. Of the 3.5 crimes saved per confinement year, 3.29 (or 90 percent) were burglaries and larcenies. Violent incidents, of highest public concern, were prevented in much smaller numbers. For example, each added person-year of incarceration was associated with a reduction of only .007 homicides and .055 rapes.[36]

Such small percentage points of violence avoidance can add up to meaningful absolute numbers in the big picture. Zimring and Hawkins' estimates suggest that seven homicide victimizations were avoided for every

1,000 inmates added to the California's prisons and held for a full year.[37] The total crime reduction estimates for the same 1,000 person-years of incarceration also included 55 rapes, 125 robberies, 2,180 burglaries, and 1,110 larcenies. And over the 1980s, California expanded its prisons, not merely by 1,000 inmates, but by a cumulative total of roughly 550,000 additional person-years of confinement across the whole decade.[38] Even treating Zimring and Hawkins' figures as the roughest of estimates, with a large margin for error, it is clear that the potential aggregate benefits of incarceration growth should carry significant moral weight with any policymaker. To the many unknowing, innocent citizens who have been saved the experience of victimization, and to their families and communities, the low-rate efficacy of violence prevention through confinement is worth a great deal.

As Zimring and Hawkins' estimates also suggest, it is easier to make the case that incarceration growth reduces property crimes, such as burglary and larceny, than gravely violent crimes like homicide and rape. If all society cared about were the prevention of nonviolent economic crimes, the conservative era of punitive expansionism would be judged a comparative success. On a national scale, since 1973, the NCVS measures of property crimes like burglary and theft bear out this hypothesis with consistency. From 1973 to 2000, a quadrupling of U.S. incarceration rates corresponded with a 71 percent reduction in burglary and a 65 percent reduction in theft, with these declines accumulating fairly steadily over the entire period.[39] To illustrate the point, Figure 4.2 compares rates of theft and imprisonment.

On the opposite end of the effectiveness continuum, incarceration has proven to be a sorely inadequate tool in the war against drug use. This conclusion, explored at length in Chapter 7, has found support among criminal justice experts from both the left and the right. Increasing incarceration has affected neither drug use nor supply. At best, it can affect drug distribution practices in conjunction with intense enforcement in selected neighborhoods. Under some conditions, drug enforcement can also reduce violence associated with competing drug markets in urban areas.

In summary, if we were issuing a report card on the crime-reductive performance of the U.S. incarceration explosion since 1972, we would assign different grades by offense type, rather than render a single judgment on the expansionist era as a whole. For property crimes, we might assign a grade of "B" or even "B plus," while recognizing that these are not the of-

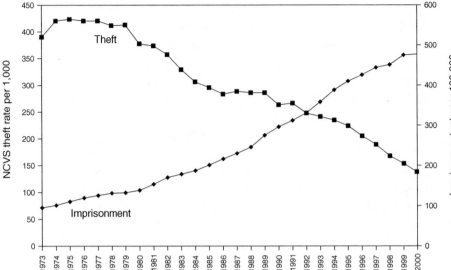

FIGURE 4.2 Theft and imprisonment rates, 1973–2000. Data from U.S. Department of Justice, Bureau of Justice Statistics, *Sourcebook of Criminal Justice Statistics, 2000* (Washington, D.C.: GPO, 2001), p. 507, table 6.27; U.S. Department of Justice, Bureau of Justice Statistics, *National Crime Victimization Survey Property Crime Trends, 1973–2000,* displayed at *www.ojp.usdoj.gov/bjs/glance/tables/ proptrdtab.htm* (visited Sept. 5, 2002).

fenses the public cares the most about preventing. For violent crimes, including the highest-priority category of serious violence, a fair assessment might be a "Gentleman C," with the caveat that *any* demonstrable level of crime avoidance among serious violent acts is a benefit to be highly treasured. For crimes of drug use and distribution, it might seem generous to award even a "D minus," except for the fact that some uses of drug incarceration may have the ancillary effect of disrupting urban drug markets and the violence that has sometimes been associated with them.

Racial and Ethnic Impacts of Incarceration

We preface this discussion with two propositions:

First, the existing and growing racial and ethnic disparities in incarceration in America *in and of themselves* are a heavy cost experienced by society. Such disparities raise a presumption that the crime response complex has failed in its highest aspirations of doing even-handed justice, and has neither earned nor deserved a reputation of legitimacy among all members of the public.

Second, existing and projected racial and ethnic disparities in punishment should not be tolerated by policymakers or members of the public in the absence of good evidence that (1) such disparities reflect real differences in the rates of crimes committed by different racial and ethnic groups, including past criminal histories, (2) the crimes in question involve serious past victimizations and the risk of serious future victimizations, and (3) the use of incarceration will address effectively the risks of serious offending in the future.

With homage to Jeremy Bentham, who argued that *all* criminal punishment was an evil to be avoided unless there was some greater and countervailing good to be realized, these propositions treat all racially and ethnically disparate punishment as an evil in itself. And yet, it is an evil that may be tolerated, justified, or even mandated in certain circumstances.[40] These principles apply differently, depending upon whether one is considering punishment for serious violence, other acts of violence, property crime, or drug offenses.

Beginning with the most serious and frightening offense category—gravely violent crimes that cause death, serious bodily harms, or forcible sexual victimizations—the evidence is compelling that most of the disparities in the criminal punishment of African Americans for such crimes are rooted in actual differences in rates of gravely violent criminality.[41] We possess suggestive information that for Hispanics too, the disproportionate use of confinement may be attributable in part to differences in past rates of offending and violent victimizations—but our information is too thin to permit solid conclusions.[42]

We will thus focus analysis on African Americans, where the available data are stronger. As William Julius Wilson has observed, "The tendency of liberal social scientists either to ignore these issues or to address them in circumspect ways does more to reinforce than to undermine racist perceptions."[43] In fact, many published studies of race and punishment tread very lightly, if not disingenuously, on the subject.[44] But, as law professor Randall Kennedy has written, it is far from clear where the interests of racial justice lie when responding to serious violent crime.[45] Demographically, more than 80 percent of violent offenses committed by blacks are directed against black victims.[46] If black homicide commission rates, in some years and in some age groups, have been ten times the white rate, black homicide *victimization* rates have likewise soared to ten times or more the equivalent white rates in the same age groups.[47] Indeed, violent victimizations of all kinds are significantly higher among the black population of this country than among whites. The more life-threatening the crime, the greater the black-white disparities in victimizations.[48] Kennedy has argued cogently that the "unequal protection" of black victims (even when the offenders are also black) can itself be a form of racial discrimination.[49]

The two principles set forth earlier press toward continued investments in incarceration as a response to gravely violent offending, even if the cost of this policy is to reinforce or exacerbate existing racial disparities in punishment. Given the enormous human costs of victimization for this category of crime, and given the data that incarceration is effective to some meaningful degree in reducing such offenses, the policymaker is forced to choose between victims and convicted offenders, both of whom have a great deal to lose in their future quality of life and their life chances. With the stakes so intolerably high on both sides, it is difficult to privilege the guilty over the innocent.

The consideration of racial and ethnic disparities in punishment leads to greater uncertainty in the area of property offending. Again, we must make resort to statistics pertaining to only blacks and whites, because those are the data that are available. Blacks are arrested more often than whites for most property crimes, and are also more likely to be property crime victims. But the disproportionalities are smaller than for violent crimes. In the 1990s, the black arrest rate for such crimes as burglary and theft exceeded the white rate by a factor of three. Black victimization for crimes such as household larceny and theft was somewhat greater than for whites, for example, surpassing the white rate by 14 percent and 47 percent in 1992.[50]

Racial disparities in incarceration for property crime do not fare well under the calculus set forth earlier. The injuries inflicted by property criminals are usually far less severe than the harms associated with serious violent offenses. This does not mean that property crime should be decriminalized, of course, but that sanctions other than confinement should be given greater emphasis in crime response policy.

The major justification for current levels of incarceration for property crimes is the fact that the prisons and jails seem to help prevent future property offenses. There is also considerable criminological research showing that few property or violent offenders specialize in one type of crime. Today's burglar might be tomorrow's armed robber (just as today's violent felon may never commit another violent act).[51] We cannot willfully ignore the fact that one reason incarceration is correlated at all with reductions in violence is that some inmates who happen to have been convicted of property offenses have criminal propensities beyond those reflected in their formal records.

If our focus is on violence, then, we need to know much more about the criminal careers of people whose convictions include only property offenses. Many such criminals present little danger of future violent acts, while some present larger risks. Rather than continue to confine hundreds of thousands of such persons in numbers that are racially and ethnically disproportionate, we should require very strong evidence that individuals subjected to lengthy confinement present unusual risks of committing violent crimes in the future.

Perhaps the clearest policy conclusion of all emerges in the area of drug enforcement. In many jurisdictions, the incarceration disparities between blacks and whites for drug crimes are as great as or greater than those for serious violent offenses. Much of the overrepresentation of Hispanics in prison populations appears to be rooted as well in the drug war. Yet these striking disparities are offset by no redeeming benefits.

First, there is no evidence of underlying racial and ethnic disparities in drug abuse that approach the degree of racial and ethnic disparities in punishment for drug offenses. As we will see in Chapter 7, the majority of users of illegal drugs in America are white—and yet incarceration policy has its heaviest effects on other groups. For example, in 1999, 77 percent of drug prisoners serving mandatory sentences in federal prisons were African American or Hispanic, and only 23 percent were white.[52] Second, although no one should dismiss the harms inflicted by illegal drug use, they must be ranked far lower than those attending gravely violent crimes. Third, there is a consensus among researchers that the imprisonment build-up has not been an effective countermeasure to drug crime. Just as importantly, there is growing evidence that the large-scale confinement of drug offenders does painfully little to reduce rates of violent or even property crime. Many drug offenders are *only* drug offenders; they do not regularly diversify into other types of criminality.[53] With the added weight of racial and ethnic disproportionalities, it becomes extremely difficult to justify the present confinement policy for drug offenses.

A Constructive Rethinking of U.S. Incarceration Policy

We offer seven principal recommendations for an American incarceration policy that is more knowledge-driven and fact-based than that currently in place. The combined effect of our suggestions cannot be quantified in advance. It is possible that the program might result in some degree of prison growth nationwide.[54] We suspect, however, depending on the data that comes from better assessment of the use of prisons and jails, that our program would overall decrease current incarceration rates in many or most American jurisdictions, in some places substantially.

1. *Prioritize the use of incarceration as a response to grave violence.* U.S. incarceration policy since the 1970s has been only half-heartedly committed to locking up those criminals whom Americans fear the most. This commitment has been diluted, if not overshadowed, by larger investments in the incarceration of nonviolent drug and property offenders. We advocate an emphasis on grave violence and its prevention.

For such offenses, greater punishments may have to be meted out, at least for the most dangerous offenders—but only if ongoing assessment indicates that violence continues to be reduced. We are not wholly confident that such findings will occur. Some researchers already posit that we are approaching the point of diminishing returns in incarceration growth, and that future crime reductions will be much smaller than those of the past.[55]

Provided that crime reductions continue at 1990s rates, we would support incarceration expansion for grave violence despite two very unpleasant consequences. First, cutting-edge research in psychology and psychiatry tells us that predictions about who will commit serious acts of violence in the future are wrong two out of three times, even when such predictions are made in the best clinical settings.[56] The blunderbuss efforts of the crime response complex will undoubtedly result in even poorer guesses.[57]

Therefore, in order to impose extended confinement on the minority of truly dangerous individuals (those who both fit a court-administered profile of future violence *and* will in fact commit violent crimes in the future), we must be willing to allow the mistaken over-punishment of quite a few "false positives" (those who fit the profile of dangerousness, but who will not in fact commit violent acts in the future). This judgment cannot be made lightly—and it is much more difficult for anyone who considers, or takes the trouble to get to know, the human beings who will be consigned to (often) needless incarceration under such a program.[58] Nevertheless, a choice must be made between intolerable unfairnesses *to someone*. The crime response complex must choose either to visit enormous costs upon a large number of persons who have been convicted of serious crimes, or to invite intolerable harms upon a substantial number of innocent victims.[59]

A second formidable concern is that a program of redoubled emphasis on incarcerating those who commit gravely violent crimes will, in the nation's present circumstances, exacerbate racial and ethnic disparities in punishment for those offenses. The most powerful justification for enduring such effects is the serious nature of victimizations that we are seeking to avoid—victimizations that occur most often in minority communities.

2. *Charter a permanent sentencing commission.* Most U.S. jurisdictions lack adequate tools for the deliberate refashioning of incarceration policy. In a growing number of states, however, the creation of permanent sentencing commissions has brought new powers of rationality, planning, and oversight to punishment practices.

Fourteen states and the federal system now operate with sentencing commissions that produce standards or "guidelines" for sentencing decisions in specific cases. The commissions also monitor sentencing patterns to assess how the guidelines are working.[60] In addition, they perform a variety of research tasks, including prison population forecasts and (in some jurisdictions) studies of racial disparities in punishment.[61]

Sentencing commissions and guidelines differ a great deal from place to place. The current federal system, for example, has many fierce detractors—including large numbers of U.S. District Court Judges who must regularly apply the federal guidelines.[62] In contrast, many of the state sentencing commissions and guidelines have won high praise from lawyers, judges, academics, and policymakers.[63]

Of immediate relevance, a number of state commissions have promulgated guidelines to increase, sometimes dramatically, the sentences imposed on serious violent offenders. At the same time, they have often instituted fewer or shorter prison sentences for nonviolent offenders, offsetting the harsher sentences for violent crimes. Some state commissions have gotten tougher on violent crime while simultaneously slowing or stopping preexisting patterns of incarceration growth.[64]

We know through repeated experience in the 1980s and 1990s that sentencing commissions are able to control prison growth if they are asked to do so. Past crime statistics, sentencing guidelines, and computer projection models can be used to determine what the future bed space needs will be if the law is changed in small ways (as when a guideline sentence is altered by a few months) or in large ways (as when the legislature proposes the adoption of new mandatory minimum penalties). In some states, legislatures have instructed or authorized their commissions to slow or halt the process of prison expansion by designing sentencing guidelines that will not overtax existing facilities. To date, every commission that has tried to do so has succeeded.[65]

In contrast, a few commissions have operated with mandates to increase the use of incarceration, for all or selected offenses. Once again, there is impressive evidence that the commissions can engineer planned prison growth, if that is what is wanted.[66] The presence of a commission does not dictate the future course of sentencing policy. But a commission's existence does make it far more likely that substantive policy decisions will be carried through and evaluated.[67] This record is remarkable in the crime response field, where the usual supposition is that "nothing works."[68]

The suggestion we offer here is important, but it is no novelty. In 1994, after five years of study, the American Bar Association concluded that every state should create a sentencing commission or equivalent agency.[69] In 2002, the American Law Institute began a multiyear project to revise the prestigious Model Penal Code to incorporate new provisions for sentencing commissions and guidelines.[70] It is time for state governments nationwide to take a close look at these institutional reforms.

3. *Reverse policies of more and longer sentences for drug offenders.* Sentencing commissions, with legislative authorization, should create a presumption against the confinement of drug offenders convicted of lower-level drug offenses, and a very heavy presumption against lengthy terms of confinement for drug offenders who are incarcerated. We are not recommending drug legalization for the United States, but rather a policy of "deprisonization" of the vast majority of persons convicted only of drug law violations. Our supporting argument for this position will appear in Chapter 7. Suffice it to note here that a major component of our incarceration policy, in conformity with the recent writings of such diverse figures as John DiIulio, James Q. Wilson, and Michael Tonry, is a large-scale reversal of the war on drugs insofar as it has overpopulated our prisons and jails.[71]

4. *Conduct a national audit of the use of incarceration.* The United States has imposed more than 28 million person-years of prison and jail confinement during the period 1970 through 2000. If no prison growth had

occurred during that thirty-year period, the country would have instead imposed only about 10 million person-years.[72] Such massive interventions were undertaken without serious and ongoing efforts to track their efficacy. Many of the added person-years of incarceration were no doubt supportable from both crime-reduction and moral standpoints. But everyone should be deeply suspicious that a considerable share of the confinement expansion since the 1970s, particularly the many additional millions of person-years visited on nonviolent offenders, would not have withstood scrutiny if ongoing evaluation had been undertaken at the time. The possibility alone renders the failure to evaluate a deeply troubling omission—and one that should be remedied at the earliest possible moment.

A national audit of incarceration policy, undertaken today, should examine the costs and benefits of confinement with respect to specific classes of offenders. The first step would be to generate a detailed census of the types of confined offenders. Suppose we wanted to find out what percentage of incarcerees in the United States have ever been convicted of an act of grave violence. No one can tell us the answer nationwide, or for any of the individual states—and the answer would almost certainly vary dramatically from state to state.[73] Instead, inmate surveys, conducted nationally every several years, tell us how many "violent" offenders are held in confinement—yet this classification tells us little about what kind of injury, if any, was inflicted by the criminal. The inmate surveys provide further statistical breakdowns for broad, but minimally informative, offense categories such as "robbery" and "assault." Except for such uniformly serious offenses as homicide and rape, which together account for only 14 percent of state prisoners, we are left largely in the dark about the extent of physical harm caused or threatened by each inmate.[74]

Assault deserves focus as one of the most commonplace of all violent felonies that land people in prison or jail. In 1998, there were an estimated 109,500 state prison inmates confined for this offense category.[75] But our ignorance concerning all these people has been impressive. Here are some of the missing elementary data: Among inmates incarcerated for assault, how many caused serious victim injury? How many caused any injury at all? How many threatened serious injury without causing it? How many used guns? What were the prior criminal records of inmates sentenced for assault? How many had prior offenses involving serious violent victimizations? For those who caused or threatened serious victim injuries, were there factors in their prior life history that would have helped to predict the assault? Among those who were eventually released from incarceration (which includes nearly everybody), how many committed violent acts again? And are there tools that can be used to distinguish the most dangerous assault offenders from those who do not present such a high risk?

Perhaps the most important project of ongoing research about whom we incarcerate will be to gather improved information about inmates' prior criminal histories and what can be done to predict their future criminality. Criminologists have grappled with such issues through a tiny number of sporadic inmate surveys and recidivism studies, which have entailed watching cohorts of prison releasees over several years. But so little work has been done in the area that it is hard to operationalize the bits and pieces of important information that we have. We know that a small percentage of all criminals are much more dangerous, and have much more active criminal careers, than all the rest, but we do not know how to identify with much accuracy the hyperactive few. We know that prison programming and post-release supervision arrangements vary a great deal from state to state and from prison to prison, yet we do not track post-release behavior well enough to know what the best programs are.

Our advocacy for much greater attention to the empirical study of criminal careers is hardly original. The list of scholars who have made this call in the past would comprise a Who's Who among eminent criminologists.[76] We add our voices because this urgent area of knowledge development remains sorely neglected.

A related series of inquiries should focus on the experience of spending time in prison and jail. In a 1999 study, Anne Morrison Piehl and her co-authors asked prison inmates in New Mexico and Arizona a series of questions about the effects of doing time. Among the most provocative of these, inmates were asked whether they agreed or disagreed with the following statements:

"Among my friends on the outside, one gains respect for having done time in a state prison" (32 percent strongly agreed or agreed).
"For someone like myself, going to prison is just another part of life" (21 percent strongly agreed or agreed).[77]

These answers are both fascinating and alarming. They support and help quantify anecdotal reports that the stigma and suffering associated with serving time have been weakening in the expansionist period, at least for some people in some communities.

One of the most startling revelations of the Piehl study was the authors' report that "such questions have never been asked of inmates before."[78] Future research should not ignore this crucially important, and accessible, source of information about the crime-reductive potential of incarceration, and the moral legitimacy of criminal punishment as perceived by offenders. Surveys of inmates can provide insight into mental processes that are otherwise distant and mysterious to the middle-class policymaker. Too often, when the government does something to or for people, no one bothers to ask the affected population how they feel about or make sense of it.[79]

We believe that the best organizations to spearhead a national incarceration audit would be sentencing commissions, acting in collaboration with many other state agencies, such as departments of correction, probation and parole services, and statistical analysis centers. In jurisdictions without commissions, other appropriate agencies would have to be found or created. (Perhaps, in some states, recognition of the need for a regularized incarceration audit would inspire leaders to charter a permanent sentencing commission.) Based simply on the dollars at stake, each state's fiscal self-interest mandates financial support for such evaluation efforts.

5. Promote effective helping programs for offenders. Prisons and jails cannot by themselves prevent all of the crimes we want to prevent—or all it is possible to prevent. As we have seen, massive confinement expansions in the past decades have brought inconsistent drop-offs in crime rates. There is little reason to expect that future incarceration policy will fare better.

A maximally effective approach to crime avoidance calls for programs that can supplement the deterrent and incapacitative effects of confinement. A diversified crime-reduction strategy should include effective "helping" programs: those designed to help prospective criminals steer a law-abiding life course, and to help past lawbreakers adhere to the law.

The most efficacious helping programs, according to current research, are aimed at children (as young as in utero) who are at high risk of becoming criminals later in life. Such "primary prevention" efforts are discussed in Chapter 8. The major practical drawback of primary prevention is that it requires long-term planning. There is no immediate gratification when a successful childhood intervention shows up in the crime statistics a decade later. In comparison, a stiff prison sentence, imposed within a matter of months after a serious crime, produces the satisfying sensation of condemnation and an immediate forceful solution.[80] One goal of this book is to encourage crime response policy that includes the long view as well as the immediate view. Under such a philosophy, it is necessary to develop the promising area of primary prevention as an important complement to incarceration.

Within the prisons and jails themselves, helping programs for inmates seek to achieve levels of crime avoidance beyond those supplied by deterrence and incapacitation alone. The history of such in-prison programming, however, is not encouraging, having produced a lengthy trail of well-intentioned programs that have collapsed because they were too expensive, ineffective, or because prison managers had competing incentives (such as to maintain discipline or turn a profit) that drove out any sustained commitment to prisoner rehabilitation.[81] Work-related prison programs have also been beset by opposition from the business community and labor unions, which have opposed the operation of many prison industries.[82]

Despite these bleak realities, it is far too soon to give up on helping programs inside prison walls. Research in the 1990s found that compulsory drug treatment programs for incarcerated inmates have yielded good results. Indeed, recovery rates among inmates who were forced to undergo such treatment seem to be indistinguishable from those among inmates who volunteered for the programs.[83] These are beacons of hope—but they also remind us how little we know about so-called rehabilitative programming. Before the 1990s, many people believed that such programs could not succeed unless an inmate volunteered to enter treatment with an honest desire to be helped.[84]

We must likewise continue to seek scientific knowledge of the variety of helping sanctions that exist outside of prison walls, including regular probation, parole, intensive probation, home confinement, outpatient drug treatment, and community service. In the era of incarceration expansion, dating to the early 1970s, funding levels for community sanctions were eclipsed by the massive financial investments needed for prison construction. During this time, however, probation and parole populations grew just as quickly as the prison and jail populations. The caseloads of probation and parole officers ballooned, but resources lagged behind. Many officers, overwhelmed with administrative details, had precious little time left over for individualized supervision of their clients.[85]

The two decades from 1980 to 2000 produced considerable interest in the development of intermediate sanctions (criminal penalties that are more serious than regular probation and less severe than incarceration).[86] During most of that period, few jurisdictions could boast newly invented programs that successfully diverted criminals from confinement.[87] By the close of the 1990s, however, there were signs of forward progress in a small handful of sentencing commission states, including Delaware, North Carolina, and Pennsylvania.[88] All three sentencing commissions had written guidelines meant to encourage judges to make more frequent use of intermediate sanctions in lieu of prison terms. In North Carolina and Pennsylvania, these guideline innovations were paired with successful lobbying efforts to acquire new state funding for intermediate treatment slots in the community.[89]

Finally, a gap exists in helping programs for the released prisoner. In the year 2000, an estimated 585,000 felony inmates returned to their home communities from state and federal prisons.[90] The crime response complex has never performed well at this transitional juncture. Parole officials have on occasion developed release "plans" for ex-convicts. Some drug treatment and sex offender programs have emphasized "aftercare" for clients newly returned to their communities.[91] Research suggests that the aftercare phase may make or break the success of a helping intervention.[92] And yet, for the vast majority of criminal sanctions, the transitional period is ignored or addressed with pro forma measures.

The transition from confinement to freedom is becoming an increasingly important element of incarceration policy. In part this is due to the growing number of persons who undergo such a life change each year. In addition, large numbers of released prisoners have been returning to the prisons and jails for violations of parole. During the 1990s, more than one-third of all prison admissions were made up of parole violators. Criminologists such as Joan Petersilia and Shadd Maruna have expressed the urgent need to address the problem of parolee recidivism and to reinvent the monitoring and helping programs we make available for newly released inmates.[93]

Implementation of all of the helping programs discussed here should be attended by rigorous evaluation. In 2000, Lawrence Sherman made the bold statement that experimental evaluations of rehabilitative programs "would be the shortest path to reducing incarceration rates" in the United States. Sherman's central premise was that policymakers and the public would invest enthusiastically in such programs if they can be proven to deliver results.[94] Likewise, we would welcome a renaissance of helping initiatives that would prevent crime and victimizations, and would assist more individuals to lead law-abiding lives, but the full size and shape of such a renaissance depends on program development and assessment that has not yet occurred, or has barely begun. Ideally, the accumulation of new knowledge may lead the crime response complex back to the general emphasis on helping programs that prevailed in the 1960s, but each step along that road (this time around) must be grounded in evaluation and self-criticism, not in unrealistic optimism.

6. *Review policies dealing with the incarceration of women.* Ninety percent of criminals who commit serious violent acts are male,[95] and 92 percent of prison and jail inmates are likewise male.[96] Accordingly, those who think about crime response policy tend to focus on the crimes and punishments of men and teenage boys.

It is a shame, however, when this male-centric view becomes exclusive. Although women have always made up a small percentage of total incarcerated populations in the United States, for each woman in prison and jail, and for her family and friends, the effect of confinement is never "a small percentage" of the male experience. When there are children involved, the effects of incarceration can be greater for women than for men. In our present society, women inmates are far more likely than men to have been the caretakers of children before their confinement.[97]

A habitual focus of attention on males has become increasingly unfortunate as the absolute numbers of female inmates have grown nationwide. Women's incarceration rates in recent years have been swelling even more dramatically than male rates. From 1980 to 1996, male imprisonment rates increased by a formidable 195 percent, but female rates exploded by 364 percent.[98] The number of women in U.S. prisons and jails at the turn of the twenty-first century exceeded 150,000, and was still growing.[99] Women's incarceration for drug offenses has in particular been on the increase, again more so than for male offenders. Between 1980 and 1996, 43 percent of all expansion in the women's prisons was due to drug incarceration, compared to 28 percent of the growth in male imprisonment.[100]

The justification for expanding female confinement, if there is one, is deficient. Women commit only a small fraction of serious violent crimes in society. If the proper priority of the crime response complex is the avoidance of grave violence, this can supply no rationale for the confinement of most women criminals. Indeed, a General Accounting Office survey of state prisoners in 1997 found that, while 48 percent of male prisoners were incarcerated for violent crimes (generically defined), the same was true of only 28 percent of female prisoners.[101] We are aware of no studies of the crime-reductive effects of incarceration growth that examine women prisoners and ex-prisoners. Most, if not all, criminologists would probably agree that the expansion of female confinement produces little avoidance of serious violent crime. Accordingly, a specially targeted audit of women's incarceration is badly needed, and this need is made more urgent because the racial and ethnic demographics of women in U.S. prisons and jails are just as alarming as those for men.[102]

7. *Require that changes in punishment laws be preceded by a statement of the racial, ethnic, and financial changes that may result.* Basic fiscal responsibility mandates that punishment laws should not be made in the absence of a commitment to pay for their foreseeable costs. A handful of jurisdictions now follow the practice, informally or formally, of requiring fiscal impact statements prior to the passage of new sentencing laws.[103] Such financial projections are prepared routinely by state sentencing commissions, and over the years, some commissions have developed reputations for being highly accurate in their projections. This is a good example of an improved information system that has influenced policy. On numerous occasions, state legislatures have tabled or modified punitive sentencing proposals when informed of their expected effects on prison growth and the state treasury.[104]

In light of the nation's unique history of racial and ethnic discrimination and distrust, the role of impact statements should be expanded. For most crime categories, technology exists to forecast the effects of changes in punishment laws on the racial and ethnic compositions of prison, jail, probation, and parole populations. Typically, however, when new sentencing provisions are proposed, there is no institutional impetus to summon the relevant data. This can make legislative decisionmakers less accountable than they should be for the predictable results of their actions. Michael Tonry, for example, has asserted that the racial disparities in imprisonment that followed the war on drugs in the 1980s were known or foreseeable to the architects of the drug war. He advocated that policymakers should be held politically and morally responsible for such effects when they are discernable in advance.[105]

Our prescriptive goal is similar to Tonry's, although we would like to see a measure of institutional regularity in the crime response complex's ongoing efforts to assess racial and ethnic disparities. The requirement of a formal impact statement, to be prepared by a knowledgeable group of researchers (usually associated with a sentencing commission), can focus policymakers' minds on issues of distributive justice and help ensure that the necessary data will be compiled and consulted.

Each jurisdiction must also specify how racial and ethnic impact statements should be used once they are produced. In some situations, the ability to make such projections will be limited. Sentencing commissions (or some parallel agency) should always be charged to monitor new laws in application, in order to assess unforeseen effects on minority constituencies. In other situations, however, impact statements will warn of probable or inevitable disproportionalities in punishment. These warnings need not always bar enactment of a new law. Rather, a signal of probable racial and ethnic disparities should be treated as a negative factor that can be overridden if the policy justifications for the law are sufficiently compelling. Consistent with our earlier discussion, the policy formula for such decisions would ask (1) whether the expected disparities in punishment reflect actual disparities in crime commission, including offenders' prior criminal records, (2) whether the crimes in question involve serious victimizations and the future risk of serious victimizations, and (3) whether the proposed changes in punishment laws are an efficacious means to address such problems.

Crime response institutions have always operated in an environment of insufficient facts and uncertain projections for the future, and they always will. The pressing need to respond to crime cannot wait for the results of the next research study or pilot program, any more than a doctor can be told to withhold treatment today because there will be better medical technology five or ten years from now.

But major crime response decisions affecting millions of lives should, at the time they are made, be informed to the extent reasonably possible. Serious efforts, commensurate with the importance of the subject, should be expended to improve our future knowledge base about incarceration policy. Even if society cannot eliminate guesswork in policy formation, we should as a nation work to reduce the boundaries of ignorance, thoughtlessness, and neglect that have to date characterized much of America's massive confinement experiment.

It is likewise important that the moral calculations that lie beneath policy choices should be made explicit and be exposed for open commentary.

Those who promote radical deincarceration should be heard to admit that rollbacks in confinement, while morally attractive on many dimensions, will come hand in hand with greater numbers of criminal victimizations. Those who advocate incarceration stability or growth, for some or all crime categories, should similarly disclose the predictable ethical costs of their choices, such as the overconfinement of "false positives" and the continuation (or worsening) of the national wound of racial and ethnic disparities in sentencing. No one, particularly those in public life, should be permitted by sleight of hand to gloss over the moral tradeoffs that are involved.

5

Public and Private
Paths to Security
from Crime

A society cannot analyze what actions it is taking to directly promote security of home, business, and person without including all private and public institutions substantially participating in those efforts. If we limit our inquiry to the traditional criminal justice apparatus, we will misunderstand the range of what we expend to protect ourselves and what freedoms we may be forgoing in the process. The narrower analysis is also probably incorrect in how it credits—or blames—a police department's efforts against crime.

Although private and public actions to directly combat crime have developed separately for the most part, those efforts have commenced to overlap in the past few years. A conjoined examination of America's total crime response will allow the necessary, wider examination of how our society should and could establish responsibility and allocate resources. Public police departments bear too much of this responsibility at present. If private efforts to maintain security prove to be a reasonable and more effective method than public law enforcement, or can aid public law enforcement, these alternatives should be designed, tested, and implemented.

Public and private efforts are now devoted to direct crime prevention and detection in different ways, with different degrees of coercive power, and with varying motivations. Whether or not we even see a police officer during our daily lives, we all encounter direct crime prevention—the security camera and the private security officer in the stores and offices we visit, the annoying security tag on the coat you want to try on, the prisonlike glass and metal encircling the pay window at the gas station, the x-ray machine that searches our bodies and our belongings at many office building entryways, the updated software we continuously acquire to protect our computers from viruses and from theft of credit card and social security numbers. The shopping malls, business development areas, and apartments we visit or occupy all include security-related aspects in their architecture, building materials, landscaping, and staffing. When we go to the bank, either inside or outside, a camera records our every move. Our automobiles all have security protection built into them. Many of us also buy numerous and often elaborate locks for our homes and apartments, or even install complex protective alarms.

We certainly feel safer with all these measures, but we also are becoming totally accustomed to and perhaps accepting of other people watching us, examining us, and preserving our actions on permanent file wherever we go. One can also argue that, in accepting a loss of privacy in both our public and private worlds, we are becoming more receptive to government and corporate intrusion into all aspects of our lives. Failure at least to analyze the social and individual effects of these new facts of life constitutes a dereliction of every citizen's duty to be conscious of and to protect our freedoms. How much privacy and freedom are we willing to surrender in order to prevent the fear and actuality of crime and terrorism? And how much money are we willing to pay when we really do not know the effectiveness of these measures, alone or combined, in protecting our safety and property?

Private Security

Although America inherited the historic English tradition of citizens individually and collectively protecting self and neighborhood, this concept slowly moved to the background in the nineteenth century with the formation of public police departments. But when crime rates were rising in America during the late 1960s, 1970s, and 1980s, citizens and commerce tried once again to develop their own ways to feel safer. Institutions created internal security measures or hired outside personnel and consultants. Individuals, organizations, and business proprietors spent money on a wide variety of security products. In 1984, one report noted that in the United States, private security personnel (guards, private detectives, private police, and so on) rose from 300,000 persons in 1950 to 400,000 in 1970, and were projected to increase by about 125 percent in the ensuing two decades even though the population was to grow only about 23 percent.[1] The report estimated that as early as 1979–1980, private protection expenditures (personnel and security equipment) exceeded moneys expended for public police protection by 57 percent, and that an estimated 150,000 off-duty police officers worked regularly as private security employees.[2] Hallcrest Systems' field study in 1989 reported off-duty private police work by more than one-half of the police officers in the Washington, D.C., Seattle, and Dade and Lee County (Florida) law enforcement agencies.[3] These moonlighting officers were providing a significant extension of police protection to citizens and businesses. And the supply is ordinarily maintained in one of three ways: the officer himself finds this second job, the police union finds an officer for the private employer, or the police department itself contracts with the private business.[4]

By 1997, a Congressional Report estimated that private security employees outnumbered public law enforcement workers by 2.4 to 1 and should grow to a three-to-one ratio by the year 2000, totaling close to 1.9 million people.[5] In trying to determine total private expenditures for security, one first confronts the problems of definition. The Hallcrest report includes nine categories: proprietary (in-house) security, guard and patrol services, alarm services, private investigations, armored car services, locksmiths, consultants, security equipment manufacturing and distributing, and a catch-all "other" group.[6] The paucity of research results in data phrased as "estimates," with a wide range of such estimates in the various security categories.[7] But probably the best and most conservative estimate of expenditures for private security projected to the year 2000 totaled $103 billion, with $63.4 billion for contract services, $23.7 billion for manufacturing sales and distribution, and $16 billion for in-house security organization.[8]

Moreover, all of these estimates preceded the expansion of identified private security needs as society and technology changed. Expenditures for computer security and for employer drug testing of both applicants and in-service employees exploded in the 1990s. Over 120 federal agencies with about 1.8 million employees, in addition to all of the U.S. military and over 80 percent of all U.S. companies with more than five thousand employees, had drug-free workplace programs, including drug testing, in place by 1999.[9] The total cost of just these programs is unknown, although one report in the late 1980s cautioned against overestimating the extent of actual administration of workplace drug testing.[10] The Hallcrest report did estimate in 1990 that computer security expenditures alone would approach one billion dollars by the year 2000; but that estimate occurred prior to the 1990s expansion of home and business computers and the universal need for, and availability of, antivirus software, which requires frequent updating.[11] And the newly created homeland security efforts against terrorism add substantial, but unstipulated amounts to the total.

These kinds of investments reflect peoples' desire for less physical danger, fear, and property loss in their everyday lives. In analyzing how to deter crimes in varying settings, Marcel Niglii urges the study of crime situations and their social constructions, focusing on not only reducing opportunities for crime, but also creating positive alternative activities for the potential criminal.[12] Niglii also points out that this private activity avoids the value maintenance and punishment goals of criminal law and focuses instead on "specific, concrete situations . . . [with a] disregard for grand theories."[13] Unlike the government's efforts in the crime response complex, the private world need not pay attention to a larger set of goals—justice, maximum efficiency, the consumer's perception of good faith and justice, and constant evaluations of effectiveness—unless the community affected by a particular business' or neighborhood's private security efforts demands these additional components. And the private world need not deal with 911 calls and answer to the public at large, a mayor or city manager, and a city council. Profits motivate the business owner, and only that factor along with a personal ethic and the potential for civil liability instill a respect for justice, privacy, and other societal goals. The business owner does realize, however, that each establishment must reckon with not only actual crime but also a potential customer's fear of crime both inside and outside the store. And each crime averted by private situational prevention also means one less crime response by the public police and court system.

John Eck examined 109 separate, privately imposed interventions instituted to reduce primarily violent crime or both serious property and violent crimes at different categories of places: residences, bars and taverns, retail stores, banks and money-handling places, public transportation facilities, parking facilities, airports, open public spaces, and public coin machines. In 90 percent of the interventions, the targeted criminal activity declined; in only 3 percent did crime increase.[14] But Eck also concluded that in most of these interventions particular preventive tactics were not sufficiently associated with crime reduction.[15] Most were single-site case studies, many of the locations had instituted multiple security-related changes, and the evaluation methodologies and statistical analyses employed by various researchers were generally not sufficiently rigorous to isolate a cause-effect relationship.[16]

Eck does conclude, however, that well-planned lighting improvements worked to reduce crime in open public places, and closed circuit television probably worked in stores and parking areas.[17] The Highway Loss Data Institute concluded that a computer-chip immobilizing device used in new, higher-priced autos and SUVs was at least partially responsible for the 74 percent decline in auto thefts in New York City during the 1990s.[18] And evidence exists that the crime prevented by these tactics is not displaced to other areas.[19]

Tactics unrelated to equipment installation also produce situational crime prevention. Marcus Felson cites a reduction in British football violence simply by causing buses to arrive just prior to the match's start, thus reducing the pre-match idle time available for spectators' liquor consumption—and in Arlington, Texas, the city reduced the street and neighborhood problems caused by teenage and youth "cruising" by designating a huge parking lot, otherwise empty on weekends, where the youngsters could race their cars and just "hang around."[20] In West Germany, passage of a helmet law for motorcyclists compounded the safety benefit by also deterring motorcycle theft because most such thieves, who did not either possess or use such helmets, were instantly identifiable.[21]

The private sector will often implement situational prevention with multiple, simultaneous tactics. Felson describes a strategy wherein the 7-Eleven chain of convenience stores hired convicted robbers and consultants to make changes in sixty stores, while sixty "control" stores remained unchanged. The experimental stores created wide visibility by uncovering their windows, moved the cash registers near the door on a platform, used timed access to portions of the cash registers, had only one access door for the public, ensured that store personnel could see all customers, and even encouraged the frequent presence of people by providing taxi drivers with free coffee and use of rest rooms. Crime levels remained constant in the "control" stores but declined 30 percent in the experimental stores.[22] Again, one cannot isolate the particular change or changes, if any, that were most related to crime reduction and one cannot state with certainty that the control stores were equivalent to the altered stores in their settings, customer flow, personnel characteristics, and outside influences. But a businessperson would probably find the study results sufficiently convincing to enact similar changes, as needed, in all stores he or she owned.

Situational strategies and tactics also have led to crime prevention through environmental design, or CPTED. By the end of the twentieth century, most land planners accorded some degree of emphasis on CPTED by designing and installing so-called defensible space (for example, walls or limited access), by creating spaces where everyone can see actual or potential negative activity, and by developing a sense of community whereby every person who lives, works, or plays in a place feels a protective duty and a desire to make that space safe. For example, one study review found promising the tactic of closing off through streets in high-crime urban areas.[23] And government decisions that public safety and a sense of community were impossible to achieve in high-rise public housing led to its large-scale replacement with low-rise, segmented "neighborhoods."[24]

As early as 1983, Barry Poyner identified thirty-one patterns using environmental principles for crime prevention in neighborhoods, housing, multiunit apartments, city centers, schools, and underground railway stations.[25] Extensive, detailed CPTED prescriptions now exist for particular high-traffic, high-crime opportunity locations, such as parking facilities, all designed to make the location one that potential offenders will find more difficult to access, more risky to approach, and more available to citizen observation.[26] And CPTED principles can be incorporated into American common law to justify civil suits against landlords, owners of public premises, and service providers who negligently fail to use these well-known and reasonable crime prevention designs and tactics.[27]

Situational prevention is also important for making people feel safe. Perhaps the best illustration of this phenomenon is the rise of gated communities in America. Edward Blakely and Mary Snyder found an explosion of such developments since 1970, reaching perhaps twenty thousand by 1997 with more than three million units and an estimated 8.4 million people.[28] Their survey of homeowner association boards found that 70 percent of the respondents listed security as "very important" in their choice of gated-community living.[29] Even if crime in gated communities is not reduced in comparison to so-called open neighborhoods (and the evidence is inconclusive as a whole), the gated residents believe that crime levels are lower than that of nearby neighborhoods, and their fear of crime is reduced.[30] But all of this comes at the price of reducing "gated" residents' sense of belonging to an American community as a whole, reducing their identification with other cultures, and reducing incentives for exercising social responsibility.[31]

Public Police Agencies

Public police officers face an enormous range of challenges and restrictions in their daily work. One researcher, who enrolled in the full curriculum of the Philadelphia Police Academy and patrolled the streets with sworn police officers for more than a year thereafter in the early 1970s, describes the challenges:

> On his first day as a policeman a rookie may capture an armed felon, be cracked on the head with a rock, be offered sexual favors, free food or money; he may be confronted by a naked woman, screaming hysterically, or a belligerent drunk who outweighs him by fifty pounds . . . He has no control over what he will learn first, and when he will learn it, because he has no control over what he must do. Regardless of what occurs, he is obliged to be immediately what he has chosen to become, although his colleagues know he has only the vaguest appreciation of what that is.[32]

When a police officer is on patrol, the constant and often bizarre mixtures of missions, carried out with society's authorization to use force when necessary and conjoined with the officer's fear of possible serious injury or death, involve difficult roles that few professions require. At the Philadelphia Police Academy, a teaching manual stated that a cop was expected to "prevent crime, protect life and property, arrest law violators, assist the public, preserve the public peace, regulate public conduct and control and expedite the flow of vehicular traffic."[33]

Egon Bittner suggests that the role of the police is best understood as a mechanism for distributing nonnegotiable coercive force with only an instant's grasp of each situation's demands.[34] As a police officer fulfills disparate missions—for example, stopping a speeding car, intervening in a violent or potentially violent domestic dispute, confronting a seventeen-year-old boy who harasses elderly ladies in the neighborhood, or contending with a mentally ill person who is waving a sharp object on a city sidewalk—the ultimate result of each encounter depends on the officer's possession of, and ability to use, some degree of authorized coercive power. Social workers, psychiatrists, psychologists, hospital aides, or others may well be more effective than cops in solving some of these problems, but these professions lack coercive power and are not likely to be available on the street and around the clock. Further, many simply are not hired to deal with such potentially dangerous situations, so police officers must accompany them to introduce the potential of coercive power and control.

Citizens call on police officers to serve various personal needs when no one else is available, maintain order in the community, and prevent and solve crimes. In doing so, cops are trained to use their educated judgment to choose wisely from an extraordinary range of possible discretionary acts; and police officers do this often by waiting patiently, resisting fear and rejecting the temptation to employ coercive force before other alternatives have failed. To supervise and control each officer's extraordinary power and range of activity, police departments formed military-type organizations where leaders conveyed mixed messages about role and mission and demanded written accountability to endless rules. Such a method of command and structure, and its accompanying reward and promotion system, has until recent times focused police goals on meeting internal organization needs—needs that discouraged a patrol officer's initiative, inhibited proactive (as opposed to reactive) strategies, and avoided outreach to the neighborhood and to other agencies to help solve those problems that most concern a community. Reducing crime was merely one among many goals.

This lack of a central focus may have developed because criminologists could not explain what part, if any, police activity plays in rising or falling crime rates. We could not measure cause and effect, and our governments did not try to do so. Instead, when crime rates rose, elected officials avoided blame by citing social ills or failures in police management or the legislative or judicial systems; but when crime rates fell significantly, police chiefs, mayors, legislators, governors, attorneys general, and presidents all flocked to the podium to take a bow. Any knowledge gaps about the real potential of police to control crime were—and are today—ignored by glory or defensiveness, political orientations, biases, and the latest theories about the causes and cures of crime. The rhetoric remains today, but knowledge is slowly making a dent.

Since we taxpayers pay police to protect us, one would think it natural that police chiefs would always want to know what our priorities are, how we assess their actions, and particularly how we as victims and neighbors of victims can help cops solve crimes. After all, we are the ones present when the crimes occur; the police usually are present only after we call them. One would also think that our police would periodically ask us who, if anyone, in the area is creating fear, bother, and harassment. In a small town, yes. But in urban areas, at state and federal levels, government institutions grow distant, self-absorbed, wrapped in bureaucracy—sometimes with a ribbon of arrogance. America's urban police came late to the idea that they must adhere to the rule of law and formulate specific crime-reduction goals, all while creating and maintaining public participation and approval. Local law enforcement undertook this long climb from a startlingly low threshold just seventy years ago.

In 1931, President Hoover's Wickersham Commission concluded, "The general failure of the police to detect and arrest criminals . . . has caused a loss of public confidence in the police of our country."[35] The report on police described a status quo of incompetent police chiefs, political corruption and pervasive political influence, uneducated and untrained patrol officers, poor communication, sloppy recordkeeping, and low salaries. The commission devoted a separate report solely to abusive police interrogation practices, proclaiming that the "third degree—the inflicting of pain, physical or mental, to extract confessions or statements—is widespread throughout the country," and "physical brutality is extensively practiced."[36]

Several decades later, after the American Bar Foundation's sixteen-year project had brought to public view the reality, low visibility, and complexity of the discretionary decisionmaking that, day to day and hour to hour, dominates the roles of the police,[37] President Johnson's national crime commission in 1967 challenged the police world, in effect, to find out for the first time what it was really doing every day.[38] One cannot overstate the persistence of pervasive knowledge gaps and lack of goal-related and operations data in policing just thirty-five years ago, nor the effects of that void.

The Johnson Commission briefly performed its own tentative research steps, for example, exploring how government could measure levels of crime incidence through victim surveys that supplement and call into question traditional crime data, which record only those crimes that citizens report to police departments.[39] The commission also recommended certain items now a staple of policing, such as a universal police telephone number (later implemented as 911), an automated fingerprint recognition system, and computer-assisted command-and-control systems.[40] Almost unknown to police operations in 1967, these developments are taken for granted today, although in still-evolving formats.

But the commission also proclaimed that neither the police alone nor indeed the entire criminal justice system could reduce crime significantly unless the underlying social causes of crime were addressed. The lack of focus on a significant crime reduction role reflected the prevailing wisdom of that era—a view that lacked credible challenge because the void in research-produced data and knowledge had left police with little to try beyond traditional objectives: better response to individual incidents, better allocation of police strength to high-crime hours of the day and week, better recruitment, improvements in personnel and training, and better supervision. Beyond these concepts of "professionalism," no one really knew what "better" was.

To the enduring credit of the police, they were the only crime response group to accept the commission's challenge to reexamine every aspect of its goals, organization, operations, and use of personnel. The courts, prosecutors, jails, and prisons became overwhelmed with vast increases in cases, offenders, and prison confinement; and the spread of sentencing guidelines vastly decreased the discretion formerly available to judges in executing their functions. But the police began to examine, and to let researchers examine, what cops really did and whether or not the existing reactive mode—that is, just patrolling and then responding to citizen calls and crime reports as they flowed into police switchboards—was effective. As many researchers have described in detail, initial in-depth studies and operational experiments of differing quality were showing tentatively that criminals were not caught by faster police response times. Nor were crimes prevented by policemen constantly patrolling by car to deter potential offenders, or solved by assigning most felony cases to detectives.[41] But most of this 1970s research examined crime control through street operations; and the role of police interaction with the community and of centralized versus decentralized police management was just a fringe focus.

Between the Wickersham Commission in the 1930s and the Johnson Commission in the late 1960s, some police departments had indeed strived for reforms resulting in what many termed the professional model.[42] Many of the reform chiefs wanted to separate themselves and their departments from the traditional overwhelming political interference with departmental recruiting, assignments, and operational priorities. This thirst for independence led to more centralization of control, higher recruitment and education standards, better recruit and in-service training, higher wages, establishment of planning and research units, and the removal of city police from jail duty and other fringe functions.[43] But these changes were not crime control strategies. They were primarily internally focused, and the riots, massive civil rights and anti-Vietnam demonstrations, as well as fast-increasing crime rates in urban areas in the late 1960s and early 1970s created a police personnel culture that saw the residents of the inner cities and the mobs of the younger, "sixties" generation as anarchic and immoral forces that could destroy our society. The desire to escape political meddling was now joined with reasons to see "the community" as the enemy.

The U.S. Supreme Court decisions restricting police actions provided more fodder for this police feeling of isolation. Then, when early research findings during this era appeared to negate the efficacy of what police departments were doing, without telling them how they should be operating, the incentive for acquiring new knowledge and for accepting research findings suffered.

In this atmosphere, Johnson Commission recommendations about a team-policing concept—which was to be implemented through a decentralized organization and with an intense focus upon the community—receded into the background.[44] Also ignored were recommendations that police join with local communities by creating Community Service Officer positions and police-citizen advisory groups in every minority-group neighborhood. Instead, the community became the adversary, particularly as police traveled to their inner-city work from the culture and quiet of their own suburban or edge-of-city neighborhoods. Soon, much of police patrol was confined to cops robotically driving police vehicles and devoting their time to an increasing number of calls placed through the now-universal 911 telephone systems, which the public was using for a wide variety of services and needs unrelated to crime.[45] The newly reinforced estrangement between police and community also served a long-standing leadership viewpoint that keeping patrols from having close contact with neighborhoods vastly reduced opportunities and temptations for broad-based police corruption and neighborhood political influence on police assignments and decisions.

Besides, police argued, there was little room for new ways. The demands of 911 calls offered a convenient justification for not even thinking about alternatives. Many police used the perceived time tyranny of 911 as an unavoidable reason to tie down police operations with constant car patrol. One study of 1977 information from 175 police jurisdictions with populations exceeding 100,000 found the great majority emphasizing the immediate dispatch of a sworn police officer to almost all citizen service calls, regardless of the reason for the call.[46] William Bratton cites an example from his days as a Boston police sergeant, where that department received and responded to 1,300 calls in one year complaining about the kids "drinking and acting up" at one street intersection.[47] But no one could fairly blame the tyranny of 911; police had only themselves to blame for the tyranny of narrow thinking and a desire not to work with the community on joint crime control. A business owner or a city water department, for example, when receiving a series of calls about a continuing problem at one location, would fully address the basic problem, not just alleviate it temporarily.

As crime continued to rise, departments began to develop priority ratings for 911 calls. As early as 1981, a research group directed by "reform" police chiefs developed a model for differential police responses to such calls. The grid determined who would respond and how quickly, by seriousness of incident and the time of occurrence in relation to the time of the call.[48]

But differential 911 responses alleviated only part of the problem. Data for the six largest cities in the United States in 1986 showed enormous variation among cities in total service calls to police per one hundred inhabitants, in the actual dispatched calls for police service per marked patrol car, and in the percent of police service calls that actually generated a patrol car response.[49] Data from other U.S. cities for the twelve-month period ending June 30, 1997 showed similar kinds of variations.[50]

But as the modus operandi of police patrol changed slowly in the 1980s, research began to confirm that police had much uncommitted time even after responding to crime and service calls, perhaps up to 60 percent free time.[51] David Bayley reported on workload studies showing that officers on patrol "have a considerable amount of uncommitted time." But he also noted that in over thirty years of police research, both before and after the advent of 911, police "from top to bottom" always reported that "frontline personnel are too busy to handle" even the externally generated demands upon them.[52] Of course, on Friday and Saturday nights, police may have little free time; but particularly during part of each weekday, a patrol officer on routine patrol assignment, or some patrol officers assigned to a shift, could work on something other than random or directed preventive patrol and response to calls. This finding is important for deflection of a police administrator's assertion that the in-box of 911 calls and crime investigation leaves no time for proactive approaches to crime control. In the old days of the business world, middle managers also claimed they had no time to think and create because their in-boxes were too full. Many business CEOs responded by simply abolishing many middle management positions, then instructing the remaining managers to find a way to meet specific corporate goals. Only a small portion of police leadership had followed this lead by the end of the 1980s.

With reported crime rates rising precipitously in the 1970s and 1980s, an unprecedented volume of police-oriented research ensued. Many program planners and researchers decided that if police were to have a direct effect upon crime, they would have to focus on developing a crime-reduction hypothesis and then implement trial-and-error experiments. The idea of a positive relationship with the community became relevant only insofar as it contributed to crime reduction.

As technology improved the development and retrieval of crime data, research revealed a heavy concentration of places, times, and offenders involved in crime.[53] Lawrence Sherman reported that only 5 percent of the street addresses and intersections in Minneapolis produced all calls to the police reporting robbery, auto theft, and criminal sexual conduct, and overall, only 3 percent of all places produced 50 percent of all crime calls to which police cars were dispatched for any reason.[54] John Eck reported on research studies showing a high concentration of robberies at just a few among all convenience stores, a high concentration of gun crimes and drug dealing in just a few places, and a disproportionate concentration of fast-food restaurant property crimes at a small number of such establishments.[55] After analyzing recent place-concentration studies, Eck suggested that "something about a few places facilitates crimes and something about most places prevents crimes."[56] In 1989, William Spelman and Eck estimated that 40 percent of all victimizations nationwide involve only 10 percent of the total victims, about 55 percent of the crimes are attributable to only 10 percent of the offender population, and 60 percent of the crimes occur in only 10 percent of all places victimized.[57] (Note, however, that for urban police departments, a small percentage of total addresses or street intersections still represents a large number of actual places at which crime needs to be prevented and detected.)

If one combines a finding of place-concentration for crimes with what is called "opportunity blocking," the potential for crime reduction evolves. In simple terms, if a man with a lengthy criminal record walks down the street one evening with an unfocused anger and a desire to throw a rock through a window and burglarize a store, one could posit that he would proceed to commit both acts even if it takes him hours or days to find the appropriate target. But others posit instead that perhaps a police tactic, community strategy, or physical alteration of the building would block his opportunity to carry out that crime long enough to allow a lawful diversion to catch his attention or to give him pause because the police have publicized their strong emphasis on arresting repeat offenders. In this hypothesis the man does not have to be "cured" or "rehabilitated" in order to lower the total number or the broad range of his criminal acts; his decision to act just has to be temporarily diverted or made harder to carry out. Those who call for police patrols focused on high-rate offenders and high-victim places necessarily assume that the offender will not just wander over to another neighborhood and commit the same number of crimes, at least for a while. Focused patrol can also mean that if he does go ahead with a retail store break-in, he will more likely be detected and apprehended.

Some police departments, realizing the ineffectiveness of random patrol, did show effective but temporary crime reduction through intensified patrol, sometimes termed "hot spots" patrol, and through temporary crackdowns at high-crime locations.[58] Other police departments developed programs to increase their focus upon known repeat offenders, in cooperation with prosecutors; and two evaluations of such programs, implemented in different ways, demonstrated a substantial increase in prison sentences for repeat offenders.[59] And if police direct their patrol efforts to both gun confiscation and repeat offenders, a reduction in firearms crime occurs during such concentrated police work.[60] In addition, when police action against retail drug markets in neighborhood buildings is linked with follow-up pressure on the landlords and possible civil, nuisance-abatement actions, a drop in drug activity appears to result, particularly in neighborhoods where landlords perceive higher future property values and thus the need to retain title to their properties for investment and income purposes.[61]

Those who have examined whether crime prevention at one place results in total displacement of crime to other places find little evidence for such a hypothesis. Any occurrence of displacement can be highly contingent on the nature of the neighborhoods, the particular crimes, and the particular offenders.[62] One can posit as well that even if a portion of some crimes being prevented in one crime-ridden neighborhood is displaced into ten nearby but different neighborhoods, that same amount of crime when diffused will cause less overall fear and disintegration of community. One can also posit a diffusion-of-benefits effect from protection of certain places or items. For example, some evidence exists that if a potential offender knows that security devices cover one portion of a place or a portion of items in a place, he may attribute that coverage to other portions as well.[63]

But even with extensive research findings, the variety of police policies, strategies, and tactics, and the settings, culture, and personnel who implement them in the United States render impossible the task of identifying *the* tactic, *the* operation, *the* policy that produces universal success. The danger of using an experimental finding as a basis for universal operational change is vividly illustrated by the research that endeavored to develop optimum police strategies for handling domestic violence. The first widely publicized controlled study occurred under Lawrence Sherman's guidance in Minneapolis in the early 1980s, where police alternately handled such complaints with a randomly distributed response mandated from three alternatives: arrest, separation of the couple (that is, the offender must stay away from the residence for at least eight hours), or advice to the couple in whatever form the officer should choose (other than arrest or separation). The result? The arrest alternative produced the lowest percentage of recurring domestic violence incidents for the six months following the randomly chosen alternative responses.[64] In the five years following release of the study, police policies in domestic violence calls changed dramatically in many departments around the nation. Fortified by state statutes permitting warrantless arrest in misdemeanor cases of domestic violence, and riding the impetus of the women's movement between 1984 and 1990, arrest responses increased dramatically.[65]

But fortunately the original researchers recommended replication. Following the completion of seven studies, Sherman offered quite complex conclusions about the short-term and long-term effects of an arrest policy for domestic violence. The relationship between arrest and later recurrence of domestic violence varied with the race, employment status, and economic status of the participants and their surroundings, with arrest actually increasing later domestic violence in some situations. These studies clearly demonstrate that research findings should not lead to actual policy implementation until the effects of variations in police response have been observed in the varieties of a particular crime's settings and participants.[66] The seven domestic violence studies did teach police not to follow a uniform mandatory arrest policy. But unfortunately, the current anticrime rhetoric has left police, the public, and lawmakers ill-equipped and ill-inclined to deal honestly and forthrightly with any finding that arrests in certain situations can increase repeat crime.

Even taken as a whole, existing research cannot produce the conclusion that police alone reduce crime or even that police action is responsible for a certain percentage of the decline in crime rates in the 1990s. As widely respected academic researchers John Eck and Edward Maguire state in summarizing the research on police operations: "There is one thing that is a myth: that the police have a substantial, broad, and independent impact on the nation's crime rate."[67]

We should place some faith in the fact that so many operational experiments in policing do seem to cause at least temporary crime reduction.[68] But even then, many contributing causes may also be present—for example, the experimental neighborhood itself becoming more crime preventive in attitude and action, businesses and schools there taking their own anticrime measures, employment rates improving, higher levels of imprisonment occurring, federal drug enforcement and drug treatment expanding, the neighborhood's new social network rejecting the social devastation observed during an older generation's hard drug culture, or after-school programs expanding. And even if a neighborhood's crime was affected most directly by a policing experiment, that experiment in itself may involve a concentration of police personnel and perhaps a downward delegation of supervisory authority that cannot and will not be sustained in the everyday police world.[69]

The search for universal remedies may well be fruitless also because cities, regions, and police departments differ in fundamental ways. For example, one can see instantly that San Diego is not New York and Seattle is not Miami. In just the police world, most large Southwest and Western cities have much lower levels of total police complement than most Midwestern and Eastern cities. For example, Baltimore, Detroit, New York City, Chicago, Newark, and Philadelphia all had more than 4.0 full-time sworn police officers per one thousand population in 1997, whereas San Diego, Phoenix, San Francisco, Seattle, Tucson, Los Angeles, Denver and Dallas all had 2.8 or fewer.[70] Only a portion of this variation reflects a greater use of civilians in some of the Western departments compared to some in the East.

One might expect at least that greater relative police strength would result in lower violent crime rates under the theory that more cops per citizen allows increased flexibility in assigning greater patrol concentrations to "hot spots" and other high-crime areas. But police strength does not correlate inversely with rates for violent crime. For example, New York City with its 520 police per 100,000 residents had a violent crime rate of 1,167 incidents per 100,000 residents in 1998, while San Diego's comparable police and violent crime figures were 170 and 725, respectively. In sum, San Diego had a 38 percent lower violent crime rate than New York City with a 200 percent lower ratio of sworn officers to residents.[71] One must keep in mind as well that probably less than 10 percent of a city department's total sworn complement will be on patrol at any particular time.[72] Unfortunately from a public education standpoint, a mayor or city manager will proudly announce the net addition of one hundred officers but not disclose, nor will the local newspaper, that ten or fewer of those new officers will be on patrol at one time.

Implementation of a research finding should also proceed slowly when researchers themselves articulate great caution. For example, the negative findings about random patrol as a crime control strategy could well have discouraged reliance on patrol and thus deterred exploration of other patrol strategies. But fortunately, such research proceeded to discover the crime prevention and detection effects of police patrols specifically directed to known high-crime places and intersections. This change may sound basic and intuitive and raise wonder that police took so long to realize the need for patrol focus. But until computers replaced pin maps, data collection and analyses about crime and about the nature and origins of 911 calls both citywide and for as long as a year's time (as opposed to weekly or even monthly changes) did not reliably exist. The concentration of crime and citizen calls at comparatively few locations was truly unknown, other than intuitively by veteran cops, until relatively recently.

Then too, research can prove what probably does not work; but can offer only probabilities and associations in describing what does work. In other words, a study can demonstrate that crime rates were unchanged in all areas where different strategies were simultaneously installed. But if some areas show a reduction in crime after introduction of an experimental police activity, the question remains: Did the new strategy cause the crime reduction in these areas, or did lower crime rates proceed from some other simultaneous, direct preventive factor or factors? And were these factors represented in the analysis, or indeed even identified by researchers as relevant? Even if control areas with no change in police activity demonstrate a different trend in crime rate from the experimental areas, innumerable questions remain about how the experiments actually were carried out and what other simultaneous dynamics were occurring in those areas. Then too, it is quite rare in crime research to have a widespread experiment with similarly widespread control areas. And finally, any kind of social experiment that works well in its initial setting is always difficult to implement on an agencywide basis, where all personnel must be "on board" and be able to implement a new approach that may well be more demanding and require duplication of a carefully planned, operated, and supervised experiment. Social science experimentation and evaluation inside and outside the crime arena are replete with small, "successful" programs being swallowed and soon forgotten in the everyday operation of a government agency.

Despite all of the warnings offered by respected researchers over time, as crime rates fell dramatically in the 1990s, large portions of the operations world of policing began to proclaim that police who are focused on crime reduction can make significant progress in that regard no matter what social, demographic, and economic conditions exist. The overt and aggressive police acceptance of responsibility for the level of crime in society was previously unknown in American law enforcement.

In fact, for almost a decade after 1992, the significant and sustained decrease in serious crime occurred in every region of the nation. And three years after the crime decrease had commenced, two widespread phenomena gradually occurred in the police world: relatively massive infusions of sworn personnel at the local level, primarily through federal funding, and the nearly unanimous use of the term "community policing" to describe almost every police chief's proclaimed "new approach." So, one should ask, did these two phenomena—as well as the focused patrol efforts described earlier—cause the crime reduction? Eck and Maguire concluded that the substantial numbers of additional police officers did not "play an independent or consistent role" in violent crime reduction. Further, violent crime reduction effects cannot be consistently attributed to various forms of community policing implemented through police-community partnerships and / or police organizational changes.[73] One always qualifies such a conclusion by noting that the addition of police officers and of the several varieties of community policing probably contributed, jointly with other factors, to the downward crime trend. But research conclusions should always be limited to the effects of certain tactical or analytical approaches on certain problems in certain neighborhoods at particular periods of a crime cycle.

One can possibly find a more direct effect of these changes in policing in the 1990s by examining national trends in the arrest rates over twenty-five years. In comparing 1974 and 1998, the national total arrest rate per 100,000 inhabitants for serious crime in the FBI Crime Index actually declined by 13 percent, but the mix between violent and property crime arrest rates changed significantly. The violent crime arrest rate in 1998 was up about 15 percent compared to 1974 but the serious property crime arrest rate dropped about 21 percent.[74] Comparably, the rate of total reported serious crimes in 1998 was down about 5 percent compared to 1974; but the violent crime rate increased by about 23 percent while the serious property offense rate dropped by almost 8 percent.[75] All of the violent crime arrest rate increase is attributable to the 68 percent rise in the rate of aggravated assault arrests; the arrest rates for murder, rape, and robbery declined between 1974 and 1998.[76] And the 68 percent rise in aggravated assault arrest rates is comparable to the rise in the rate of aggravated assault offenses reported to the police. The rape offense rate, however, also rose 31 percent from 1974 to 1998, even though the rape arrest rate declined.[77]

But police arrest activity reflected in FBI data compiled from agencies covering over 50 percent of the population, including most large urban areas, shows that for the period 1996–2000, total serious violent crime arrests dropped about 11 percent and serious property crime arrests declined 21 percent while the overall population was increasing at just under 4 percent during those five years. Even the aggravated assault arrest volume declined more than 7 percent during those five years.[78]

So, if rates for serious crime and arrests for those crimes were declining at the same time that federal funding was just commencing to recruit, train, and then add police street personnel in large numbers nationally for community policing, what were police departments doing with all these expanded resources? The following increases in arrest volume between 1996 and 2000 for certain crimes outside the FBI serious crime index offer evidence: drug abuse, 7 percent; liquor law crimes, 12 percent (excludes drunkenness and driving under the influence); embezzlement, 23 percent; vagrancy, 10 percent; miscellaneous offenses, 3 percent. Unexplained, and certainly puzzling, is the 25 percent decline in state and local arrests for any kind of weapons offense from 1996 through 2000.[79] The increased personnel appear to have been devoted at least in part to the lesser crimes not included in the FBI's serious crime index. No one has documented how much of this lower-level arrest activity is connected to locating and attempting to disrupt potentially more serious crime.

These statistics, of course, do not tell us what is happening in any particular city, suburb, or rural area. But they might well reflect changes in police tactical or strategic priorities. Since crime response is always slow to follow crime rate variations, huge increases in crime troops were promised in the 1992 presidential political campaign, but ironically did not actually begin to flow into battle until 1996 or 1997, even though the violent crime rate had peaked by 1993–1994.[80] Coincidentally, "new" phraseology for basic concepts of policing gained national visibility: aggressive order maintenance, zero tolerance, community policing, problem-oriented policing, "broken-windows" policing, and quality-of-life policing. Community policing, "broken windows" policing, and problem-oriented policing entered the research world in the 1980s. "Order maintenance" has been a long-standing concept with different emphases. The original concept described police emphasis upon keeping the neighborhood peace, including at times enforcing the law.[81] Addition of the word "aggressive" to "order maintenance" radically altered the concept by emphasizing peace through widespread arrests, stops, and frisks. Zero tolerance and quality-of-life as broad concepts of policing were new.

The popular uses of all these labels became particularly confusing and often misleading because they mix together goals, policies, strategies, and tactics. Some are aimed at immediate crime reduction, perhaps only in certain neighborhoods and for a short period of time. Others, such as "broken windows," reflect an overall, long-term and short-term approach for high-crime, disintegrated neighborhoods, peopled usually by racial and ethnic minorities. Pure "zero tolerance" removes police discretion to decline arrest for even lower-level crimes. Overloaded prosecutors and judges soon cry out against prolonged, widespread zero tolerance policing and dismiss many arrests.

Even the word "community" in community policing conveys no particular direction. We are each a member of many "communities": a family; neighborhood; business; school; special interest group pushing one particular social, gender, racial, or ethnic goal, political party or orientation; ethnic group; service group; or religious institution. Indeed, each of our "communities" helps form our views, and vice versa, and what is "good" for one of our communities may be "bad" for another one. All of the labels attributed to policing in our various communities recognize basic goals of crime reduction and fear reduction. Some seek also to dispense justice in a rational way and through actions that the citizenry as a whole perceive as just and effective. Some minimize or downgrade these goals. All purvey their programs as the promised land in controlling crime, even though the crime drop commenced before each new approach had been in widespread use and even though, as we have seen, research cannot credit conclusively police strategies and tactics for being the cause or even the prime cause of the overall drop in crime. Let's look at each label more closely.

In 1994, after the rate of reported serious crime had commenced its descent, a community policing consortium published a fifty-three-page monograph outlining the goals, core concepts, and plans for community policing.[82] Chiefs of police, sheriffs, local government officials, academicians, national organizations, and the U.S. Department of Justice all participated in this launching of an initial five-year program using federal moneys to fund state and local community policing programs and add 100,000 sworn personnel to state and local police departments, roughly a 16 percent addition to the national total. All grant recipients pledged themselves to "community policing," thus perhaps unintentionally lending that single, mandatory label to what proved to be a wide variety of programs around the nation. Three goals were established as measures of effectiveness: reduce neighborhood crime, decrease citizen fear of crime, and enhance the quality of life in the community.[83] Implementation of these goals depended upon two core concepts: community partnerships with the police and police adoption of a problem-solving methodology.[84]

During the fifteen years preceding this program there had been many variations of what various police chiefs had termed community policing. Most were experiments loosely attached in some fashion to the business-as-usual departmental operations. Examples include police storefronts, some police teams permanently assigned to specific neighborhoods, some neighborhood meetings, and crime prevention lectures or home visits by police. Many evaluations of these efforts were summarized in 1992 with Mark Moore's statement that no police organization in the nation had successfully made the strategic changeovers required by community policing doctrine.[85] In 1997 researchers Wesley Skogan and Susan Hartnett could report a 50 percent success rate in achieving desirable outcomes in five diverse areas of Chicago using 1,800 officers who were community policing a combined population almost equal to the size of Boston.[86] Outcomes involved such issues as visibility of police to citizens, alleviation of fear, reduction of one or more named kinds of crime, and elimination of one or more presences (such as prostitutes) or signs of decay (like abandoned autos). But Skogan also found that ten of eleven such experiments in six other cities, conducted on very small scales with a 50 percent "success" rate, had all disappeared over time as funding lapsed, 911 call demands increased, police officers and leaders opposed the change, and politicians objected.[87] And in Chicago, Skogan and Hartnett found few positive outcomes in Hispanic neighborhoods.

In 1997, Maguire and others identified among police departments thirty-one different types of activity that had acquired the label of community policing. These ranged from Neighborhood Watch to different police partnerships with schools, or with civic or business groups working together to combat some defined criminal activity.[88] On May 12, 1999 the Office of Community Oriented Policing Services (COPS) in the U.S. Department of Justice funded its one hundred thousandth police officer, or equivalent, after 6 billion grant dollars had been awarded to 11,300 state and local law enforcement agencies that serve more than 87 percent of the American public—all this in just five years.[89]

One may find it difficult to believe that the police came late to the concept of community. After all, we are the communities of citizens who are the victims, the ultimate boss of the police, and the payer of police officers' salaries. Further, some of the highly trumpeted new practices in policing are well known to the world of public corporations, whose leaders realized long ago that their communities—customers and shareholders—had to be satisfied and that good results, that is, quality products, excellent service, and net profits, resulted from empowering employees through decentralization, from increasing productivity, and from not only meeting, but anticipating, customers' needs partially by staying in constant contact with the customer. If corporations have a problem, they identify it, analyze it, design a remedy, and implement the necessary change. Herman Goldstein has been articulating such a problem-oriented approach for the police world since 1979. He later joined with other institutions and organizations to design such a process for police use. The SARA process instructed police to *scan* the data to detect and identify the problem, *analyze* the elements of the problem from cause to consequence, design and implement an appropriate *response*, and *assess* the degree of effectiveness of the response—really a version of what businesses have done for many years.[90] The concept of problem solving gives focus to the too-broad umbrella of generic community policing programs. The street corner, residence, bar, store, or city block that produces 20 or 50 or 1,300 calls to police per year is addressed as a problem to be solved, not just an annoyance taking too much police time. Using SARA, this or any other neighborhood problem jointly identified by police and citizens can be attacked with a comprehensive response that may involve other city departments and local businesses.

Under this problem-oriented process of community policing, direct crime prevention efforts become as important, or more important, than solving a particular crime incident. These prevention efforts can more readily involve the police world in wider interactions with other city agencies, environmental design changes, and private security actions and programs. Police can also address a wide range of problems: significant burglary reduction in a 500-unit apartment complex (Newport News); rapid crime reduction in slumlord apartments by forcing the use of competent apartment managers (San Diego); reducing police service calls in child-custody disputes (Fresno); lessening drug traffic offenses, auto theft, vandalism, and burglary in a 77-block inner-city neighborhood through combined efforts of police, neighborhood groups, city agencies, and service organizations (Minneapolis); reducing chronic truancy at certain high-risk schools and thereby reducing neighborhood daytime crime and delinquency (San Diego and Baltimore); restoring order at a business intersection plagued by aggressive panhandlers, litter, graffiti, and other signs of decay (Vancouver); and taking a run down, tavern-dominated, three-block inner-city business district and, with police leadership to mobilize the community, creating instead a district with low-crime conditions, low 911 call demand, vital business and retail activity, and anticrime environmental design (Green Bay).[91]

But the consortium had articulated a third goal for community policing apart from crime reduction and lowered fear of crime: improvement in the community's quality of life. The Justice monograph admitted that such an improvement was difficult to measure, citing only examples such as ridding the streets of gangs, drunks, panhandlers, and prostitutes as well as removing signs of neglect—abandoned cars, derelict buildings, and garbage and other debris.[92] But quality of life also became the very clever label deliberately attached to "aggressive order maintenance" policing, which was geared to implement the crime theory articulated in the now-famous 1982 "broken windows" essay of James Q. Wilson and George Kelling.[93] Although Wilson coined the phrase "broken windows," Kelling has carried the research and promotion role continuously since 1982. Explaining his advocacy for aggressive order maintenance activities by the police, Kelling wrote in 1987:

Research showed that maintaining order—keeping subways free of graffiti or keeping dirty and messy people off the street—was not merely a cosmetic treatment. Drunks, gangs, prostitutes, obstreperous youth, as well as panhandling and other behaviors considered disorderly, were linked in citizens' minds to personal danger and serious crime. Moreover, as James Q. Wilson and I have argued, citizens may be right. Just as unrepaired broken windows . . . may signal that nobody cares and lead to additional vandalism and damage, so untended disorderly behavior may also communicate that nobody cares (or that nobody can or will do anything about disorder) and thus lead to increasingly criminal and dangerous predatory behavior.[94]

Jack Maple, however, crime control director for Police Commissioner William Bratton's highly touted twenty-seven-month tenure in New York City in the mid-1990s, sees flaws in the "broken windows" rationale:

Rapists and killers don't head for another town when they see that graffiti is disappearing . . . The average squeegee man doesn't start accepting contract murders whenever he detects a growing tolerance for squeegeeing. Panhandling doesn't turn a neighborhood into Murder Central. In fact, panhandlers don't work in bad neighborhoods. In Midtown Manhattan, a beggar might be able to act like a bully. In a bad neighborhood, he'd be set on fire. Literally.[95]

Maple, who also sees community policing as a concept "hatched by academics" and "full of holes," calls his strategy and tactics "quality-of-life-plus," in which every arrest on a "maintenance of order" offense has a known relationship to more serious criminal activity or to serious offenders.[96] That is, he promotes making arrests for low-level types of disorder crimes only when this strategy leads to the apprehension or deflection of real criminals such as repeat offenders, gun law violators, drug offenders, or those with an outstanding arrest warrant.[97] This approach severely undermines the justification for implementing "zero-tolerance" policing—universal arrest for any kind of "broken windows"–type crime. Under zero tolerance, all of the "dirty and messy" people described in Kelling's broken-windows rationale, including all of the homeless and the mentally ill vagrants, would be swept into arrest and court processing. Zero-tolerance practices for lower-level crimes remove the "harm" element of crime and thus fail to distinguish between a dirty and messy person who harasses another person and a dirty and messy person who stays outside because he or she simply cannot find or tolerate an "inside." A Department of Justice–sponsored evaluation of community policing nationwide noted the "recent and growing trend toward zero-tolerance policing" and stated that what would have been termed a "crackdown" in 1995 is now billed as a zero tolerance or order maintenance policy carried out under the umbrella of "community policing."[98] The authors noted that the aggressiveness and intensity of a zero-tolerance philosophy could well alienate the community and negate the community partnership goal. The authors also found that so-called problem-solving operations in many jurisdictions are merely traditional investigative and enforcement actions that neither address the underlying cause of repetitive, widespread criminal conduct nor build the community support necessary to help create and, as important, maintain the solution.

A practitioner like Jack Maple disdains zero-tolerance policing because mass arrests lead to time-consuming court processing, which diverts police time away from the street. And anyone concerned with supremacy of the law and regulated, supervised exercise of police discretion must refuse to let an aggressive order-maintenance strategy turn into "zero tolerance" or "kick-ass" modes of operation.[99] Unfortunately, in practice, aggressive order maintenance slides easily into those modes and even into racial profiling and stereotyping. Indeed, some police chiefs' dedication to "broken windows" policing may well be reflected in the large increases in nonfelony arrests for order-maintenance-type crimes during the economically prosperous years of 1995–2000.

It is important to strip the "quality of life" label from the police activity that it cleverly masks: aggressive order maintenance and zero-tolerance policing.[100] Who could be against improving everyone's quality of life? Order maintenance has always been a police role and should be discussed as such not only because of its propensity for abuse and for its often discriminatory exercise in practice but also, just as important, because police undeniably play a role in preserving civic morality and the freedom of citizens to walk the streets without fear of undue harassment, intimidation, or physical harm. We want order to be maintained where we work and live, but the meaning of "quality of life" depends on whose life and what activity we target. For Kelling and Wilson, quality-of-life policing should target the "dirty and messy people" who commit the offenses of public urination, public drinking, squeegee operations on city streets, panhandling, prostitution, and disorderly conduct. The New York City Police Department's Operation Clean Sweep adopted that purpose and included a quality-of-life hotline for citizens to call in their complaints. In fact, in 2001 less than 2 percent of the citizen calls were related to the Wilson-Kelling examples and over 80 percent of the calls, totaling 97,000, were related to noise.[101] Police will always have to balance maintaining justice for all and implementing the majority's legally enacted will. Once police and the public refuse to limit the phrase "quality of life" to just one or two forms of police activity, they will reinforce the proper use of the phrase, which represents a major goal of all police activity: improving each citizen's quality of life through reducing crime, undue disorder, and fear of crime.

Indeed, the apparently inevitable quest for a popular label to define policing approaches is self-defeating and quite harmful. Good and bad zero tolerance, problem-solving, aggressive order maintenance, and other strategies are not analyzed as such because each is identified as an overall policy. In fact, each takes many forms in different areas and cities, and analysis should focus on which forms of each are most effective in what kinds of situations and for what length of time, not which overall form is better than the other. One can have a fruitful zero-tolerance crackdown, even one of a long duration, if it is planned jointly with the community and targets a neighborhood's persistent problem.[102] But sweeping a park of homeless men for three nights in a row is not good problem solving. In Chicago's Alternative Policing Strategy, as described by Skogan and his associates:

[A] problem is defined as a group of related incidents or an ongoing situation that concerns a significant portion of those who live or work in a particular area. A problem is also persistent . . . and must potentially be solved using police and community resources . . . A problem need not be a criminal matter . . . [T]he police mandate would coordinate responses to a broad range of community concerns, including social disorder, municipal service problems, and code enforcement matters.[103]

If each label were to be independently and not competitively analyzed in different contexts, one police chief probably would use each form at different times, in different parts of a jurisdiction, and in different formats for various lengths of time. Even problem solving as an overall approach is too ambitious when a police department is depleted, inexperienced, or overtaxed temporarily by excessive 911 demands, or when a mayor, city manager, or police chief will not support it. The national evaluation of the community policing projects discovered enormous variation in community partnerships, problem solving, police crime prevention projects, departmental organizational change, and adaptation of the police culture to these changes.[104] The report concluded that change in the initial four years of the federal community policing program was too diverse and it was too early for any assessment of even potential long-term effects on the original goals of crime reduction, fear reduction, and improvement of quality of life.[105] Indeed, although COPS funding added 100,000 police officers directly, and indirectly by funding the technology and / or civilian hiring intended to free up existing sworn personnel for street duty, one cannot predict how much of the net gain in officers will remain five and ten years from now.

The degree of change sought in policing poses unprecedented issues in making a police officer accountable and reward-eligible for his or her performance. The traditional measures—arrest numbers, traffic citations given out, patrol officer accidents, citizen commendations or complaints, absenteeism, and compliance with rules—bear little relationship as a whole with the goals and policies of crime reduction, fear reduction, partnership with the community, problem solving, achievement of just results, and creation of an appearance of efficiency, effectiveness, and justice. But in general, the new high-tech collection and retention of data about any operation promotes visibility that, in turn, provides ample data for assessing police performance. Community policing and problem solving encourage police chiefs to make more permanent assignments of officers to one beat or one district and to hold the officers and their superiors accountable for results: lower crime, lower citizen fear of crime, greater citizen satisfaction with the police service, increased use of successful problem-solving, maintenance of ongoing relationships with various groups within the neighborhoods or the district, fewer citizen complaints and civil suits against police, and/or more citizen commendations for police performance.

The highly publicized COMPSTAT, or "compare stats," methodology, exemplifies how technology assists accountability for goal achievement. New York City's COMPSTAT is in theory a supervisory process and a comprehensive database offering continuous help to managers who cite specific problems in trying to implement the NYPD's self-defined four steps to crime reduction: accurate and timely intelligence, rapid deployment, effective tactics, and relentless follow-up and assessment.[106] COMPSTAT review processes also help top management identify talented young managers. But the COMPSTAT manual is quite clear about its two key components: empowering the precinct commander, and then holding that commander responsible for crime reduction in his or her area of command.[107] COMPSTAT is also very confrontational, using a technique familiar to every national and international corporation's sales personnel and managers: periodic gatherings of all commanders in a big room, huge data presentations on the wall showing results or lack of results, cheers and boos by peers and superiors, and an immediate demotion or warning for lack of results. The message to precinct commanders in New York is simple: We have delegated to you the authority to manage your area. Now, get those crime statistics down or else!

The COMPSTAT technique has spread in various forms to many areas of the nation, although most police chiefs in America probably will reject its confrontational aspects and single focus. But many have used its data-related ideas and processes as well as some concept of regular accountability sessions. Many police departments had their own data systems, analytic processes, and measures of accountability already in place.[108] One danger of COMPSTAT pressure, particularly with its focus on only one primary goal—crime reduction—is the temptation to tamper with the crime statistics, just as tampering by salesmen who were rewarded or punished solely through sales statistics has brought trouble to publicly owned business corporations. Although most departments have crime statistic audit procedures, crime figures are somewhat readily adjustable through procedural changes in how citizens must report a crime, police classifications of crime reports, and other forms of subtle manipulation. Under COMPSTAT, at least two commanders in New York City were demoted for elevated crime conditions in their areas even though an immediate predecessor to one of the displaced commanders had himself been demoted for manipulating crime statistics.[109]

The more fundamental danger of single-result accountability is that, once serious crime does decrease to levels that are difficult to lower, the accountability measure may switch over to number of arrests—which would definitely result in more aggressive policing, as well as an emphasis on "zero tolerance," which in turn might lead to severe police-citizen hostility in minority neighborhoods and other areas where low crime levels do not justify aggressive practices. Too little attention was paid initially in New

York City to community resentments aroused by widespread frisks of minority youth, pretext arrests to justify searches, and use of summary punishment induced by Friday evening arrests that would jail their subjects until the next arraignment opportunity on Monday morning. Methods of accountability that are heavily weighted toward reducing citizen fear and achieving citizen satisfaction with overall police performance avoid these pitfalls. If citizens have high levels of satisfaction and low levels of fear in a neighborhood, a punishment for police commanders with lower arrest levels in these situations would be self-defeating and absurd. Further, maintaining outdated accountability systems that fail to measure the efforts of police officers to achieve the goals of these new policing approaches will mean that only those officers who follow too narrow a set of goals will be promoted.

Abuse of Police Discretion

Police leaders' search for positive change must cope with a fundamental downside. Throughout America's history, African Americans have had a unique experience. Whites treated blacks violently in urban and rural settings for 350 years, first with deliveries from the slave trade and the maintenance of slavery until the 1860s, then with thousands of lynchings, then with white resistance to any proper form of rights and equality under the law—always using racial segregation and police, court, and other forms of governmental power until the law commenced reining in those practices under the Civil Rights Acts of 1964 and 1965.[110] As society should realize after that kind of tragic history, the ensuing thirty-five years of implementing laws to correct 350 years of white violence against blacks, and to change white law enforcement's inattention to black-on-black violence, does not rid black society of the consequences of these historical horrors. Nor does it create the overall foundation for nonviolent, stable family-building that may well be the essence of a peaceful society, peace both inside the house and outside on the street.

As a consequence, black-on-black violence has proceeded at a higher rate than that of other groups in America. Blacks in the year 2000 constituted 12.3 percent of our population but, where the offender's race was known, committed over 50 percent of the murder offenses. Where a victim's race was known, 48 percent of all murder victims were black, with 94 percent of black victims slain by black offenders.[111] Fifty-four percent of robbery arrests and 38 percent of all arrests for violent crime involved black suspects.[112] But some research studies have found that police arrest black suspects more than whites who are equally arrest-eligible.[113]

Using these and other statistics, most cops say they are merely going where the violent crimes, drug crimes, and weapons crimes are and arresting those who commit those offenses. Black victims and their fearful neighbors no doubt appreciate police focus on their crime situations, but too often this focus is carried out with tactics and intensity that cops do not bring to white crime. Inner-city policing too often lacks any true partnership with the community and proceeds with a random quality that portrays an arrogance and lack of informed selectivity, even perhaps an internal fear of the unknown on the part of the 81 percent of municipal police officers who are white. The result?—stop-and-frisk tactics that at least seven out of ten times produce nothing but humiliation and shame for the victim; racial profiling in auto stops and bus and train searches; racial stereotyping in auto and pedestrian stops; and the occasional killing of unarmed minority males.

For community-police partnerships to work, training and education have to reflect the fact that the police community observes primarily the underside of the larger citizen communities. Nobody calls the police to report a peaceful day in the family, a young man without a gun, or a voluntary street clean-up by a youth group. Police see the worst of human nature. And they mistake the fearful, helpless failure of a neighborhood to act against crime and disorder as neighborhood-wide complicity. As one police sergeant told us: "They don't care about their own communities. Why should we? And besides, when we help them, they hate us anyway." This perception can proceed from innate bigotry in some white police, frustration with high crime levels, or stereotyping by police of every race and color; but the despair and contempt reflected in these views by white, black, and Hispanic police officers demonstrate a problem that extends beyond issues of racial and ethnic bias. Let's look at two examples.

On June 16, 1999, Alton Fitzgerald White was preparing to leave his landmark building in Harlem to go to the bank. Fresh from a standing ovation the previous evening as the star of a hit Broadway show, *Ragtime,* White was accosted in his own lobby, forced to his knees and, with three other black men who were moving into the building, handcuffed by police officers. Someone in the building had just reported two unknown Hispanic men with a gun. Even though two Hispanic men were also arrested in the lobby by the same police officers, the four black men were kept in hand-cuffs, transported to the precinct station, strip-searched, and placed in a cell intermittently between sessions of questioning that revealed the cops' knowledge of White's stardom on Broadway. For Alton White, the five-hour ordeal produced humiliation, embarrassment, shock, and exhaustion, which destroyed his lifelong assumption that skill and hard work will be rewarded in our society with dignity and justice. The police ironically called it "standard procedure."[114] That standard procedure had its basis in a stereotype that four black men do not belong in a well-maintained fancy building, even in Harlem.

On February 4, 1999, Amadou Diallo, a twenty-two-year-old Jamaican man who was five-foot-six and 160 pounds, came home late in the evening with a day's earnings in his pocket from a street vendor job in downtown New York. Diallo carried no weapon and had no criminal record. A few minutes later, he lay dead. Four white plainclothes police officers, allegedly looking for a young, black male rapist or robber, ripped Diallo's body with nineteen bullets as he stood pulling out his keys in an alcove by the front door of his apartment house. Twenty-two other bullets from police guns missed their human target. The white cops had a stereotyped idea that any young, black male must be reaching for a weapon rather than for ID or apartment keys to show a confronting cop.

Alton White lived, Amadou Diallo died. What was their crime? Being black and at home in their own communities. The officers testified that Diallo failed to react correctly to their plainclothes commands (commands that may well not have been heard, believed, or understood by Diallo) and that, when a confronted and perhaps fearful young black man reaches in his pocket for the keys to his own apartment in his own vestibule in a high-crime neighborhood, a gun might be there and so, cops have the right under law to kill him. An Albany, New York criminal case judge and jury agreed, and so did New York City's police commissioner.[115] In other words, if police are looking for a young, black male suspect at night, all of the young, black males in the neighborhood, when coming home from an er-rand or from work or play, risk loss of life if they do not immediately hear, comprehend, and react precisely as police expect.

It should not be news to police officers that even in relatively high-crime neighborhoods many young black males get out of bed, go to work, pursue everyday lawful tasks, and arrive home from work. But White and Diallo only mirror an enormous race problem in the policing of America. Although blacks made up only 12 percent of the U.S. population in 2000, blacks in that year were the subjects of 37 percent of all weapons arrests, 22 percent of all vandalism arrests, 35 percent of all drug abuse arrests, 64 percent of all gambling arrests, 33 percent of all disorderly conduct arrests, 43 percent of all vagrancy arrests, and 39 percent of all prostitution arrests.[116] These are classic "aggressive order maintenance" arrest classifications and are clearly disproportionate to relative conduct by race. For example, reports of once-or-more and current use of any kind of cocaine by high school students in 1999 showed that almost 10 percent of whites used cocaine at some time during their lives with 4.1 percent at current use, while 2.2 percent of blacks used cocaine at some time with 1.1 percent showing current use.[117] In 1996, 19.67 million whites were in high school, but only 3.64 million blacks.[118] Applying the 1999 percentages of current use, 610,000 white high school students were currently using some form of cocaine compared to 25,410 black students, a 24 to 1 ratio. And yet blacks under eighteen years old represented 28 percent of total drug abuse arrests in that age group.[119] Although these statistics represent only a portion of the drug user population, the discrepancies in use and arrests cannot be explained by any proper crime response rationale.[120]

The stereotyping in inner-city policing has a counterpart in racial profiling on the highways of America. In the mid-1990s, researchers observed traffic along a portion of Interstate 95 in Maryland and recorded the driver's race and the car's speed. Of 5,741 observations, 16.9 percent of the cars had black drivers, 75.6 percent were white. Almost 95 percent of the autos exceeded the speed limits, 17.5 percent with black drivers and 74.7 percent with white drivers. During a twenty-month period in 1995–1996, Maryland state troopers stopped and searched 823 motorists on the same I-95 stretch, 72.9 percent of whom were black—almost a total racial flip-flop from the observed speeding violation rates. Seventy percent of the searches produced nothing. And this occurred *after* a court settlement of racial profiling charges by the Maryland State Police.

During the same time period, statewide auto searches conducted by state troopers outside the I-95 corridor showed 32 percent black drivers and 64 percent white. In comparing both I-95 and statewide results of such searches, a controlled dangerous substance (drug offense) was found in 29.9 percent of the stops on I-95 and in 27.1 percent of the statewide stops. The "contraband find" rates statewide were 28.4 percent for black motorists and 28.8 percent for white motorists, that is, equal drug offense rates for white and black, totally negating the I-95 "strategy" of focusing 75 percent of the stops on black drivers. The concept of grossly discriminatory racial profiling in drug cases, based on a flawed police theory that drug offenses are primarily a black crime even beyond the inner city, was thus established beyond a reasonable doubt as a practice and its theoretical basis for drug law enforcement refuted.[121]

Also in 1996, revealing yet again its apparent ignorance of police-public interaction on the streets of America, the U.S. Supreme Court affirmed car stops by plainclothes drug officers for feigned enforcement of traffic laws that department regulations forbade them from enforcing. The purpose of the stop was to follow an instinct that the car's driver was committing a crime. The Court's upholding of the feigning practices, along with a subsequent holding in 2001 that police may actually arrest, book, and jail a motorist for a traffic violation that carries only a fine, mean that patrol officers can justify an actual arrest and search of virtually any car and its passengers by alleging any kind of motor vehicle violation, no matter how trivial.[122] Police officers may now lawfully stop and search cars, drivers, and passengers on a hunch about other criminal activity that falls far short of reasonable suspicion or probable cause, without having to admit to using race-based factors alone.

What actually happens on the street? In Volusia County, Florida, a newspaper obtained 148 hours of county sheriff tapes of traffic stops on I-95. The sheriff, presaging the Supreme Court's ignorance of actual practices on the street, said the stops were for traffic enforcement. The reality? Although blacks and Hispanics were about 5 percent of the drivers on the county's portion of I-95, they were 70 percent of all drivers stopped and 80 percent of all cars searched. Stopping the minority drivers also induced police searches that on average took twice as long as searches of white people and their cars. Only nine of the 1,100 drivers who were stopped received traffic tickets.[123] In 1995, Eagle County, Colorado officials settled a lawsuit by paying $800,000 to a class of plaintiffs whom a court had found to be victims of the Sheriff Department's unconstitutional racial profiling. Using traffic stops as a pretext for random drug searches, the officers had actually issued no traffic tickets during the time period in question.[124] The Supreme Court tells governments now that they need not settle such class actions.

The racial profiling practice also includes police drug "sweeps" of bus stations, bus passengers, and trains.[125] And New Jersey agreed to federal monitoring in a court settlement of a pattern of racial profiling by state police on the New Jersey turnpike, a practice that included a shooting by police of three unarmed black men.[126]

A study by the attorney general of New York State, conducted under rigidly constructed methodology and analysis with the aid of independent national experts, examined 175,000 stop-and-frisk forms filled out by New York City police officers. In gross terms, whites made up 43.4 percent of the city's population and 12.9 percent of the stops. Blacks composed about one-quarter of the population and 50.6 percent of all stops.[127] Even after adjusting the race-specific and crime-specific arrest rates by precinct demographics, police stopped blacks 2.1 times more often than whites on suspicion of violent crime and 2.4 times more often than whites on suspicion of carrying a weapon. These two categories made up 53 percent of all stops. Police stopped Hispanics two times more often than whites on suspected weapons violations.[128] And this analysis measured only the stops actually recorded on forms by the police. Unrecorded stops probably involved an even greater proportion of minority subjects.

And what about our overall goal that the crime response complex create a public perception of equal justice administration? In the fall of 1999, a Gallup poll demonstrated that 56 percent of whites and 77 percent of blacks believed police to be guilty of "widespread" racial profiling.[129] And the U.S. Justice Department was exercising its power under a 1994 federal statute to investigate and seek to enjoin by court mandate or by consent order local police actions that demonstrate "a pattern or practice of conduct by law enforcement officers" in violation of citizens' constitutional rights.[130] In Pittsburgh, city officials signed such an order, including eighteen pages of directives about how the police department shall conduct itself in citizen contacts, arrests, and searches, and a directive mandating oversight by an independent auditor for a minimum of two years. As of May 2001, the Justice Department was investigating twelve cities for alleged unconstitutional patterns and practices of police conduct, including New York City and Washington, D.C.[131]

In 1991, the Christopher Commission's investigation of police brutality in Los Angeles produced sweeping recommendations for change. Commission members believed that the most important factor in forecasting how fully the recommendations would be implemented was the attitude and the actions of police leadership and city leadership.[132] Just eight years later in Los Angeles, an LAPD officer alleged police beatings of minority gang members, the manufacture of false evidence and crimes, the use of the arrest power to achieve deportation of "undesirables," awards to officers who wounded or killed gang suspects, and other abuses in the so-called CRASH unit in the Ramparts area of Los Angeles. CRASH was an acronym for Community Resources against Street Hoodlums, and the Ramparts area was one of the largest of the LAPD operational commands, with more than four hundred officers working a density of 36,000 people in each of the area's 7.9 square miles. Ramparts had high crime rates (particularly violent crime), high gang concentration, and high narcotics activity. Significant portions of its population were undocumented aliens from Central America, many of whom spoke only Spanish and carried a distrust of law enforcement from their experiences with military dictatorships in their home nations.[133] After investigation of a few of the allegations against the Ramparts CRASH officers, the internal LAPD Board of Inquiry produced a lengthy document full of conclusions about pervasive police mediocrity, lack of leadership, an out-of-control Ramparts CRASH culture, lack of proper supervision, and no actual controls on police discretion.[134]

This internal report did address enormous gaps in police leadership and significant problems engendered by an arrogant, closed police culture—two of the areas in which we believe the police have made the least progress in the past thirty years and in which significant improvements are necessary if any permanent change in police practices is to result. But in both its analysis and recommendations, a glaring and puzzling void exists in the Board of Inquiry report. No narrative explores the apparent total gap of understanding and appreciation by the LAPD police of the history, culture, and goals of Ramparts's ethnic minorities, other than a reference to distrust of police. And none of the recommendations suggests educating police to distinguish between the law-abiding Central American community, including the law-abiding youth, and the violent gang members. Once again, we read of the need for better training, better supervision, better personnel practices, better controls, better audits—all of these words have been written over and over again for the past thirty years. Even though the report acknowledged that "this scandal has devastated our relationship with the public we serve and threatened the integrity of our criminal justice system," the recommendations and analysis never dealt with the fundamental issue of understanding and involving the larger community in defining and implementing a neighborhood's policing.[135]

The Ramparts investigation's internal report did suggest changing the CRASH name to something less inflammatory. Instead of investigating the very concept of special police units invading a neighborhood on a permanent basis—as opposed to incorporating all anticrime activity and personnel under the regular precinct or district command, perhaps at times with a larger but temporary police presence, the LAPD opted for a change of name and a retention of the special unit concept. Not surprisingly, two days after the report's release, the Los Angeles police chief abolished all CRASH units and announced they would be replaced in a month with "special enforcement units" carrying another name and tighter supervision.[136]

Even when police wish to form a true partnership with the communities they patrol, the neighborhoods must then create some formal and informal practices to decide what they want from their police. David Cole notes with insight that liberal residents of comfortably safe streets can express indignation about police abuse of constitutional rights because, for those residents, safety is not a problem; and financially secure conservatives living safely beyond high-crime areas can self-righteously proclaim their defenses of police action because their rights are not infringed by police invasions.[137] Aggressive and intensive police action that will inevitably to some degree affect innocent lives in a high-crime neighborhood, particularly the lives of young, minority males, probably helps reduce high levels of crime and fear there, at least temporarily. Police should listen and respond to the formal and informal neighborhood voices about when to start *and* when to stop such activity, including neighborhood advocacy about which parts of police activity could and should be changed, and why, and what other approaches could be taken to combat various crime and disorder problems in the neighborhood.

In New York City, despite all the aggressive order maintenance and the trumpeting of COMPSTAT, there were 6 percent more murders in 1999 than in 1998; but reported serious crimes other than murder did not rise.[138] Some police chiefs worry about the integrity of their crime reporting statistics when the hardest-to-hide crime, that is, murder, rises but other violent crimes decline. Some chiefs would also begin to think that perhaps they need more help from the community and from other organizations, both government and private. Others would merely intensify the aggressive tactics. One thing is certain, however: most police leaders now taking credit for lower crime rates are not going to accept blame for any rise in crime, even though their COMPSTAT-like systems tell the precinct commanders that their jobs and status depend upon crime reduction in the areas under their command.

With so many government agencies operating in each city, with mayors and city managers often interacting with police, and with the police interacting every day with all those who implement criminal case processing, the police obviously do not act alone. The Los Angeles Police Board of Inquiry report includes one isolated conclusion that states unobtrusively what should be shouted from the rooftop:

> [T]he entire criminal justice system has [the responsibility] to ensure that each of its component parts is operating properly. Every one of these cases [of improper police actions] went through that entire system virtually unchallenged by anyone . . . [T]he criminal justice system itself must take a serious, introspective look at itself.[139]

This paragraph represents a rare public call by the police to confront the hypocrisy of both the justice system and the political environment in which police operate. Here the board report is saying to the local prosecutors: cops know when you are subtly coaching them during interviews and trial testimony; cops know that prosecutors understand when cops are figuratively winking at them; cops know that prosecutors did not contest the illegal deportation strategy in the Ramparts area for those gang members whom police could not catch committing crimes, and prosecutors know very well that the police narcotics case testimony has a familiar, repetitive ring about how all those defendants just dropped all those drugs right at their feet. And why is the judiciary silent, asks the report, as they hear and nod affirmatively during incredible, repetitive testimony from the prosecution side in narcotics cases? And why were elected political leaders unresponsive when some in the neighborhood complained about Ramparts practices?

Cops know that they do not act alone; they need a system that supports them. And cops also know that when their indefensible practices finally surface in the media or in an investigative report, the rest of the system's formerly cooperative participants are far away professing shock at those offensive and indefensible police actions. Police know who the corrupt politicians are, and which city officials, criminal justice officials, and self-appointed indignant reformers are drug abusers, spouse abusers, regular prostitute customers, or regular recipients of tainted money. Cops know who among the "pillars of the community" are corrupt or debased, and which well-connected citizens, and their relatives and friends, are getting "passes" from criminal justice treatment. The hypocrisy, corruption, and complicity that police officers quietly view in the world of power around them make it very difficult to change the insular police culture. Nor does this outside world present to cops any apparent practical reason for changing any corrupt police practices that may exist.

In 1972 the Knapp Commission investigating corruption in the New York City Police Department was remarkably prescient about the depth of resistance to making the fundamental changes necessary to truly reform the police. At the conclusion of its investigation and hearings, the commission stated: "Police corruption was found to be an extensive, Department-wide phenomenon, indulged in to some degree by a sizable majority of those on the force and protected by a code of silence on the part of those who remained honest."[140]

In summarizing its recommendations and expectations for change, the commission then asked the right question:

> The present situation is quite like that existing at the close of previous investigations. A considerable momentum for reform has been generated, but . . . [a]fter previous investigations, the momentum was allowed to evaporate. The question now is: Will history repeat itself? Or does society finally realize that police corruption is a problem that must be dealt with and not just talked about once every twenty years?[141]

Twenty-two years later, in 1994, history repeated itself. The Mollen Commission investigating police corruption in New York City found: "Today's (police) corruption is far more criminal, violent and premeditated than traditional notions of police corruption suggest and far more invidious than corruption of a generation ago."[142]

The Mollen Commission cited its analysis of the persistent basic problems: the police culture, willfully blind police leadership, the demise of the principle of police accountability to various constituencies, and a hostility and alienation between the police and community in certain precincts of New York City.[143] These are lessons that can be carried over at least in part to racial stereotyping and racial profiling, as well as to all basic police reform.

At present, society and its politicians tell the police to control crime. But as we continue to demand too much peace and order from the police alone, we too often get the public oratory of community policing and the hidden street enforcement of aggressive arrogance, "beat-and-release," lead-lined police gloves, POPOs (pissed-off police officers), "kick-ass," patrol officers who regard policing as a contact sport, and even good cops who carry a "put-down" knife or gun to plant beside a citizen who was hurt when the cop made an honest mistake that he or she knows the larger world, both inside and outside the police department, will never countenance as such. We also hear the police force's self-defined need to patrol after sunset with the uncompromising proclamation: "We own the night."

The gaps in police accountability must be filled. In giving police the responsibility for reducing crime and improving our quality of life, we citizens have introduced the kinds of pressures that mandate more regulation of police discretion in how they employ their authority—through arrest, use of force, education, warnings, commands, searches, and "informal" actions. During Douglas County, Nevada's 2001 New Year's Eve celebration, the police made only fifty arrests among the rowdy 60,000 revelers. Said one sergeant: "There's the letter of the law and there's the spirit of the law. On New Year's Eve, we go by the spirit of the law."[144] In fact, cops routinely choose actions ranging from enforcing the letter of the law to fulfilling the spirit of the law. And they need administrative regulation to help guide their choices.

The need and possible reform path presented in Frank Remington's and Herman Goldstein's writings for the Johnson Crime Commission in 1967 bear a striking resemblance to those belatedly promoted by George Kelling in 1999 to regulate the discretion exercised in aggressive "broken windows" policing of abandoned cars, "messy people," prostitution, noise, graffiti, public drinking, and disorderly conduct.[145] Kelling's 1999 effort reprinted as good examples the New Haven, Connecticut Training Bulletin for the exercise of order maintenance powers and the San Diego, California Policy Statement guiding police action when encountering undocumented persons.[146] In the past three decades, various local police regulations have been constructed to address issues such as use of force, auto pursuits, use of nonlethal weapons, roadblocks, and stopping and frisking residents. But many regulations need regular updating. For example, we have learned over time that every nonlethal weapon has its potential shortcomings as well as its lifesaving potential. Cops have seen that choke holds can kill and that pepper spray and beanbags filled with lead can produce serious citizen injury, often to innocent bystanders. Rubber bullets, stun guns, wooden bullets, and stingball grenades add to police options and also to the need for close regulation.

The enormous difficulties in regulating aggressive and proactive policing are illustrated by Chicago's creation and enforcement of loitering ordinances to deal with the street presence of youth gangs and narcotics trafficking. The city's intense efforts in the early 1990s led to over 40,000 loitering arrests.[147] But the U.S. Supreme Court declared the ordinances and the police department's administrative regulations unconstitutional.[148] In so doing, one "conservative" Justice, joined by a more "liberal" Justice, issued a concurring opinion to suggest narrowing the coverage of the law. In early 2000, Chicago's City Council then built the Justices' exact language into two new gang-loitering and narcotics-loitering laws.[149] The Chicago Police Department issued detailed regulations further guiding when use of the new loitering laws' group dispersal and citation provisions was appropriate.[150] This litigation and reissue process for antigang and antidrug enforcement took over five years and the redrafted ordinances and regulations no doubt will face renewed challenge.

Problem solving by police faces the same issues. In San Francisco, an innovative police officer, disgusted with the frequent rearrest and release of public drunks, took photographs of them, posted the photos with local store merchants, and issued orders that those so depicted not be served or sold liquor. The practice was challenged in court as unconstitutional and the city settled with the depicted persons for a payment of about $900 to each.[151] The do-not-serve police practice was stopped in both San Francisco and some nearby towns, and the revolving arrests presumably resumed with the problem unsolved. The police in Green Bay, Wisconsin adopted a do-not-serve policy, but limited their exercise of enforcement discretion to alcohol consumers who, within a three-month period, had both three arrests for intoxication plus sufficient public intoxication on three occasions that required transport to a detoxification center, plus conduct that generated a citizen complaint in the geographic area covered by the policy. At the time of this writing, this more confined police policy had not been tested in court.[152]

These good-faith efforts to control the exercise of discretionary power while endeavoring to solve a persistent problem proceed quite slowly and then sometimes abruptly cease when new commanders surface or political opposition emerges. The process should offer a way for communities to help create the regulations and guide the police action that follows on the street.

Federal Policing

In the United States, public law enforcement at the state and local levels has always been decentralized, and the only potential for a national, centralized police power affecting all of us emanates from the various federal law enforcement agencies. But within the federal system, the lack of interagency cooperation and information sharing between law enforcement agencies and departments significantly lessens what could be either a very effective force against certain criminal activity or a very destructive public power source that affects most of us through surveillance and a national, centralized intelligence system.[153]

Until September 11, 2001, when terrorism perhaps temporarily became an overwhelming priority, the broader effects of federal policing were visible in two areas: drugs and firearms. (These efforts are examined in separate chapters.)[154] But the increasing and extensive reach of the crime response complex through policing in our federal, state, local, and private sectors includes a dramatic rise in federal criminal law and its enforcement. The U.S. Congress enacted about 59 percent of all existing federal criminal statutes in the first 180 years of our history and about 41 percent of all such laws in the past thirty years.[155] No one even knows how many such statutes exist, although the more recent estimates range from 3,000 to 3,300 separate federal criminal laws plus some additional prohibitions every year.[156]

This statutory expansion has led to the development of an unprecedented federal policing apparatus. One hundred forty-eight separate agencies have federal law enforcement functions. Just thirteen of the largest such agencies (excluding the Bureau of Prisons) employed about 60,000 sworn personnel authorized to carry firearms and commanded a combined fiscal 1998 budget exceeding $6.7 billion for law enforcement functions.[157] Indeed, in 1992 one of every thirty federal employees was a criminal investigator; by 1999, one of every twenty federal employees was so employed.[158] But all of this effort and all of these dollars, only a portion of which are highly focused on national priorities, still produce less than 5 percent of all prosecutions in the United States.[159]

The federal expansion in criminal enforcement poses puzzling and sometimes disturbing questions that few in public life bother to ask or to answer. For example, the decade-long series of problems in the Federal Bureau of Investigation—failure to produce court-ordered documents; FBI agents spying for other nations; obsolete computer systems; faulty lab performance; lack of information-sharing with other enforcement agencies; woefully deficient internal investigations; faulty espionage investigations; court-ordered mandates dealing with discrimination in hiring and promotion of blacks, women, and Hispanics—failed to gain proper public attention until long after the harm was done.[160] Police power in a democratic society can best be observed by the populace and controlled by civilian authority when that power resides as close as possible to the people from whom it is derived. Law enforcement against crime in the streets has always been viewed as a local matter where local people set the priorities and establish the boundaries of enforcement. Modern technology, world commerce, individual mobility, and federal regulations certainly raise a need for federal enforcement against violent terrorist activity, cybercrime, commercial and financial fraud, and some aspects of interstate drug traffic and gun flow. But with the expansion of the federal system into crimes that have almost identical form at the state and local levels, federal prosecutors and investigators can now choose to act directly against 3,300 different forms of criminal conduct. With more than ninety separate federal prosecution offices in America exercising this vast range of statutory options, unexplained, unrationalized, and disparate justice can easily result. Little comparative benefit to crime control results from the increasing state-federal overlap, and the federal options often impose greater criminal penalties than their state and local counterparts for essentially similar conduct.[161] In practice, between 1947 and 1997, the percentage of all federal criminal cases filed under federal statutes having no state or local counterpart has dropped from twenty-six to five. And the number of federal drug defendants in terminated cases more than tripled between 1982 and 1999.[162] For those who want to rationalize the build-up in federal investigative and prosecution capacity, along with the enormous prison expansion, as a necessary step in the war on drugs, the argument stumbles on the fact that the federal monolith prosecuted only about 1.5 percent of the nation's approximately 1.5 million drug arrests in the mid-1990s.[163]

As a result, two prestigious and ideologically balanced groups, one created by the American Bar Association and the other created by the U.S. Congress, have recently arrived at identical conclusions: the expansion of federal law enforcement scope and power is largely wasteful and ineffective against violent crime, and it threatens both the appropriate federal-state-local balance and the public's confidence in our justice system.[164] One of these groups, chaired by a former director of both the FBI and CIA, recommended a law mandating that every federal criminal statute must justify any federal-state overlap and must contain a sunset provision whereby each criminal law expires after five years absent Congressional reenactment.[165] The report also notes that effective and focused law enforcement against national and transnational crime, such as terrorism and cyber-crime, "may be compromised" by mass federal creation of crimes dupli-cated and enforced at the state and local levels.[166] The tragedy and propin-quity of terrorist acts may now prove to be the unwelcome catalyst for longer-lasting change in the focus of federal enforcement efforts and for more intense outside scrutiny of federal agency performance.

The best use of federal agencies for combating crimes that now overlap federal and state law is to have them give support where needed to state and local policing. For example, as illustrated in other chapters, the federal Alcohol, Tobacco, and Firearms agency serves an important role in the tracing of firearms recovered at local crime scenes; and federal prosecutors support local efforts in gun and drug enforcement by imprisoning those offenders who create and operate interstate and international enterprises.

The Melding of Private and Public Crime Response

Most Americans do not directly encounter a police officer in their daily lives. But almost all Americans interact every day in varying combinations with private security efforts in stores, malls, banks, schools, office build-ings, computers, and our own automobiles. Many of these private ef-forts are beneficial. For example, almost all elderly persons benefited when banks agreed to accept direct deposit of social security and other kinds of payments, thereby ending the hazards of check theft and of sometimes slow and therefore vulnerable walking trips to and from the bank while carrying one's entire monthly compensation. But the implications of the often subtle and concealed private security efforts as they affect the private and public exercise of power in our society are just beginning to be dis-cernible. And even the theoretical debate spawned by the combined pub-lic-private nature of law enforcement and crime prevention only compares controls and potential dangers of each, rather than the combined totality of their power, benefits, and dangers.[167] Indeed, David Bayley and Clifford Shearing suggest that a fundamental restructuring of the policing function is already under way in a direction that makes the historic separation of private security and public police obsolete.[168]

Design and use of research to learn the single best universal approach to controlling crime may be impossible and is undesirable in both the private and public security worlds. In public police operations around the nation, the personnel, police culture, ethnic and age mix of the area's population, pedestrian volume, crime mix, number of citizens per square mile, use of space, economic development, local police traditions, forms of local government, relationships between the police department and the elected officials, levels of education, drug use, ideological contrasts, police union strength, rigidity of police organization and diverse leadership qualities of police chiefs—just to name a few factors—all exist in various and ever-changing forms and mixes within and among regions and urban areas. And with private security efforts, an owner of a twenty-four-hour convenience store does not want to know about all thieves, or about thieves who steal from cars, or even about thieves who generally prey upon convenience stores. That storeowner wants to know how to reduce theft at each hour of the day and night in his particular store in its particular neighborhood.

Even though research findings will not inform them sufficiently to make rigid choices, if crime is a real problem affecting profits, business owners might install better lighting, TV monitoring, a new alarm system, or a new cash management system; rearrange the store; and hire an extra clerk all at once perhaps without regard to whether one or two of them alone might have reduced robberies, shoplifting, and employee theft the same amount. And usually a comparison to a control property where no changes are made in roughly equivalent premises is unavailable. An owner probably will not plan a security response jointly with competitors or even with neighbors. Nor will business operators hire a researcher to measure all aspects of the new security strategy. Each owner just wants his or her own crime situation to improve quickly through situational crime prevention. Business associations can help, but their agendas are lengthy and have a wide scope.

The site-specific focus of the private world and the vast differences in police departments and the environments in which they must function suggest that both research and operational experiments should abandon attempts to find the "magic bullet" against crime and focus instead on site-specific, problem-specific analyses and solutions. If such were the focus, analysts would quickly see that any analytical effort and program implementation for better crime control efforts must join the private and public security worlds. New programs might choose private over public remedies, or vice versa, for specific sites or areas or ascertain how they must work together to achieve the best results in the most cost-effective and just manner. Local governments could survey public-access businesses and facilities and then publicly rate their safety for potential customers. Or these governments could mandate specific crime prevention measures and / or devices for certain kinds of businesses and assign levels of penalties for violations, including lower police priority for nonpersonal security calls from noncompliant businesses. If the public and private world locally focused attention on the 10 percent of places that produce 60 percent of the crime calls to police, public-private cooperation in devising and carrying out prevention and enforcement would certainly improve. Mayors and city managers, for example, could direct specific agencies to work with businesses, neighborhoods, and the police to solve the particular crime concern at a problematic street corner, bar, youth gathering place, or neighborhood. A national pooling of information could then share local analyses and results for others to either reject or adapt to their particular situations.

Despite a decade-long decline in crime rates, both the public and private sectors have been separately expanding their personnel, technology, and expenditures devoted to crime response. The rationale for this increase, along with the total effect upon citizen security and privacy, have not yet been examined, but they should be. Private security efforts on balance certainly help to reduce the kind of citizen fear of crime that can, more than any other existing factor in society, destroy our freedom of movement and thus also deter the presence of local retail business establishments serving neighborhood customers. When an open or closed space feels safer, and is in fact safe, more people will use it and probably thereby make it even safer.

The most destructive aspect of the private efforts, in conjunction with the public efforts, may well be our loss of privacy and our increasing tendency not to appreciate how such a loss can dramatically increase the potential of our losing other freedoms and expectations. The most dangerous example of this may well be the use of a crime or security justification for massive privacy invasions and control techniques that have more to do with public regulation or private marketing efforts. One can see that examination of only the "criminal justice system" can be quite misleading and that one must view private and public efforts together as the totality of our crime response complex—its financial costs, its positive influences, and its existing and potential dangers. Today, one should not assume that privacy accompanies the home computer and its transactions. In the office, with security cameras and computer tracing that can relay to the boss every confidence you have typed into your computer—even those you have deleted—the nature of work is changing in ways we cannot yet understand. In addition, schools are educating each child over a twelve-year, crucially formative period with the sense that privacy does not exist in a school bag, coat, locker, notebook, or in what one says to one's friends—and with the premise that each student should be wary of all other students. Zero tolerance has invaded our workplaces, our schools, and portions of public policing. It in turn breeds the urge and demand for immediate results in discovering the lawbreaker or other kind of "offender," and then punishing him or her often without regard to actual harm or intent. This trend has larger, unexplored implications for all human and social interaction.

But as Eck and Maguire note, very little theory development or fact research is examining the relationships among various institutions' direct and indirect responses to crime.[169] This gap is surprising given the era of the 1990s when astute observers could easily discern that America's recent high degree of crime reduction was almost universal and was occurring in cities with very different police cultures, strategies, policies, and tactics.[170] When truly divergent police tactics and approaches produce similar results in truly divergent urban settings, one would think that researchers would try to ascertain how crime incident changes relate to police tactics *and* their interactions with private and public crime prevention activities. A recent research approach endeavors to measure how police activity may affect the social norms of a particular community, such as a violent juvenile gang or a drug-consuming neighborhood; but even this approach deals only with the effects of public enforcement-related activities without including and measuring other direct public and private crime prevention actions and social reactions, which could well have more significance for these social norms.[171]

Much of the debate about police performance and effectiveness ignores the basic issue of deciding the proper role of the police. Melding the actions of public police and private security constitutes only a partial reform. Research must also explore how police can and do relate to their mayors and city managers, to their city councils and county boards of supervisors, to various city agencies, to those who claim to represent a neighborhood, and to other kinds of "communities" bound together by some kind of common thread, be it ethnic, business, social, or political. Police act because they have to answer 911 calls and meet demands caused by crime, fear, chaos, and clashing "communities." Police also act many times be-cause other parts of government, business, and leaders in the private world flee from their responsibilities of both defining the crime and security problem and then accepting their role in creating and carrying out solutions. Why should police be responsible for a citizen's quality of life beyond addressing directly the factors of safety, equal justice, and lack of fear? With police officers' power to adversely affect each of our lives on every street in America, and the harm to which society exposes its police officers, isn't it dangerous to tell them they are in charge of maintaining the quality of life of residents in high-crime areas? Abandoned buildings, abandoned automobiles, homeless human beings, drug addicts, alcohol addicts, the mentally ill, unattended juveniles—these subjects are all discussed in the police literature about aggressive order maintenance, community partnerships, and problem-oriented policing. The larger political world and its various executive departments responsible for the health and welfare of the citizenry ignore or at least deflect responsibilities when these problems are visible in the streets.

But the answer is not for police to goad the public and private world into devising more permanent solutions.[172] Instead, for example, the Boston Ceasefire Working Group showed how juvenile gang violence could be reduced when city, state, and private agencies, as well as neighborhood organizations, work in conjunction with police actions.[173] And the government in Charlotte, North Carolina is demonstrating how parking lot owners can approach vandalism and thievery on their premises through municipal regulations mandating private security measures.[174] Mandatory security requirements at other locations, such as construction sites, could also reduce theft there. The private and public organizations among us must lead without waiting for the initiative of an imaginative police officer.

The federal program evaluation noted that community policing has assumed enormous variations around the nation and that true community partnerships involving shared power and decisionmaking between police and community are rare. Further, the concept of problem-solving has wide variations and too often takes on a short-term pure enforcement orientation that fails to invite broad-based community support.[175] Once the federal funding for additional police officers under the COPS program expires or is significantly reduced, and state and local budgets are unable to pick up the slack, the future of police-neighborhood partnerships and problem-solving goals becomes even more in doubt.

Even for those police departments open to change, the growing knowledge base has not yet provided clear guidance on future paths. Research has focused police on addressing concerns in key areas of activity and organization, but in so doing has intensified police debates rather than created a consensus. Different police departments make different choices about centralized versus decentralized organization; use of special street units; the proper degree, timing, forms, and location of aggressive policing; the role of the community; and the ability and rationale for asking police to solve problems rather than just solve crimes. And even for the task of solving crime incidents, as well as the more recent problem-solving efforts to reduce crime, the police are making vastly insufficient progress in areas that unfortunately are difficult to measure and yet crucial if basic change is to occur: (1) creation of a new police culture that will nurture and value a true partnership with the community; (2) building a police leadership that embraces the ideas of decentralization, problem-solving, community partnerships, full accountability, and a sharing of crime responsibilities with the larger private and public world; and (3) taking action with a devotion to equal justice under the law, a devotion that may proceed only when police officers develop a fundamental understanding and appreciation of the history, culture, and goals of each segment of the increasingly ethnically diverse mix of people in America. If these changes took place, the police job would be more challenging, more satisfying, more conjoined with the community, less corrupt, less brutal, and more effective. The details of change would flow naturally.

Some progress has been made toward these long-term goals. In particular, police are now using technology to serve analytical, accountability, field support, and leadership purposes. In addition to aiding accountability measures, technology has led to enormous advances in the creation, flow, and analysis of data and the collection and analysis of tangible evidence. Automated fingerprint identification systems, computer-assisted dispatch, collection and analysis of DNA, computerized and layered crime-mapping tools for many purposes (including problem-solving strategies and "hot-spot" tactics),[176] computerized face-identification programs, computer simulations of street encounters for police training, and patrol officers' instant access to stored data through car-mounted digital computers and terminals already exist and have been improving rapidly.[177] And the widespread COPS grants have helped to spread mobile computer and other technology further.[178] One can foresee the day when every murder, rape, sexual assault, and even burglary crime scene will be examined in order to collect evidence for DNA analysis, with permanent preservation of that evidence for identification of suspects.

For many reasons, reforms appear to have been adopted more quickly in some areas and in some cities. But the willingness of police to be accountable for levels of criminal activity could quickly change once crime inevitably begins to rise. The police world could well be the leading dynamic force in the future of crime response in America. But the police need much more help than they are receiving from the political world around them. We are currently asking the police to welcome research that asks them to redefine their role, develop new relationships with the community, and free officers from traditional duties so that they can identify and solve persistent crime problems, as well as evaluate solutions. The elected political leaders must take the lead in devising, allocating, and linking with the police other government agencies, the business community, and private organizations that can assist in preventing and controlling crime. No longer should anyone glibly delegate the crime problem solely to the public police. That strategy is unfair to every police officer, limits the effectiveness of society's crime response complex, and carries societal risks.

6

Guns, Crime, and Crime Gun Regulation

On March 19, 1998, an eleven-year-old student and his thirteen-year-old companion hauled ten guns to a wooded area adjacent to the Jonesboro, Arkansas, middle school. That same morning, they killed five human beings and wounded ten others. This tragedy and other highly publicized multiple shootings since the early 1990s have fueled the outrage among those advocating strict gun control. They contend that one basic problem leads directly to much of the human loss caused by violent crime: the presence of an estimated 200 to 240 million guns in America. Maybe we cannot know the causes of crime, the argument goes, or solve the broader individual, social, family, and mental conditions that are related in some way to crime, but surely we can take away the guns and thereby reduce the loss of life resulting from violent encounters.

But others argue, with some irony, that the sheer proliferation of guns proves that they are not the problem. Why try to ban 200–240 million guns, they argue, if only a small percentage is actually used in crime, particularly when most guns are bought and held for lawful citizen protection or for sporting purposes? Why not just enforce the law against the comparatively few gun owners who misuse them for criminal purposes? Both sides of the issue justify their positions with selective use of available facts. And unfortunately, the full facts about gun crime and gun ownership often become lost in the emotions and enflaming rhetoric of the ongoing public debate.

The single-interest ideology of each contrasting view has produced a barrage of public relations and lobbying efforts. Pro-gun advocates seek to convince us that gun control represents the government's path to tyranny through an ultimate, unconstitutional denial of firearms to all. On that path, it is said, lies the criminals' dreams of a disarmed citizenry, helpless to protect themselves. The antigun organizations promote the ultimate answer to violent crime as government control of firearms through bans on gun ownership, controls over gun access, and significant deprivation of gun availability and use. Unfortunately, as with all single-interest politics, the partisan advocates do not provide full truths. If one were to ask an American on the street "How many of our nation's 280 million people were murdered with firearms last year?" or "How many firearms accidents resulted in loss of life last year?" one suspects that the offered responses would be wildly divergent and probably dramatically inaccurate. So let us proceed with the basic facts, such as they appear to be known, and try to bury the emotions, the rhetoric, the politicization, the regional biases and, one can hope, the subliminal prejudices one way or another. In this discussion, the words "guns" and "firearms" are used interchangeably as a generic reference to pistols, revolvers, rifles, and shotguns. "Handgun" refers to pistols and revolvers as a group. "Semiautomatic" refers to an autoloading weapon that will fire just one shot for each pull of the trigger.

Guns and Crime

In 2000, residents reported to the police and the police, in turn, reported to the Federal Bureau of Investigation, 1,424,000 violent crimes—or about five such crimes for each one thousand residents in the United States. These violent crimes were robbery (29 percent) and aggravated assault (64 percent) with rape adding 6 percent and willful killings 1 percent. About one-quarter of these reported crimes involved firearm use by the perpetrators.[1] Accordingly, less than 0.15 percent of all residents faced a firearm during a violent crime in 2000, with urban areas, particularly low-income, minority neighborhoods, having a far greater risk for violent victimization by firearms than suburban or rural locations or areas with primarily white urban residents.

For the murders in 2000 for which supplemental data are available (more than 80 percent of the 15,517 total), about 65 percent involved firearms, including 52 percent with handguns. The victim and offender knew each other in 44 percent of the deaths, with the victim-offender relationship unknown in 43 percent of these felonious homicides.[2] About 41 percent of the robberies and 18 percent of the aggravated assaults reported to the police involved offenders with firearms.[3] In sum, roughly 341,000 of

280 million U.S. residents faced a firearm during a reported violent crime in 2000.

Although the national survey of victims showed about 6.6 million violent victimizations in 2000, four million of these incidents were "simple assaults," which by definition excludes use of any firearm. Of the remaining incidents, 23 percent of the aggravated assaults and 26 percent of the robberies involved firearms.[4] If one adds to these firearms crimes the total firearms-related killings estimated by the FBI for 2000, about 500,000 U.S. residents faced firearms during violent crimes that year, or less than 0.2 percent of the estimated U.S. population. Put another way, even if one places full faith in the reliability of victim survey sampling, as opposed to the data from crime reported to the police, a resident of America in 2000 had more than a 99.8 percent assurance of not facing a violent crime committed with a firearm, with an even higher assurance for rural, suburban, and white urban residents. Looked at from a longer perspective measured by a recent national survey, nine of every one hundred Americans reported that they had been shot at (including sports hunting incidents), and another 14 percent report having been threatened with a gun, at some time during their lives.[5]

How has violent crime changed since the 1960s in terms of the percent of crimes involving firearms? Firearms were the weapons used for 55 percent of all murders in 1964. But since then, that figure has ranged from 58–59 percent in the mid-1980s up to 70 percent of all murders in 1993.[6] The FBI reports that firearms-related robbery since 1974 peaked at 45 percent of all robberies in 1974–1975, bottomed at 33 percent in the late 1980s, and sustained itself at 40–42 percent during all but two years of the 1990s.[7] For both robbery and murder, then, the lowest percentages of firearms use during the past quarter century occurred in the 1980s but persisted at comparatively higher ranges for most of the 1990s. For aggravated assault since 1974, the firearms-use portion peaked at the 24–25 percent range in the mid-1970s and the early 1990s, but declined to the 19 percent level in 1998. Thus, in 1998, four of every five reported aggravated assaults did not involve a firearm.[8]

In trying to explain fluctuations in these firearms-usage percentages over time, one has to examine what is occurring among different age groups of offenders. For example, Alfred Blumstein's extensive analyses demonstrate that, within age groups, the increases in the homicide rate from 1985 through 1993, peaking from 1990 through 1993, can be accounted for totally by the growth in homicides committed by young people with handguns.[9] Jeffrey Roth reports that in 1990 the firearms murder victim rate for black males ages fifteen to nineteen was 105.3 per 100,000, a rate almost eleven times higher than the level for white victims in that age group.[10] The enormous racial disparity occurred only after 1985 and only for young black males, and may well reflect the crack cocaine and youth gang violence of the post-1985 period. Philip Cook and Jens Ludwig cite the racial and ethnic differences for gun homicide in 1996 for male victims ages eighteen to twenty-nine, with the Hispanic rate about seven times, and the black rate about twenty-five times, that of white men in that age group.[11] Garen Wintemute cites a homicide victimization rate for gang members sixty times higher than the rate for the general population.[12] In contrast to youth homicide, as James Alan Fox notes, the level of gun homicide of and by those ages twenty-five and older has declined steadily since 1980.[13] As a result, effective enforcement against juvenile drug and gun crimes, declines in the crack cocaine markets, and apparent changes in the social dynamics among the young high-crime age groups (especially those located in high-crime, minority-populated urban areas) themselves apparently served a major role in reducing the overall national homicide rate after 1993. But as Philip Cook, Mark Moore, and Anthony Braga state, little evidence exists that the level of gun ownership in our society itself has much effect on the overall violent crime rates.[14]

The influence of gun use by young people is further evidenced by the 65 percent increase in juvenile homicides in the seven years from 1987 through 1993, when overall homicide totals increased about 30 percent. Nearly all of the increased juvenile killings occurred in the number of older juveniles killed by guns. In 1980, 41 percent of juvenile homicides involved guns; in 1993, one of the peak years of homicide, that figure rose to 61 percent and then fell to 56 percent by 1997 as the homicide rate generally declined.[15] The California experience adds more evidence. The weapons offense arrest rates in 1988 per 100,000 persons in the relevant age groups were 161 for juvenile males and 133 for adult males. By 1994 the juvenile arrest rate had risen to 350, but only to 147 for adult males. By 1998, the arrest rates for both groups had declined as homicide levels declined. Nevertheless, during the ten years prior to 1998, the felony weapons arrest rate for juveniles in California increased 76.1 percent while the rate for male adults declined 13.4 percent.[16] Nationally, total juvenile homicides from 1993 to 1997 declined to a level just 20 percent above that of 1987, the year the total figure began to climb from its normal range.[17]

Although the prevailing national rhetoric did not so inform us, the level of risk posed by guns in our society declined significantly in the last seven years of the twentieth century. The total number of incidents of both violent crime and the use of guns declined dramatically, and although the percentage of murders and robberies occurring with firearms is still at higher levels compared to the mid-1980s, the share of aggravated assaults with firearms has returned to the lower mid-1980s level of about 20 percent. On a wider level, the national death rate from criminal injury by firearms had as early as 1995 returned to a level below that of 1980, and the willful homicide rate per 100,000 population in 1999, which was 39 percent lower than that in 1990, had reached a level not achieved since 1966.[18] Significantly as well, the forty-two law enforcement officers feloniously killed while on duty in 1999 represented the lowest total on record and a 30 percent decline in just one year.[19]

Widespread citizen knowledge of the actual risk of gun victimization is so very important because the level of fear, induced partially by highly publicized shootings, may well persist much longer than the actual risk. We know that the number of willful gun homicides declined by more than one-third from 1991 to 2000. But what about nonfatal wounds suffered in criminal gun violence? Comprehensive injury data covering only crime-caused gun injuries is somewhat elusive because most relevant studies cover all gun-related injuries no matter what the cause. And although more laws now require hospital workers to report gun injuries to law enforcement, emergency room and hospital admission personnel have no independent need or incentive to make detailed records about the criminal or noncriminal nature of the firing of the gun that caused the wound. Data from 1993 to 1997 do show that of all victims faced with nonfatal violent crime, excluding simple assault, fewer than 1 percent suffered a gunshot wound, even though 28 percent of such victims faced a firearm and 4 percent suffered some injury.[20] And the number of assault-generated gunshot wounds treated in hospital emergency departments fell by 39 percent, from 64,100 to 39,400, between 1993 and 1997.[21]

But is it not logical to think that a violent crime committed with a firearm would be more injurious more often than the same crime committed with another weapon or by strong-arm tactics? One study for the Bureau of Alcohol, Tobacco, and Firearms (ATF) noted a growing body of research since 1975 showing that attacks with guns become lethal far more frequently than do attacks with other kinds of weapons.[22] One expert cites data showing the overall fatality rate in gun robberies—four deaths per one thousand robberies—to be three times the death rate for knife robbery and ten times the rate for robbery with other kinds of weapons. In assaults, use of a gun increased lethality in one study by a factor of five compared to knife assaults.[23] Researchers have considered whether or not these differences in result reflect user motivation and determination, rather than the mere instrumentality effect of the weapon itself, and agree for many reasons that the lethality of the weapon itself is the principal cause of the differences in fatality rates.[24] In other words, offenders who choose guns over knives, for example, do not do so because they are more motivated to inflict lethal results. But recently, the numbers of robberies and aggravated assaults by firearm have been decreasing by similar or higher percentages than such incidents committed with other kinds of weapons or with no weapon at all.[25] Thus, the national trend since 1995 has been a decreasing percentage use of firearms in a total number of violent crimes that is decreasing as well.

The presence of a firearm is not inevitably detrimental to crime victims. When death does not occur, a victim is actually more protected from injury in a robbery and assault by firearm than victims confronted with knives, other weapons, and even no weapon at all. Employing national victimization survey data from 1973 through 1982, the 14 percent injury rate from nonlethal robberies and assaults by firearm was much lower than the 25 to 45 percent injury rates occurring when offenders use knives, other weapons, or no weapons.[26] And the 1998 survey demonstrated that for both robbery and aggravated assault, injury from a weapon occurred in lower proportions of firearm use than the injury proportion when another weapon or no weapon is used.[27] But no one knows if this result occurs because victims offer resistance less often against an armed offender or because the armed offender feels more self-assurance with a firearm, or both. At any rate, robbery victims confronting a gun face a higher risk of death compared to a confrontation with other kinds of weapons, but a lower risk of injury if the incident is not one of the four-per-thousand firearms robberies where death results.

Proponents of gun ownership theorize that more prevalent gun possession creates deterrence through offender fear of gun retaliation by victims. Studies do exist on defensive uses of a gun by a victim against an offender while a crime is in progress, but their results are so divergent as to preclude meaningful conclusions or policy implications. Various polls conducted with varying samples conclude that the number of persons employing a firearm in self-defense each year ranges from 108,000 to 3.6 million.[28] A Gallup Poll in 2000 produced a 7 percent affirmative response to the question of whether or not (apart from military combat) the respondent had ever used a gun in self-defense either by firing it or threatening to fire it, but this covered lifetime use and could include defense against animals as well as instances where no human perpetrator was actually viewed. Data from the victimization surveys (which also showed the 100,000-plus defensive use figure) show that only 3 percent of the victims who had been home during an actual or attempted residential break-in were able to deploy a weapon, even though 35 to 40 percent of residences possessed a firearm at that time. The data divergence on defensive use of guns thus far negates the degree of reliability needed by policymakers as a proper basis for firearms laws and regulations. But such survey and other research should continue.

Guns and Criminals

If the government knew how and why criminals obtain their firearms, the focus of regulation and law enforcement could then be more narrowly drawn, perhaps with greater effectiveness, compared to remedies that may inhibit all gun acquisition, both legal and illegal. Some data from law enforcement's tracing of guns used in crime have led gun-control advocates to conclude that the nation can inhibit crime gun supply successfully by controlling primarily the flow of recently manufactured semiautomatic handguns to "straw purchasers" at retail outlets. Such "straw" buyers are qualified under the law to procure handguns for themselves, but instead do so for a friend, relative, or acquaintance who is disqualified by law. By 1993 pistols supplanted the prior preference for revolvers and had become 80 percent of the handguns produced in the United States, up from 28 percent in 1973.[29]

But contrary to any contention that most crime guns are purchased at retail, theft of guns by criminals appears to play a major role. Some studies ask only how an offender acquired his most recent firearm or whether the criminal has ever stolen a firearm. The studies then cite a percentage proportion for each of the different modes of gun acquisition or for the gun used in the criminal's most recent crime, including various sources such as theft, family, friends, "the street," a drug dealer, a retail store, and others. But James Wright and Peter Rossi in the 1980s followed up by asking the next logical question: whether the offender knew definitely or probably that the weapon conveyed was stolen. They learned that 32 percent of the felons had acquired their most recent weapon through their own theft; an additional 14 percent knew that their friend, family, or street source had stolen the weapon before conveying it; and an additional 24 percent thought that the weapon probably had been stolen by his source. At least 46 percent, then, and possibly as many as 70 percent of felons' most recently owned firearms had been stolen either by the offender himself or by the source from whom he acquired the weapon. In addition, 47 percent of the respondents quizzed as to whether they had ever stolen a firearm during a crime admitted to so doing and 86 percent of the felons who admitted prior stealing of firearms reported multiple thefts.[30]

The finding that survey respondents who reported acquiring a firearm from a "friend," family member, or "the street" are likely to be actually using an originally stolen firearm was confirmed by asking those who had stolen one or more firearms whether they had sold or traded them and, if so, to whom. Ninety percent had sold or traded firearms and 66 percent of the gun thieves mentioned disposition to a friend, with lower percentages mentioning distributions of stolen guns to pawnbrokers, licensed dealers, fences, drug dealers, and strangers on the street.[31] In another study, interviews of over seven thousand persons arrested in eleven cities during the first six months of 1995 revealed that 13 percent had stolen a firearm. But 25 percent of the juveniles and about 30 percent of both gang members and drug sellers stated that they had done so, and over half of all those interviewed stated that guns are easy to obtain illegally.[32] Still another survey, this one of juvenile inmates in 1991, found that 83 percent owned at least one firearm just prior to incarceration and 65 percent owned three or more. At least one-half of the respondents had stolen a firearm at some time. Although a much lower percentage reported stealing their most recent handgun, 39 percent stated that they would steal one if they wanted a firearm in the future. But again, significant percentages also mentioned friends, "the street," drug dealers, and addicts as likely sources and, according to the Wright and Rossi findings, these sources probably had themselves stolen at least a portion of the firearms they were selling or trading. The surveyed juvenile inmates also stated that when they had sold or traded firearms that they had stolen, they did so to friends or other trusted persons. Another national gun survey estimated that over 500,000 weapons are stolen each year, including more than 200,000 handguns.[33] These figures do not demonstrate the percentage of crime guns originally stolen or acquired from a legal source because presumably criminals steal from each other. But they do show, for example, that hypothetically one thousand lawful guns from the legal primary market could migrate to the illegal secondary market and eventually support two thousand or more criminals who are stealing guns from each other. In other words, a small diversion of legal guns into the secondary market could have larger criminal consequences as each gun is passed around the criminal community.

Each of these studies affirmed the criminals' belief that acquisition of a firearm is neither too expensive nor a difficult, time-consuming task. Most criminals acquire guns primarily for self-protection, and a very high percentage at some time engaged in drug dealing and / or some version of an organized gang. More than one-half of the offenders have been threatened themselves with a gun or actually had gunshots directed their way, and most appear to possess more than one gun. Handguns are the most desired weapon and offenders want guns that are reliable, easily concealed, relatively new, and powerful. As a result, a criminal's firearm is more than likely a handgun and to a significant extent, one of recent origin ("recent" being defined as the gun's first retail sale having occurred within three years of its known use in crime). For example, ATF analyses of material submitted from twenty-seven local communities between August 1997 and July 1998 showed that 8.1 of every 10 successfully traced guns were handguns, 52 percent of them semiautomatic, with higher semiautomatic percentages for guns involving juvenile suspects. Recent guns represented 25 percent to 49 percent of those successfully traced, depending on the offenders' age group. And one-half of the successfully traced guns had originally been acquired by "straw buyers," who were making the purchase on behalf of an undisclosed, disqualified person.[34]

Those who believe that theft of guns is not a major source for criminals cite these gun trace studies. And some seize upon the tracing data as justification for their argument that reformers need control only the straw purchases of recent handguns from licensed and unlicensed gun sellers and not the universe of firearms. But for many reasons, guns traced by ATF represent less than one-fifth of the total number of crime guns recovered by police, and recovered guns do not begin to account for either all crime guns employed or all guns actually in possession of criminals. Consequently, as ATF readily admits, such tracing studies fail to provide valid sampling about the universe of crime guns. Nor has anyone yet discovered a good way to identify which legal buyers are "straw" buyers.

No study has shown that criminals have ever had difficulty in acquiring firearms in the past forty years, no matter what the level of gun production, gun regulation, or the type of gun currently in favor among manufacturers and users. So long as firearms are so easily acquired by criminals, directly or indirectly, legally or illegally, even effective regulation of handguns recently manufactured probably would not have a significant effect on gun use by criminals. And because most criminals appear to possess firearms for self-protection, one cannot justify an assumption that they would forgo acquisition, possession, or use of an older gun just because the supply of recently made guns dwindled or the retail or "street" price of weapons increased.

Because criminals acquire their guns swiftly through primary and secondary markets, through indirect means, and through direct and indirect theft, we must return to the universe of firearms to devise a means for controlling the gun supply to offenders and perhaps offender demand for firearms. An analysis of how to reduce firearms-related crime must first address issues of supply, demand, and distribution of all guns and discover where they are, how many exist, and how many are added to the national supply every year.

In the late 1960s, the National Commission on the Causes and Prevention of Violence found that one-half of the nation's households contained America's 90 million guns.[35] By 1994, when Cook and Ludwig analyzed a national telephone survey performed for the Police Foundation, about 192 million firearms—including 65 million handguns—were in civilian hands in the 35 percent of American households that possessed a gun.[36] Between 1968 and 1994, then, with the nation's population increasing 30 percent, total gun ownership more than doubled even though the percentage of households with a weapon apparently dropped 30 percent, and the handgun percentage of total firearms owned in the population at large increased from 26 percent to 34 percent. Although these figures demonstrate sufficient available guns to equip each adult with a firearm, the adults who each own four or more firearms (about 19 million, or 10 percent of the nation's adults) in fact possess 77 percent of America's civilian firearms inventory. One-quarter of adult residents own one or more firearms, which means that any general gun regulation would affect about 50 million owners.[37]

Handgun production figures from ATF show that pistol manufacturing peaked in 1993 at about 2.1 million and declined to under one million by 1998; handgun importation also dropped by more than half, to about

500,000 handguns imported in 1997.[38] Many researchers, as originally summarized by the national Violence Commission and repeated by others up to the present time, conclude that violent crime decreases when and because gun availability decreases. They reinforce their conclusion by noting the recent studies by ATF and others showing the preference of offenders, particularly youth offenders, for newer weapons. Further, they note that handgun production commenced its downward slide in 1993, when gun violence generally started to decline.

But the studies also show that juvenile and adult criminals tend to have more than one gun, including handguns, and that they do not find it difficult to acquire an additional firearm. No study of which we are aware demonstrates that offenders of any age cease their gun violence when they cannot buy a relatively new handgun. Nor have we found any study that finds that between 1993 and the present, as handgun production declined, offenders' ability to find a firearm, including a handgun, declined. In fact, the total number of firearms manufactured in 1997 was still higher than the figures for 1986, even though 1986's murder rate was 25 percent higher than that in 1997 and even though the number of murders in 1986 exceeded that for 1997, when the population was larger.[39] In addition, if violent crime is declining and most people, offenders and law-abiding alike, acquire their guns for self-protection, perhaps the market for new guns declines partially because crime declines. In that scenario, the crime decline causes the gun production decline as manufacturers deduce less of a market potential for guns. For example, handgun sales in California peaked in 1993 at 419,000 after the Los Angeles riots of 1992. Such sales had fallen to about 205,000 by 1997 even with an intervening population increase. Various experts speculated different reasons for the decline: greater concern about guns and safety, lower crime rates, crackdowns on retail licensees and new city regulations governing licensees, the aging of the prime gun-buying generation in the public at large, and a marketplace where people who wanted guns already had them.[40] The aging issue is intriguing: the 1994 Cook-Ludwig survey found that a high percentage of households with guns have members who are military veterans or members whose parents owned a firearm. As military veterans decline in number and proportion in our society, therefore, so should the level of household gun ownership.

Although some commentators assert that household ownership of firearms has declined since 1993, they are citing polls that the Cook-Ludwig analysis and polling in 1994 found as probably overstating household gun ownership. As noted above, the Cook-Ludwig percentage for 1994 was 35 percent, and different polls for 1998 and 1999 found the household firearms percentages to be 36 percent, 35 percent, 39 percent, and 37.8 percent.[41] The drop in gun production since 1993 thus may not have significantly affected the percentage of households owning guns in subsequent years. In fact, one recent study found that in telephone polls of married-couple households, females report 12 percent lower household ownership than do males. The researchers concluded that if only males answer the telephone in such households, the polls might conclude that American residents own 43.3 million more firearms than is now believed to be the true figure.[42]

Proponents of gun regulation should try as much as possible to isolate criminals' gun ownership from the universe of gun ownership. Although about 7 percent of all crimes of violence are committed with a firearm, the 1999 crime victimization survey tells us that 90 percent of the violent crimes using a firearm involve a handgun.[43] As a result, intensive regulation of crime-related guns need focus only on handguns. Sixteen percent of all adults own handguns and 80 percent of that ownership is male. About two-thirds of the people owning a handgun acquired it primarily for protection against crime.[44] As a result, regulation limited to handguns could still affect the 32 million adults who possess about 65 million handguns, in situations where about 22 million of those possessors acquired the weapons primarily for defense against crime. New guns are manufactured, distributed, and sold every year, and preferences change. ATF records show the manufacture of about 1.3 million new handguns (pistols and revolvers) in America in 1998, with about 35,000 exported and over 450,000 imported. Although handgun production by manufacturers has decreased since 1993, the Brady Law, which requires licensed retailers to initiate a state or federal search of records to find out if a criminal conviction or other relevant prior act by the prospective gun buyer bars his gun acquisition, provides another source of information about the flow of guns. Retailers initiated 8.8 million Brady requests in 1999, including about 2.9 million checks regarding handgun transactions, so at least close to that many firearms changed hands in that year.[45] Although we do not know how many firearms are sold at gun shows by nonlicensees without Brady processing, we do know that over 4,400 such shows occur each year, most over a two-day period, and that gun shows draw an average of 2,500–5,000 people examining weapons for sale by sellers, up to half of whom are not licensed dealers. It is thus safe to say that the gun stock inventory in America is served by over three million handgun transfers each year.[46]

But how many of these guns are owned for criminal purposes? Although an armed criminal who happened to have been called during the 1994 "Guns in America" survey, or any of the other firearms surveys, may have responded to the firearms questions, our guess is that did not happen very often. And even if it did, the one or more current offenders who may respond probably would represent too low a sample for generalization. Surveys of gun ownership therefore probably exclude the nature and volume of current offenders who possess guns. The Cook-Ludwig analysis of the 1994 survey does show that of the almost 7 percent of respondents admitting to a past arrest for an offense other than a traffic violation, 37 percent (representing about 4.7 million people) currently owned a gun, but this admitted past included any kind of minor offense and does not indicate convicted criminals or suggest an ongoing criminal career.[47] We also know that in 1999, estimated arrests for weapons offenses—that is, when the lead charge is the carrying or possessing of a deadly weapon (not necessarily a firearm)—were about 172,000.[48] But this does not include firearms charges added on to charges such as robbery, aggravated assault, or drug selling.

So, can we even guess at the number of handguns possessed by current criminals? The victimization survey numbers suggest about 500,000 separate crimes using a firearm in America in 2000. The 1991 survey mentioned earlier did show that 83 percent of confined juveniles possessed a firearm just prior to arrest and 65 percent owned three or more, but confined juveniles are a small portion of all arrested juveniles. Another survey reported that 37 percent of persons (a sample of both juveniles and adults) arrested and booked (not released prior to formal police charge) in 1995 in eleven major urban areas admitted to owning a gun at some time in the past.[49] Can we apply the 37 percent figure to the number of persons arrested in 2000, indicating that no more than 5.2 million identified, alleged offenders (37 percent of the estimated 14 million total arrests in 2000) owned a firearm? Unfortunately, we have no way of knowing whether the 37 percent lifetime gun ownership figure would apply to the portion of total arrests that did not result in a booking. And of course, ownership at some time during one's life bears an unknown relationship to current ownership figures. But 14 percent of the booked arrestees did say they carried a gun almost all of the time and 23 percent stated they had used a gun to commit a crime. Projected to total arrests, these percentages yield about two to 3.3 million offenders carrying or using guns to commit a crime in 2000.

But inmate surveys also show that criminals probably own more than one gun and believe that they can always obtain an additional firearm easily. And ATF tracing of seized criminal guns, admittedly not a representative sample of all guns possessed by criminals, showed that recent sales by licensed dealers to qualified buyers were a significant proportion of successfully traced firearms that ended up being used for crime.[50] This fact demonstrates the need to face the "straw buyer" problem, as well as gun theft and the offender-to-offender gun market, in trying to control the supply of guns used for crime. We must also realize that we are dealing with annual figures: new offenders join the crime scene every year, others cease their activities either voluntarily or because of incarceration and, although the overall use of firearms in crime was down during the latter half of the 1990s, no reason exists to suggest a permanent downturn in crime (other than the proportionate aging of America). And the percentage of the total violent crime that is committed with a firearm fluctuates separately for murder, robbery, and aggravated assault over the years. We also do not know nearly enough about gun turnover—that is, how long criminals keep a firearm, how many firearms become disabled, or how many just become recirculated among the criminal element. A final key question: If young offenders cannot locate a new handgun in a hurry through a friend or "straw buyer," do many then abandon firearms crime or do they use an older gun that they already own, go to the "street" to find a gun source, or steal a firearm?

Despite limitations in what is known, policymakers must do their best at least to place factual boundaries upon the problem under analysis. One study discussed earlier concluded that gun ownership among criminals is most closely related to selling drugs, gang membership, and just being a young male offender. But carrying guns is not associated with mere use of an illegal drug. A 2001 report of the Office of National Drug Control Policy estimated a total of 14.5 million current drug users in America.[51] So, even if one drug seller exists for every five users, that would result in three million gun-owning dealers.

All of these approaches produce numbers suggesting that total crime gun ownership falls somewhere between the 500,000 number of violent firearms crimes in 2000 and the probably high projection that 5.2 million arrested offenders in 1999 possessed a weapon sometime during their lives. If we choose two-thirds of the difference between these two extremes, or about three million offenders, and project that they currently own an average of two firearms each, most of which are handguns, we place at least six million weapons in at least three million criminal hands separate and apart from the estimated 32 million residents who own handguns and the 50 million residents who own any kind of firearm for lawful reasons.

Gun Regulation

In designing a gun regulation policy, we must first examine any social purposes apart from reduction of crime-related gun injuries and deaths. Most experts cite the broad category of safety. Indeed, with over 200 million guns in circulation, one would probably estimate a rather large accident rate. But accidental death rates from use of firearms are dwarfed by higher rates for deadly accidents caused by motor vehicles, fire, falls, drowning, and poisoning.[52] In 1999, about nine hundred people died in firearms accidents—68 percent fewer than the 2,800 such deaths reported by the Violence Commission in 1967 when the national population was lower by 70 million and the gun ownership total was probably less than one-half of the 1999 figure. The firearms accidental death rate is down 29 percent just since 1992, even though "unintentional deaths" by all causes other than road accidents during those seven years rose by 21 percent to 95,500 in 1999.[53] In further contrast, the number of accidental deaths by firearms in 1999 equaled only about 6 percent of the total alcohol-related traffic deaths in 1998. Over one-half of our annual suicides occur by use of firearms, an especially lethal weapon, to be sure, but no one knows how many of these suicides would occur in the absence of firearms.

Policymakers can rightfully believe that, even though lethal gun accidents are decreasing dramatically and the suicide rate has been relatively steady for two decades, greater gun safety precautions would still help prevent some gun deaths, gun suicides, and gun injuries. Indeed, guns are still the second leading cause of injury-related death in America when willful homicide is combined with accidental gun deaths and suicide.[54] Given the low numbers involved as compared to total firearms crime incidents, however, firearms accidental death and suicide programs could well be directed to training, safety devices and safety storage, education, and counseling rather than comprehensive gun regulation. For example, the elderly are the age group most prone to suicide by gun, and antisuicide programs could well be directed at that group.

These figures demonstrate that crime deserves primary blame for most of the social costs of gun use. But as a society we try to offset the "gun problem" by regulating guns at all points in their manufacture, distribution, and sale. Legislators and executive branch officials rarely possess evidence about how and why a particular regulation or prohibition will lead to a particular result or how and why that particular result would reduce or increase gun crimes or crime gun injuries. Only recently have researchers even commenced to explore these questions

Indeed, extensive federal firearms regulation itself is relatively new in our history. Gun statutes enter the books only when violent events induce political responses, so most federal gun regulation laws have been enacted in election years. The violence of Prohibition brought some gun regulation in 1934 and 1938, primarily affecting the machine guns and other automatic weapons publicized by the actions of Al Capone and the federal enforcement teams. The assassinations and urban riots of the 1960s brought about the Gun Control Act of 1968, which today remains the most comprehensive law and still the heart of national gun regulation—the ATF was established to assume the firearms regulatory and enforcement responsibilities established by that act. And the peaking of reported violent crime in 1993 brought greater strength and depth to gun regulation in 1994. But at other times, the U.S. Congress enacted laws to ensure that firearms regulation cannot develop into overall firearms control and that no national registry of gun ownership can be created. The anti–gun control ideology has triumphed with the prevailing national policy that no federal official should be able to learn who in America possesses guns, promoting the fear that such government knowledge will lead to government confiscation and loss of individual freedom.

The history of ATF provides a central illustration of the ambivalence of federal gun regulation, where each proregulation step is accompanied or followed by a rigid limit on such regulation. Since its inception, ATF has been collecting taxes and enforcing criminal laws relevant to the liquor, wine, beer, tobacco, explosives, and firearms industries. In fact, as of 1996, ATF was a revenue-producing mechanism collecting $13 billion annually in various taxes.[55] But periodically, study commissions and presidents—for varying reasons—have sought ATF's abolition or partial dispersal into other federal agencies. (President Reagan wanted to abolish ATF in the

1980s, for example, but Congress overruled him.) In fact, every formal review of ATF functions since its birth has supported the dispersal of its law enforcement activities elsewhere. The latest such commission, chaired by a former FBI and CIA director, put it bluntly: "ATF lacks a clear mission and sense of purpose because of the clash of disparate jurisdictional responsibilities . . . This small agency has for more than thirty years attempted to reconcile the irreconcilable. The same organization houses functions that are at cross purposes, feeding internal competition for resources and detracting from a unified law enforcement policy."[56] A former ATF official summarizes his views just as bluntly: "In short, ATF is not a cohesive, rational, and focused organization but an accident produced by a highly fragmented system obsessed with the dispersal of government authority."[57]

One should begin the discussion of gun regulation with this history because, too often in law enforcement and regulation, we separate analyses into the legal structure of the regulations and then separately, the powers given to the implementing agency to administer and enforce those regulations. Yet in this case the Congress of the United States has created an agency legally unable to fulfill its mission. Over and over, Congress compels ATF to limit its regulation and to destroy, or even to refrain from creating, records that could be helpful in achieving its goals of keeping guns out of criminal hands and helping apprehend criminals who acquire guns.

In particular, the statutes tell ATF to regulate importers, manufacturers, distributors, and retail dealers. But the law also commands: do not regulate retail sellers of firearms unless they have "a regular course of trade or business with the principal objective of livelihood and profit through the repetitive purchase and resale of firearms."[58] This definition keeps the ATF from regulating the formal and informal secondary market, which is so important to crime gun acquisition. And although the statutory apparatus requires licensed sellers, manufacturers, and importers to create and maintain records, ATF is prohibited by law from requiring that *any* such record or *any* portion thereof be recorded at, or transferred to, a facility owned, managed, or controlled by the federal government or by any state government in a way other than the law itself provides. The law further prohibits establishment of any system of registering firearms, firearms owners, or firearms transactions or dispositions. The only exception to these prohibitions is federal inquiry into gun disposals in the course of a criminal investigation.[59] Further, except for court-ordered warrants and for records needed in criminal investigations, the law prohibits ATF compliance personnel from inspecting the inventory and records of a licensed firearms manufacturer, importer, or dealer more than once each year.[60] State and local enforcement personnel who receive firearms purchase records from ATF must destroy them within twenty days of receipt unless the purchaser is barred by federal law from acquiring a firearm or shipping one interstate.[61] If a licensed importer, manufacturer, dealer, or collector is indicted for a felony, the law dictates that the criminal defendant may continue in the gun business until any conviction becomes final, perhaps years later.[62] Swap meets, flea markets, and the four thousand gun shows held each year are unregulated at the federal level except for federal licensees who may be participating in them. And under the Brady provisions of the law, if a dealer request for a records check about a potential gun buyer shows no reason to bar the purchase, the implementers of the records check must destroy all system records relating to the call (other than an identifying number and date) and all system records relating to the person and the transfer.

Finally, the most recent strengthening of federal gun regulation is subject in some instances to automatic repeal in 2004. The prohibitions banning both semiautomatic assault weapons and large capacity ammunition feeding devices (a feeder of more than ten rounds) will self-destruct in the year 2004; even the statutory clauses defining such weapons and devices will disappear. And such weapons and feeding devices already in existence in 1994 have been exempted from regulation. Also exempted from the ban are almost seven hundred rifle and shotgun makes and models specifically listed in the act—an extraordinary bit of specificity and commercial identification in congressional legislation. Also self-destructing by automatic repeal, this one after fifteen years, is a law banning any firearm that is not detectable by metal detectors or by x-ray machines (such as the ones we see at airports) in a way that accurately shows the shape of the component.[63] The automatic repeal provisions of these protections may best illustrate the emotions, fear, and distrust of governmental power that firearms regulation has generated in the minds and hearts of some legislators, members of the National Rifle Association, and ordinary citizens.

Within these mandatory constraints, administered by an agency bluntly told by legislators to fight crime while tiptoeing through this minefield of limitations, gun regulation does truly exist. But the extent of these restraints may well indicate that the best regulatory course for the future should lean toward their removal, rather than the imposition of new laws. ATF does manage to perform some duties effectively despite the legislative chains. Each licensed importer and manufacturer must identify its firearms products with unique serial numbers recorded in its records. Interstate sales are generally prohibited both to licensees and nonlicensees except under specified allowances, which rarely include a retail sale. Dealers who have a federal firearms license (FFLs) must make and retain records of all firearms acquisitions and dispositions and turn over those records to ATF when the dealer goes out of business. Retail licensees retain their federally licensed status only if they comply with all applicable state and local laws, including zoning. And for each retail sale, an FFL must view a government-issued photo of the purchaser and initiate a government records check under the Brady Law. Any retail sale of two or more handguns to one person within five business days generates a report to ATF, and every licensed dealer must respond to a federal request for information necessary to trace a crime gun, gun projectile, or ammunition shell casing.

All licensees and nonlicensees are prohibited from conveying firearms to specified persons—for example, a felon, a drug addict, an adjudicated "mental defective," and any person who has ever been committed to a mental institution or who has ever been convicted of a domestic violence misdemeanor. And FFLs cannot transfer a handgun to anyone under twenty-one years of age. Nor can anyone lawfully transfer or possess certain kinds of semiautomatic assault weapons or ammunition feeding devices, such as a firearms magazine capable of accepting more than ten rounds of ammunition.[64]

But even after all of this regulation, the federal government as a whole has no permanent records of licensees' firearms transactions other than records from out-of-business FFL's, reports of multiple handgun sales, and the records of firearms traces and images. And the relatively few regulatory provisions that apply to nonlicensees who sell or trade guns—that is, people who say that they are not "engaged in the business" of selling firearms "with the principal objective of livelihood and profit"—do not require these sellers to secure information from their purchasers and establish sellers' liability only if they know or have reasonable cause to believe that the buyer is legally prohibited from purchasing the gun. This level of knowledge is difficult to prove.

Crime Gun Regulation

Despite the deliberate loopholes in gun regulation legislation, several relatively recent actions could now help launch fact-based inquiries into the possible effectiveness of different kinds of crime gun regulation. In developing fact-based regulation as part of its crime response policy relative to guns, America must change the focus by discarding the overly broad and rhetorically destructive "gun control" label and establishing instead the goal of "crime gun regulation," a title that centers policy orientation on firearms used in crime. Gun ownership by the law-abiding would be subject only to those restrictions proven to be directly related to enhancing safety and to curbing gun violence.

First, the 1994 Brady Law, in requiring licensed dealers to initiate a records check of prospective gun buyers, was extended after November 1998 from just handgun coverage to all guns. Under the law, if a record check is not completed within three business days, the dealer-licensee may proceed with the firearm transfer. During the seven years from 1994 through 2000, about 30 million Brady checks occurred and 689,000 applications, or about 2.3 percent, were rejected. Almost 70 percent of these rejections occurred either because the prospective buyer was a felon or under pending felony charges (by far the primary reasons), or a domestic violence record existed.[65] Brady Law supporters posit that a gun purchase denial dissuades offenders from carrying out crimes either by making them postpone and then drop their plans or by preventing acquisition of the needed weapon. But Brady's effectiveness in reducing actual crime gun violence has yet to be demonstrated. One study concluded that Brady screening did not affect homicide rates; another analysis did show that when persons with felony arrest records, but no records of conviction, were cleared for gun purchases, and another group of convicted felons were rejected under Brady for such purchases, the group cleared for gun purchases was more likely than the rejected group to be convicted of gun and violence offenses within the next three years.[66] The increasing efficiency of Brady in its nationwide application to all firearms acquired through licensed dealers may increase its direct relationship to prevention of gun violence and to inhibition of some gun traffickers who try to purchase crime guns in states with lax gun transfer regulation for shipment to states with strict controls.

Yet Brady's delays may well affect the number of defensive gun uses when lawful buyers who want a firearm merely for self-protection instead quit the market. Only future research will tell us if any of those effects truly occur. At any rate, built-in limitations now exist to limit anticrime effects. Until Brady extends its reach to gun shows and other secondary market sales, that law cannot affect the estimated 2.5 million secondhand guns sold annually in the United States through buyer-seller exchanges where no licensed dealer is involved. Offender survey research would help demonstrate how conduct is affected when Brady does deny a gun. Does denial act as a complete crime deterrent or a complete firearms crime deterrent? Is it a temporary delay that reduces only immediately contemplated crime? Or do offenders easily and quickly obtain arms from another seller or from a family or friendly donor in the secondary market?

A second encouraging step in recent years is widespread acceptance of ATF's significant role in gun enforcement efforts. The agency's lukewarm, tenuous reception in the halls of Washington, D.C.'s executive and legislative branches was reinforced in 1993 by the agency's highly publicized, tragic raid against the Branch Davidian complex at Waco, Texas. But the peaking of the crime rate, the public's delayed realization that violent crime was declining after 1993, and the highly publicized, multivictim firearms killings at schools and offices in the last half of the 1990s brought focus upon ATF's ability to perform needed, effective action. The agency has developed close ties with state and local police to enforce the crime gun laws, particularly those for juveniles and young adults. Joint task forces exist under the Youth Crime Interdiction Initiative in key urban areas, and crime gun programs are developed jointly with differing strategies and emphases depending upon the nature of each local problem. A system now also exists for state and FBI referral to ATF of Brady's "default proceeds"— that is, situations where a firearm was released to a buyer because disqualifying information about the buyer was first produced beyond the three-business-day limit allowed by law for the records check. ATF now also pursues possible prosecution of gun buyers who falsified the ATF forms they had completed at the dealers' stores for the Brady records check. To avoid an overwhelming flood of cases, federal prosecutorial guidelines limit prosecution of Brady-related false statements to known felons and other serious situations.[67] But the proof of the reality of even partial control is in the pudding of government's ability to actually enforce a criminal law. For example, use of a false ID can get a prohibited buyer through a Brady check. Research will have to pursue what level of prosecutions under the Brady law would lead to significant deterrence of Brady-related falsifications and to prohibited persons' deciding not to even try to obtain a gun from licensed dealers.

ATF has also made progress in tracing crime guns to help identify both gun offenders and gun dealers who traffic guns to criminals. The agency and the FBI have developed a unique national system of automated ballistics identification. The barrel of a weapon leaves a distinct marking on any bullet traveling through it, and the firearms breach mechanism leaves distinct markings on ammunition cartridge cases. Previously, technicians labored for days to manually trace such items against a file of previously submitted materials. Now, with the unification of the FBI and ATF identification programs, accomplished in December 1999, almost 800,000 images became available by computer at 225 sites. And early on, the system had produced over eight thousand "cold hits" using stored images of cartridge cases and bullets to match a newly submitted case or bullet to a crime gun, evidence matches that would not have occurred under the old manual system. In the ATF automated system alone, as of September 30, 1998, fourteen firearms specialists using the new system produced results that would have required 2,575 firearms examiners under the displaced manual system.[68]

ATF can also initiate the trace of a recovered crime gun when its serial number is readable, but obliteration of serial numbers occurred in about 11 percent of the trace submissions analyzed by one ATF study. The agency is improving its ability to restore such obliterations, and local agencies receive training in this restoration process. With a serial number, the gun is traced first to the manufacturer and then, if possible, through the distribution chain to the first initial retail purchaser. But in this process ATF must send a trace request each step of the way from the manufacturer through distributors to the retail dealer, and even if the name and address of the first civilian retail purchaser is located, the paper trail usually ends and ATF agents must conduct time-consuming witness interviews to investigate subsequent movements of the weapon until a crime suspect is identified. Although more recent guns are easier to trace successfully, in most cases the tracing trail of used firearms sold or transferred through private channels is too "cold" to lead to identification of a criminal buyer or transferee.

Even with all of these difficulties, gun tracing—particularly as the system becomes more automated—is becoming faster, more available to local police, more conclusive, and thus far more useful to the crime-solution process. In the case of a pre-1990 weapon, ATF may not even commence the trace process because of the low potential for success. But in 1998, ATF received tracing requests for almost 200,000 crime guns.[69] And tracing is very helpful in locating the relatively few licensed dealers who are the initial sellers of a high volume of recently sold crime guns. In February 2000, the Treasury Department authorized much more intensive inspection schedules for these dealers. An ATF study showed that about 1.2 percent of current FFLs accounted for 57 percent of the crime guns traced back to the dealer population, and just 132 dealers had fifty or more crime guns traced to them. In addition, about 450 dealers who had been linked with high numbers of crime guns were directed to provide to ATF specified information about secondhand firearms they acquire. Even with these efforts, ATF recognizes that over two million used guns sold annually in the United States do not proceed through licensed dealers and are now largely untraceable. Recent agency requirements now command any dealer who fails to respond to an ATF crime gun trace request to send in all their firearms sales records so that ATF will have access for future trace searches.[70] The increased gun tracing allows ATF for the first time to focus its inspections and regulation on the licensed dealers most closely tied to the nation's supply of crime guns.[71]

The new knowledge acquired through tracing also has useful policy implications. For example, police departments routinely had placed their used weapons back into the marketplace as trade-ins when the departments purchased new weapons. Until 1994, even federal agencies were selling their used firearms and thus enhancing the supply of guns at the same time that they were fighting gun crime. When law enforcement's used guns began showing up in crime gun traces, the theoretical disadvantage to these gun trade-in policies finally became clear, and many police departments replaced their trade-in practices with gun destruction.[72] But the largest policy implication is the now obvious necessity for Congress to untie some of the bonds on ATF records gathering and retention. Gun tracing becomes more effective and much more efficient if gun-buyer records and records retention are mandatory for all sellers. And regardless of the ideological battle over guns, handgun registration would provide the best gun-tracing, crime-solution methodology.

A third promising development is the maintenance of a law enforcement focus on gun violence. This emphasis commenced as analyses began to reveal that the 1985 through 1993 increase in gun violence occurred almost exclusively among juveniles and young adults, and was associated with their gangs and illegal drug activities. As discussed in our chapter on police, and described by John Eck and Lawrence Sherman in their surveys of the effectiveness of various police actions, the "hot spot" and directed patrol tactics used to address different crime problems in various communities can also be focused toward reducing both gun violence and the burgeoning presence of guns.[73] In certain areas of Kansas City, for example, police engaged in intensified car stops, pedestrian stops, and arrests and stops directed toward known or likely offenders, particularly gang members and drug dealers, with a dual goal of weapons confiscation and offender arrest for any provable offense.[74] Also well publicized is the police, prosecutor, church, and community mobilization project Operation Ceasefire in Boston, where all of these constituent elements met with gang leaders to announce and then rigidly enforce all gun laws.[75] Another variation is Project Exile, begun in Richmond, Virginia, in March 1997, when that city had one of the five highest murder rates nationwide. Police there began to refer gun cases to federal prosecutors who had available under federal law mandatory minimum prison punishment. With intense publicity, the federal prosecutors then prosecuted all locally arrested felons-with-guns and all drug trafficking and domestic violence cases involving guns. About 75 percent of these defendants were denied bail and an equal percentage pleaded guilty without prosecutorial concessions on the gun charge.[76] The murder rate dropped precipitously. Finally, and also well publicized, are the New York City Police Department's directed patrols that enormously increased stop-and-frisk incidents to implement gun confiscation, drug enforcement, and apprehension of drug and gun offenders. Research evaluations of these tactics conclude that they have contributed to some extent to the lessening of gun violence between 1993 and 1999. But those experts who exercise proper caution point out that violent crime and gun crimes were down almost universally in urban areas over the last five or more years of the 1990s even though enormously variant police tactics existed in those cities.

The overall significance of these figures, then, is difficult to ascertain. As the volume and rate of crime declined since 1993, so too did the number of arrests for weapons violations—they were down about 25 percent from 1990–1999.[77] And federal firearms prosecutions from ATF case referrals also declined between 1992 and 1998, although the average prison sentence increased through 1995 and thereafter declined to levels still above that of 1992.[78] Government figures showed substantial increases in total numbers of federal firearms prosecutions and firearms defendants for 1999. But one must be careful of prosecution and court-related statistics. For example, the FBI, the ATF, the Justice Department's administrative office for federal prosecutors, the federal courts' administrative office, and the widely respected private efforts of TRAC (a Syracuse University–based research team on federal criminal justice statistics) often show significant differences in these numbers. But everyone agrees that from 1992 through 2000, America had declining gun crime and declining gun arrests, along with increases in directed police patrol and, for some areas, intense stop-and-frisk police activity in high-crime "hot spots" and zero-tolerance arrests for low-level crimes. The years since 1994 have also produced a large decrease in juvenile gun violence.

Finally, society brought a broad range of strategies to the task of controlling gun crime in different cities. In explaining the positive developments in gun violence, no research has compared, for example, the relative roles of law enforcement; culture change; changes in both residents' and offenders' perceptions about the need to be armed for self-protection; reduction in the crack trade, which had produced gun violence, especially among youth; gun availability; juvenile and youth gang prevention programs; community attitudes and programs; and full employment conditions in the bubble economy of the 1990s. But more research should become available in the next five years. In 2002, the Justice Department authorized Project Safe Neighborhood, a crime gun project in each of the ninety-three federal districts based on variations of the Exile or Ceasefire models.

A fourth encouraging trend for crime gun regulation is the decline in the number of retail gun dealers with a federal firearms license (FFLs), particularly since 1994, and the decline in the volume of newly manufactured pistols, the gun preferred by criminals. The ATF reports about 69,000 FFLs in the United States as of May 2000, a dramatic decline from the 247,000 figure in August 1992.[79] A firearms owner's redemption of his weapon from a pawnshop also requires a Brady check as of November 30, 1998; the National Pawnbrokers Association estimates that the 12,000 to 14,000 pawnshops in the United States take in about ten million firearms annually, holding about three million in their vaults at any given time.[80] Even if a felon slips through an initial Brady check at original acquisition—for example, by using a qualified "straw buyer," stealing the gun, or buying it from a "street" source—that person now faces a Brady check often when he pawns it (at the store owner's discretion), but always upon redemption.

The lower number of FFLs means that ATF has fewer locations to inspect. The dealer decrease probably resulted from a combination of higher dealer license fees, better ATF enforcement, and more stringent statutory requirements for the FFLs, particularly the need to comply with all state and local laws (including local zoning laws, which mostly prohibit the large number of "dealers" who were really just homeowners selling guns in residential neighborhoods). The increased likelihood that an FFL will be inspected by ATF, along with the intense efforts by ATF and others to identify crime gun traffickers through expanded computerized crime gun tracing and the application of the Brady Law to all firearms as of December 1998, make it more likely that an FFL who ignores the law will be detected.

These factors, in combination with the lower production of those firearms most favored by criminals, should have some inhibitive effect on the ability of potential offenders to acquire the guns they want when they want them. At the least, such weapons may not be as quickly and easily available to offenders as studies have shown them to be in the 1980s and early 1990s. The trend toward lower handgun production will probably continue so long as the later-discussed pending litigation against gun manufacturers by various levels of private and governmental entities is sustained. In particular, California's concentration of handgun producers in the Los Angeles area will disappear as the strengthening of state and local requirements endures and particularly as endless litigation produces legal costs that small companies cannot survive. New companies may slowly emerge in less regulated state environments. But even large companies could follow Colt Manufacturing by assessing which portion of their firearms production relates most to eventual crime (even if the manufacturer denies causation and fault), and then discontinue production of those firearms models in order to end bad publicity, legal costs, and management time devoted to litigation issues. Indeed, in spite of temporary production increases expected during any subsequent national crime wave or after a tragedy caused by international terrorists in the United States, mass marketing of handguns generally may well not again reach the peaks achieved in the mid-1990s.

An aging America also could reduce the demand for rifles and shotguns if hunters, target shooters, and collectors continue to retire from these avocations and new generations turn to other interests.[81] Yet the Women's Shooting Sports Foundation reports that the almost 2.5 million female hunters in the United States in 1998 represented an increase of 40 percent since 1989, and target shooting with handguns by women increased by 19 percent, to 3.1 million females, during those years.[82]

A fifth focused development in the last half of the 1990s is the expansion of state and local efforts to regulate firearms. Wintemute reports that eighteen states and Washington, D.C., prohibit firearms purchases not just by felons, but also by those convicted of certain misdemeanors, such as ones connected to drugs, alcohol, or violence.[83] As of July 1, 2001, twelve states had a waiting period for handgun purchases; sixteen states and Washington require a license or, in some cases, a permit to purchase a handgun; three states and Washington have handgun registration and three others have local jurisdictions with this requirement; and in twenty-five states and Washington records of certain or all firearms sales are sent to local police.[84] As of October 1999, Connecticut law permits police to enter a home or business to seize weapons for up to one year after a court finds that a person with access to guns may do harm to himself or others. The law was implemented at least seven times in its first two months.[85]

But many state laws also protect the existence and use of firearms.[86] Almost every state has a constitutional provision establishing some version of a citizen's right to bear firearms and a legislative provision prohibiting certain local firearms ordinances more restrictive than state laws. Most states also have laws prohibiting interference with lawful hunting activities and protecting firearms ranges from nuisance and noise control enforcement. In the ongoing litigation battles between various levels of government and the firearms industry, progun interests also have caused enactment of laws in twenty-seven states that forbid local jurisdictions from suing firearms industry entities. Equally as controversial are laws in thirty-three states permitting a citizen with a license to carry a concealed gun.

More and more state legislatures are exploring the concept of prohibiting the sale of certain firearms manufactured after an effective date unless they meet prescribed standards of quality and / or safety. Maryland and California have already done so. Even executive branch regulations are under consideration. For example, using the state's consumer protection laws, the Massachusetts attorney general mandated that all handguns sold there include such items as childproofing, tamperproof serial numbers, and consumer safety warnings. These laws may well lower firearms production and sales by increasing production costs and therefore consumer price.[87]

Although multigun sales are crucial to those who traffic in crime guns, very few states have enacted a proposed law barring the sale of more than one handgun a month to any retail buyer. Sometimes, local jurisdictions with high gun crime try to control gun supply to a greater extent than their states do. Very strict firearms regulations have existed for many years in New York City, Chicago, and the District of Columbia. Yet although such laws can be effective for a time immediately after enactment, they soon become overwhelmed by the sale of guns in local jurisdictions surrounding the cities.

Public opinion about specific kinds of gun regulation represents a sixth and final encouraging trend relating to guns, gun violence, and crime gun regulation.[88] A 1999 Gallup poll found that 87 percent of the respondents favored mandatory background checks of all gun purchasers at gun shows; 85 percent wanted safety locks or trigger guards in all new handguns; and 79 percent favored registration of all firearms. A 1998 poll by the National Opinion Research Center (NORC) found that 88 percent wanted all new handguns to be childproof and 70 percent desired all new guns to be configured to allow only the owner to fire the weapon. In six of the national NORC polls between 1990 and 1998, between 78 percent and 82 percent of the respondents favored a law requiring persons to obtain a police permit before acquiring a gun. And a *Newsweek* poll in August 1999 reported that 81 percent of non–gun owners and 66 percent of gun owners favored gun registration with a government agency. Mandatory gun safety courses received favor from 88 percent of non–gun owners and 80 percent of owners. But only 18 percent of the people, when asked to identify the most effective deterrent to violent incidents, cited "stricter gun control."[89] And this poll occurred almost immediately after a series of multivictim murders around the nation. Equally important, these views do not differ significantly by political party affiliation. For example, in the NORC poll asking who favored mandatory police permits for gun purchasers, 86 percent of Democrats and 75 percent of Republicans favored such a provision. But three NORC polls between 1996 and 1998 demonstrated that only 15 to 16 percent of the respondents favored a handgun ban, even though 43 to 46 percent believed that such a weapon made the home less safe.[90]

Yet even if government wanted to further refine gun regulation to focus on crime prevention and detection, anti–gun control advocates have raised two barriers. First, John Lott, Jr., an economist, has attempted to demonstrate, in his regression analyses, the harms produced by gun regulation and the benefits produced by laws promoting citizen carriage of concealed weapons (CCW laws). Lott advocates widespread adoption of "shall issue" CCW laws, which require a state or local community to issue such a permit to anyone who fulfills the law's explicitly stated, simple qualifications. Lott says that the more the general public is armed, the less confident and secure criminals will be in committing violent crimes.

The second edition of Lott's book responds to the antigun challenges that had greeted the publication of his initial findings and conclusions. The author addresses all criticisms with new, expanded regression analyses that endeavor to demonstrate that enactment and citizen use of these CCW laws did not just correlate with the drop in violent crime from 1993 forward, but is also statistically associated with a finding that CCW laws are the most cost-effective means of reducing violent crime. Lott does this by statistically controlling for other possible factors such as police practices, demographic data, arrest and conviction rates, prison sentences, the earlier forms of the Brady Law, existing gun regulation and criminal laws, and income levels.

Lott also analyzes the effects of other kinds of gun regulation. For example, he finds that the Brady Law is significantly related to a 3.6 percent *increase* in rape. He also concludes that laws mandating safe storage of guns are significantly related to almost 9 percent more robberies and rapes and 5.6 percent more burglaries, and thus an additional 3,600 rapes, 22,500 robberies, and 64,000 burglaries in 1996 in just fifteen states with safe storage laws, presumably because potential victims cannot gain access to their guns in time or refrain from buying useless guns, and offenders take advantage of this. Lott also finds that existing laws restricting buyers' handgun purchases to one per month were associated with increases in murder, robbery, and aggravated assault.[91] Several researchers have performed studies with results radically different from Lott's, and most reject his findings.[92] A more detailed pursuit of these regression analyses and their conflicting results is not within the scope of this book. Suffice it to say, one cannot base social policy on one proponent's heavily disputed findings.

In the ongoing evolution of academic data analysis, the more thoughtful scholars are now realizing that statistical analyses showing that X condition, when compared to other possible explanations, is most strongly associated with Y's presence, require the additional base of a valid theory and perhaps historical logic to form a factual foundation for social policy. Too often, regression analyses result in 'tis-'taint battles, as illustrated by John Lott and his critics and by the conflicting results produced by Wesley Skogan's and Bernard Harcourt's regression analyses of a possible relationship between "broken windows" policing and levels of serious criminal conduct.

In addition to John Lott's research findings, gun advocates cite the absolute "right of the people" to keep and carry arms, a concept they perceive in the Second Amendment to our Constitution: "A well regulated Militia, being necessary to the security of a free State, the right of the people to keep and bear Arms, shall not be infringed."

Gun-control advocates, for their part, view this amendment as establishing a collective right, not an individual right, serving solely the now-obsolete purpose of arming a well-regulated militia. But the militia is not an obsolete concept. Today, American males from ages seventeen through forty-four probably would be surprised to learn that under federal law they are all militia members, with some few exceptions, and they and their ancestors have been so since the Constitution was ratified.[93] The president can summon any state militia at any time for specified purposes; throughout the twentieth century Congress has provided assistance to make sure that target practice, guns, and ammunition are available to the unorganized militia at supervised ranges.[94] But unlike the late 1800s, today's militia members need not bring along their own firearms when they report for duty.

Despite the enduring academic, public, and political debates, no one can solve the constitutional question under the Second Amendment until the U.S. Supreme Court speaks finally and comprehensively. In the authors' opinion, prior cases are inconclusive on this question and no insight has become available from the Court in over fifty years, when the Court last ruled on this issue.[95] We can guess that ultimately the Supreme Court will find that, whatever the extent of the right established under the Second Amendment, that right can be "infringed" by local, state, and federal governments for compelling reasons of public health and safety. But if some degree of an individual right to bear arms is established, one could also foresee the Supreme Court prohibiting any level of government from barring all guns either on one's own person or in one's home. If so, the ideological gun war could at least be tempered.

Optimum Crime Gun Regulation

It is a false idea of utility . . . that would deprive men of fire because it burns or water because it drowns . . . The laws which forbid men to bear arms are of this sort. They only disarm those who are neither inclined nor determined to commit crimes. Can it be supposed that those who have the courage to violate the most sacred laws of humanity . . . will respect the lesser and more arbitrary laws, which are easier and less risky to break, and which, if enforced, would take away the personal freedom—so dear to man and to the enlightened lawgiver—and subject the innocent man to all the annoyances which the guilty deserve?[96]

Writing these words over two hundred years ago, social philosopher Cesare Beccaria reflected upon a danger ever present in criminal law. Historically, in the endeavor to regulate one condition, society's rulers and legislatures have reached too wide and regulated too much. To control the two to five million people who may be carrying handguns to assist in committing crimes, strict gun control adherents would ban anyone from owning the 65 million handguns already in American homes. To find one thousand guns, society humiliates ten thousand or more people with police searches on a city street. And instead of using the criminal law to build public support for crime gun regulation, disrespect for gun enforcement is fostered in large segments of its populace. Broad-based support for government action causing privacy invasions, intrusive searches, and delays, such as airport screening, develops only if an unacceptably high cost of inaction and the unavailability of effective alternatives are clearly demonstrated—such as not finding a gun or explosive carried by a terrorist who seeks to destroy an airplane in flight.

Examining all the data, one justifiably wonders why enacting crime gun regulation is a problem. The polls clearly show that most Americans favor the kinds of gun regulation that all states employ for driving and owning cars: registration, training, permits, and safety requirements. But most Americans also do not favor a ban on even handguns and most do not believe that stricter gun control is the most effective deterrent against gun violence. As a society, we exacerbate the difficulty in finding solutions by constantly employing the term "control," as in "gun control." The implications of "control" feed the ideology that touts a secret government goal to take away our guns, which are proclaimed the last and best defense of each person against those who seek to harm us and against government tyranny threatened from both within and without. Whence springs the flaming oratory at National Rifle Association annual conventions, where the speaker proclaims with rifle held high, "only from my cold, dead hand," followed by a standing ovation that ignores the fact that crime handgun laws would not affect rifles. The oratory by itself feeds the political rhetoric of exploitative politicians who fail to educate either themselves or potential voters about gun issues. At the end of his presidency, Bill Clinton explained that the most powerful gun lobby, the National Rifle Association, by making fear of gun control the principal voting issue for 15 to 20 percent of voters in both parties in many congressional districts, leads to the postponement or defeat of gun control legislation.[97] And unfortunately, too many politicians will continue to speak on gun issues with too little knowledge and using careless, inflammatory language.

Gun control advocates create similar problems. All too often, without any evidence or proof, they proclaim that gun control is the key to lowering criminal violence and guns' social costs. No proof exists to establish such a nexus, however, and gun safety in practice has improved enormously in the past twenty years without much regulation directed to that goal. Gun control advocates often brand their opponents with ad hominem nomenclature that does no service to the search for compromise. And when a criminal shoots many people, thereby violating numerous existing federal and state gun laws, the control advocates inexplicably blame the lack of federal gun control legislation. The gun control lobbyists also give no respect to gun owners' reasonable demands that society enforce and evaluate existing gun laws before deciding upon possible new ones.

The initial step toward breaking this lockstep trail of ideological opposites is the choice of a new battlefield. The phrase "gun control" is inherently so broad as to be meaningless. Control what? What kinds of guns? The total number of guns? The number of guns in criminal hands? The method of disposition of all guns? The safety of guns? Or other forms of control? Gun control can also mean, for some, making sure that most law-abiding people own and carry guns to deter and possibly retaliate against criminals and their guns.

Society must instead shift the debate to "crime gun regulation" and insist that legislators either prove that a particular crime gun regulation will lower violent crime (or at least the extent of injury from violent crime), or show that the regulation's resulting inconvenience, expense, and delay for law-abiding gun buyers and owners is an appropriate trade-off in government's search for answers to the volume of violent crime and the injury levels inflicted by gun crime.

Most existing regulations affect the law-abiding populace who want guns for self-protection or for enjoyment of some kind. As the Brady statistics show, 97.7 percent of retail buyers from federal firearms licensees wait for a government records check but bear no disqualifying conditions. We have little evidence as yet that denying a licensed retail source of guns to criminals prevents crime or deters gun acquisition elsewhere. Yet especially since September 11, 2001 and because of possible deadly consequences for all passengers, all air travelers willingly endure time-consuming, often intrusive searches at airport gates, even though 1.8 billion individual searches in 1999 produced only 1,552 weapons.[98]

Some gun regulation addresses safety issues, but safety remedies can make a firearm less immediately available for self-protection, requiring removal from locked storage or the unlocking of various kinds of gun locks and trigger guards. Some of the regulation does affect criminals' conduct. The Brady Law forces a criminal with sufficient funds for retail purchase of a gun to undergo the inconvenience of either finding a "straw purchaser"; stealing a gun; finding one among his family, friends, or acquaintances in "the street"; or just using another one from his existing stock. Yet we know that only about 60 to 70 percent of the approximately ten million guns sold annually are transferred through FFLs and that up to 5 percent of even the Brady Law records checks cannot be completed before the retail dealer is authorized to release a gun to a purchaser. Also, a Brady records check through state channels can be more thorough than an FBI one, because many state laws authorize their records to contain information about a noncriminal status, such as prior mental illness, that can disqualify a potential gun purchaser. But as of February 2000, about one-half of the states were not prepared to perform any portion of the Brady records checks, leaving that chore to federal hands where the information is less complete and the rejection rate is lower. Government investigation also finds that a large number of crime guns are traced back to unregulated gun show sales, and that more than 46 percent of the ATF investigations involving gun shows led to felons buying or selling firearms there.[99] But no one knows Brady's crime deterrence or even violent crime deterrence, or what percentage of crime guns pass to gun offenders through the four thousand annual gun shows, half of which occur in only ten states.

What kind of crime gun regulation should we want? One should start by reducing expectations that gun regulations, particularly the kinds that are politically and culturally realistic in our society, will greatly reduce crime. Recall that only a small percentage of total crime in America involves firearms and that only 1 percent of even violent crime victims suffered gunshot wounds. Further, 80 percent of aggravated assaults do not involve a firearm. We must narrow expectations by focusing on homicide reduction as the primary goal of crime gun regulation, followed by reductions in armed robberies and armed aggravated assaults (along with reductions in the extent of injury from armed robbery and serious assaults). We should also explore safety measures that can prevent gun deaths and gun injury, and use the law to keep guns from both violent hands and those of the mentally ill.

We can also justifiably focus on handguns used in crime. The regulation should have the least possible effect on the 65 million handguns owned solely for lawful purposes by about 16 percent of the adult population, so that these owners will support it. Public acceptance of such a regulation may well depend on convincing the American public and its politicians that a right to a firearm, undeniably a dangerous instrument, carries with it an enforceable responsibility to take care. The regulation should intend a severe constraint on the up to six million firearms, probably mostly handguns, that we estimate to be in the hands of criminals. ATF has shown that probably a small percentage of all licensed retail gun dealers are responsible for trafficking most crime guns sold through regulated retail sales; but an unregulated secondary market annually transfers up to 2.5 million guns to a variety of markets, including offenders. To be effective then, crime gun regulation and crime gun enforcement, or both, must penetrate this secondary market.

This brief outline focuses attention on a policy framework of four subjects: (1) handguns; (2) persons who convey handguns to criminals in great quantity; (3) handgun safety and tracing technology; and (4) the offenders who use handguns.

On the action level, we should first focus upon the best use of federal law and federal enforcement. The ATF inspection process for retail licensees should be intensified with more personnel and more computerized alert systems identifying for each retailer high levels of multiple handgun sales, handgun sales to females in a much higher proportion than the normal female-male ratio (in order to identify straw purchasers), a very low level of reported sales, ongoing tracking of any FFL connection to traced crime guns, and other indicia of improper dealership status or conduct. Resources should also be provided to make ATF crime gun tracing universally available to state and local police, and every manufacturer should be required to fire one round from every weapon so that a fired round and its shell casing, with their distinctive markings, can be submitted to ATF's computerized database. ATF has already established this goal, and Congress should provide the necessary legislation and resources to achieve it.[100] These federal laws and procedures would obviate the need for individual states to pass varying kinds of tracing-related regulations, which could create chaos for manufacturers and dealer-licensees. Indeed, every enforcement gap identified by ATF as affecting the battle against violent crime should be legislatively examined and then, when appropriate, cured by repealing existing laws that prevent full enforcement of regulatory goals and by providing the funding and new laws that permit their full enforcement. In December 2001, the U.S. attorney general claimed that the Brady Law prohibited him from checking any temporarily retained records to see if a suspected terrorist had recently bought a gun at retail.[101] In other words, a disputed interpretation of federal law was protecting terrorists. That absurd and perverse barrier should be explicitly removed by Congress.

The Justice Department budget also needs to be revised in order to fully fund the battle against gun crime, so that federal agents and prosecutors in each federal district, in cooperation with state and local officials, could make gun crimes, particularly those committed by illegal gun acquirers and suppliers, a priority. Long prison sentences should be the first option for any adult using guns in ongoing, sustained drug trafficking or gun trafficking and for any previously convicted felon who uses a gun while committing a violent crime—and all local prosecutors should emphasize weapons prosecutions in these situations. In addition, federal moneys should be available to fully fund the technology research geared to limiting a handgun's use to only its lawful possessor.

The Brady checks should be extended to all exchanges at gun shows, not just to those checks now required for FFL sales. Legislators could take this step even as research proceeds to identify the effects of Brady, if any, on violent crime, suicide by means of a gun, and harm caused by mentally ill persons using guns. Congress has balked at applying Brady's three-day maximum wait to a non-FFL, gun-show seller because a typical gun show ends after one or two days. But legislation requiring a Brady check for each gun show's sales could provide a maximum wait no longer than the show's duration and still capture most of the transactions. And if legislators balk at including rifles and shotguns, they should still proceed with Brady application to all handgun exchanges at gun shows. Greater enforcement of laws against the use of false identification when buying firearms at retail is also necessary.

At the state and local levels, private and public litigants have turned to the courts to claim damages caused by guns and to seek rulings that would require changes in manufacturing and marketing practices. By January 2002, more than thirty-two counties, municipalities, and states had filed negligence, product liability, and / or public nuisance lawsuits against gun makers and sellers; and in about one-half of the filings, the courts have rejected early motions to dismiss.[102] But several states bar city and county litigation against the gun industry. And although lawsuits may well bring reckless gun marketers under control, court action probably will not produce directly either timely or significant changes in the practices of large gun manufacturers, wholesalers, or retailers without some kind of breakthrough in existing concepts of liability. In fact, safety-related gun changes will probably have occurred prior to the completion of any litigation. As for gun acquisition by criminals, the existence of the government-mandated Brady check of each gun buyer may help protect defendant manufacturers from future nuisance liability suits. Most manufacturers', wholesalers', and even retailers' inability to control secondary market sales may also deter any widespread applicability of liability findings once safety-related changes have been made.

An extended federal "wish list" for increasing controls over the flow of crime guns is best reflected in the settlement papers of one of the civil litigation cases filed against firearms manufacturers by the federal government (and joined by some state, city, and county parties). There, Smith & Wesson acquiesced in early 2000 to many requested changes.[103] To meet the problem of serial number obliteration, which inhibits crime gun tracing, the settlement agreement provides that the serial number will be placed on the gun interior as well as the exterior. And within three years, if mandatory research on technology has produced such a capability, all new firearms designs will have to be "smart"—that is, allow actual gun use only by an electronically authorized user. Other crime-related measures bar the settling manufacturer from selling guns readily convertible to illegal fully automatic ones or from designing guns able to accept ammunition magazines exceeding ten rounds. These provisions, when combined with existing and proposed regulations of multiple handgun sales, sales to straw purchasers, and devices especially attractive to juvenile offenders, as well as wider Brady Law coverage, are all crime-related and do not deter gun possession by the law-abiding gun owner or customer. Although in the spring of 2001 Smith & Wesson was sold to an independent safety-lock manufacturer that may or may not be subject to the agreement, all of the changes in policy should be widely instituted without any need for litigation.

To achieve gun safety, the clearest route on the federal level is to extend the regulatory power of the Consumer Product Safety Commission (CPSC) to include guns. The anti–gun control lobby has thus far succeeded in preventing even congressional consideration of this step. But Congress should at least explore the idea of authorizing CPSC's reasonable regulation of handguns. Firearms, so potentially deadly to humans, certainly need at least as much safety regulation as that now given to toys and ladders. If Congress refuses to act, more and more states may well proceed individually and in so doing create differing standards.

Gun reform advocates also search for ways to reduce the numbers of deaths in mass killing incidents by limiting the firing capacity of automatic weapons. This seems reasonable but probably not effective. Most multiple-killing incidents are committed by offenders, many with mental illness, who possess a variety of guns, many of which were lawfully acquired. (Even in Hawaii, where the highest level of state gun regulation exists, an office employee killed seven of his coworkers in 1999. He possessed at least eighteen firearms, all of which had been duly registered with the police.)[104] The current federal legislation banning fully automatic guns and certain firepower levels of semiautomatic firearms must not be permitted to expire as is now provided through sunset provisions.

For gun regulation below the federal level, we prefer state regulation over local regulation simply because the local laws are easily evaded by traveling to the next town or city. In Hawaii, if you want a firearm, you go to the police station and submit to a fourteen-day waiting period that includes a background investigation plus disclosure of information for identifying and registering your desired firearms. No "shall issue" CCW law exists there for victim self-protection. And the high-volume tourist nature of the state would portend an unusually elevated rate of violence. In 1999 Hawaii's rate of serious crime, measured according to the FBI's eight-crime index covering violent and property crimes, was indeed high in comparison to other states'. But Hawaii's rate of violent crime, and its percentages of violent crimes committed with firearms, are among the lowest of all states.[105] With over 1.2 million residents, as well as a $10 billion annual tourist trade, the state of Hawaii had only thirty-five murders in 2000.[106]

Each state should examine Hawaii's regulations and adapt them as needed for use in its jurisdiction. Probably only handgun registration would be appropriate and acceptable in most states even though Hawaii covers long guns as well; again, most crime guns are handguns. Time-consuming police background checks of each gun buyer, apart from Brady checks, will also not be practical in most places. But some kind of gun registration, perhaps with an owner's card, appears to be the only sure way to begin control of the secondary market in crime guns. Registration would enable broadly enhanced tracing of crime guns, and the failure to register a handgun, or the possession of a gun registered to someone else, would be an easily provable crime. Also possible is a law requiring notice to a government registry about a handgun transfer, along with its serial number and identity of recipient. States that are predominantly rural do not need nearly the degree of regulation that could best serve primarily high-crime urban states. And even within some states, registration exemptions for rural residents and licensed rural dealers by population density of particular areas should be examined in an effort to find an exemption path that would not bring flocks of traffickers to rural areas. (Any undue handgun activity in such an exempted rural area should be easy to detect, and federal regulations would still apply.) Finally, any safety regulation should be monitored and documented with improved methodology to examine if a particular aspect of that regulation has in fact inhibited defensive uses of a weapon that likely would have prevented a death or serious injury during a crime. If the restriction has had a significant effect, the benefit-harm balance can be reassessed by the legislature. Objections to government intervention through handgun registration or transfer notice might be met by creating at the state level a quasi-public corporation that could acquire and distribute certain information only under strictly drafted legal guidelines and restrictions. The board of directors of such a corporation could include representatives of both pro-gun and anti-gun organizations. Unlike the registering and regulating of autos and their drivers, which is a privilege and not a right, crime gun regulation must ultimately survive Second Amendment scrutiny by our highest court. One route to upholding handgun registration, a simple act if allowed by mail or the internet, is convincing American politicians that the right to bear a deadly handgun carries a responsibility of making sure it does not end up in the hands of criminals. This type of regulation does not, and will not ever, represent a disarming of America.

As the polls demonstrate, each reform proposed here is backed by a sizeable majority of all Americans, including most Republicans and Democrats, as well as gun owners and non–gun owners. Everyone realizes that gun issues today are debated in a highly charged atmosphere of raw emotion, political wrangling, political contributions, and special-interest lobbying. The community and its crime response apparatus must force the participants in this debate to focus on the relationships among improving the effectiveness of various regulations and enforcement efforts against crime guns, continuing the availability of guns to law-abiding residents who want to acquire them, reducing the social costs of firearms violence and the volume of handgun-related crime, and maintaining the safety of children. Only when we address all these issues of crime gun regulation with objective analysis and rational action will we begin to make real progress toward more effective legislation and regulation.

7

Crime, Alcohol, and Illegal Drugs

In trying to confront crime and health problems caused by alcohol, tobacco, and drugs, American legislatures over time have enacted various laws ranging from criminalization to regulation to revenue-raising. The governmental efforts to eliminate or at least control these quests for pleasure engender intense reactions of approval and disapproval, ideology and rhetoric, culture and religion, and in some cases, racial and ethnic effects. But for the past seventy years, the basic response structure has endured intact. Using alcohol and tobacco for pleasure is legal; using drugs for pleasure is illegal. To justify this radical contrast, government asserts a need to control crime and public health problems by criminalizing drug sale and use, with no need to control such problems through a criminal ban on the adult sale and use of alcohol and tobacco. But when the government punishes Americans for engaging in conduct they want or feel a need to pursue, it needs to have a compelling reason or such action will eventually falter. The political failure of alcohol prohibition, for example, led to its repeal in 1933.

At the end of the twentieth century, survey estimates told us that slightly more than one-half of America's population over eleven years old was drinking alcohol, slightly more than 30 percent used tobacco, and 6 to 7 percent were using an illegal drug. With this background of contrasts in control and use of these substances, we must examine the drug-crime and alcohol-crime relationships, along with the consequences of criminalization, regulation, education, and treatment in controlling the usage and crime potential of these substances and of tobacco products.

David Musto recounts three eras of relatively severe alcohol consumption in our national history. The worst peaked during the 1830s with a rate of consumption more than twice that in each of the two subsequent peaks in 1910 and 1980.[1] In the 1830s, temperance movements, new medical knowledge, and state laws intervened. In the early portion of the twentieth century, temperance movements, medical developments, and eventually fourteen years of Prohibition moderated use until 1933. Decline in alcohol use from its third historical peak in 1980 occurred without a national temperance movement and without widespread serious criminalization other than an enforcement emphasis on drunk driving laws, the minimum age for alcohol purchase and use, and other laws prohibiting certain public behavior while under the influence of alcohol. The alcohol industry is taxed and regulated at the federal, state, and municipal levels of government, and mandated health warnings appear on their products and where their products are sold. Public and private agencies appear to have succeeded in lowering total alcohol consumption in the last twenty years through massive public education campaigns warning of the risks of driving and drinking, a rise in the minimum age for use of alcohol, the spread of public awareness about health and pregnancy risks, and private and public funding of alcohol treatment programs. Changes in social preferences for achieving joy also may have affected alcohol use. Nevertheless, usage remains quite high and many experts still regard alcohol as the nation's most dangerous and deadly substance.

Tobacco farmers enjoyed many years of federal subsidies and, although heavily taxed at both state and federal levels, the tobacco industry has received a persistent exemption from regulation by the Food and Drug Administration. The federal government did mandate that every pack of cigarettes contain warnings about certain health risks, and use of tobacco has declined significantly among the adult population over the past thirty years as publicized experiences of specific health and mortality risks, particularly lung disease and fetal harm, weighed on the public. The settlement of far-reaching litigation against the producing companies mandated the funding of more antismoking advertisements, specific limitations on marketing tactics, and more emphasis on devising and publicizing ways to prevent juveniles from taking up smoking and from having access to tobacco. Law enforcement contributed almost nothing to the dramatic change in the use of tobacco by Americans.

Drug use was quite acceptable in the United States in the nineteenth century. But during the late 1800s, high levels of opium use suddenly produced public alarm, even though morphine was still considered the medical hero of the Civil War. Cocaine was producing consumer joy through some very ordinary products on market shelves such as Coca-Cola, advertised as a soft drink to "ease the Tired Brain, and soothe the Rattled Nerves and Wasted Energy to both Mind and Body." In 1885, the Parke-Davis company advertised that cocaine "will free victims of the alcohol and opium habit from their bondage." Just prior to the twentieth century, one year before its introduction of aspirin, Bayer Pharmaceutical heralded heroin as the new "nonaddictive" drug to combat tuberculosis, coughs, and pneumonia. After 1906, Food and Drug Act labeling requirements for the first time informed consumers how many popular patent medicines contained one or more of morphine, opium, other opiates, alcohol, cannabis, and cocaine. By 1910, the State of New York had outlawed cocaine. In 1915, the federal Harrison Act required physicians to purchase tax stamps in order to prescribe medicines containing the drugs now viewed by the public as harmful. The executive branch then used the act to devise a regulatory scheme that evolved into a federal enforcement policy that effectively prevented physician-supported drug maintenance of addicts. In 1919, the U.S. Supreme Court upheld the Harrison Act as a proper exercise of Congress's power to tax even though the Court accepted the doctor-defendant's contention that the act's real mandate was termination of a physician's right to maintain addicts.[2] In the 1920s, marijuana came to city streets as "loco weed," and by 1930 New Orleans was the first city to outlaw its sale. The federal government followed with the Marijuana Tax Act of 1937. Franklin Roosevelt in 1940 cited narcotics sales as the "worst of all crimes except murder."

From 1930 to 1962, the federal cry to battle was led by Harry Anslinger, who as director of the Federal Bureau of Narcotics became the J. Edgar Hoover of drug enforcement. If few perceived a drug crisis during portions of this era, Anslinger could create one with sudden, alarming testimony before Congressional committees.[3] Just like cocaine in the 1930s, heroin in the 1950s then swept into many of the nation's inner cities, especially Harlem, in an epidemic nearly invisible to most Americans.[4] Nevertheless, the high degree of heroin abuse led to the federal Boggs Act of 1951, establishing the first mandatory sentencing laws applicable to drugs at the federal level.

The federal Controlled Substances Act of 1970 commenced the most intense, most enduring federal battle against drugs, which has now become a permanent war. By June 1970, the *New York Times* was citing narcotics as the leading killer of persons ages fifteen to thirty-five years in that city.[5] Heroin was devastating many cities, cocaine was deemed just a probably nonaddictive stimulant, and marijuana reigned as a symbol of youthful revolt to some and decay to others. But by the 1980s, heroin had been almost forgotten, powder cocaine had become king in the young-adult portions of the middle and upper classes, and crack, a much less expensive and smokable derivative of cocaine, had become a health and homicide threat in primarily black inner-city areas.

In 1986, Congress added a comprehensive schema of mandatory minimum prison sentences to the drug laws and strengthened their reach in 1988. These sentencing provisions increased the incarceration length for drug offenders in accordance with stated increases in the weight, not of the drug itself, but of the mixture or substance containing the drug; these prescribed weights, in variations statutorily prescribed for each drug, became the benchmark for all the federal drug sentencing guidelines established and currently maintained by the U.S. Sentencing Commission.[6] Congress wanted ten years of mandated confinement for drug traffic leaders and a five-year benchmark for serious traffickers at the retail level, with double those levels for repeat drug offenders. By then, most states had enacted their own drug laws imposing mandatory minimum sentences for some drug offenders.

After 1970, presidents kept reinventing the fight against drugs primarily with special study groups, ever-changing White House drug abuse offices, and changes in the federal drug enforcement agency—from the Federal Bureau of Narcotics to the Bureau of Drug Abuse Control, to the Bureau of Narcotics, to the Bureau of Narcotics and Dangerous Drugs, to the Drug Enforcement Agency (DEA), to competing efforts of DEA and the FBI, and then to placement of these competitive drug efforts within the Justice Department, while retaining each as separate agencies.[7]

In 1988, a federal act establishing the impossible, soon-discarded national goal of a drug-free America by 1995 also gave birth to the White House Office of National Drug Control Policy (ONDCP). The office and its director, media-labeled as the drug czar, establish a national strategy against drug use; set goals, objectives and targets; prepare a consolidated federal drug control budget, including a certification of the budget of each participating agency; and measure the effectiveness of anti-drug efforts. Fifty-two federal agencies participate in these efforts, ranging from drug prevention to treatment to education to law enforcement to prisons to foreign drug crop controls to drug interdiction at the U.S. border. The drug czar proclaimed that a war on drugs is misleading because wars end, but the fight against drugs, like the fight against cancer, must endure.[8]

The laws that created and reauthorized ONDCP assigned to the term "drug" the same meaning given the term "controlled substance" in a federal drug act of 1970.[9] That act places each drug in one of five separate schedules, in effect a ranking in descending order of a substance's assessed potential for abuse, potential for creating dependence, and acceptance for safe medical use. With some dosage and other exceptions, basically heroin, marijuana, GHB, and ecstasy are in the most dangerous category, Schedule I. Opium, cocaine, and some methamphetamines are Schedule II drugs, and basic amphetamines are Schedule III.[10] In defining the term "controlled substance," Congress specifically excluded distilled spirits, wine, malt beverages, and tobacco.[11] As a result, except for underage use, the extensive federal battle against substance abuse affords relatively low priority to alcohol and tobacco use. Legislators addressing crime control specifically omit alcohol and tobacco in lists of substances having a high potential for abuse and a high potential for inducing dependence with no safe utility in medical treatment, even though they indeed have exactly those characteristics. Drugs, alcohol, and tobacco have all proved deadly in one way or another. But the only common criminal provisions are those at state and federal levels banning their sale to juveniles.

For many reasons, except during the early 1960s and the early 1970s, law enforcement in the past forty years has constituted the focal point and by far the most costly portion of antidrug efforts. As a society, we should be—but are not—continually reexamining that approach. Law enforcement is a crime-control device. But we rarely examine the reality of what portion of crimes against victims are truly caused by drug use, other than the offenses that drug criminalization itself creates through illegal drug markets and their reasonably foreseeable violence. Nor do we debate the use, forms, and outcomes of the criminal sanction itself. And when we broaden the scope further to include the harm that drug use causes to the user, other individuals around him or her, and society in general, we fail to jointly compare the harm caused by drugs, alcohol, and tobacco and devise alternative and even conjoining remedies that society could adopt for the harms caused by each.

For drugs, use of the crime response complex is indeed increasing. Unlike even Prohibition days, where possession and use of alcohol was not criminalized, we increasingly punish the possession and use of drugs. Despite the enormous increase in police manpower during the 1990s, the total number of estimated arrests in 2000 for any crime at the state and local levels had returned to the 1991 figure, but the percentage of total arrests attributed to drug abuse violations rose 50 percent, to over 11 percent of all arrests.[12] Even the arrests of juveniles for drug abuse violations soared by 145 percent during those 10 years.[13] By 2000, the percentage of all drug abuse arrests attributable to possession had risen to 81 percent, meaning that only 19 percent of all drug arrests were directed against someone who was selling or manufacturing drugs.[14]

From 1989 to 2000 America also vastly increased its use of prisons for those possessing or selling drugs. The total number of adults in the custody of state and federal prisons doubled during that period, to about 1.4 million prisoners, and the percentage of those who were drug law offenders rose to 61 percent of all federal inmates and 21 percent at the state level.[15] Mandatory sentencing produced a portion of that increase and generally, the higher the weight of an offender's substance containing illegal drugs, the higher the length of the prison stay.

Crime control involving alcohol abuse rests more upon the traditional harm-based rationale. Alcohol-related criminal laws punish conduct that threatens other citizens, such as sale to juveniles, physical injury, creation of fear, and neighborhood decline. The resultant crimes include driving under the influence, disobeying regulatory liquor laws, public drunkenness, vagrancy, and disorderly conduct. This focus gives priority to arrest followed by a relatively small penalty. As a result, although law enforcement efforts against violators of alcohol-related crimes accounted for about 24 percent of all arrests for state and local crimes in 1999, most of these offenses either do not authorize a prison sentence or, in the case of driving under the influence, do not result in a high percentage of prison sentences.[16] For example, in 1997 an estimated 513,200 offenders were under correctional supervision for driving while intoxicated (DWI), but about 88 percent were on probation, with just 41,100 in jail and 17,600 in state prison.[17]

Drugs, not alcohol, have driven up our imprisonment rates. Arrests for driving under the influence (DUI) of primarily alcohol (partially narcotics as well) declined 20 percent from 1991 through 2000, but remained level for the last five years of that time. During the ten-year period, arrests for drunkenness declined by 27 percent, disorderly conduct by 12 percent, and vagrancy by 29 percent. Only liquor law violation arrests—that is, all direct liquor violations other than drunkenness and DUI—increased, by 13 percent.[18] Law enforcement's battle against drugs has escalated to a dominant position in the crime response complex in comparison to the uncoordinated, much less expensive law enforcement effort against alcohol-related harm. The most focused use of alcohol-related law enforcement—DUI patrols, publicized arrest numbers, and prosecutions—have helped reduce the percentage of alcohol-related crashes in motor vehicle fatalities from 57 percent in 1982 to 38 percent in 1998, even though the rate of arrest for DUI per 100,000 licensed drivers declined substantially. Since 1986, the number of DWI offenders under some kind of correctional supervision per one thousand arrests rose from 151 to 347, but the sentencing priority rests with the probation systems of the nation's states and counties.[19]

How well have the contrasting control methods worked in reducing drug, alcohol, and tobacco use since 1980? One has to pursue such a search with skepticism. Surveys about usage necessarily build their conclusions upon samples. But if one is surveying conduct labeled by society as illegal, such as use of drugs, one can expect some hesitation in admitting to this conduct, while readily admitting legal conduct involving alcohol and tobacco. As a result, an incorrect negative reply about history of use or current use is projected out perhaps to hundreds of thousands of people—more so when the percentage of people who participate in the conduct under study is low compared to the total population. Further, if one is attempting to measure hardcore use, a household survey probably undercounts through its failure to reach "street people." The effort to make a survey more representative of each segment of the population adds to this problem. For example, according to the General Accounting Office, one survey's population weighting formula in 1991 projected the heroin use of one seventy-nine-year-old white woman as representing one-fifth of all estimated heroin users in America.[20] This alertness about possible inaccuracy leads many policymakers and researchers to regard survey results of controversial conduct such as drug use more as evidence of trends over time, rather than actual proof of conduct by a certain number of Americans.[21]

In the surveys of alcohol use between 1980 and 1997, annual per capita consumption in gallons dropped somewhat for beer and wine and lowered by one-third for distilled spirits.[22] For tobacco, among those eighteen years old and older, the percentage of persons who currently smoke dropped by one-fifth between 1985 and 1998.[23] For drugs, between 1979 and 1999, the percentage of total population twelve years old and older who had used any illicit drug within the month prior to the surveys dropped from 14 percent in 1979 to below 6 percent in 1992, but increased to 6.3 percent by 2000.[24] These trend figures for the 1990s show that increased drug enforcement does not appear to correlate with any significant lessening of drug use. In fact, overall usage of tobacco, alcohol, and illicit drugs have all remained relatively stable since 1995.[25]

Most disturbing, however, are the high percentage increases in the number of new users of each drug and tobacco, when comparing 1990 to 1998.[26] During the 1990s, three separate indicia—medical emergency room incidence, drug use among arrestees, and user death rates—show that the hardcore cocaine-user population was aging as a percentage of total hardcore cocaine use.[27] This should afford us some optimism that younger cocaine users are now more able to cease their use early on. Other data also demonstrate that, although marijuana users as a percentage of the relevant population remained constant from 1993 to 1998, the adolescent user percentage was increasing but the adult measure was declining.[28] This represents a possible trend showing that the aging process is most relevant to discontinued marijuana use. Yet in one survey inquiring about student use of an illicit drug in the past thirty days, the number of twelfth-grade students reporting such use had increased over 50 percent from 1991 through 2000. And the percentages of increased use were even higher for tenth and eight graders, up 94 percent and 109 percent respectively.[29]

Other analyses can also demonstrate differences by age groups over time in current use of particular drugs, changes in total numbers of first-time use, and average age variations in first-time use. These results can assist evaluations, for example, of drug education programs in schools. Surveys by age groups can also demonstrate the introduction and popularity, and dangers, of new drugs. Such surveys, for example, identified the increased use of the synthetic "rave" drug ecstasy between 1996 and 2000.[30] So-called pulse checks, whereby interviewers talk to epidemiologists, ethnographers, law enforcement personnel, and treatment providers in cities around the nation, also help identify new drug use trends.[31] These surveys can help law enforcement define their priorities.

How do the numbers of drug-induced and alcohol-induced deaths compare? In age-adjusted rates per 100,000 population, drug-induced deaths soared from 3.0 in 1980 to 6.3 in 1998 (and higher in 1999), moving up to the alcohol-caused death rate—which had dropped from 8.4 in 1980 to 6.3 in 1997.[32] The recent prevention and treatment efforts against alcohol-related deaths appear to be more effective than the law enforcement dominance of the battle against drugs. But America in 1999 had substantially more people dependent on alcohol (an estimated 8.2 million) when compared to those who are dependent on illicit drugs (an estimated 3.6 million).[33]

Certainly if a society is pretending to mount a truly comprehensive national effort against drugs, a ready and willing individual should expect to receive drug treatment when it is needed. But we all know that has not happened in America. Potential treatment dollars are awarded instead to the supply-side effort against drugs. Leaders in the drug war remain skeptical about demand-side spending because drug abusers and drug dependents believe that they do not need treatment. The ONDCP tells us that fewer than 20 percent of drug abusers and dependents received treatment in 2000.[34] One must consider as well that, based on a national sampling of short-stay hospitals, the number of emergency room episodes related to drug abuse rose over 60 percent, to a total of 602,000 from 1990 to 2000.[35]

Mark Kleiman reported in 1992 that of the 17.7 million Americans who are estimated to have a "drinking problem," only about 1 percent pass through residential treatment each year, with another 7 percent undergoing outpatient therapy. Another 800,000 "alcoholics" in treatment were frequently attending Alcoholics Anonymous (AA) meetings, with unknown numbers of other persons using irregular AA visits to bolster prior intense participation.[36]

In sum, 52 percent of Americans over eleven years old use alcohol, about 30 percent smoke, and under 7 percent use illicit drugs. But the percentage of drug users characterized with dependence or abuse is much higher than those so characterized by alcohol use, and the death rate from illicit drugs is increasing while the alcohol death rate is declining. Despite the massive infusion of law enforcement and prison resources into the drug war in the last seven years of the 1990s, the population's drug usage percentage since 1992 has remained about the same. Usage percentages for alcohol and cigarettes fell or remained level during the 1990s without a massive law enforcement and prison approach. But for those who are dependent on alcohol or drugs, or both, we know that treatment availability is woefully deficient in meeting the possible demand.

Crime, Drug Use, and Drug Criminalization

In society's determination of what to do about the drug problem, the crime question must address whether drugs cause crime apart from the crimes of illicit drug sales and possession and apart from the thefts, assaults, and murders that occur only in an illicit drug market. Oddly enough, given our decades-long war on drugs, research endeavoring to draw a causal connection between violent crime, particularly murder, and drug acquisition and consumption is relatively recent. Paul Goldstein and his fellow researchers noted the lack of major national data collection efforts and concluded that, although local studies offer a strong association between drugs and crime, the researchers cannot explain the degree of that association or the causal direction. Different definitions, guiding theories, and use of indicators also inhibit proper comparisons over time or between locations and regions.[37]

The national drug control strategy report for 1997 noted that the increase in persons convicted federally for crimes involving the sale or possession of an illicit drug is responsible for nearly three-quarters of the total growth in federal prison inmates since 1980.[38] The 1998 report proclaimed that state prison inmates convicted of drug sales or possession increased by 478 percent between 1985 and 1995.[39] Of course, this says nothing about drugs and violent crime apart from the fact that society has chosen to criminalize drug sale and use and thereby to create these illegal drug markets.

One should first note that the dramatic drop in violent crime from 1993 to 2000 was not accompanied by a drop in overall illicit drug use or in marijuana, heroin, or cocaine use during that period. Indeed, during the precipitous decrease in illicit current drug use from 1985 to 1990, the rate of reported serious crime was rising in the United States, with violent crime rates increasing more than those of property crime.[40] Although one may be tempted to conclude an inverse ratio between the level of current drug use and the level of serious crime, that conclusion is premature without first exploring what research can teach us about drugs and crime.

For example, the crack markets and their violence in the nation's inner cities peaked during those five years. The FBI noted that drug-related murders reached just over 1,400 by 1989 and then descended to 669 by 2000.[41] Alfred Blumstein's analysis shows that the increased national murder rate from 1985 through 1993 was attributable largely to young, urban offenders, particularly black juveniles, youths belonging to gangs, and armed youths serving in the crack market.[42] Goldstein and his fellow researchers explored in detail the murders in New York City in 1988 and classified three different kinds of drug-related murders: psychopharmacological (related to drug effects on either victim or offender); driven by economic compulsion (related to addict crime); and systemic (related to the illicit drug market). Within these three models, only 7.5 percent of the total sample of homicides involved a psychopharmacological cause, with most of these involving alcohol only. In only about 2 percent of the total were economic considerations the motivation of the drug-affected offender, all relating to crack use. And nearly 75 percent of all the drug-related homicides (about 39 percent of all the homicides studied) had connections only to the illicit drug market itself, two of every three of these being crack related. The researchers concluded that in 1988 in New York City, just over half of the homicides in their sample were drug related in one or more of several ways, a majority of those involving crack or cocaine. The drug-related percentage is conservatively stated, because whenever doubt existed as to whether or not an illicit drug was an important and causal factor in the homicide, Goldstein and his colleagues classified it as non–drug related.[43]

This study shows only what happened in one large city in one region in one year. But the research analyses investigating drugs and crime demonstrate how crucial it is to use appropriate subcategories when exploring what portions of drug-related homicidal activity, and indeed of drug-related violent and property crime, resulted from the illicit drug marketing system itself, what percentage of the victims were truly strangers to that system, and what portions of that criminality resulted from the addicts' need for money to buy drugs (a partial effect of the illicit drug market) or from the effects of each particular drug on the mind, body, and actions of the drug-based offender. The lack of national event-specific data hampers any firm conclusions about drugs and crime, apart from the devastating effects that intra-drug market location and disputes appear to have on some neighborhoods in some cities. Franklin Zimring and Gordon Hawkins note that even the police estimates of killings related to drugs are low, ranging just below 10 percent with an occasional peak just over 50 percent in New York City and Washington, D.C. The authors also note the lack of killings in many other urban drug markets in the United States and in many cities around the world.[44] Research must now compare the nature of the drug markets themselves, the marketing participants, the users, the particular drugs, and the overall traditions of violence and gun use in the different drug markets of many cities.

Jan Chaiken and Marcia Chaiken report that one cannot discern a "simple general relation between high rates of drug use and high rates of crime."[45] The authors define predatory crimes as those committed for material gain, such as robbery and theft, with some being violent and others not. And not all violence is classified as predatory crime—for example, a violent domestic dispute is not. Research has yet to support a conclusion that drug use generally precedes the beginning of a criminal career or that drug usage causes predatory criminal activity. In fact, state the Chaikens, 50 percent of delinquent youth gained offender status prior to their drug use and the other half commenced their drug use and delinquent conduct at about the same time or became delinquent thereafter. Preventing persistent use of drugs other than heroin, and also cocaine in some environments, is probably unrelated to reducing persistent predatory criminal activity.[46] Of course, many long-time drug users and many long-time career criminals issue from the same environment, primarily inner-city neighborhoods with such problems as child abuse, lack of parental supervision, poor schooling and drop-out status, lack of employment status, and no marital partner. But often career criminals are not involved in drug use. The Chaikens do conclude from their research, however, that among those persistent predatory offenders who are also high-frequency drug users, the offense rate is very high and they commit many different types of offenses, including violent crimes, as well as use many different drugs.[47] Drug selling has a stronger relationship to predatory crime, but little is known nationally how much of the predatory crime committed by sellers is a product of their drug market environment and disputes.

The federal Bureau of Justice Statistics reports that in 1997 33 percent of state prisoners and 22 percent of federal prisoners were using drugs at the time of their crime. And over one-half of state prisoners were users within the month preceding their crimes.[48] But the Chaikens note that persistent drug-using offenders are subject to arrest at much higher rates than persistent offenders who use no drugs or use drugs occasionally. As a result, one must avoid making drugs-and-crime conclusions based on surveys that capture only the self-reports or testing of these arrested offenders. The Chaikens conclude that criminal justice programs focused on high-rate predatory offenders should include among the selection criteria those who persistently and frequently use multiple types of illicit drugs.[49] Even a reduction in a persistent user's dosages of drugs, particularly heroin, and frequency of use appears to lower their predatory criminal activity.

Many researchers caution against an overemphasis on the tristructured Goldstein homicide model. They note how tentative any drug-crime model can become unless it incorporates variations caused by the particu-

lar era, the specific drug, the specific neighborhood, the age-range participation, the nature of the drug distribution process (for example, open-
market street operation versus indoor markets), and the history and practice of cultural violence in a particular neighborhood.

Ethnography can help us understand this interaction of so many factors,
for example, in inner-city black neighborhoods. Elijah Anderson's *Code of
the Street* presents a compelling and detailed picture of a North Philadelphia black community.[50] But William Bennett, John DiIulio, and John
Walters, in their book *Body Count,* contend that inner-city blacks do not
commit crime because of poverty, desperation, lack of jobs, and the accompanying lack of a stable family environment and good schools. These
authors maintain that black youth merely make a rational choice to commit crime because its rewards vastly exceed its penalties. They find that society's only answers are either to punish them with imprisonment, have
them develop and then adhere to a moral code, or both.[51] They state their
book's simple creed: "As we have argued throughout . . . , moral and not
economic poverty is the real 'root cause' of the nation's drug and crime
problem."[52] The authors then decide that morality is almost impossible to
develop in the black inner city, so a principal remedy is interracial adoption plus incarceration of 150,000 juvenile superpredators in the years following 1996. Their argument proceeds on the fundamental belief, shared
by many, that so many children in the inner city are bad because they have
no parents who function by a moral code. Another principal remedy,
therefore, is religion. These expressed views are important because the authors are the former head of a White House office on faith-based programs
and a present and former national drug czar.

But these authors also apparently assume, curiously without analyzing
or dealing with the parenthood problems, that the assumed moral chaos of
the parents' lives has nothing to do with economic poverty. In recommending instead that the principal remedies are to find God and interracial, surrogate parents for these children, the authors do not allow for other
possibilities. They deny the possibility that if the parents had jobs, the
neighborhood had government services, the education system was func-
tioning correctly, and a reasonably-priced, job-producing retail market of
goods and services were available, family love and stability would exist to a
much greater degree. The authors fail to even entertain the notion that if a
child can participate in positive group activities offering one or more role
models, whether faith-based or not and whether parental or not, these

positive attachments between children and adults can offer a building block for a child's faith in a future and a belief that the larger society will accept them—in other words, faith that they will be able to extract themselves from their violent, dirty, unserved ghetto. These authors also do not even allude to any idea that moral, religious families in fact do live in the ghettos. And they voice no message that the concept of morality must include social justice, not just individual moral character.

In contrast to this position, Elijah Anderson became immersed in the inner-city culture and found a hardy presence of strong, loving, "decent" (a term common in the inner city), and "moral" families interspersed among the unemployed, runaway fathers and those welfare mothers desperately raising children in a totally disintegrated single-parent environment. But he also describes the overpowering street culture with which every young male resident has to contend from the moment he walks that street alone, a culture and code in which violence and aggressive conduct predominate and indeed precede the young man's possible drug use. This culture and code has its own stringent set of rules that often prevail over the "decent" neighbor's or parent's moral code.

When one grows up having no access to the dominant society and no faith in any government institution, especially the police and the courts, the resulting alienation is profound, in some cases unshakable, and in too many cases a source of firm belief in no positive future but rather a very possible imminent death or certainly an eventual short life. Surround that alienation with alcohol, drugs, and physical abuse and with the sense of being alone, young, and without potential, add the lack of education and training as well as spotty job availability and the nagging persistence of racial discrimination, and we have what Anderson calls the challenging persistence of an oppositional ghetto culture.

For many of those youth, the drug trade seemingly will supply money, power, and group togetherness. But in fact disputes are constant, violence settles many kinds of issues, just as it does for other activities in the streets, and too often, the drug trade itself reinforces the sense that life may end abruptly and violently. Just imagine young persons establishing an ongoing mental norm dominated by the thought that at any age, on any given day, at any minute, fate may well bring them instant death.

In further analyzing the drug and crime problem, researchers have available the statistics from what is now labeled the Arrestee Drug Abuse Monitoring Program (ADAM), run by the federal government's National Institute of Justice with its private research contractor. The ADAM program conducts voluntary interviews of persons arrested and booked in over thirty-five cities and counties and also employs urinalysis drug testing from consenting arrestees. Given anonymity, over four-fifths of arrestees agree to participate. The ADAM testing is able to detect ten separate drugs. The drug detection period varies, ranging from use within two to three days before the test for cocaine and opiates and, for marijuana, up to ten days for infrequent users and up to thirty days for chronic users. Definitive conclusions are difficult. For example, some forms of opiates, such as morphine and codeine, appear in medicines and thus a positive screening for these drugs does not prove illicit use. And the presence of drugs after arrest does not necessarily indicate what the arrestee's condition or motivation was at the earlier time of the offense.[53]

For now, then, one can only note the extraordinarily high percentage of adult and juvenile booked arrestees, male and female, who used one or more drugs shortly prior to their arrest. Overall at thirty-five sites in 1998, between 50 and 75 percent of the tested arrestees had drugs in their system when arrested. And at twenty-two of those sites, between 20 to 30 percent of the tests demonstrated presence of more than one drug. The median rate for presence of cocaine in participating arrestees at all sites was 36 percent; and at eleven of the thirty-five sites, cocaine was the drug most commonly found in the tests. But national data do not reveal the significant regional and even intraregional variations in drug use. For example, 8 percent of San Jose arrestees tested positive for cocaine, while Miami arrestees were 47 percent positive. And methamphetamines appeared only sporadically in states outside the nation's western and southwestern region.

Age differences were also important for each drug. Marijuana showed a use concentration among the fifteen- to twenty-year-old group of arrestees, but most sites still had an overall marijuana use rate close to one-third of all arrestees. The marijuana domination prevailed among juvenile arrestees as well, offset by a very low rate of opiate use and with cocaine use rates significantly lower (2 to 15 percent of the juveniles) than the rate for adult arrestees. Opiate use existed disproportionately among older offenders, that is, those over age thirty.[54] ADAM's preliminary findings for 2000 revealed that between one-quarter and one-half of both drug and alcohol users at the sites needed treatment for high risks of, or actual, substance abuse or dependence.[55]

Ignoring all of the qualifiers discussed here as cautions against making general conclusions about drugs and crime from surveys and tests of arrested and imprisoned populations, the ONDCP Drug Strategy Report for the year 2000 instead threw caution to the winds: "A large percentage of the twelve million property crimes committed each year in America is drug related, as is a significant proportion of nearly two million violent crimes."[56]

But even this undocumented, indeed unprovable, conclusion shows the lack of precise data: a "large percentage," a "significant proportion," and "drug related" are all subjective terms. The ONDCP also fails to analyze how many of these crimes are "related" to society's establishment of drugs as illicit. In addition, we must learn more about drugs and specific crimes involving strangers versus crimes involving people who know each other. In particular, we need to know more about drugs and aggravated assault, inasmuch as that crime alone accounts for about 60 percent of all reported serious violent offenses. More important, in analyzing where drug response resources should be allocated, as Jan and Marcia Chaiken and Elijah Anderson and Mark Kleiman have taught us, the drug trade and the drug-crime nexus have to be viewed in the specific context of their occurrence. In the black neighborhoods of the inner city, even if drugs were removed, the gangs, the underlying conditions, and the oppositional culture would remain. Surely life would be better for some, and the illicit drug market violence and other crimes would not have a reason to exist. But violence and other crimes existed in the poverty-driven inner-city communities of various immigrant waves and in deprived, broken-family black communities before the widespread illicit drug trade, and presumably would still exist to some extent if the drug trade disappeared.

Even though a high percentage of offenders had used drugs recently, that does not mean that a high percentage of drug users commit crime. In fact, one national household survey in 1998 showed that a maximum of 77 percent of America's drug users—more than eight million—were employed full or part-time and a high percentage were only marijuana users.[57] No one claims that a high percentage of such users engage in widespread or persistent criminal activity. The National Drug Control Strategy report for 1998 pointed out that "sixty-one million Americans who once used illegal drugs have now rejected them."[58] No research has established that a significant percentage of that drug rejection by former users was related to law enforcement's crusade against drugs. One could probably speculate with accuracy that a high percentage of the middle-class and upper-class cocaine users in the 1980s just "moved on" without ever having committed a crime apart from drug use, because the fad was over and many started families and new jobs. And even in New York City's ghettos, those who substituted marijuana for crack use in the 1990s did so primarily because the crack generation had created intensely negative role models for the succeeding generation.

Drug users abandon their custom for many reasons, but researchers have not adequately analyzed these reasons. Yet when such a large percentage of drug users are not engaged in violent crime or acquisitive property crimes, drugs in themselves obviously do not "cause" crime. The story of drugs and crime can be told only by analyzing *for each drug*, for multiple drug use, and for drug-alcohol use the different cultures, subcultures, and locations, as well as the different age groups, in which drug use and drug selling occur. Then one must consider further that most offenders in prison for serious crimes were jobless or lacked a steady job, lacked a high-school degree, were unmarried at the time of their latest offense, and are disproportionately of minority backgrounds. To this, one should then add specific local and individualized issues such as the degree and influence of gangs, an individual's aggressive acts and behavior prior to drug use, child abuse, parental and peer factors, varying neighborhood influences, and regional differences in drug availability, price, and markets.

In considering the issues of drug and crime, policymakers also must recognize that their labeling as criminal all nonmedical drug sales and use created the competitive illicit market that actually increases crime. Juvenile and youth gangs thrive in an illegal drug environment, and violence results. Public health problems increase as users contract the AIDS virus from impure needles and contract other illnesses induced by undisclosed drug adulteration and consumer ignorance about a drug's strength and purity level.[59] And those devising a crime response must recognize and analyze the social animosity and injustice caused by disparate law enforcement treatment of certain racial and economic classes. Instead, policymakers today react to their frustration about persistent drug usage and the failures of drug prevention and treatment programs with recommendations to build much more prison space or find some new, untried way to intensively supervise drug offenders.

Finally, although the ONDCP Drug Strategy Report for 2000 boldly stated that a high percentage of violent and property crimes is drug-related, subsequent documents from the same office qualify this statement.

ONDCP's Performance Measures admitted in 2000 that "current Federal data systems cannot provide the foundation for tracking drug involvement" in the violent crimes of rape, robbery, and assault.[60] Earlier, in April 1997, ONDCP issued a paper stating that "the drug / crime relationship should be interpreted cautiously," noting that many different factors induce an offender's crimes, that the term "drug-related" has different definitions in different studies, and that self-reports may be subjectively influenced. The office did conclude, however, that drug users are more likely than nonusers to commit crimes (a questionable assertion given its universal nature), that many arrestees and inmates were under drug influences at the time of their most recent offense, and that drug trafficking itself generates violent crime.[61]

In looking at available data and research, no set of clear drug-and-crime facts or cause-effect findings emerge to even suggest that law enforcement should be the prime emphasis of the drug war. In fact, the high percentage of even hardcore addicts and prison-bound addicts and abusers for whom no treatment programs are available appears to demand a more balanced use of resources against drugs. Treatment for this hardcore group does not have to cure permanently in order to reduce crime; even temporary crime abstinence would help. As ONDCP has concluded, one million "offenders under criminal justice supervision need, and are not getting, drug treatment," and "with treatment, during and after incarceration, . . . (the high) level of recidivism can be sharply reduced."[62]

Alcohol, Crime, and Law Enforcement

Alcohol is an imposing presence in our society. Bridget Grant found that about one in four children under eighteen years of age in America had been exposed to alcohol-related abuse or alcohol dependence within the family.[63] A 1998 analysis shows that just over 60 percent of people ages eighteen through thirty-four are users of alcohol, even though annual overall per capita consumption of alcoholic beverages dropped about 10 percent between 1990 and 1995.[64] In a somewhat different conclusion, Thomas Greenfield, Lorraine Medanik, and John Rogers found that current drinking, weekly drinking, and weekly heavy drinking all declined from 1984 through 1989 but then remained steady in the first half of the 1990s.[65] A federal survey of all the nation's known alcohol treatment facilities in 1995 found about 800,000 abusers of alcohol receiving treatment services, a figure regarded as a substantial understatement of the total abuser population.[66]

Most of the 105 million Americans who consume alcohol do not commit violent crimes. In contrast to the drug market, alcohol is widely available as a legal product and neither its sellers nor its buyers have to become criminals to market and consume this product. But even with specific findings of widespread use and abuse of alcohol, researchers have found no general basis to conclude that either use of alcohol or intoxication caused by alcohol constitutes an overall risk of crime or represents a general risk of violence.[67] As with drug use, we do have figures about alcohol use by those who do commit crimes. In the national victimization surveys about violent crime committed from 1992 to 1995, including simple assault, 70 percent of the victims reported that they could perceive whether or not the offender was using drugs or alcohol at the time of the crime. Of those respondents, 56 percent reported no offender use of drugs or alcohol, 28 percent reported offender alcohol use, and another 9 percent detected either drugs or alcohol. When a victim of violence was able to describe possible alcohol or drug use by the attacker, 67 percent of those in an intimate relationship reported such use, but only 31 percent of those who were strangers to each other did so.[68] Alcohol use by the criminal, according to the national victimization surveys of those ages twelve and older, occurred on average in 183,000 rapes, 197,000 robberies, 661,000 aggravated assaults, and 1.7 million simple assaults each year for the 1992–1995 period studied. For each of these crimes, except robbery, many more victims perceived their attackers to be using alcohol than using drugs.[69] For reasons not explained or analyzed by researchers generally, surveyed victims indicated a percentage of violent offenders using illicit drugs that was more than four times lower than that compiled in the ADAM surveys and testing. In contrast, self-reports by offenders under correctional supervision and victim perceptions of their criminal attackers are quite similar in establishing that close to 40 percent of violent crimes were accompanied by an offender's alcohol use.[70]

Even though state and local law enforcement efforts have conjoined with public education programs to lower the percentage of alcohol-related highway deaths, those deaths annually are still equal to the number of murders nationwide and exceed by a factor of ten the number of drug-related murders. And since two-thirds of murders are committed with firearms, alcohol-related traffic deaths clearly exceed gun-related murders.

Finally, although death rates from drug-induced causes rose and those from alcohol-induced causes fell between 1980 and 1998, the alcohol death rate was identical to the drug rate. How curious it is, then, that the national legislative and executive branches, when addressing the crime problem, focus almost entirely upon fighting drugs and guns, when alcohol in fact kills more people just on the highways. Mandatory minimum imprisonments meted out for drug possession and sale and for violent offenses committed with guns contrast dramatically with the light "punishment" for driving under the influence of alcohol (DUI). Legislators should confront this contrast and determine not only why they tolerate the life-endangering reality of drunk driving, but also why their policy to deemphasize incarceration (by substituting correctional supervision in the community for prison) seemed to contribute to or at least not prevent a decline of alcohol-related traffic deaths from 22,000 in 1990 to about 17,000 in 1996, even as the number of licensed drivers increased and the rate of arrest for DUI declined 24 percent.[71]

Researchers have strived to define a more exact relationship between alcohol and aggression. Measuring various influences, studied both separately and in conjunction, they have tried to gauge genetic factors, brain functions and brain chemicals, family environmental factors, temperament, personality, and social environmental factors to determine what contribution, if any, use of alcohol or intoxication makes to increased violence.[72] Two tentative conclusions are appropriate. Alcohol consumption and intoxication do increase the tendency of some individuals in some circumstances to exhibit more aggressive behavior and, in some cases, to commit violent acts. In addition, a general decrease in the availability of alcohol appears to be significantly related to a reduction in violent criminal acts. Many different kinds of actions can decrease alcohol availability, for example, much higher taxes on beer and spirits, strict zoning requirements limiting the density of alcohol-purveying retail outlets and bars, family surveillance, and trained bartenders who regularly and diplomatically "cut off" those customers exhibiting signs of intoxication.[73] Many Chicago neighborhoods have exercised their precinct's referendum option to ban all liquor sales in any bars, restaurants, and retail stores.[74] David Boyum and Mark Kleiman suggest alcohol prohibition limited to those previously convicted of alcohol-related offenses, enforced by special markings on driver's licenses (or other required ID) and by requiring sellers to view identification from all alcohol buyers.[75] Daniel Yalisove, noting the one-problem focus of many programs, cites the need for alcohol treatment programs to also investigate and then treat any client's violent tendencies, particularly the existence of marital violence, and for battered spouse programs to also investigate and seek treatment of either or both spouses' alcohol problem as well as any violence problem.[76] With a high percentage of criminal offenders reporting alcohol use at the time of the crime, legislators should perceive the same kind of need for alcohol treatment as for drug treatment in correctional and prevention programs.

America's Response to Drugs

In contrast with government's responses to the prevalence of alcohol, ONDCP has mobilized an enormous federal program to combat drugs. The total federal drug control budget request for fiscal year 2003 was $19.2 billion. Only a minute portion of these moneys goes toward lowering tobacco and alcohol use, primarily among juveniles. The functional budget allocates $9.45 billion for drug law enforcement, $3.8 billion for drug treatment and research, $2.47 billion for drug prevention and research, $2.3 billion for drug interdiction, and $1.15 billion for international programs. The last category includes a fresh infusion of over $731 million for the Andean Counterdrug Initiative in South America, primarily as continued aid to the government in Colombia to counter the cocaine production and distribution market operated through civil war insurgents there and also as aid to Colombia's neighboring nations to counter the spillover effects of Columbia's drug war.[77]

This federal drug budget has increased about 75 percent since 1991, and yet the rate of illicit drug use in America held relatively steady comparing 1990 with 2000, and a significant increase occurred in the rate of adolescent drug use by the end of those years (despite a decline from 1997 to 1999). And yet, the 75 percent funding increase built in no change to the government's basic priorities. Since 1984, about one-third of the drug control budget has been devoted to reducing consumer demand for drugs, with 60 percent of that portion going toward drug abuse treatment and treatment research. Two-thirds of the federal drug budget continues to be devoted to controlling the drug supply, primarily through domestic law enforcement, interdiction efforts to prevent drugs from entering the United States, and international programs to control foreign drug production and shipment.[78] But during the 1990s, budget allocations within this supply control function changed, so that by 2001 domestic law enforcement expenditures rose while interdiction moneys dropped.[79] The federal drug control budget will be drastically revised in 2004 so as to reflect only agencies with a primary mission of drug law enforcement or demand reduction. This conceptual change will remove, for example, the costs of detaining and incarcerating federal drug prisoners. The overall drug control budget will be thereby reduced on paper about 40 percent.[80]

To achieve its goal of reducing illegal drug use and drug availability, along with their adverse consequences, the ONDCP has established basic strategies that change as presidential administrations change. The George W. Bush administration has basically established three such strategies: (1) preventing drug use, (2) placing treatment resources where they are needed, and (3) disrupting the drug market.[81]

The Bush ONDCP does not set specific crime reduction goals. Even if researchers could identify what portion of violent crime is drug-related, they still could not identify whether a particular reduction was caused by law enforcement efforts or by other contemporaneous actions and factors in society and government. These limitations create a huge gap in an agency's ability to assess the worth of drug control expenditures. Law enforcement efforts consume the highest proportion of the federal drug budget with no way truly to assess the effects on crime. And the decade-long persistence of the drug use percentages among the youthful and the general population, in addition to the alarming percentage increases in first-time use of each illicit drug, indicate how difficult it may be to relate drug law enforcement, drug treatment, or drug prevention efforts to any reduction in drug demand. A recent National Research Council study concluded: "It is unconscionable for this country to continue to carry out a public policy of this magnitude and cost without any way of knowing whether and to what extent it is having the desired effect."[82]

Equal difficulty emerges in evaluating drug interdiction and international efforts. The relevant figures are created using estimates derived from drug crop destruction, intelligence and investigative operations, drug cultivation figures, computer models, money laundering accounts, sampling, and other devices. State Department figures show opium production, for example, to be about the same for 1991 and 1998. Estimated coca leaf production in Latin America declined substantially between 1991 and 1998, with lowered net cultivation in Peru and Bolivia offsetting production increases in Colombia. But revised coca leaf production estimates for Colombia in 1999 soared to more than six times the 1998 number, casting doubt on the entire estimation process.[83] Indeed, any independent researcher will admit that for any given year no one really knows what quantity of any particular drug actually reaches American shores from overseas and how much eventually reaches which drug markets. Nor can anyone explicate the significance of, or definitive reasons for, fluctuating drug purity and prices from year to year, between different parts of the same city at the same time, or indeed for different kinds of retail customers. And how the retail drug market is maintained, as dealers are imprisoned, shot, physically and mentally burned out, or as they simply retire, remains a mystery.[84]

Most disturbing of all, very few in public life are focusing even on the ONDCP analyses and its admitted limitations in allocating public resources to the illegal drug problem. Since the 1980s, about two-thirds of the federal drug control budget has been directed toward drug supply reduction, with the remaining one-third devoted to demand reduction. But in the 1970s, the supply reduction programs received only a 31 to 53 percent share of those moneys, with demand reduction emphasized.[85] Why aren't policymakers comparing the results and merits of these two very different approaches, particularly because the 1970s' emphasis on treatment programs was achieved primarily during "law and order" Republican administrations? And how does government, in designing a drug control policy, learn from the prevention and focused correctional policies addressing the harms of alcohol and tobacco? Further, how do we weigh the harm caused by each now-illicit drug, separately considered, against the harm and the crime caused by making the possession and sale of each such drug illicit? The George W. Bush administration apparently seeks to avoid these drug-and-crime relationship problems. Its strategy report in 2002 focuses only on two-year and five-year goals for reducing drug use, perhaps because drug use can be directly measured, though imperfectly, through national surveys.[86] Rather than focusing on reducing crime and improving public health, the Bush program appears to echo past alcohol temperance movements in establishing the drug war as a moral effort to save the souls of drug-using Americans.[87]

Drugs and Law Enforcement

No one has been able to quantify the results or benefits of law enforcement's fight to control illicit drug flow. According to the National Research

Council study: "The nation possesses little information about the effectiveness of current drug policy, especially of drug law enforcement."[88] But we do know that the effort to stem the tide of illicit drugs has been massive—and expensive. On the local level, 93 percent of county police agencies and 82 percent of all municipal agencies with more than one hundred police officers contained a full-time drug enforcement unit, as did about 60 percent of the state police agencies and almost 70 percent of all sheriffs' departments. New York City alone in 1997 reported over 2,500 police officers dedicated to drug units and task forces. More than 90 percent of all these police agencies received moneys and property forfeited by drug sellers for use in law enforcement operations; about three-fourths of all local departments, along with about half of state police agencies, participated in some form of a multiagency drug enforcement task force.[89] State and local police made about 1.6 million arrests for drug abuse violations in 2000, four-fifths of them for drug possession, in addition to an unknown number of other arrests for violent and property crimes induced directly or indirectly by the illicit nature of the drug market.[90] And in 1998, drug offenders were 35 percent of all felons convicted in state courts.[91] But in a 1996 poll of police chiefs conducted by the Peter Hart organization for the Police Foundation, just under 75 percent of the chiefs expressed the opinion that mandatory minimum penalties either have been only somewhat effective in reducing, or are not really the answer to, drug trafficking in their respective communities.[92] The Commission on the Advancement of Federal Law Enforcement concluded: "Despite a record number of seizures and a flood of legislation, the Commission is not aware of any evidence that the flow of narcotics into the United States has been reduced."[93] The report also noted that federal prosecutions of domestic drug trafficking, which were 28 percent of all federal case filings in 1997 and accounted for over 60 percent of all federal prison inmates, resulted from only 1.5 percent of all drug arrests in America in 1997 and were less than 2 percent of all drug prosecutions in the United States.[94] Of the federal convictions where the drug type was reported in 1998, 34 percent involved marijuana and 28 percent were for powder cocaine; crack cocaine constituted 16 percent of the total.[95] And despite the large increase in the law enforcement portion of the national drug budget, federal convictions for drug offenses lingered in the 18,000 range from 1992 through 1997 but suddenly jumped to 21,571 in 1998. Prior to September 11, 2001, the FBI's increased emphasis on drug enforcement was evidenced by the fact that 8 percent of its total federal convictions involved drugs in 1984 but such convictions were about 25 percent of the FBI's total in 1998.[96] Total federal drug prosecutions tripled between 1981 and 1998.[97] The FBI's drug priorities have now been reduced, however, as the agency's antiterror activities increase.

On the level of local enforcement, John Eck and Edward Maguire examined the research on the effectiveness of police operations against retail drug sellers and concluded that police enforcement "when coupled with civil action against landlords, appears to have a powerful impact on drug dealing."[98] The police world appears to agree that effective drug enforcement must involve a heavy concentration of efforts and units in specific areas, rather than a drug bust here or there or an occasional sweep of the streets. When community policing is effective, key residents of a neighborhood will assist the police to a greater degree. City and town attorneys must help approach landlords or other owners whose structures house drug operations and either persuade them to take action against their drug-involved occupants or sue the owners to secure nuisance abatement.[99] As Eck and Maguire point out, a thriving economy assists these efforts because rising property values and future economic promise give landlords incentives to preserve their ownership even in a "bad" neighborhood. One controlled experiment demonstrates the importance of follow-up tactics. After the San Diego Police Department took drug enforcement action against 121 separate locations in residential neighborhoods, some landlords received no follow-up (control group); some received a letter from the drug abatement response team explaining the police action, the owner's legal liability for a drug operation, and the availability of police help; and others received that letter as well as a request for a meeting with the drug-response team.[100] In the last group, most landlords did attend the meeting. After six months the fewest drug and crime events had occurred for the letter-and-meeting group. But after the initial six months, the number of crimes in each group's properties became similar for thirty months.

Again, we do not know if breaking up a drug market itself lowers violent crime other than that occurring within the illegal market operations. And less housing for drug dealing could potentially increase drug market violence as dealers compete for fewer locations and operate more on the street. One can also plausibly argue, however, that if society drives an open-air drug market into one or more buildings and then makes indoor locations less available and less accessible, fewer people will buy drugs in that area and more users, particularly casual ones, may use drugs even less. We simply do not know how much an increase in the general "hassle" of finding and buying drugs lowers the actual use of drugs, particularly considering the difficulty of measuring over time how much drug markets are displaced to other geographic areas.

One research institute used information from the New York City area to trace the rise and decline of the heroin injection market from 1960 to 1975 and the cocaine-crack market in the 1980s, along with the rise in the 1990s of the marijuana-blunts era (marijuana wrapped in cheap cigar paper). The research assessed the effects of intense police and court actions and of changes in the subculture of drug-using, inner-city areas of the city.[101] The authors describe the unprecedented, intense response to crack by law enforcement and the use of mandatory minimum prison penalties. This response partly resulted in New York State's 100 percent rise in prison population during the 1980s, and contributed to the rise in the percentage of the African American portion of those under criminal justice supervision from 25 percent to 33 percent in just the period 1989–1994.

The study's analysis used birth data from the ADAM study in New York City and research data to establish that arrested inner-city youths born in the 1970s had shown disdain for both crack and heroin. As a result, given the more peaceful and lower-priced nature of the marijuana market compared to the crack market, and with marijuana being used primarily as a social drug along with alcohol, the marijuana-blunt generation produced fewer drug sellers, much less need for handguns, much lower levels of robbery and violence, and a more placid and participatory domestic situation.[102] Most interesting, the authors note: "The primary reason that the BluntGen gives for avoiding crack and heroin is the *negative* role models in their lives. They clearly do not want to emulate their parents, older siblings, close relatives or acquaintances who were ensnared by crack or heroin. Indeed, the BluntGen typically blame much of the poverty and other difficulties of their predecessors on heroin and crack."[103]

The study also found that crack use persisted among many older users, but with a different, controlled pattern that often included several days of abstention. Although this finding puts a dent in the statements of many "experts" that crack is so much more dangerous than other drugs—because its users, in obtaining very quick "highs" followed by very quick "lows," are believed to necessarily engage in constant crack use, property crime, and violence—Congress has refused to alter its policies. As a result, federal sentencing guidelines continued to incarcerate crack sellers and users in the year 2002 up to six times more severely than the length of sentences involving powder cocaine. The New York researchers describe how, despite the 1990s generation switching to nonviolent marijuana use as its principal drug, police department tactics in New York City became more severe in 1998 through an increase in marijuana arrests and the transporting of apprehended public marijuana smokers to a central area for booking and detention prior to bail hearings.[104] Ironically but not surprisingly, this law enforcement pressure on the marijuana market may itself be inducing higher prices and therefore higher violence.[105]

Andrew Golub and Bruce Johnson analyzed the results of drug testing and interviews of federal arrestees in urban areas around the nation between 1989 and 1996 and found that significant declines of 10 percent or more in crack use had occurred among the arrestees in East Coast and West Coast cities, with either a plateau or a slow decline in Midwestern cities.[106] Many locations demonstrated substantial declines in crack use among younger arrestees, for example, a decline in Washington, D.C., from 39 percent to 10 percent. But even with these reductions, estimated drug abuse arrests nationally rose about 16 percent from 1989 through 2000 as total criminal arrests declined; and the percentage of possession arrests for marijuana rose from 23 percent to 41 percent of the total arrests for drug abuse violations.[107]

The Downside to an Emphasis on Supply Controls

The dominance of supply-side controls in America's response to drugs induces a significant downside. The litany of negatives for law enforcement is lengthy and destructive: police perjury; police corruption; police cynicism about the law and its processes; unhealthy and inefficient law enforcement agency competition; racial profiling and stereotyping; the ratcheting up of statistical achievement figures by arresting low-level drug possessors and sellers; the use of relative leniency for higher-level drug dealers in exchange for testimony convicting more lower-level participants; increased use of intrusive surveillance techniques such as wiretaps, electronic eavesdropping, and no-knock house entries (sometimes into the wrong house with deadly results); identification of targets based on potential assets to be forfeited to police coffers; and informant practices that lead to various kinds of abuses, including perjury and virtual immunity for some to continue in the drug business. One federal informant alone "made" 295 cases involving 445 drug dealers in a sixteen-year career that netted him $1.9 million in federal compensation, and that ended only when a defense attorney finally proved the man had lied about his personal background.[108] No one will ever know for sure whether that government witness' perjury influenced juries and infected his more substantive testimony about particular defendants and their actions.

Nor has anyone adequately studied whether, in general, mandatory minimum penalties for drug possession and sales are inflicted on the so-called drug kingpins. Anecdotal evidence suggests otherwise. In Michigan, the 240 drug offenders sentenced under the mandatory life-without-parole provision turned out to be primarily fringe participants—female couriers, addicts, and lower-level sellers sentenced for conspiracy with the higher-level people they may have never met. Political courage on both sides of the aisle in the Michigan legislature led to some reform of the law through lower maximum sentences.[109]

The issue of race also pervades drug enforcement. The danger of the crack form of cocaine is the rationale most often cited for the longer prison sentences of black drug offenders. William Bennett, John DiIulio, and John Walters state that claims of racial bias are a sham because crack by far attends the most serious criminal and life-threatening situations and is most dangerous and pervasive in the black communities of our cities.[110] But we now know of the decline in crack's use and effects in the 1990s. If one projects by race from household surveys of population percentages involved in current drug usage (use within the past thirty days), blacks constitute less than 13 percent of the population and probably constitute less than 15 percent of the total number of drug users in America. Even though the percentage of blacks using crack-cocaine is higher than the percentage for whites, only 10 percent of current illegal drug users identify cocaine as one of their drugs.[111] And crack-cocaine usage is attributable to less than one-third of all cocaine usage. With more than 95 percent of current drug usage in America involving an illicit substance other than crack, that danger clearly cannot justify a severe drug enforcement emphasis toward blacks. Of all persons arrested for drug abuse violations in America in 2000, 35 percent were black, even though arrests for any form of cocaine and heroin sale or use between 1989 and 1999 were declining from 54 percent to 34 percent of total drug abuse arrests and even though crack use and violence in the largest cities had declined precipitously.[112]

The incarceration figures are even more disparate than the arrest figures and cannot be justified. Remember that blacks using drugs make up only

15 percent of the numbers reporting drug use. In contrast, 63 percent of those admitted to state prison for drug offenses are African Americans, and relative to population, black men are confined in state prison for drug offenses at a rate 13.4 times greater than the rate for white men.[113] Racial minorities of all types account for 79 percent of all state prison drug offenders. In part because of this disparity, state and federal prison populations combined contain one of every twenty black males over eighteen years old in America and one of every 180 white men.[114]

Looked at another way, of all federal convictions sentenced in fiscal year 1999, 41 percent were for drug trafficking offenses. In these cases, the drug offenders were 25 percent non-Hispanic white, 31 percent black, and 42 percent Hispanic.[115] The comparable representations in the total population were 72 percent, 13 percent, and 12 percent. In 1999, the National Household Survey on Drug Abuse showed current illicit drug use for those twelve years and older to be 6.6 percent for whites, 6.8 percent for Hispanics, and 7.7 percent for blacks, still resulting in about five times more white than black illicit drug users and over six times more white illicit users than Hispanic.[116] Nevertheless, just these two minority groups with almost 25 percent of the national population accounted for 73 percent of the federal drug convictions in 1999. And this disparity continues even as the violent crack market wars subsided years ago, the violent crime rate has declined 33 percent since 1991, and drug-related murders have decreased 60 percent in just eleven years through 1999.[117]

Drug sentencing is also unusual. In the federal system, 57 percent of the prison inmates in September 2000 were serving sentences for drug offenses.[118] In fiscal year 1999, for all federal offenders the mean sentence was about 48 months with the median at 24 months. But for drug trafficking offenses, which represent most federal drug cases because trafficking includes possession with an inferred intent to distribute, the mean sentence was 73 months and the median figure was 48 months.[119]

Federal law mandating minimum sentences in specified drug cases, and the sentencing guidelines implementing that law, aggravate the numbers disparity by establishing as a basic starting point for the length of a prison sentence a ratio that equates each gram of crack-cocaine, used in far greater proportion by blacks, with one hundred grams of powder cocaine.[120] Partially as a result, in fiscal year 1999, the mean sentence for crack violations was 120 months but for powder cocaine, 79 months. And the median sentence for crack offenses was 57 percent longer than that for powder cocaine.[121]

The disparity is further aggravated by the sentencing "safety valve" law added by Congress in 1994, providing for a waiver of the mandatory minimum sentences for those least serious drug offenders who fulfill stated conditions, such as having a prior imprisonment record of no more than a certain few days.[122] This provision is obviously unavailable for those blacks who have previously been subjected to racial profiling and stereotyping, disparate arrest practices, and disparate sentencing at both state and federal levels. As a result, in fiscal 1999, 34 percent of powder cocaine defendants eligible for mandatory minimum prison sentences received the benefit of this safety valve provision, but only 15 percent of crack cocaine defendants were so treated.[123]

Americans thus far have responded to the racial disparities of the drug war with suppression and silence, in part, we believe, because of their frustration with the drug problem and unwillingness to face racism. And because white majorities have not borne the burden of overwhelming imprisonment, legislators have accepted the traditional and now mendacious law enforcement rationale. As a result, police crackdowns on alleged drug-related violence, such as murders supposedly caused by the influence of crack, continue long after the original rationale for racial disparity has been overturned and long after the statistics have proven its irrelevance and burdens.

The disparity has other severe consequences even after drug felons have completely changed their lives. In particular, many states deny such convicted felons the right to vote, and the federal government bars the opportunity to receive college financial aid, and the chance to receive temporary aid for needy families. Society will not let such people forget or participate even though their prison terms have ended.

Interdiction and International Controls Programs

In the federal drug budget requested for fiscal year 2003, the two components of drug interdiction and control of foreign production consume about 18 percent of the total $19.2 billion.[124] Drug interdiction can slow a supply temporarily, as happened with heroin after the famous French Connection convictions in the 1970s. But world markets have a way of constantly adjusting to obstacles and temporary interruptions. International crop control efforts and interdiction seek to negate a basic principle in a competitive economy. If the demand exists, the supply will exist. One or more nations increase their production and shipment, as Colombia did with an enormous increase in coca production from 1997 to 1999 after interruptions in Peru and Bolivia; one or more nations commence shipping a drug new to America or expanding such shipments, as with the enormously profitable trade in "ecstasy" tablets; a domestically produced drug originally used in a legal therapeutic way suddenly becomes a recreational drug, is criminalized, and then becomes popular regionally, then nationally, as occurred with methamphetamines in the 1990s; or new methods and new routes of shipment are devised, as occurred when the U.S. success in interdicting air shipments in the 1980s induced a market shift to maritime and ground shipments. Law enforcement has even uncovered elaborate drug supply tunnels under the Mexico-U.S. border and the construction in Colombia of a submarine for drug transport. (And just a few freighters could probably bring into the United States a year's supply of heroin.) Finally, the main drug of choice shifts when enforcement or social culture and attitude changes render people more averse to one drug while more accepting of another whose prior ill effects have been lost in social memory, as happens periodically between cocaine and heroin or with a shift to relatively new drug markets.

Those who pursue good feelings through drugs also do not hesitate to seek new sources. At times, an effective new, legal drug quickly leads to widespread abuse, as happened with illegal sales of a slow-release legal drug trademarked as OxyContin, which had over $1 billion in medically prescribed sales in 2000. In the latter part of the 1990s, the U.S. illicit drug market was hit by an expansion of synthetic drugs, such as domestically produced methamphetamine, ecstasy tablets imported from Western Europe, and GHB, the "date rape" drug that federal legislators in 2000 temporarily reclassified to the most dangerous controlled substance class pending permanent classification under federal drug law.

We pay a price far beyond today's budget for interdiction. These efforts are quickly expanding the federal bureaucracies dedicated to that purpose with well-meaning, hard-working career civil servants whose organizations will be more and more difficult to shrink if America ever decides that reallocation of drug control resources is merited or necessary. A large, entrenched federal bureaucracy always builds its own constituency in Washington, D.C.

We also pay a price in foreign policy and credibility. The estimates of international drug production are subject to major errors, as the ONDCP discovered in the fall of 1999. Colombia's coca crops, previously assumed to be low yield with three years of required cultivation, were actually high yield and carried only a one-year cultivation period. The resulting jump in estimated Colombian coca production required ONDCP's reexamination of goals, measures of performance, and claims of success versus failure in interdiction; indeed, just the area under coca cultivation in Colombia expanded by over 140 percent from 1995–1999 with a 126 percent increase in cocaine production.[125] In 2000 President Clinton launched an additional $1.3 billion in U.S. aid to Colombia for sixty helicopters and for other kinds of assistance to a military seeking to destroy drug production by revolutionary forces that have been fighting a civil war there for over thirty years. Clinton expedited the launch with waivers of human rights compliance goals mandated in the aid legislation, thereby disturbing the leaders of many South American nations who acknowledge the mobility of the drug trade.[126] By 2002, Colombia's government was asserting that the prior year's coca acreage had decreased while the United States was declaring that such acreage had in fact increased by 25 percent.[127]

U.S. drug actions often create foreign policy embarrassments and crises. The list of such incidents is long, including the U.S. drug czar vouching for the integrity of Mexico's drug enforcement czar just prior to his arrest and eventual seventy-one-year prison sentence for corruption, and the U.S. drug czar imperiously blasting the Dutch government for its domestic drug policy.[128] As a result, our country loses credibility with other nations' governments, not to mention each foreign country's populace. Americans and their government have no idea how humiliating and enraging it is for Mexican, Colombian, and other Latin American leaders and citizens to have U.S. representatives march arrogantly into their countries and demand lower production of coca, whose crops at least provide some sustenance for their farmers, when America does so little to control or even admit abroad its high demand for illicit drugs. The United States periodically adds to the overseas outrage with programs that American citizens would not accept within their own shores, such as spraying potentially harmful fungal herbicides in Colombia on food crops grown interchangeably with coca or opium, with no one truly knowing the danger to future cultivation of each sprayed area or to the environment generally.[129] The U.S. participation in aggressive drug surveillance flights in Peru was suspended for a time only after the United States assisted in the fatal shooting down of an American missionary flying with his family in a small plane having no connection to drugs.[130] Nor does the United States offer significant aid to help cultivate crop alternatives to drugs, and to build and equip the transportation network to ship the new, legitimate crops to seaports and other international destinations. The European Union had to step in to help fill that gap.

So, after years of costly efforts to interdict drugs and control their foreign production, where do we stand? In comparing 1981 to 1998, the purity of both heroin and cocaine in the U.S. market is way up and the price is way down.[131] In other words, the market seems to have become better for the illicit drug customer.

Real Alternatives to Ongoing Drug Policies

When government decides to inhibit society's use of drugs, tobacco, and alcohol, policymakers have to determine how much to emphasize controls over supply, restrictions on demand, and consequences for offenders. To implement these policy emphases and objectives, legislators and administrators then prioritize among research, prevention, treatment, education, civil and criminal law, and administrative regulations. But for reasons never articulated, legislators at all levels of government take divergent routes in dealing with alcohol use, tobacco use, and drug use. Occasionally, when a decades-long government "solution" to one of society's problems proves to be faulty, ineffective, or fraught with unacceptable harms, government reframes the policy. Other times, government constantly reorganizes the responding agency framework without ever questioning whether the assumptions underlying existing policy need reframing. Sometimes from stubbornness, sometimes in frustration, the government simply adds more resources to the existing policy and expands some or all aspects of the traditional response. Government drug policies have unfortunately followed this path.

One of the most vivid examples of policy paralysis is the Rockefeller drug law passed by the New York State legislature in 1973. At that time, many of us working for New York City's mayor knew and stated strongly precisely what was going to, and did in fact later, occur: nonviolent drug users would receive long, mandatory prison sentences; fifteen-year-olds, not subject to the new law, would be recruited en masse as drug couriers the day after the law was passed; and the law and its effects, once in place, would endure perhaps for generations because future legislators would want to demonstrate that they were as "tough on crime" as their predecessors. Several legislators from both political parties, just prior to their votes in favor of the bill, whispered to us in state capitol hallways that they appreciated the merit and factual basis of our warnings but just could not vote against "tough" drug enforcement and survive the next election.[132] Ironically, when the bill passed and the juvenile drug couriers immediately "hit the streets" for the first time, the heroin crisis that had rightfully preoccupied New York City had already started to wane. In 2002, the Rockefeller drug law was still in place.

How do we learn from this "war on drugs?" Unfortunately the reform debate centers mainly upon only two alternatives: either preserve and strengthen the current response, or legalize drugs. Too little discussion proceeds on a drug-by-drug level or on a step-by-step process of change. Indeed, Americans are discouraged about the ability to control illicit drug demand but do not want to stress the arrest of drug users.[133] And too many politicians run scared, dutifully followed by timid or narrow-minded administrators. Drug reform proponents could only cringe when both President Clinton and his drug czar, who had for eight years helped to cram federal prisons with drug offenders, waited until the eve of their departures to suddenly recommend that their successors expand drug treatment and reduce drug imprisonment in America's programs.[134] On the other hand, John DiIulio set a courageous example in letting the facts change his drug priority from enforcement to prevention and to help for drug addicts.[135] Others may well follow in his footsteps. As prisons continue to consume so much of the drug response dollar, as efforts to control drug supply promote enforcement's racial stereotyping, and as it dawns on Americans that supply control consumed two-thirds of every drug control dollar throughout the 1990s without much progress in overall drug use and without a provable connection to any positive result, perhaps American society and its politicians can at least begin to examine real facts and explore real alternatives.

In so doing, we decline to deal here with overall drug legalization or decriminalization. No large, modern nation with a diverse population has yet tried it. Further, legalization alternatives for each drug range from prohibition to decriminalization to different regulatory approaches to unregulated general use. Even with one now-illicit drug, marijuana, Americans approve of legal use for medical treatment, are almost evenly divided over legalizing a person's use of small amounts, and reject legalization of its general use.[136] Different drugs and their derivatives also have different effects, tolerance levels, and potentials for abuse and addiction.[137] Every existing and new form of drug as it comes upon the market would need separate evaluation regarding its legalization potential. Complicating the separate analyses are simultaneous multidrug usage and the use of one or more drugs with alcohol. As a potential for incorporation into America's crime response policy, legalization is years away from reality.

For crime response policies during the next three decades and perhaps beyond, we suggest the following changes. First, this nation must decide what priority to place on criminalizing harmful substances. In particular, America cannot articulate why it makes all nonmedical drug sale and use criminal, with unprecedented volumes of mandatory minimum imprisonment, when alcohol presents similar public health and crime problems (once you eliminate the violent criminality related solely to the illegality of the drug markets). The Clinton administration stated that its drug criminalization policy was an effort to minimize crime and public health problems. But the White House drug control office then admitted that they had no specific quantification of the relationship between drugs and crime. Nor would they acknowledge that widespread legalization of drugs, comparable to the legal availability of alcohol, would eliminate most of those forms of criminality, particularly criminal violence, that accompany all activities in a competitive illegal market. In contrast with his immediate predecessor, George W. Bush sees drug control primarily as a moral crusade, saying: "We must reduce drug use for one great moral reason. Over time, drugs rob men, women, and children of their dignity . . . and character . . . When we fight against drugs, we fight for the souls of our fellow Americans."[138] But in pronouncing this moral crusade to save the 4.3 million Americans either dependent on or abusing drugs, the Bush administration fails to explain why all alcohol consumption should not be similarly criminalized. These government officials must know that the number of alcohol-related traffic deaths is equal to the total number of murders in America and that 45 million Americans engage in "binge" alcohol drinking (five or more drinks on one occasion in the past thirty days), including 12.4 million who are robbed of their dignity and character by heavy drinking (five or more drinks on each of five or more days in the past month). And everyone now realizes that tobacco smoking kills people, but no one proposes criminalization of tobacco farming. Total criminalization of drug use is merely chosen by fiat, and the emphasis upon criminalization and punishment responses has continued for decades without our knowing what we have accomplished. In analyzing why drugs should be criminalized, no one draws from the experience of the political collapse of Prohibition. For now, no matter what the purpose, the goals appear to be to limit drug, alcohol, and tobacco use, without policymakers' explaining why they choose different routes to meet those goals. Indeed, most legislators and administrators simply ignore the contrast. Perhaps the striking policy differences are submerged by the power structure in the larger society because the punishments dictated by the drug policy (and to a smaller extent, parts of the alcohol policy) fall heaviest upon the same ethnic and racial minorities. But the drug and alcohol policies must be rationalized and then explicated together—a process that could and should produce changes in each.

A second proposal mandates more balance in the response to drug supply and demand. As researchers learn more about the medical effects and the physiological, psychological, and social causes of drug addiction, expanded treatment, prevention, and research become primary emphases. Treatment results, until recently, have been frustratingly poor. Indeed, a recent thirty-three-year follow-up study of 1960s heroin addicts found a high death rate and a high percentage of survivors still using heroin.[139] Improvements may come as law enforcement, special courts, and shorter confinement are joined with a treatment focus. For example, in 1989 drug courts were created in one jurisdiction by combining judicial authority and supervision with multiprogramming to persuade arrested drug users to become "drug-free," obtain a high school degree, find or maintain employment, and meet all financial obligations. By 2002, 782 drug courts were operating in forty-nine states with many more programs in the planning stage. The program retention and graduation percentages, as well as the employment percentages, are significantly higher, and the positive urinalysis rates of program participants are significantly lower, than those for other drug programs. The recidivism rates are difficult to compare among these programs because different drug courts have varying criteria for entry and for measuring success, and a much higher percent of drug court participants already have a high school degree or GED certificate and are older (over twenty-five years) than most violent offenders who are using drugs.[140] But this is one of the few programs that rightfully persists in dealing with its clientele in every area of life: family, work, the community, and leisure choices. As of the end of 1999, 122,000 of 175,000 people who entered drug court programs had graduated from or remained in treatment, and evaluations have thus far shown that the felony participants remain in drug treatment or other kinds of structured services at about double the retention rate of other forms of community drug programs.[141] New York has mandated a drug court program as of 2003 for all nonviolent drug offenders not subject to the Rockefeller drug law.[142] Through a proposition opposed by law enforcement agencies and many judges, but approved by 61 percent of its voters, California in 2001 commenced mandatory drug treatment in the community in lieu of confinement for first and second offenders charged only with drug possession and use.[143] As they did with welfare reform, states have moved far ahead of the federal government in exploring alternative drug policies. For those offenders who were merely drug users and do not require drug treatment but are on probation or parole status for their crimes, Kleiman and Boyum advocate national implementation of a program that involves frequent drug testing, then punishment of those who fail a test with immediate incarceration in jail or prison space made available by releasing those now confined simply for drug use.[144] Such a program would require some basic systemic changes in our drug response policies.

For those sentenced to confinement, residential treatment programs conducted apart from the normal prison population, and followed by work release supervision, also have produced lower recidivism rates.[145] But between 1991 and 1997 in state and federal prisons overall, even though a higher proportion of inmates were current illicit drug users at the time of their offense, the percentage of total inmates in drug treatment dropped, and for those who had used drugs within one month of their current offense, dropped by more than 50 percent.[146] There have been some increases in funding since 1997, but drug treatment for inmates should exist for everyone who needs it. Columbia University's Center on Addiction and Substance Abuse estimates that an additional $6,500 per year per inmate would provide intensive drug treatment, education, and job training.[147] An ONDCP study estimates a per-inmate cost of $3,000, representing just a 15 percent increase in the existing $20,000 per inmate maintenance costs, for adding drug treatment in prison to all prisoners who need it.[148] Both studies state that such treatment costs would more than pay for themselves through lower recidivism and the tax payments and other economic benefits resulting from prisoners becoming productive community members.

Treatment programs also need more flexibility in order to reduce the harm of illicit drugs as well as stop offenders from using them. Methadone maintenance for heroin addicts is an example of this flexibility. Many view drug maintenance as the first step toward widespread legalization and therefore oppose it. Others oppose this supervised maintenance because it represents another form of addiction. Methadone is a controlled substance under Schedule II, which lists drugs found to have a high potential for abuse possibly leading to severe psychological or physical dependence. But the federal government has permitted methadone maintenance treatment programs with daily walk-in doses for heroin addicts since the late 1960s, and evaluations show a 70 percent reduction in heroin use, a 57 percent reduction in criminal activity, and a 24 percent increase in full-time employment.[149] Those who oppose chemical maintenance programs should support research leading to longer-lasting maintenance doses, the negation of a drug's sought-after effects, or even a cure for specific forms of addiction.

The unwillingness of politicians to give more priority to the goal of reducing drug demand, with a return to the balance of the 1970s drug control budgets at 50 percent each for supply and demand programs, is puzzling. This radical dollar reallocation would reduce current law enforcement, interdiction, and U.S. international crop control programs only by 24 percent but would increase treatment and prevention budgets by 50 percent. The National Center on Addiction and Substance Abuse has exhaustively documented how at the state level almost ninety-six cents of every dollar spent on substance abuse involving alcohol, tobacco, and drugs is spent on the burden of such abuse on public programs (like education, police involvement, health care, and so on), while at the same time less than four cents is devoted to prevention, treatment, and research for reducing the incidence and consequence of abuse.[150]

A third basic recommendation revokes mandatory minimum sentences for all but major drug trafficking, drug money laundering, and career criminals. Under the existing drug statutes, prosecutors too often enhance their statistical conviction numbers by granting sentencing concessions to a single high-level drug trafficker in return for assistance in convicting a group of lesser subordinates. Too many lesser drug market participants are caught in the wide net of mandatory minimum years of prison confinement. A further required step would follow the lead of California and New York by eliminating prison and jail confinement in every state for those whose first- or second-time drug convictions are limited to drug use. The staunchly conservative crime expert John DiIulio said in 1999: "Research . . . suggests that the nation has 'maxed out' on the public-safety value of incarceration . . . [A]s America's incarcerated population approaches two million, . . . [i]t's time for policy makers to change focus, aiming for zero prison growth . . . Current laws put too many nonviolent drug offenders in prison."[151]

DiIulio cites reliable estimates demonstrating that at least a quarter of state prison admissions have been people whose only crimes were low-level, nonviolent drug offenses. Since 1973 in New York alone, he said, the Rockefeller drug law has been confining "legions" of nonviolent drug offenders in prison for mandatory terms of fifteen years to life. The author concludes by offering policy suggestions aimed at *reducing* the prison population even as he points out that by 2006 America will have the largest number of teenagers, a high-crime age cohort, since 1975.

In order to reduce the enormous disparity in sentencing between powder cocaine and crack-cocaine cases, a fourth basic change would raise the amount of crack substance necessary to reach higher sentencing guidelines levels. These amendments would permit application to crack sentencing of the same departures from the normal sentencing range that the guidelines now permit in judicial determination of prison sentences for powder cocaine. With drugs, the sentencing starting point is based for the most part on weight of the substance in which the drug is mixed. In addition, the courts should permit the lowering of sentences for limited participation in drug selling or delivery and for other relevant factors.[152] Sentencing guidelines for drug offenses also should eliminate punishment for "relevant conduct," a system now in force to permit sentencing an offender for conduct for which he was not convicted, including conspirators' conduct reasonably foreseeable by the sentenced offender. Pursuant to "relevant conduct," for example, a judge may sentence a defendant for involvement in a one-thousand-pound drug shipment even though that defendant was convicted of actually participating in a much lower quantity. A recent Supreme Court decision may require at least a partial change in this procedure in order to bar longer sentences for facts not determined by the jury.

The ONDCP itself in both its 2000 and 2001 strategy reports advocated certain crack-cocaine sentencing adjustments to reduce the disparity with powder cocaine sentencing. ONDCP also recommended eliminating mandatory minimum incarceration for a first offense of simple crack possession.[153] But in 2002 the Bush administration reversed that proposal and instead aggressively disputed the need for any reduction in crack-cocaine punishment.

A fifth recommendation mandates reexamination of the placement of marijuana in the most serious drug schedule, Schedule I. To so qualify, a drug must have the highest potential for abuse of all drugs and no acceptable medical use. Schedule I status equates marijuana with heroin and establishes it officially as a national danger larger than cocaine. Only federal law enforcement people would so contend today. Absent placement of marijuana in a lower schedule, exceptions to the consequences of such placement should exist for its casual sale and use, especially for the alleviation of pain induced by a certified lingering illness. President Nixon's own Shafer Commission recommended an exemption for casual sale and use in 1971, but he buried any efforts to implement these recommendations. They then totally disappeared in the drug war of the 1980s and beyond.[154] A 1999 Institute of Medicine Report, issued by a prestigious eleven-member advisory panel, found that the primary adverse effect of acute marijuana use is diminished psychomotor performance—so it is inadvisable to operate a motor vehicle or other dangerous equipment while under the drug's influence. The chronic effects lay mostly with the dangers of smoking; but for a few chronic users, and only a few, dependence can result.[155] As to the contention of ONDCP and other drug experts that marijuana requires dangerous drug status because it acts as a "gateway" to more serious drug use, the Institute's report stated: "There is no conclusive evidence that the drug effects of marijuana are causally linked to the subsequent abuse of other illicit drugs."[156] The report does note that for drug addicts, the common course of use commences in childhood with smoking and alcohol, then marijuana, and then the more serious drugs. But the authors refuse to portray this as causality. And ONDCP has never recommended that tobacco and alcohol be classified as Schedule I dangerous substances. The Institute's report suggests medical use of marijuana for particular conditions, such as chemotherapy-induced nausea and vomiting and complications from AIDS, but only until research produces an effective, rapid-onset cannaboid drug delivery system lacking unacceptable side effects. Such a system avoids the dangers of smoking. But we have trouble envisioning a terminally ill person fretting over the dangers of smoking while securing pain relief from marijuana.

The electorate no longer punishes politicians for prior casual marijuana use, and neither should the crime response complex. Over 46 percent of all drug abuse arrests in America are for marijuana, with almost 90 percent of such arrests involving possession only. But 58 percent of high-school seniors in 1999 had already used marijuana and 70 million Americans have used it during their lifetime. Criminalizing such widespread use obviously has led to selective enforcement, and reinforcing the idea that marijuana is an unqualified menace to society makes a mockery of the law. At least nine states have voted to permit medical use of marijuana, but the federal government stubbornly ignores that public mandate and instead raids marijuana clinics serving patients and threatens the drug-prescription license of any physician who authorizes marijuana pain therapy for anyone.[157] In so doing, the national law enforcement apparatus diverts resources from the fight against terrorism to make sure sick people cannot use marijuana to relieve persistent, excruciating pain. Such a ridiculous policy choice serves only to promote general contempt for law enforcement.

For a sixth proposed change, our government must help decrease disease among those who use drugs. When the government refuses to provide free needles to addicts in order to prevent the spread of AIDS, the government becomes a co-conspirator in death, particularly when, as now, insufficient treatment programs and long waiting lists exist. Government officials, even in undercover status, could also purchase small quantities of drugs on the street and analyze them for dangerous impurities in order to issue warnings to the consumer. Parents who worry about a child's potential drug use would particularly appreciate this alert. Package warnings for both tobacco and alcohol, and warnings in bars and restaurants about the dangers of alcohol, have set a precedent in this regard.

Seventh, America must pursue extensive research to evaluate the worth, accuracy, and effectiveness of drug testing schoolchildren and of testing adults both when they apply for jobs and during their employment. Effort must also be devoted to ensuring fairness in the use of test results and in implementing widespread use of noninvasive test vehicles, such as a hair sample. Drug testing is now a norm in the ordinary lives of millions of Americans, presenting an invasive, sometimes humiliating, process with potential, and some actual, cases of faulty findings and unfair consequences. More than 73 percent of America's illicit drug users were employed either full-time or part-time in 1998. Drug testing exists in over one-half of America's work sites employing fifty or more people, and many schools have adopted a zero-tolerance policy toward drug use enforced by drug testing ever greater numbers of the student body. If so many of America's drug users are employed, the effectiveness of such testing is at issue. Drug tests reveal marijuana use within the preceding thirty days and the use of other drugs, within two or three days. Perhaps research can also discover ways to permit identification of whether someone used an illicit drug immediately before a harmful event. If such a new test vehicle were available, society would more easily accept enforceable targeted criminal sanctions, such as punishments for driving vehicles and operating other dangerous equipment under the influence of marijuana, rather than criminalizing possession and use of even small amounts of the drug.

An eighth step requires expanding government funding for medical research on the effects of drugs and alcohol on the brain and on possible pharmacological solutions. An ongoing debate pits those who contend that addicts choose their way of life and must bear personal responsibility for the consequences against those who research and explicate the brain-disease theory.[158] Medical research could solve many questions about when punishment is appropriate and about when brain disease makes punishment counterproductive and treatment the only effective alternative. With drug addiction now a priority in government programming, medical research about addiction as a possible brain disease must itself receive a higher priority in drug dollar allocation than at present.

For a ninth change in approach, America must increase research to help improve the effectiveness of drug prevention programs, and to develop different approaches, particularly to address the needs of children. Administrators must accept the recent National Research Council findings that although a lot of money is spent on drug prevention programs, evaluation has been limited. Further, those programs based in school classrooms have been carefully evaluated, but have not shown significant longer-range positive effects. The most popular program, DARE, exists in 48 percent of America's elementary schools but has little influence on student drug use.[159] Although widely popular with parents and police, DARE felt compelled to change its program in 2001 and now awaits new evaluations.

A tenth new approach requires examination of the overall public-private strategy now employed to reduce tobacco and alcohol use. For example, how did society drastically reduce alcohol-related motor vehicle fatalities without widespread use of prison confinement? And why did its disease potential steer so many people away from tobacco, while the horrors of drug addiction fail to penetrate the public consciousness in the same way? A recent national survey found that the percentage of eighth-, tenth- and twelfth-grade students who smoked tobacco had dropped by significant percentages between 1996 and 2001, with better prevention programs and higher product pricing.[160] Why is that strategy working for tobacco but not for drugs? We can only guess that drug-specific prevention programs might be more effective than just a general exhortation about "drugs."

An eleventh innovation requires that the White House Office of National Drug Control Policy give significantly more national attention to alcohol use and abuse. In September 2000, just prior to his retirement, the then drug czar stated in a little-noticed forum that "alcohol is the most dangerous drug in America" and that alcohol abuse is America's top drug problem.[161] He did not explain why the ONDCP had failed during his tenure to concentrate significant resources on the problem. But the parameters of alcohol control must also be included in any national priority focus and policy. The wine, beer, and spirits lobbying apparatus would resist such a national focus and already fights any attempt at further regulation. But politicians should realize that they are lending more credibility to drug control policies when they also focus upon alcohol harm and possible control strategies. That route would most likely lead to a more selective use of criminalization and punishment for both alcohol and illicit drugs. It would also cause the development of prevention programs and ensure that treatment is available at least to all those drug and alcohol users who also bring harm to society.

A twelfth step commands government funding mechanisms to implement the fundamental recommendations issued in March 2001 by the National Research Council in a presidentially commissioned report. The council—a group of fifteen economists, criminologists, and psychiatrists—found that data on drug consumption, drug markets, drug pricing, and drug distribution are so inadequate that, in their opinion, effective courses of action to deal with drugs are impossible to formulate.[162] They recommended specific ways to assemble a more useful bank of basic drug data and to judge the effectiveness of drug enforcement and drug interdiction. Too often, government funding mechanisms live in a separate world, ignoring the findings and pleas of impartial special study groups that have no stake in the funding institutions and their ongoing agenda and advisory committees. The historical rut of our national drug policy must be fixed with new knowledge, and funding the needs expressed in the National Research Council report would represent an excellent start.

Finally, the federal legislative process for drug budgeting should be consolidated, at least at the initial stages, just as ONDCP each year proposes an overall federal drug control budget reconciled from the submissions of various executive branch agencies. Legislators now approach drug use principally as a crime problem. They outlaw almost all drug use and enforce those laws with extensive reliance on mandatory minimum imprisonment. Only America's citizens and their leaders can force the average politician to focus on a wider range of possible priorities, to draw on existing knowledge and develop new knowledge, and then to reexamine the present approach. Congress scatters drug control budgeting among all the various appropriations committees and subcommittees that deal individually with cabinet-level and other executive branch agencies. Under this system, the committees and their subcommittees each view the drug problem only through the lens of one federal agency. Such a fragmented budgetary process obscures analysis of possible responses and appropriate priorities. An alternative exists. Just as it normally passes an overall federal budget that guides individual committees, Congress each year should debate and formulate an overall drug control budget that the various appropriations committees and their subcommittees must at least recognize, explore in hearings, and then either follow or publicly justify any changes. The creation of tobacco-control and alcohol-control budgets would also be useful, but we think that lobbyists and most politicians simply will not allow this further step.

Right now, government drug policy represents merely "more of the same." Americans deserve much more than that. Our proposals for the most part are not individually new, but taken together could make a difference. Drugs, like guns, raise emotional issues, ill-defined problems, and irrational responses. A comprehensive approach to drugs, alcohol, and tobacco must supplant those emotions with programs based on constantly increasing knowledge and a selective use of criminalization that pays close attention to all the goals of the crime response complex.

8

Juvenile Crime

The "juvenile justice system," as it is commonly called, is a diverse and often uncoordinated collection of responses to juvenile crime (and to other problems involving juveniles) that differ markedly from state to state, and even from urban to rural areas within the same state.[1] We will not make frequent use of the misleading term "juvenile justice system" for the same reasons that we disfavor the complacent trinomial "criminal justice system." Instead, we will speak most often of "juvenile crime response." This subcomponent of the overall crime response complex includes juvenile courts, juvenile probation services, child-protection agencies, and institutions of juvenile custody and out-of-home placement.

For the last century or so, the United States has segregated its arrangements for juvenile and adult crime response. In all American jurisdictions today, the overwhelming majority of criminal offenders who are under a specified age (eighteen in most states, but sixteen or seventeen in a number of others) are not charged, tried, and convicted in the adult criminal courts, nor are they subject to punishments in the adult correctional system.[2] Instead, they are haled before a court with separate jurisdiction over juvenile offenses, generically called the juvenile court (although technically called something else in many states).[3]

All juvenile courts originally were founded on the theory that the court should address the needs of each juvenile who came before it, act in the "best interests of the child," rehabilitate the juvenile if possible, and intervene in the circumstances of the juvenile's family life that had contributed to the delinquent behavior. The juvenile courts reflected beliefs that children were less responsible for their actions than adults, and more malleable.

In most states, the early juvenile courts were not even classified as criminal courts at all—and this remains true today. Instead, the juvenile courts were formally conceived as *civil* tribunals. According to the approved terminology, they did not "convict" juveniles of "crimes"; they merely "adjudicated" juveniles of "acts of delinquency." Instead of inflicting punishment, the official theory was that the juvenile courts were child-saving operations: They claimed to be acting for the offender's own good, for the good of his family, and for the good of society, all at the same time.[4]

As early as the 1820s, before the juvenile courts had become established across America, some cities and states began building separate "houses of refuge" for underage criminals. This policy took root, spread across the nation, and by and large remains an important basis of juvenile corrections today. With rare exceptions, juvenile criminals who are placed in custody are held separately from adult offenders. By the end of the nineteenth century, facilities for juvenile custody were generally called "boys' schools," "reform schools," or "homes," and the inmates were called "scholars," "residents," or "clients."[5]

As a chorus of historians have documented, the benign-sounding theories of juvenile courts and juvenile corrections have seldom been realized in practice. Even in the founding era of juvenile courts nationwide, during the early decades of the twentieth century, only a few juvenile court judges seem to have run their courtrooms with genuine empathy for the needs of each child offender, or were willing to devote the time to discover nuances in the personal background of the juvenile or his family.[6] Juvenile probation officers, who were supposed to provide needed information to the judge, were terribly overworked, ludicrously underqualified, or both. Psychiatric therapists who according to the early proponents of the juvenile court were supposed to provide a sound scientific basis for the court's dispositions, were never employed at all by most of the juvenile courts nationwide, and in any event were ignored by judges in the few courtrooms that were lucky enough to receive psychiatric recommendations.[7]

As for corrections, all histories agree that juvenile "homes" and "schools" in general were institutions of punishment and warehousing, and that concentrated efforts to educate and reform the "scholars" were rare indeed. It was difficult to recruit qualified educators and counselors to work in reformatories, and few jurisdictions were willing to fund the salaries necessary to change that reality. Rather than caring and compassion, the average child in custody could expect neglectful and even abusive treatment from his jailers—and even worse from his fellow inmates. In a watershed decision in the 1960s, the U.S. Supreme Court found that the child-saving rhetoric of juvenile corrections had long been unrealized in practice, and it mandated new procedural safeguards for delinquency proceedings that could lead to such punishments.[8]

Up-to-date evaluations of confinement facilities for juveniles suggest that the Progressive ideal was still far from a reality in the late twentieth century. One study of the conditions of juvenile custody in 1988 found that the "homes" and "schools" were ruled by violence and intimidation, although they were "not as uniformly bad as adult prisons."[9]

At the end of the twentieth century and the beginning of the twenty-first, the juvenile court and the "juvenile justice system" as a whole have been criticized heavily. Increasingly, there have been calls to abolish the juvenile court, to prosecute and punish some (or all) juvenile offenders "as adults," or in other ways to erase the present-day distinctions between juvenile and adult crime response.[10] Some people charge that juvenile crime response has already become barely distinguishable from the adult machinery, as legislatures nationwide have toughened juvenile sentencing laws, expanded legal mechanisms to transfer the most serious juvenile offenders to the adult courts, and even extended the death penalty to some adolescent offenders.[11] Recently, broad charges have also been made that the juvenile system is infected with racial inequities much like those in the adult crime response complex.[12]

Before laying out suggestions for the future of juvenile crime response in America, it is important to note that many of the current critics seem to be getting their facts wrong. Depending on who is lambasting the juvenile court, we have at times heard considerable exaggeration about the quantity and overall seriousness of juvenile crime, with doomsday prognostications for future "waves" or "bloodbaths" of juvenile violence. Some other critics greatly exaggerate the degree to which the juvenile court has merged into the increasingly punitive practices of the adult crime response complex. Still others, in seeking to level the strongest possible attack on racial disparities in the juvenile system, have overstated the case of demonstrable race-based discrimination, and have failed to recognize the relatively muted effects of racial disproportionalities in juvenile as opposed to adult crime response. In general, the critics badly underrate the continuing justification for and practical importance of the separate juvenile crime response program.

The Facts of Juvenile Crime

Via the national media, our most vivid images of juvenile crime are formed by a small number of events. The juvenile offenses that inspire the greatest fear, and receive the most public attention, are crimes of lethal violence, including homicides by shockingly young killers, usually involving guns. Recent examples include the murder of six-year-old Kaylah Rolland by her six-year-old classmate, and a seeming plague of school shootings by older juveniles, the worst of which have resulted in multiple fatalities.[13] It often happens that the victims of such crimes are children themselves—similar in age, race, and background to their attackers. These murders, in part because of their ghastly incongruity, and in part because of the heartbreaking youthfulness of their victims, become deeply etched in the public mind and receive saturation coverage by the media. The effect is especially potent when such events occur outside the inner cities. A tragedy such as the Columbine High School massacre in April 1999 can become a dominant icon of the (supposedly) disintegrating character of the nation's youth. The thirteen innocent victims of the Columbine shootings stand out in public perceptions over the other fifteen thousand homicide victims of 1999, and eclipse public concern for the far more numerous nonfatal criminal events. As Franklin Zimring has said, without irony or exaggeration, "One Columbine is more important to people's sense of insecurity than 100,000 housebreakings."[14] In the wake of Columbine, parents nationwide reported that they were afraid to send their children to school, high schools everywhere developed acute sensitivity to students who seemed potentially dangerous, and federal and state programs dedicated to school violence proliferated across the country.[15]

Any complete picture of juvenile crime in America must reach beyond the most infamous atrocities. Policy response should attend to *all* victims and potential victims, not only those whose tragedies are compounded by the indignity of media obsession. To focus on a few highly unusual cases is to risk paying too little attention to the larger share of human misfortunes that unfold in more "routine" circumstances. Moreover, if we limit our view solely to juvenile offenders who have committed the most appalling and inexplicable crimes, we are guilty of looking away from the millions of children and adolescents whose delinquent careers will never approach such fearsome acts.

There is ample reason to be concerned about juvenile crime in the contemporary United States. Since the 1970s, approximately one quarter of all serious violent victimizations across the nation have involved a juvenile offender—and this fraction brimmed as high as 30 percent in the mid-1990s. A substantial number of crimes involving juveniles are committed under the guidance of adult criminals—and most crimes committed by juveniles without adults are committed by groups of adolescent offenders.[16] The single most common motive for juvenile crime—from petty theft to homicide—appears to be the desire to gain status in a peer group.[17] Recklessness, short-sightedness, and susceptibility to peer pressure all seem to peak at the same time in the life cycle.

It is a well-documented fact in the United States—as in other nations worldwide—that adolescent males ages sixteen through eighteen are more likely to be mixed up in crime than human beings of any other age or gender.[18] According to one nationwide longitudinal survey of adolescents in the 1970s and 1980s, as many as one quarter of all males admitted involvement in at least one "serious violent offense" while age seventeen, defined by the survey as an aggravated assault, robbery, or rape. For fifteen- and sixteen-year-olds, the levels of annual participation in serious violence were a bit lower, but still above 20 percent in those age groups.[19] Almost all of these serious violent acts among adolescent males were assaults rather than robberies and rapes (rapes were exceedingly rare), and most of the incidents were never reported to the police. Still, this is a great deal of violent crime committed by a large segment of our young population.

Our portrait of the juvenile crime problem in the United States is also informed by data from other countries. In the early 1990s, for example, seventeen-year-olds in the United States were arrested for homicide at six times the rate of seventeen-year-olds in England and Wales.[20] The Justice Department reported that, for the mid-1990s, juvenile arrest rates for property crime in the United States were similar to those in Canada, but juvenile arrests for violent offenses were twice the Canadian rate, and juvenile arrests for homicide were six times the Canadian rate.[21]

This news is not in every respect as bad as it first sounds. Some criminologists believe that, on average, acts of juvenile violence are less harmful than acts of adult violence. Adolescents commit large numbers of assaults (usually directed at other adolescents), but most are not terribly serious. A majority would be graded by the law as misdemeanors rather than felonies. And fewer juvenile assaults result in the deaths of their victims than when adult criminals attack somebody.[22] Similarly, juveniles who commit robberies are less likely than adults to carry firearms or seriously injure their victims. Even the property losses that result on average from juvenile offending are lower than for adult property crime.[23]

Based on a Justice Department analysis of homicide statistics for 1997, we calculate that 91 percent of all homicides nationwide for that year involved adult offenders—4 percent of whom acted with juvenile accomplices. Only 8.7 percent of homicides in 1997 were committed by juveniles acting without adult "supervision," and that small percentage share has probably been falling off in the years since 1997.[24] Adult violence may be less prevalent, but it is more lethal, than juvenile violence.

Delbert Elliott, perhaps the nation's leading researcher on youth violence, has found strong evidence that the seriousness of violent behavior escalates among those juveniles who continue their criminal careers into young adulthood. Thankfully, most youthful offenders never reach such a point. More than 80 percent of white juveniles who have committed a violent crime as an adolescent simply stop—or "age out" of the behavior—by their early twenties. The same is true of two-thirds of African Americans with a juvenile history of violence.[25]

The Juvenile Homicide Spike of 1984 to 1994

The present debate of juvenile crime policy has been shaped most by a single phenomenon: From 1984 to 1994, America suffered through a terrifying decade of escalating homicide among juveniles and, to a lesser extent, young adults ages eighteen to twenty-four.[26] Along with increases in homicide came surges in certain other forms of near-lethal violence, such as aggravated assaults with firearm injuries. In many ways the nation is still reeling from the shock of this experience. As the "juvenile homicide spike" hit its peak, and just before it began to drop off again, conservative academic John DiIulio made a widely publicized announcement that "moral poverty" in America had created a wave of "juvenile superpredators," and that "a sharp increase in the numbers of super crime-prone young males" was "just around the corner." Among DiIulio's suggestions, he wrote that "we will have little choice [but] to pursue genuine get-tough law-enforcement strategies," including, by his estimation, a doubling or even tripling of the number of juveniles held in custody.[27]

In the mid-1990s, other academics like James Q. Wilson joined in the dire prediction that there would be large upswings in juvenile violence by the first decade of the twenty-first century.[28] Criminologist James Alan Fox, frequently quoted in the media, foretold a "crime storm" and a "bloodbath of teenage violence that is lurking in the future."[29] In a report written for the Justice Department in 1996, Fox included a projection that by the year 2005, juvenile homicides could reach a level of five times their numbers in 1984.[30]

The early and mid-1990s were years of great concern about juvenile violence even before the invention of the "superpredator" imagery. It was a period in which proposals to toughen juvenile crime response intensified—and a certain amount of punitive legislation resulted. Following a "summer of violence" in 1993, Colorado governor Roy Romer called a special legislative session to rewrite the state's juvenile sentencing laws. A number of states began passing laws to make it easier to prosecute juvenile offenders as adults, and to fund tougher sanctions such as "boot camps" for young criminals.[31]

Some people have argued that the turn toward more punitive measures in juvenile crime response was political and part of the ideological change that has produced large effects in adult crime response.[32] Instead, it is important to recognize the underlying factual basis of the get-tough movement in juvenile crime response that gained momentum in the early 1990s. The realities of adolescent homicide and grave violence were well documented and dramatic, and were far from the product of the imaginations of conservative "ideologues."

The first four years of the 1980s brought a welcome period of declining homicidal acts among both adults and adolescents. After 1984, and through the 1990s, adult homicide rates continued their steady downward drift in almost every year. Between 1984 and 1994, in contrast, rates of juvenile homicide roughly *tripled*, following a course horribly divergent from the adult pattern. Then, in 1995, juvenile murder rates began to fall off even more rapidly than they had accrued: By the end of the 1990s, the flare of adolescent homicide had subsided back to the levels of the mid-1980s.

No one fully understands what caused the youth homicide spike of 1984 to 1994, or what caused it to reverse direction. The statistical record offers some powerful clues, however. We know that nearly 100 percent of the increase in juvenile homicide was comprised of gun-related deaths. Every year from 1980 through the late 1990s, there have been close to five hundred homicides committed by juveniles without firearms. Juvenile gun homicides, by contrast, increased from several hundred per year in the early

1980s to an incredible peak of 1,800 in 1994. In symmetrical fashion, the entire decline in juvenile murder since 1994 has matched the swift drop-off in firearm deaths. From 1994 to 1997 alone, the annual total of adolescent killings with guns plummeted by more than one thousand.[33]

The unavoidable conclusion is that the juvenile homicide spike of 1984 to 1994 was directly attributable to increased gun possession by some children and adolescents, the increased willingness of those young people to use their guns against human targets, or some combination of the two.[34] The decline in juvenile homicide since 1994 may be traceable to reversals in much the same factors. No one knows with certainty why such wild fluctuations in gun possession and use occurred, although they may have been tied to the rise and fall of the crack-cocaine markets in the inner cities, and gang activities related to those markets.[35]

There is also reason to believe that the juvenile homicide spike was not accompanied by comparable increases in juvenile crimes below the level of homicide and near-lethal attacks. The best empirical analysis of juvenile violent crime in the 1980s and 1990s was presented by Franklin Zimring in his 1998 book, *American Youth Violence*. Zimring concluded that there have been no long-term trends, or dramatic short-term trends, in juvenile offending rates for the crimes of robbery, rape, and assault since 1980. Instead, Zimring posited that a tiny fraction of all assaults committed by juveniles became greatly more dangerous because a small but meaningful number of teenagers were suddenly complementing their assaultive behaviors with handguns. Out of hundreds of thousands of juvenile assaults each year, Zimring estimated that only ten to fifteen thousand extra "gun wound" cases in the assault statistics would have produced all of the extra gun homicides that pushed the juvenile homicide spike to its upper limit in 1994.[36]

Considering all of the evidence, the juvenile homicide spike in the late 1980s and early 1990s seems to have been a powerful but isolated phenomenon. It involved only juveniles and young adults, it was restricted to killings and grave assaults with firearms, and it did not significantly extend across less serious juvenile offenses. It was also geographically and demographically centered, largely in the poorest sectors of the black inner cities. As the spike hit its peak, the number of homicides committed by African American juveniles had soared upward by a factor of four (from 1984 to 1993), while white juvenile homicides at their peak had increased by a factor of two (from 1984 to 1994).[37] Homicide victimization rates were the starkest indicator of what was happening: In the early 1990s, the risk of death by murder experienced by a young black male ages fourteen to seventeen was 8.6 times that attending a white male of the same age group, and the murder risk of black males ages eighteen to twenty-four was ten times the comparable white risk.[38] The risk of homicide victimization in white America changed very little compared to the changes in risk among blacks.[39]

The juvenile homicide spike of 1984 to 1994 produced a wave of legislative activity during the 1990s, but it is hard to judge how powerful an effect it will have on juvenile crime response into the 2000s. In some ways, the juvenile homicide spike can be compared to the surge in all crime categories that occurred in the 1960s and early 1970s, which fueled the conservative agenda on adult law enforcement and punishment.

Like the earlier crime wave, the juvenile homicide spike was shocking and frightening, it unfolded rapidly, and, to many people, it seemed to portend a crisis spiraling out of control. In other important ways, however, the juvenile homicide spike bore little resemblance to the general crime wave of twenty years earlier. For one thing, the juvenile crime rise was limited to homicide and near-lethal violence, whereas the crime surge beginning in the 1960s included all categories of violent and property crime. Second, the spike, after reaching its peak in 1994, fell back even faster than it rose. There is no sign that adolescent killings will level off at a new high plateau similar to the "plateau effect" for general crime rates experienced throughout the 1970s and 1980s.

The punitive character of the conservative revolution in adult crime response has been sustained by the fact that violent crime went up from 1960 to 1975 and then stayed up from 1975 through the early 1990s. The opposite has been true following the juvenile homicide spike, which immediately reversed itself. For this reason, unless serious juvenile violence turns back upward, we see little reason to forecast that the politics of juvenile crime response will become fixed in a get-tough mold.

Serious Juvenile Violence Today

Based on homicide estimates published by the U.S. Justice Department, it can be calculated that, for every one million juveniles in the nation ages ten to seventeen, there were ninety-two juvenile offenders involved in a homicide in 1997, either as principal actor or accomplice.[40] In other words, only

.0092 percent of all juveniles were involved in a homicide in 1997, which is another way of saying that 99.9908 percent of all juveniles were not. If one extends this calculation over the full span of years from age ten to seventeen, we can estimate that as many as .074 percent of all juveniles will be involved in a homicide prior to adulthood—but 99.926 will not. (This assumes that 1997 murder rates will remain constant into the future, when they have in fact been coming down.)

This very low probability that any given child or adolescent will ever commit a murder also provides a window into the likelihood that a person in this age group will ever inflict an extreme, life-threatening injury. Suppose there are twenty very serious assaults (those with an injury presenting significant possibility of death) for every one that results in the death of the victim.[41] Based on the numbers of juvenile homicides we have been seeing in recent years, this twenty-to-one ratio yields an estimate that 98.5 percent of all juveniles will never commit such an act of grave assault at any time before reaching eighteen.

The rarity of extreme violence by juveniles must be matched against high rates of lower-level criminality in the thirteen through seventeen age group, including acts of violence that do not produce grave injuries. By age eighteen, approximately 30 percent of white male teenagers and 40 percent of blacks admit in surveys to at least one act of violence in their past histories.[42] Juvenile involvement in property crime is still more commonplace.[43] Yet nearly all of this prolific criminality falls far short of the grave violent offenses that the public fears the most.

The policy implications of this analysis are straightforward: America's juvenile crime response should be formulated primarily to address the mass of commonplace cases, rather than the rare tragedies we hear about most often in the media, and should be fashioned with sensitivity to the fact that most juvenile offenders voluntarily desist from crime without outside intervention. At the same time, society must remain aware that a small percentage of youthful offenders are capable of visiting harms upon the community that rival those committed by the hardest adult criminals. An important segment of the business of juvenile crime response must be devoted to detecting these offenders and protecting the public from them.

In short, the facts of juvenile crime do not support either a unified punitive approach or a uniformly child-saving approach in crime response. Run-of-the-mill adolescent offenders should not be grouped with the worst of the worst, nor should the public be asked to tolerate a restrained, nurturing orientation toward those few youthful criminals who break the mold.

Punishment of Juvenile Criminals

Much liberal commentary on juvenile crime response alleges that juvenile courts and corrections have become more punitive and crime-control oriented in recent years. It is relatively common to hear that these changes have been so severe that any differences between the "juvenile justice system" and the adult "criminal justice system" have vanished or are in the process of disappearing. The people who take this view usually point to a cluster of legal and policy developments that have occurred in the past decade or two, including the following:

Most states have expanded the mechanisms by which juvenile offenders may or must be transferred to the adult courts to be tried as adults and made subject to adult punishments. The states vary in how transfer is achieved, but there is a nationwide trend toward more juveniles being tried and sentenced as adults. Overall, prosecutors and legislators, rather than judges, have increasingly become the key decisionmakers in this process.[44]

Many state legislatures have revised their juvenile codes to stress punishment and public protection over rehabilitation. All of the original juvenile codes, written in the late nineteenth and early twentieth centuries, claimed to place the best interests of the juvenile offender above other goals. By the late 1990s, forty-two states had added the statutory goal of punishment to their juvenile codes, sometimes to the exclusion of treatment and diversion, and sometimes as an additional objective.[45] Eighteen states now provide that protection of the public is a goal of equal or greater importance than rehabilitation.[46]

Authorized punishments for juveniles have become more severe, and there has been some movement toward using more mandatory minimum penalties and sentencing guidelines for juvenile sentencing. At least twenty states have introduced some form of "blended sentencing" for juveniles, which allows juvenile court judges to select between adult and juvenile punishments when passing sentences, or to impose some combination of juvenile and adult punishments.[47]

Legislation reducing the minimum age for adult court jurisdiction has been passed in many states, across the board or for specific cases. Young offenders are treated as adults at age seventeen in ten states and at age sixteen in three states. Many other states have statutory exceptions to their age boundaries, and define some juveniles under eighteen as adults, depending on such factors as the crime charged and the youth's prior record. For example, youths as young as ten can be tried as adults on charges of homicide in a number of states. The overall trend toward lowering the age limit has been slow in recent years. Only three states have done so since 1975, although all three changes were made in the 1990s.[48]

The old rules regarding the confidentiality of juvenile court proceedings, the expungement of records of delinquency adjudications, and the bar against the use of juvenile court records in later adult criminal proceedings have been giving way. By the late 1990s, forty-seven states had passed laws allowing juvenile court records to be accessible to police, prosecutors, social agencies, schools, victims, and / or members of the public. All fifty states, by legislation or court decision, had made prior juvenile records available as factors to enhance sentencing in later adult criminal trials, including some states that now allow juvenile adjudications to count as "strikes" under the states' three-strikes laws.[49]

Death sentences and executions of offenders who committed murders while juveniles have been increasing. The U.S. Supreme Court has ruled that the Constitution prohibits the execution of a person who was fifteen years old at the time of the crime, but there is no bar against executing persons who were sixteen or seventeen years old.[50] Since the 1970s, nearly two hundred capital sentences have been imposed on defendants who were sixteen or seventeen at the time of their crime, although this amounted to only 3 percent of all death sentences.[51] At the end of 1999, eighty of the 3,232 inmates on death rows nationwide had been seventeen or younger at the time of their arrest.[52] In 2000, four inmates were executed for murder who had been under age eighteen at the time of their crimes.[53] Since 1990, only six countries worldwide are known to have executed persons who had been younger than eighteen at the time of the crime: Iran, Nigeria, Pakistan, Saudi Arabia, Yemen, and the United States. Among these six, the United States has carried out the most executions—fourteen from 1990 to 2000.[54]

Proposals have surfaced in favor of processing all adult and juvenile suspects and offenders through a unified machinery of investigation, prosecution, and punishment, thereby abolishing juvenile courts in America. Among those who advocate such consolidation, there is little agreement over why or how this should be done.[55] Alongside the abolitionist proposals are recommendations to reinvent the juvenile courts while maintaining their separate existence. Many, but not all, of these suggestions would push the juvenile courts to more closely resemble the adult criminal process.[56]

Many people are unhappy about these developments (or threatened developments), and assemble them as proof that there are serious and ongoing threats to the basic mission and operation of juvenile courts nationwide.[57] Nonetheless, the degree of change in the juvenile sector has been seriously overstated. It is a little-known fact that our processes and punishments for youthful offenders have changed comparatively little since the mid-1970s when measured against the conservative shift that has taken place in adult crime response. The two spheres are not "converging," as some have suggested. Instead, the separate existence of a "juvenile justice system" has continued to matter a great deal.

The Continuing Importance of a Separate Juvenile Court

Claims that the juvenile court has become, is becoming, or should become extinct, would be impressive if even a single U.S. jurisdiction had abolished its courts of separate jurisdiction for youthful criminals. The abolition "movement" will not constitute a force to be reckoned with until at least several states have taken the plunge—and we are aware of no jurisdiction that is seriously considering such a radical change. The crucial issues of future policy, to the extent they are knowable today, focus instead on legislative changes that have been whittling away the scope of juvenile court jurisdiction, and changes in the punitive effects of the juvenile process itself.

There is little evidence so far that juvenile courts have lost their distinctive character. The transfer of juvenile offenders into the adult courts for prosecution and punishment has clearly been on the rise in the past ten to fifteen years, but it remains a small-numbers phenomenon. The traditional way that juvenile cases are reassigned to adult courtrooms is through "judicial waiver," where a juvenile court judge decides whether a specific case should be transferred, usually following a request by the prosecutor.[58] Nearly all states expanded their waiver laws in the 1990s, or adopted new waiver provisions, which may account in part for the 73 percent increase in use of judicial waiver nationwide between 1988 and 1994.[59]

From 1994 to 1997, however, the number of cases that were judicially waived dropped by 28 percent. As of 1997, waiver cases made up only 0.84 percent of all formal juvenile delinquency cases across the country.[60] Even at the high point of judicial waivers, in the earlier 1990s, they never amounted to much more than 1.5 percent of all formal delinquency cases.[61] Such figures hardly threaten to eviscerate the jurisdiction of the juvenile courts. In 1997, 8,400 delinquency filings were waived to criminal courts, including roughly 3,360 alleged violent crimes, 3,200 property crimes, and 1,260 drug offenses. These numbers must be compared against the 1.8 million delinquency matters handled by juvenile courts in the same year, including 996,000 that resulted in the filing of formal petitions.[62]

A number of states, however, have adopted laws allowing for the transfer of juveniles to the adult courts by mechanisms other than judicial waiver. These include statutes requiring that cases of certain offense types (such as murder and aggravated rape) be prosecuted in adult courts, provided the offenders meet the minimum age criteria in the statutes. This method of transfer is sometimes called "statutory exclusion," but we prefer the simpler term "legislative transfer." In addition, a number of states have chosen to allow prosecutors, for certain offenses, to decide whether to file charges in juvenile or adult court. This practice is known as "direct file" or "prosecutorial transfer."

There are no national data tracking the annual numbers of delinquency cases that are subject to legislative and prosecutorial transfer. Single-jurisdiction studies show a wide variety of effects. New direct file procedures in Florida in the 1980s appear to have affected many cases, but new legislative transfer laws in Pennsylvania seem to have had almost no net effect on transfer overall.[63] Nationwide effects are thus hard to judge. We do know, however, that transfers of all three kinds—judicial, legislative, and prosecutorial—amounted to only about 1 percent of all felony cases in adult courtrooms across the country in the 1990s, even at the height of the juvenile crime scare.[64] Once again, this statistic hardly suggests that a large segment of youthful offenders have been shunted over into the adult crime response complex.

This conclusion is bolstered by information concerning what happens to transfer cases after they arrive in the adult courts. Fully one quarter are dismissed.[65] Among those that proceed to conviction, it is by no means guaranteed that criminal court judges will sentence juvenile criminals more harshly than juvenile court judges would have done. A number of studies have shown that juvenile property offenders who are reassigned to adult courts, on average, receive punishments less severe than those meted out in similar cases by the juvenile courts. Juvenile violent offenders, in contrast, seem likely to receive a stiffer penalty in the adult courts.[66] It is difficult to assess the net effect of all transfer decisions, but there is no overwhelming shift toward greater severity.

Like transfer cases, death penalty cases involving juveniles are few in number—exceedingly so. In the last decade there have been more than fifteen thousand juvenile offenders implicated in homicides, yet only fourteen executions.[67] Such cases raise raw questions of morality and the legitimacy of law. But given the small fraction of delinquency cases involved, it cannot be said that capital prosecutions of juvenile offenders have much bearing on the nearly two million subcapital cases that otherwise move through the juvenile courts each year.

Finally, it is important to weigh the claim that the juvenile courts themselves are becoming more punitive, and are increasingly handing out sentences that resemble those in adult courts. In 1997, the U.S. Justice Department reported that there were 105,790 juveniles held in approximately 3,400 public and private "residential placement" facilities because they had been either charged with a crime or adjudicated for an offense.[68] In the same year, there were 1,725,842 inmates in the nation's prisons and jails.[69] Incarceration ordered by the adult criminal courts is clearly a much bigger business than juvenile confinement when looking at the absolute numbers.[70]

Do the relative incarceration or confinement rates match the proportions of crimes committed by adults versus juveniles? Significantly, there are roughly sixteen times as many persons incarcerated by the adult criminal courts than by the juvenile courts, but there is not sixteen times more adult crime than juvenile crime. In 1997, juveniles were 19 percent of all persons arrested for offenses tracked by the FBI, which means that adult arrests outnumbered juvenile arrests by about four to one.[71] For violent index offenses (murder, rape, robbery, and aggravated assault), juveniles made up 17 percent of arrest totals—including a whopping 30 percent of all robbery arrests.[72] If sheer numbers of arrests could be used as predictors of confinement, and if we applied the adult incarceration standard to juveniles, then there should have been 326,884 juveniles in custody in 1997 instead of only 105,790. This crude yardstick suggests that juvenile court punishment outcomes are considerably more lenient than outcomes on the adult side of the line.

Some may argue that this calculation exaggerates the relative lenity of juvenile court punishment. As noted earlier, the typical juvenile crime (be it an assault, a robbery, or even a property crime) is less harm-producing than the typical adult crime of the same type. Thus, for every one hundred juveniles arrested for robbery one would expect to see fewer incarcerations, and shorter average sentences, than for one hundred adult robbery arrests. One way to gauge the possible extent of this crime severity difference is to look only at the most serious offenses, where the harm produced is most uniform: murder and nonnegligent manslaughter. Yet here adult arrests outnumbered juvenile arrests by slightly more than six-to-one in 1997, which is still a good distance away from the sixteen-to-one punishment differential.[73]

Another way to compare juvenile-court and adult-court punishments is to look at trends in confinement over the last two or three decades. In adult incarceration, this has been a period of unprecedented and explosive growth. From 1975 to 1997, the adult inmate populations in our prisons and jails skyrocketed from 388,037 to 1,725,842, an increase of 344 percent.[74] The history of change in juvenile custody has been strikingly different. In 1975, there were a reported 74,270 children and adolescents in juvenile custody facilities, and 105,790 in 1997.[75] Thus juvenile-court incarceration grew by only 42.4 percent in this period—a diminutive rate of change by adult-court standards. There were one-fifth as many juveniles as adults confined in the mid-1970s, and less than one-sixteenth by 1997.[76]

This is not to say that the juvenile courts have been immune from the conservative policies that have prevailed in the last three decades. Along with moderate growth in total confinement numbers, juvenile facilities since the 1970s have become more focused on security and less likely to try to promote the inmate-friendly atmosphere of a "home," "ranch," or "school." Consequently, more juveniles in custody today experience a prisonlike environment than twenty-five years ago.[77] In addition, the increasing (but still proportionally small) frequency of transfers of juvenile cases to the adult courts has resulted in an upswing in juvenile inmates held in adult correctional facilities. For example, the number of prison inmates under the age of eighteen grew from 2,300 in 1984 to 5,400 in 1997, and dropped somewhat to 3,147 in 2001. Even when looking at the higher number for 1997, however, juvenile inmates still amounted to only 0.5 percent of all prisoners for that year.[78] Most of these underage inmates were older juveniles—seventeen is by far the most common age—but it is not unknown to find prison inmates as young as fourteen cohabiting with adult convicts.[79]

The intermixing of adult and juvenile criminals—especially younger juveniles—is morally wrong, gratuitously harmful to the teenagers involved, and more likely in the long run to produce crime than to prevent it.[80] The topic at hand, however, is whether the policies of the current conservative era have affected as many juveniles, or have hit them as hard, as punitive developments in the adult sector. The answer is no, not by a long shot.

How then can one explain the extreme claims of many people that the juvenile courts are no longer distinct from the adult criminal process? It is possible that the liberal critics of the modest transformation in juvenile crime response, who have had the dominant voice in this issue, object to any shift toward a more punitive orientation, and their rhetorical strategy has been to overdramatize the reality of incremental change. If so, such hyperbole misleads those who care to think seriously about the future of juvenile crime response in America, and ultimately is not helpful even to the liberal cause. Despite the rhetoric, juvenile justice remains an area in which liberal crime response policy, while embattled, has held onto much of its dominance through the conservative era. The central policy issue for the future is whether this persistent separateness of approach should be maintained.

Race, Ethnicity, and Juvenile Crime Response

As in adult crime response, racial and ethnic disparities are stark facts of life in juvenile case processing and punishment. Although African Americans make up only about 15 percent of the nation's juvenile population ages ten to seventeen, in 1996–1997 they made up 40 percent of juveniles held in residential placement, 46 percent of juvenile cases waived by judges to the adult criminal courts, and 60 percent of the state prison inmates under the age of eighteen.[81] Corrected for population, the black juvenile custody rate, considering juvenile facilities alone, was five times the white rate, and the black juvenile imprisonment rate (in adult institutions) was more than fourteen times the white rate.[82]

Although data for other races and ethnic groups are often not available,[83] we know that 1997 confinement rates in juvenile facilities were two-and-one-half times greater for Hispanic and Native American youths than for whites, while the Asian juvenile confinement rate was virtually identical to the white rate.[84] In adult prisons in 1997, 13 percent of inmates under the age of eighteen were Hispanic, the same as the percentage of Hispanics in the national juvenile population for that year—but still roughly three-

and-one-half times the white juvenile imprisonment rate. Although in 1997 white juveniles were 67 percent of the U.S. population between the ages of ten and seventeen, they made up only 19 percent of all juveniles held in adult prisons.[85]

There is also evidence that racial and ethnic disproportionalities in juvenile crime response have been worsening in recent decades. In 1977, African Americans were 28 percent of youths held in the nation's juvenile custody facilities. By 1985 they were 33 percent of the total; in 1997, 40 percent. Hispanic juveniles were 8 percent of all juveniles confined in 1977, 11 percent in 1985, and 18 percent in 1997.[86] By 1993, there also were large differences by race and ethnicity in the amount of time juveniles spent in such custody. The average length of stay for white juveniles was 193 days, for black juveniles it was 254 days, and for Hispanic juveniles it was 305 days.[87]

The statistics of racial disparities in juvenile crime response are sometimes cited as evidence that the juvenile courts are in deep crisis, are infected by racial bias, and are (once again) becoming increasingly indistinguishable from our agencies of adult prosecution and punishment.[88] Such claims raise serious issues, but they are overstated in ways that make it more, not less, difficult to address problems of racial inequality.

First, no adequate effort has yet been made to correct the disparities in juvenile arrest, prosecution, and punishment in terms of racial and ethnic differences in crime commission. Part of the problem is that we lack high-quality information about crime in general, and juvenile crime in particular, that is as clear and accessible as court and corrections statistics. Another problem is that people are reluctant to talk about the crime data we do possess for fear of being charged with racism.[89] It is quite common for discussions of disparate outcomes in the legal process to be laid out with little or no attention given to the underlying crime statistics.[90]

Racial and ethnic differences in offending, however, do in fact exist, and for some crime categories they are very large. The most reliable indicators are for black / white differentials in homicide. In 1997, the black juvenile homicide rate, based on arrests, was roughly six times the white rate.[91] In 1993 and 1994, at the peak of the juvenile homicide spike, black males ages fourteen to seventeen committed homicides at rates ten to eleven times the white male rates in the same age groups.[92] As discussed earlier, the homicide statistics are also strong circumstantial evidence of rates of life-threatening violence that stops short of killing the victim. In 1997, black juveniles were arrested for aggravated assaults at nearly three times the white arrest rate—and homicide statistics make it difficult to avoid the conclusion that black assaults on average were more deadly than the average white assaults. Aggravated assaults by black youths were more than twice as likely to result in the deaths of victims than aggravated assaults by whites.[93]

For armed robbery, another highly feared crime, African American juvenile arrest rates in the past two decades have been as high as thirteen times the white juvenile arrest rate.[94] In 1997, after a number of years of declines in juvenile crime, the robbery arrest rate for black juveniles was still six times the white rate.[95] If one thinks of incarceration as being most appropriately used for the most serious violent crimes, then some significant portion of the racial disparities in confinement—among juveniles as well as adults—can be traced to racial disparities in grave criminality.[96]

As in adult crime response, the evidence of improper discrimination against juvenile offenders is strongest for those offenses that are the least serious, with especially egregious patterns of disparate treatment appearing for minority juveniles accused of drug offenses.[97] Our existing knowledge suggests that such outcomes are impossible to justify either in terms of crime commission or expected crime prevention.

Stepping back for wide-angle perspective, it is clear that the raw disproportionalities in juvenile crime response are lower overall than those in the adult setting. In 1997, the black juvenile custody rate was five times the white rate. But in adult prisons for the same year, the black / white incarceration disproportionality was greater than seven to one. Indeed, according to the U.S. Justice Department, black male imprisonment rates in 1999 for some age groups exceeded nine times the white rate.[98] Among Hispanics in the juvenile courts, rates of arrests, adjudications, and commitments have been rising since the 1970s, but Hispanics are still only barely overrepresented in the juvenile system when compared to their numbers in the general population.[99]

More important, the total societal effect of racial and ethnic disparities in juvenile crime response must be assessed in light of the slow growth in juvenile punishment overall since the 1970s. Readers will recall from Chapter 1 that the percentages of African Americans in prison and jail populations have been edging steadily upward (a trend that goes all the way back to the nineteenth century). But the truly massive racial effects in the adult system have occurred not because the black slice of the pie has gotten larger, but because the entire "pie" of adult incarceration has expanded so remarkably in the past two or three decades. Not so in the juvenile domain, where the "pie" of confinement has enlarged only slightly. At the turn of the twenty-first century, black juvenile incarceration rates are only marginally higher than they were twenty-five years before. While a subject of legitimate concern, the modest changes in black juvenile custody bear no fair resemblance to the devastating racial effects that have resulted from changing patterns in adult punishment.

The Significance of Early Prevention

Historically, our society has been willing to expend far more effort and dollars for after-the-fact law enforcement and criminal punishment than for measures of early crime prevention.[100] There is something seriously wrong with this picture.

The main goal of early prevention is to forestall criminal careers before they begin, to head off the losses experienced by crime victims, and to intervene before the legal and behavioral baggage of past guilt has leadened the life chances of young people and complicated our reactions to them. Early prevention responds to the anticipated probabilities of future crime. It is often focused on youths, families, and communities that are peculiarly "at risk" of future criminal events. Indeed, the more successfully such programs can identify at-risk populations, the more cost-effective they can be. Early prevention programs with demonstrated track records of success include prenatal and infancy home visitation by nurses (into homes where there are high risks of health and developmental problems in infants), bullying prevention programs in primary and secondary schools, the Big Brothers and Big Sisters mentoring program for children ages six to eighteen (most from disadvantaged, single-parent households), certain forms of family-oriented therapy that address problems affecting youths at home, school, and within peer groups, and some programs of early drug abuse prevention (designed to decrease rates of onset and prevalence of substance abuse among young adolescents).[101]

The decisive advantage of early prevention programs is that they do not force society to make agonizing tradeoffs between the interests of offenders or potential offenders, on the one hand, and victims or prospective victims of crime, on the other. Successful early prevention is a rare instance of a positive-sum strategy in that society can help both groups at once.[102] All of this, when effective, can help avoid the substantial racial and ethnic disparities in crime commission, crime victimization, and criminal punishment that our culture now experiences.

There is reason to think that the financial expense of the better early prevention programs is comparable to, or even lower than, the cost of after-the-fact criminal punishment. A study by the RAND Corporation published in 1998 compared the crime-reduction potential of California's three-strikes law with that of several leading early prevention programs. The report also looked at comparative dollar costs. The RAND researchers estimated that the three-strikes law, if fully implemented (that is, if applied in every possible case), could reduce serious crime in the state by about 21 percent, or 329,000 offenses each year, at a cost to California taxpayers of about 5.5 billion dollars each year.[103]

By combining the two most cost-effective early prevention programs, however, RAND's estimates suggest that the state could achieve as much as an additional 22 percent reduction in crime at an annual cost of roughly 900 million dollars. Looked at another way, the three-strikes incarcerative approach can be expected to spend about $16,000 for every serious felony averted, whereas the combined early prevention programs were projected to prevent serious felonies at a cost of less than $4,000 per offense.[104]

It is important to note that to argue in favor of early prevention is not to argue against the confinement of juvenile or adult criminals once they have committed crimes. Early prevention supplements confinement policy and is not a substitute for it. No matter what position one takes on the punishment of crimes after the fact, there should be widespread interest in exploring the greater use of effective early prevention programs because they seem to be spectacular financial investments that can add to the health of communities and avoid victimizations before they happen.[105]

Among the most prominent conservative and liberal academics, a consensus in favor of early crime prevention has been materializing in recent years.[106] James Q. Wilson, who at one time expressed a blanket dismissal of the idea that society should attack the "root causes" of crime, wrote sympathetically in 1995 about interventions targeted at the risk factors that can lead young children into crime:

> We must confront the fact that the critical years of a child's life are ages one to ten, with perhaps the most important being the earliest years. During those years, some children are put gravely at risk by some combination of heritable traits, prenatal insults (maternal drug use and alcohol

abuse or poor diet), weak parent-child attachment, poor supervision, and disorderly family environment.[107]

It is encouraging that intellectuals from different points on the ideological spectrum are finding common ground on this issue. Early prevention may well become an area in which improving empirical knowledge will succeed in breaking down customary political divisions.[108]

One major problem in our past attitude toward early prevention must be solved, however. In recent decades, American policymakers have been willing to throw dollars at a patchwork of family-based, school-based, or community-based prevention programs whose effectiveness had never been established by careful research. Many of the initiatives favored by Democrats in the federal crime bill of 1994, for example (such as millions of dollars for midnight basketball, arts and crafts classes, and gender sensitivity training) were unproven at best, and were embarrassingly vulnerable to the charge of being nothing but "pork."[109] Too often, programs that sound good, and win avid political supporters, simply fail to deliver results. The most notorious ongoing example may be DARE, the most popular school-based antidrug educational program in the country. Although school districts around the country have spent many millions on the DARE curriculum, numerous evaluations have found no evidence that the program yields any short-term or long-term reduction in substance abuse or crime.[110]

The strong case in favor of prevention cannot be separated from a commitment to program evaluation. It makes no sense at all for governments across the nation to dedicate billions of dollars to childhood interventions without also spending, along the way, the millions necessary to ensure that the efforts are based on successful models, are implemented faithfully, and continue to deliver results. Early prevention has gotten a bad name because we have not created a marketplace that demands (or even detects) success. This is an area in which America could *easily* be doing much better than current experience—and the winners would far outnumber the losers.

Banish the Euphemisms

Our first suggestion for the criminal prosecution and punishment of juveniles is that we do away with the multiple euphemisms that are now used pervasively in most courts of juvenile jurisdiction. The juvenile courts do not call a crime a "crime," but an act of "delinquency." Juvenile offenders are not "prosecuted" and "convicted"; instead, their cases are "adjudicated." Juveniles held in confinement are not "prisoners" or "inmates"; they are "residents" or "students." The accurate and proper terminology for juvenile crime and punishment should be no different than for adults.

From a justice and legitimacy standpoint, the juvenile courts should speak in a language that respects the perceptions of victims of juvenile crimes, whose injuries are trivialized when our legal vocabulary fails to acknowledge the core criminality of what has happened to them. Part of the perception that the juvenile courts "coddle" offenders may well be keyed to the fact that the courts are getting the symbolism wrong.

The dissembling use of language also sends an unfortunate signal to juvenile offenders. To the extent that we hope the experiences of arrest, prosecution, sentencing, and punishment can carry moral weight with young criminals, we subtract from the moral communication by the use of fudge words. It may also be the case that an important component of rehabilitation is the juvenile's appreciation of the deep wrongfulness of his past criminal activity. Furthermore, we doubt that many juvenile criminals misapprehend the coercive, stigmatizing, and punitive nature of the proceedings. The juvenile courts act hypocritically—and lose credibility—when they deny their criminal-court attributes, and when they claim to be engaging in a child-saving mission that is little in evidence.

Related to the point that juvenile crime and punishment should be treated as such, it is necessary to the reform of both juvenile and adult crime response that the records of juvenile adjudications not be sealed, expunged, or otherwise made unavailable to decisionmakers in subsequent criminal prosecutions. The traditional practice of making the past lives of juvenile offenders invisible once they reach the age of majority is based on impulses of kindness, on the belief that juveniles stand a better chance of successful transition to adulthood without the baggage of a criminal record, and on strong doubts about the procedural safeguards accorded in the juvenile courts.[111] These are weighty concerns, and militate in favor of thoughtfulness about how an offender's prior juvenile record should be incorporated into the adjudication and sanctioning processes of adult criminal courts. But a complete bar on the availability of the information imposes high costs on rational decisionmaking. Much of the difficulty in sentencing determinations, especially at the top end of punishment severity, turns on the quality of predictions we are able to make about the future behavior of offenders. Such predictions can be improved, or hampered, depending on the availability of knowledge about the past history of offenders. The crime response complex can debate how properly to incorporate such information, but should eschew legislative bans upon its availability.

Forbearance and Helping versus Punishment and Control

Once a young offender has come under the jurisdiction of a juvenile court, a number of philosophies might be consulted for the imposition of sanctions. First, crime-response authorities might take an attitude of forbearance with respect to a particular juvenile criminal, or whole classes of juvenile offenders, and impose a sanction that is as light as possible, require no sanction at all, or divert the case from adjudication entirely. A policy of forbearance rests chiefly on the premise that many juvenile offenders dip only lightly into criminal activity, and soon grow out of law-breaking on their own accord. The operative goal in such cases is to avoid disrupting the natural maturation process, and to preserve intact the life chances of the adolescent.[112]

Second, juvenile sanctions can provide programming designed to help offenders become more law-abiding. Many young criminals do not spontaneously grow out of crime, and some do considerable damage to themselves and others before finally desisting. Helping sanctions try to push offenders toward crime desistance more quickly and more certainly than the alternative of letting nature take its course.

Third, juvenile sanctions may be fashioned on a model of punishment and control. The sanction of choice under this theory is secure confinement, on the plausible view that an offender behind locked doors cannot victimize anyone in the free community, and on the moral supposition that incarceration is deserved by some young criminals.

This rationale should not be underappreciated. A small but meaningful minority of juvenile criminals commit acts of grave violence that are every bit as harmful as the worst adult offenses—and it is no consolation to their victims that their attackers were underage. It should be noted, however, that there need not be total separation between helping measures and punishment-control strategies. Helping programs are frequently found in custodial settings, although they are often not a first priority. In addition, some people think the very harshness of confinement can teach offenders a lesson that will improve their future conduct. Despite these possibilities for offender change, the difference in emphasis between helping and punishment-control strategies is very real. As a general matter, punishment-control objectives are willing to submerge the best interests of the juvenile offender to the interests of potential victims and their communities.

All of the options described here for juvenile sentencing involve painful and sometimes dangerous tradeoffs. Compared with secure incarceration, juvenile court outcomes that return offenders to the street, or place them in community programs with light supervision, are hardly foolproof as anticrime measures. Some advocates of helping programs see them as benefiting everyone: offenders, victims, and society alike.[113] This appealing dream comes true once in awhile, making it all the more attractive. But there are also many cases of failure and recidivism, where hindsight reveals that victims could have been spared if the juvenile courts, at an earlier juncture, had responded more forcibly.

On the other side of the coin, sanctions that overreact in the direction of punishment and control carry their own heavy risks and costs. In privileging the interests of prospective victims and communities, confinement sanctions overpunish some juveniles who could have been restored to a law-abiding lifestyle with considerably less invasion into their lives. When policymakers choose to expand punishment and control, to cover gray-area cases that might otherwise be routed to helping sanctions or forbearance, this places ever greater numbers of juvenile offenders at risk of unnecessarily severe restraints.

Juvenile sanctioning choices ultimately call for moral judgments but, as with so much else in crime response policy, it is important that such judgments be built upon knowledge and information. The following sections consult the empirical research on two relevant questions: First, how well and how often do helping programs seem to change the law-breaking behaviors of juvenile delinquents? Second, how accurately can we identify those juvenile offenders who are especially dangerous, thus enabling decisionmakers to select them for sanctions involving punishment and control?

Success Rates among Helping Programs for Juvenile Offenders

In the 1970s, the best-known statement on juvenile rehabilitative programming was the multistudy review prepared by Robert Martinson titled "What Works?"[114] Based on his analysis of 231 studies of existing programs, he popularized the conclusion that most of them achieved little or no improvement in the future behavior of their clientele—and some made matters worse. The sound-bite capsulization of Martinson's argument was that "nothing works" in juvenile rehabilitation, or rehabilitation in general. Ever since, researchers (including Martinson himself in the late 1970s) have toiled to document that "nothing works" was in fact an overstatement.[115] But how much of an overstatement?

The most highly regarded assessment of helping programs for juvenile offenders available today is the meta-analysis performed by Mark Lipsey and his colleagues throughout the 1990s.[116] Lipsey and his coauthors selected two hundred studies of rehabilitative programs for juveniles, culling from thousands that had been conducted from 1950 to 1995.[117] In order to be included in the meta-sample, the original studies had to meet minimum standards of methodological rigor.[118] Within the selected body of research, 117 of the programs were in noninstitutional community settings, and eighty-three were in confinement institutions.

The overall findings were consistent with the view that rehabilitation "sometimes works." For all two hundred programs, Lipsey estimated that, on average, 12 percent fewer juveniles recidivated (that is, committed another offense or probation violation) after undergoing treatment, when compared with other juvenile offenders who did not receive the program treatment. The follow-up periods in the studies gathered by Lipsey were typically short, so that youths were deemed to have recidivated, or not, within one or two years of program completion, or even shorter periods.[119]

The 12 percent effect perhaps sounds larger than it really is. As explained by Lipsey, if one assumes that approximately 50 percent of all juvenile criminals will recidivate if not treated (this figure is roughly consonant with existing research), then the average effect of all offender change programs in the meta-analysis is to reduce that 50 percent recidivism rate to 44 percent.[120] For 94 percent of all the juveniles enrolled in the average helping program, there would be no discernable change in their future compliance with the law.

Lipsey's evaluations of specific types of programs were occasionally more encouraging than the averaged-out 12 percent effect, and a number of the programs in the meta-analysis looked to be ineffective or even crime-productive. This lends fuel to the argument that a more intelligent investment in helping programs that work well, coupled with the abandonment of ineffective options, could raise significantly the total amount of crime avoidance achieved. The most successful programs outside of institutional walls reduced juvenile recidivism by as much as 40 to 50 percent. Within confinement environs, the best programs reduced recidivism by 30 to 35 percent.[121]

Lipsey's findings must be put in policy-relevant perspective, however. For one thing, there is no evidence that it is currently possible to widely replicate the most successful programs identified by Lipsey. So far, researchers have had little success in producing solid, real-world interventions that actually bring home the top-of-the-chart juvenile crime reductions that seem available in theory.[122]

If helping programs in the aggregate are ever going to perform significantly better than Lipsey's 12 percent baseline, the supportive research must go back to the ground level to test the measurable effects of particular programs, as well as their replicability.[123] Although hundreds of programs exist nationwide for helping juvenile offenders, only a handful have been subject to the kind of rigorous evaluation necessary to make an informed judgment about program effectiveness.[124] As a 2001 report on youth violence issued by the U.S. Surgeon General put it:

> The scientific community agrees on three standards for evaluating effectiveness: rigorous experimental design, evidence of significant deterrent effects, and replication of these effects at multiple sites or in clinical trials. . . . Unfortunately, this level of evidence has not been routinely required by agencies that recommend or fund youth violence prevention programs.[125]

Despite the paucity of assessment research, the Surgeon General's report was able to identify several successful or promising programs for reducing rates of reoffending among juvenile delinquents. These included behavioral and skill development interventions,[126] family clinical interventions,[127] and the Intensive Protective Supervision Project.[128] Overall, however, the report was able to endorse only seven programs nationwide that qualified as proven "model" youth-violence interventions, and this total included four early prevention programs.[129] The record of successful helping programs for juveniles who have already entered their criminal careers remains tissue-paper thin.[130]

Moreover, the identification of individual programs that work is of limited value until there is additional proof that such programs can be reproduced in other places and with different personnel. Research on replication has been ignored almost completely in the past, although enlightened so-cial scientists have been making a strong push for change in this arena.[131] In the meantime, policymakers cannot be expected to rest decisions on mere expectations. The proponents of rehabilitative programming have been saying for a long time that better knowledge and technologies will bring substantial improvement on low success rates. But until persuasive research shows otherwise, Lipsey's averaged-out findings of recidivism re-ductions are a better policy guide than the hope that we can surpass prior experience.

Another important caveat is that the 12 percent recidivism reductions calculated by Lipsey are not corrected for any decay factor over time. Earlier in this chapter, we discussed a RAND Corporation estimate of the crime-reduction benefits of several early prevention programs. In the RAND study, the researchers assumed (as much prior research has shown) that one- or two-year reductions in recidivism tend to wear off as youths reenter their prior life patterns. In their calculations of the total crime re-duction that might be won by early intervention programs, the RAND team discounted substantially for such decay factors in program effective-ness.[132] Lipsey's numbers incorporate no such adjustments—nor do we know how to build in the necessary discounts. But it is likely that a one-time measurement of a 12 percent drop-off in criminality among certain juveniles will not by itself translate into a lasting 12 percent reduction. The long-term effect will be lower than that, and perhaps much lower.[133]

Finally, one must acknowledge that the research collected by Lipsey, and rehabilitation research in general, tells very little about the total numbers or seriousness levels of crimes that are avoided when offender-change pro-grams are successful. Virtually all recidivism studies measure reoffending as a binary variable: Youths who commit any post-treatment offenses or violations are counted as failures; youths who stay out of trouble alto-gether are counted as successes. This tells us almost nothing about how much damage the failures go on to do.

The binary measurement may underreport the amount of crime avoid-ance that has taken place. It could be that, among the failures, some are committing less serious crimes, or are offending less frequently, than they would have without the benefit of programming. An optimist might argue that such effects are substantial. There is another possibility, however, that is equally plausible: It could be that the successes are largely youths who would have been low-level offenders even if they had continued their criminal behaviors.[134] If the failures who continue their criminal careers are the worst of the bunch, and the ones whose crimes will do the most damage to victims in the future, society has gained less in crime avoidance than the percentile breakdowns would suggest.

Our discussion has taken a hard-nosed attitude toward the juvenile rehabilitation literature for a reason. Any policy consideration of helping sanctions must be realistic, and realistically skeptical. People who are predisposed to *want* such programs to work (as we are), are frequently guilty of puffing up the evaluation data and thus the prospects of doing better in the future. If there is a strong case to be made for implementing forbearance and / or helping strategies for most juvenile criminals, it must start with a careful and even conservative assessment of empirical knowledge and past experience. Rigor and skepticism are not the enemies of helping programs—they are their best hope of achieving credibility and a more widespread application.

Identifying Dangerous Juvenile Offenders

Perhaps society ought to tolerate a great deal of juvenile crime (most of it male) on the theory that "boys will be boys," and because most troublesome youths eventually grow out of their deviant behavior. Certainly, the bulk of juvenile offending, at the low end of the crime gravity scale, should not prompt the heaviest hammer of criminal sanctions: long-term confinement. Where alternative approaches of discipline and helping are plentiful, the prison cell should be reserved as a measure of last resort. Yet no matter how much adolescent crime society is prepared to treat as incidental to the developmental process, there will remain a subset of young criminals who murder, rape, and cause or threaten grave physical harm to their victims. It is impossible to conceive of such injuries as acceptable facets of adolescent development, and it is irresponsible not to consider the evidence that we can forecast and prevent some of these injuries.

As Norval Morris has said, psychologists' powers to predict future serious violence by individuals are spectacular by scientific standards, but not so impressive that they can be incorporated into the law of criminal sanctions without moral reservations. The best social science for adult criminals tells us that, for every three criminals who fit the profile of future "dangerous offender," only one of the three will actually confirm our fears. The other two, who appear just as convincingly to be high-risk types, will turn out to be false positives. Thus, in order to be reasonably sure that the incapacitation net is wide enough to catch one true future offender before the crime is committed, society must be prepared to accept the human cost of the needless confinement of two innocent people.[135]

The research for predicting violence among juveniles presents a similar picture. Mark Lipsey, in yet another meta-analysis, assembled the state-of-the-art knowledge about successfully identifying serious juvenile offenders before they commit the worst of their crimes. Much of the research examined in his study involved children as young as six to eleven years old, although he also evaluated the predictive literature for the eleven to fourteen age group. Lipsey estimated, based on the most powerful known risk factors for serious offending, that an incapacitation program would have to target more than 25 percent of the total at-risk group in order to be sure that it had included substantially all of the "true" serious offenders, who in turn make up only about 8 percent of the group.[136] It may be helpful to imagine a barrel of one hundred apples containing eight bad apples. According to Lipsey's estimates, one cannot simply pluck out the eight that are rotten. If one uses the best science to carefully select and remove twenty-five apples, however, one can now be reasonably sure to have gotten six or seven of the bad ones. Much like the adult predictive studies, the false-positive ratio in juvenile violence prediction is, at best, two for every one true positive.

The forecasting errors associated with selective punishment-control cannot establish that such policies are "wrong."[137] Such is a moral judgment that cannot be resolved by numbers alone. The truth is that hard tradeoffs are involved when we decide whether and how to use the available predictive technology. The punishment-control model delivers better serious-crime avoidance than the forbearance-helping model, sparing many future victims, but aggressive control measures visit predictable injustices on large numbers of needlessly incarcerated persons.

Choosing between Unacceptable Alternatives

In the domain of early prevention, considered earlier in this chapter, the empirical balance of costs and benefits was sufficiently compelling to provide a firm sense of policy direction without encountering difficult moral tradeoffs. In after-the-crime sanctioning policy, there is no similar positive-sum equation. It is unacceptable to expose innocent victims to risks of serious harm that we know how to diminish. It is also unacceptable to inflict unnecessarily severe punishment on young people who (if only we knew for sure) will never commit a serious crime in the future. And yet, policymakers must choose.

When dealing with thousands of cases in the juvenile courts, just as in the adult criminal courts, decisionmakers must devise frameworks for sorting cases into the sanctioning categories of forbearance, helping programs, and punishment-control. Everyone can agree that some cases belong in each category, but how should the balance be cast and where should lines be drawn? This section will offer the following limited argument: Wherever the policy balance should be set between forbearance-helping and punishment-control in the adult courts, it should be repositioned in the juvenile setting to give greater emphasis to forbearance and helping, much as has been done for the past thirty years.

This is not simply an argument for the status quo. Instead, society should further develop and use knowledge concerning which helping programs work best for which young offenders, and concerning the accurate identification of dangerous offenders whose interests will be sacrificed to the goals of punishment and control. Society also has a special obligation, more so for juvenile offenders than adults, to explore and provide meaningful helping programs even for those consigned to long-term incarceration.

The reasons for a "different balance" in juvenile sanction policy are partly empirical, but primarily matters of moral intuition. The full history of the American juvenile court, stretching across all of the twentieth century, and reaching back into the nineteenth, provides evidence of a deep-seated cultural reluctance to blame juvenile criminals in the same way as adults, or to subject them to punishments and controls with the same instrumental abandon that we sometimes employ for adult offenders. Steven Schlossman has remarked upon this theme. Even as theories of adult criminality have cycled and recycled across the eras, from an emphasis on sinfulness, witchcraft, lack of industry, biological inferiority, or moral irresponsibility, public attitudes toward juvenile criminals have remained remarkably unchanging in their focus on the influences of family, poverty, and community that are believed to mold defenseless children into juvenile offenders.[138] Franklin Zimring has also noted the long-standing and consistent theme in juvenile crime response that youthful offenders should be sanctioned less harshly, and separately, from adult criminals.[139]

The present-day inclination depends in large degree on the continuing

viability of perceptions that children and adolescents are less morally responsible than adults for their mistakes, indiscretions, and even the criminal offenses they commit. To some extent this question of blameworthiness can be addressed by experts in developmental psychology, but no
definitive answers are supplied from that quarter. Teenagers have not yet
had a full opportunity to cultivate their knowledge of the world, and to develop their judgment, impulse-control, and resistance to peer pressure. Yet
most teens have highly developed senses of right and wrong, not so different from adults, and most are able to govern their behavior accordingly.[140]
The answer to the moral question of how much, or how little, to blame
juvenile criminals for their transgressions cannot be resolved entirely
through the tenets of psychology.

Many existing institutions reflect a general understanding that society is
obligated to guide children and adolescents through their formative years.
Our school systems, child-health programs, and child-oriented welfare
policies respond to the tandem beliefs that young people are less capable of
independent moral agency than adults, and that the adult community has
a collective duty to make resources available to assist the often difficult
process of personal development. Such instincts are particularly strong,
at least for some people, when considering the poor and disadvantaged
young people who most often find their way into the juvenile courts.
Significantly, such a deemphasis on punishment-control in the juvenile
setting can also alleviate racially and ethnically disparate incarceration patterns.

No one can prove that these attitudes are "correct." They either exist
within a culture or do not. But even in the absence of such strong beliefs,
the case in favor of separate sanctioning philosophies for juveniles and
adults finds a measure of empirical support: Juvenile crimes on average are
less harm-productive than adult offenses; most juvenile delinquents desist
from crime without legal intervention, and some young people appear to
become more crime-prone after arrest or incarceration; and some people
believe that juvenile offenders are more malleable than adult criminals,
and thus more likely to be rehabilitated through helping programs.

The true test of a moral (rather than an empirical) position on juvenile
sanctioning policy is whether one is willing to accept increased risks of
criminal victimization. There is little doubt that, if the United States were
suddenly to transpose its current adult sentencing policies onto juvenile
offenders, there would be less juvenile crime in the immediate future.

Crime-avoidance would occur from greater incapacitation alone.[141] Still, for the vast majority of juvenile offenders and offenses, where the main risks cluster below the level of serious violent victimizations, the moral imperative of treating young people differently is enough, for us, to tilt the scales in doubtful cases toward forbearance and helping.

No across-the-board policy should foreclose the extended incarceration of juveniles for crime-preventive purposes, however. Some juvenile criminals present much higher risks of future dangerousness than most others, and have already demonstrated their capabilities by committing serious violent crimes. A sensible sanctioning policy should make an empirically informed effort to identify the small group (the six or eight percent) of high-risk offenders, provided the net is not cast so broadly that it guarantees a vast pool of false positives. The search for these hardcore offenders should be kept within bounds that resemble in size the small group we are trying to identify—say 5 to 10 percent of the juvenile court workload. Society should be willing to accept the resulting two-to-one false positive ratio, and some further drift in the direction of sentencing severity, because in such cases the greater moral weight lies with potential crime victims and their communities.

The result of the analysis in this section is a two-track system of juvenile sentencing with painful consequences at both ends. Some people's views of just crime response will cause them to be more victim-sensitive than this analysis has been. Alternatively, some people's sense of justice to juvenile offenders will make them much more reluctant to endorse long-term incarceration for even a small group of young criminals.[142] Whatever one's preferences and moral beliefs, everyone must draw a balance somewhere between forbearance, helping strategies, and punishment and control.

The single most important recommendation of this chapter, and perhaps of the entire book, is the call for greater investment and investigation in early prevention. Such measures are the most victim-friendly form of crime response in existence, because they take place prior to criminal events. They are also the greatest offender-friendly form of intervention, because there is no gift greater than to spare a person a criminal career that he otherwise would have had. In order to mobilize resources toward early prevention, however, policymakers have to overcome human nature and short-time-horizon politics to take actions now that will redound to the benefit of victims, offenders, their respective families, and their communities ten to fifteen years in the future.

The Future

We have no intention to predict the future. The undulant nature of crime and crime response bear witness to the foolishness of such efforts. Nor is it possible to build a future construct of society's vision, comprehension, and attitude toward these subjects. When looking ahead to the coming decades, it is perhaps most helpful to look back and assess the effects of the past punishment revolution.

As this book has described in greater detail, over a one hundred year period, 1880 to 1980, the nation added a total of about 285,000 inmates to its prison systems. During just the ensuing twenty years, 1980 to 2000, the nation added about 1.1 million inmates. From 1850 through 2000, the nation's prison system expanded about 206 times over, during a period of only about twelvefold population growth. Total people on probation or parole status rose almost ninefold between 1965 and 2000. Public dollars for crime response reached almost $150 billion by 2000, up from $36 billion in 1982, and about 6.5 million people were under official confinement or supervision following their criminal convictions. With the help of an unprecedented flow of federal dollars in the 1990s, the federal, state, and local policing complement probably exceeded one million by 2000, and over 700,000 prison and jail guards were serving in the crime response complex. The correctional officers union was the largest public employee union in the state of California—and the largest single donor to candidates for statewide office. The priority of a law enforcement approach to drug use has produced a situation whereby over one-quarter of state prison admissions result from only low-level, nonviolent drug offenses, with a degree of racial disparity in arrests and incarceration that bears little relationship to actual drug use figures. As of 2002, over 600,000 prisoners reenter our communities each year, unprepared for the daunting contrast between prison rigor and the sudden freedom of choice among life's joys, sorrows, demands, and responsibilities.

Even with these dramatic changes, the need for an ambitious reassessment of American crime response policy is not obvious. Looking only at the past decade, it is tempting to declare victory over criminals. Although the radical turnabout from an emphasis on rehabilitation to a focus on punishment produced scanty positive results during its initial twenty years, the crime rate declined for eight years after 1992, seeming to justify the change. The prosperity engendered by the bubble economy of the 1990s had also permitted lavish, unprecedented spending at federal, state, and local levels on the two principal dollar-eaters of the governmental portion of the crime response complex: police and prisons. That economic prosperity also induced high levels of private spending on both direct security measures to prevent and detect crime and on creating jobs for everyone who wanted to work, including ex-convicts. But in the end, research could not tell us which of all these changes, among other changes in society, actually caused the crime decline and to what extent any particular factor contributed.

One fact bearing on the future is clear: America's crime response strategies of the past three decades will have to change. As the first few years of the twenty-first century unfold, the threat of international terror will draw resources away from traditional crime response functions, and the downturn in the economic cycle will mean fewer constant employment opportunities for the offender population. Even though reported crime began to rise in 2001, universal state and local governmental budget crises have already signaled the end of resource prosperity for crime response. Compounding this portrait is the fact that, even if the past steady rise in incarceration rates stabilizes, during the first decade of the new century there will still be many more prison years served than in the high-growth period of the 1990s because the 2000s began with more prisoners and longer average sentences. The decades-long pattern of expansionism in punishment will not be sustainable much longer.

Indeed, change has already commenced. As with welfare reform in the 1990s, the states are moving ahead of the static federal government in developing new approaches to crime response. State governments either on their own initiative or at the mandate of their citizenry are slowly adopting changes reflecting the view that crime response is much more than retribution and punishment; much too complex to delegate just to police, courts, and prisons; and much too fundamental in its consequences to address simply by imprisoning a large proportion of the young males of one race and an increasing proportion of one ethnic group. Many states have been creative in designing, implementing, and monitoring sentencing guidelines that balance several goals of crime response; establishing mandatory drug treatment instead of prison for first- and second-time drug possession; enacting standards and regulations for the manufacture and distribution of guns; creating a range of responses to marijuana use; and reacting to numerous vindications of death-row prisoners through DNA analysis by reexamining the death penalty issues of structure, defendant eligibility, and extent of use. In 2000–2001, while federal prison populations continued to expand rapidly, state imprisonment rates edged upward by the smallest margin since the early 1970s.

In this book we have sought to offer goals, facts established by data analysis and recent research, and recommendations that can contribute to positive changes in the crime response complex. The need for constant knowledge-building through research and evaluation, and for actual use of new knowledge and data, must constantly contend with the emotions induced by crime and the deceptive simplicity of terminology and solutions advocated by many politicians and special interest groups. That is why, for example, we want to change the debates from gun control to crime gun regulation, from drug use to drug and alcohol crime reduction, from the concept that only the police fight crime to the concept of crime reduction missions that include businesses, citizens, and the government.

Research and innovative experimentation during the past thirty-five years have produced great advances in what society knows about the various forms and effects of crime and about the relative effectiveness of various crime response approaches. These data and building blocks have served to temper, if not control, the ideological battles between liberal and conservative thinkers. The search for knowledge and solutions has slowly become more of a joint endeavor, less politicized and less adversarial. Yet more data and more knowledge are necessary if we are ever to build a political and public consensus about the kinds of choices to make in a restrained budgetary environment.

New knowledge can also raise new dilemmas and choices where ideological focus will be necessary, though in a narrower frame. In the chapter on juveniles, a discussion of two findings raised such a dilemma. Society now knows that even for juveniles who have already committed a violent act, 80 percent of whites and 66 percent of blacks will cease such activity on their own after their eighteenth birthday. Society also now knows that for every three persons predicted by experts to become a future violent criminal, only one will actually fulfill that prophecy. Those facts led us to recommend an emphasis on prevention programs during the early and teenage years for those whose broad range of conduct serves as a predictor of future violence. Such a choice addresses all five goals of proper crime response: that is, it reduces crime; lessens citizens' fear of crime; uses a criminalization approach only where it is needed, enforced, and effective; and pays close attention to the dual goals of just rules and the perceived legitimacy of legal institutions. Others might choose the alternative remedy of severely punishing every act of violence by everyone at every age—a form of crime response we would employ only sparingly in the juvenile sector, and only when serious injury occurs. Our intent has been to convince the reader that this book's choices of future direction, regardless of ideology, are more factually based, more cost effective in the long run, and more just than the alternative choices.

Increasing data and knowledge should also narrow inevitable differences in viewpoint regarding just rules and just enforcement of those rules. In examining black-white disparity in prison confinement for violence, liberals can see a partial justification for that condition from crime data showing that a higher percentage of blacks than whites commit gravely violent acts. Indeed, African Americans know the effects of this violence firsthand, since they are its victims for the most part. Conservatives, too, can now see from crime data that by 2000 drug law enforcement had deviated from any concept of equal justice, given the percentage of blacks in our total population, the proportion of drug use attributable to blacks, and the much higher proportion of blacks in the national totals of drug abuse arrests and imprisonment. A greater consensus in defining the requirements of justice can emerge from better understanding of the causes and effects of racial disparities for different categories of crime.

In changing the focus from the government's so-called criminal justice agencies to the much wider public and private sweep of a crime response complex, we have sought to demonstrate with current examples of private security and public governance how each resident and organization in every community can assist with crime reduction. Research has shown that reduction in the number of criminals is not the only way to reduce the amount of crime. If direct prevention efforts reduce an offender's success from twelve crimes a year to six, those efforts reduce crime even though the offender may not as yet be apprehended. And we have offered examples showing that when law enforcement starts focusing more on discrete crime problems, rather than just separate incidents, crime can be reduced even more and the quality of life can be improved without the downside of persistent aggressive order maintenance.

For offenders, the widened concept of a crime response complex can have perhaps the greatest future effect by addressing much more successfully than at present their transitions from jail and prison to the free world. Indeed, in the offender-centered world of crime response prior to the 1970s, the failure to address adequately the challenges of offender transition contributed significantly to the decline and eventual demise of the rehabilitation concept itself. Since we know that in most cases, no matter what the degree and length of punishment, each offender will eventually rejoin the community, crime control is best served by ensuring that this reunion is successful. This view is strengthened by research showing that the massive incarceration of the 1980s and 1990s was responsible for, at most, 25 percent of the 1990s decline in crime. As criminologist Lawrence Sherman has argued, rigorous evaluation may show that crime-avoidance for some group of offenders is better advanced by nonprison sanctions than by incarceration.

For the two million people incarcerated by 2000, preparation for transition must start within prison and jail walls. No research has shown, and indeed logic rebels at the concept, that two, five, or ten years of dehumanization, total dependence, and isolation from free-world realities can successfully prepare a man or woman for the outside world. Inside and outside jail and prison walls, ex-offenders must acquire what most Americans already have access to: a job skill, a job, a high-school degree, and drug or alcohol treatment if appropriate. Far more often than the social norm, offenders have lower mental agility, a past history of parental abuse, lack of a spouse, mental illness, and other conditions that increase the barrier for achieving an ordinary life. At a minimum, corrections institutions need to provide basic schooling and drug and alcohol treatment to those offenders who can benefit from these services.

These programs need to continue after the prisoner-students graduate to freedom. As some businesses already do now, the commercial world, perhaps with some government subsidy, could locate jobs, job training, and job discipline in prisons and jails. The considerably lower pay rate in the less-developed countries now receiving jobs from the American business community would not be excessive for American prisoners and would not compete with existing American jobs and job-seekers or with the pricing of equivalent products produced by companies not using prison job programs. Finally, when freedom inevitably comes to prisoners, it is counter to transition goals to deprive them of the government benefits available to others in the community.

All of these approaches to boost the success of prisoner transition have nothing to do with coddling criminals or with turning prisons into country clubs. None of the programs "take it easy" on prisoners or make it easier for them to slip back undetected into lives of crime. On the contrary, the discipline and rigor of these programs make it harder work for prisoners to succeed, but more likely that they will accomplish that goal.

Political leaders and legislators must give more focus to why and in what situations they truly believe the resort to criminalization is necessary and appropriate. Absent this leadership, state and federal governments will continue to take the easy political step of branding additional forms of conduct criminal without exploring lesser alternatives, the adequacy of enforcement resources, and the new burdens thrust upon the crime response complex. Many existing criminal provisions also require reexamination.

This book has also depicted the many ways in which existing administrative practices now fail the test of just enforcement, and how many of these courses of action could be remedied. It is no accident that judges in our courts, operating in some cases and in some jurisdictions without much discretion to choose among alternative actions, possess the least power in the crime response complex. Over the past thirty-five years, police and prosecutors have become far more powerful agents in choosing whom to arrest, whom to criminally charge and with what offenses, and what sentencing ranges will bind the judge's sentencing process after a conviction. Today, police, prosecutors, and legislators are for the most part setting the justice standards and administering the justice rules in America. They will be guiding the accountability and the community outreach so necessary to just enforcement of the law.

Positive change in the crime response complex will depend on a continuous flow of improved data and a more expansive understanding of this information. Much of the significant funding for crime and crime response research currently proceeds through the U.S. Justice Department. The National Institute of Justice has played a positive and increasingly important role over the past twenty years, but its placement necessarily includes political accountability to the attorney general and the president. Researchers in all fields agree that a national research function can best be discharged by a relatively independent institution, even if publicly funded, such as are the National Institutes of Health and the National Academy of Sciences. Such a change of venue would be an important step toward improving the continuity of research about crime and crime response. As a start, the Uniform Crime Reporting system and the National Crime Victims Survey could be combined under one administration and located in this separate research facility.

Our analyses and agenda have addressed primarily the past thirty-five years and pointed to an equivalent future period of time. Crime and crime response will always be controversial, emotional, politicized in varying degrees, evolving, and infused with a sense of urgency. Fortunately, one does not need unique wisdom to try to improve the nation's knowledge about crime and the nation's effectiveness and maintenance of justice in crime response. We propose in this book a series of changes, based on current and historical research, that can help achieve the five enduring goals of proper crime response—all with the idea of improving the plight of crime victims in ways that residents of every race and background in America can perceive as just.

Notes

Abbreviations

ATF   U.S. Department of the Treasury, Bureau of Alcohol, Tobacco, and Firearms

BJS   U.S. Department of Justice, Bureau of Justice Statistics

FBI   U.S. Department of Justice, Federal Bureau of Investigation

GAO   U.S. General Accounting Office

GPO   U.S. Government Printing Office

NIJ   U.S. Department of Justice, National Institute of Justice

OJJDP   U.S. Department of Justice, Office of Juvenile Justice and Delinquency Prevention

OJP   U.S. Department of Justice, Office of Justice Programs

ONDCP   The White House Office of National Drug Control Policy

USSC   U.S. Sentencing Commission

1. Crime and Punishment: A Brief American History

1. See Samuel Walker, *Popular Justice: A History of American Criminal Justice*, 2nd ed. (New York: Oxford University Press, 1998), pp. 31, 74; Lawrence M. Friedman and Robert V. Percival, *The Roots of Justice: Crime and Punishment in Alameda County, California, 1870–1910* (Chapel Hill: University of North Carolina Press, 1981), pp. 170–171.

2. Michael Stephen Hindus, *Prison and Plantation: Crime, Justice, and Authority in Massachusetts and South Carolina, 1767–1878* (Chapel Hill: University of North Carolina Press, 1980), p. 30.

3. Lester Bernhardt Orfield, *Criminal Appeals in America* (Boston: Little, Brown, 1939), pp. 215–216.

4. The first specialized juvenile court was founded in Chicago in 1899. See Robert M. Mennel, *Thorns and Thistles: Juvenile Delinquents in the United States, 1825–1940* (Hanover, N.H.: University Press of New England, 1973), chap. 5.

5. In addition to the sanctions mentioned, fines were commonly employed for minor offenses such as public drunkenness, and sentences of transportation were sometimes employed as inexpensive means to rid communities of unwanted convicts. See Adam Hirsch, *The Rise of the Penitentiary: Prisons and Punishment in Early America* (New Haven, Conn.: Yale University Press, 1992), p. 5; Edward L. Ayers, *Vengeance and Justice: Crime and Punishment in the Nineteenth-Century South* (New York: Oxford University Press, 1984), p. 42; and Lawrence M. Friedman, *Crime and Punishment in American History* (New York: Basic Books, 1993), pp. 174–175.

6. Allen Steinberg, *The Transformation of Criminal Justice: Philadelphia, 1800–1880* (Chapel Hill: University of North Carolina Press, 1989), pp. 25, 52; Friedman, *Crime and Punishment,* pp. 179–187; Hindus, *Prison and Plantation;* Ayers, *Vengeance and Justice,* pp. 121–124, 135, 137, 181; Bertram Wyatt-Brown, *Southern Honor: Ethics and Behavior in the Old South* (New York: Oxford University Press, 1982).

7. See Steinberg, *Transformation of Criminal Justice,* p. 2.

8. The U.S. population across the nineteenth century grew more than fourteen times over. U.S. Census Bureau, *Historical Statistics of the United States: Colonial Times to 1970, Bicentennial Edition* (Washington, D.C.: U.S. Census Bureau, 1975), pt. 1, p. 8, ser. A 6–8. During the twentieth century, the general population nearly quadrupled once more. U.S. Census Bureau, *Population by Race and Hispanic or Latino Origin for the United States: 1990 and 2000,* PHC-T-1 (Washington, D.C.: U.S. Census Bureau, 2001), table 1.

9. See Eric H. Monkkonen, "The Organized Response to Crime in Nineteenth- and Twentieth-Century America," *Journal of Interdisciplinary History* 14 (1983): 124.

10. Friedman, *Crime and Punishment,* p. 174.

11. Eric H. Monkkonen, *Police in Urban America, 1860–1920* (Cambridge, Eng.: Cambridge University Press, 1981), pp. 49–64; David R. Johnson, *American Law Enforcement: A History* (Saint Louis, Mo.: Forum Press, 1981), pp. 26–27.

12. See Friedman and Percival, *Roots of Justice;* Steinberg, *Transformation of Criminal Justice.*

13. See Lawrence M. Friedman, "Plea Bargaining in Historical Perspective," *Law and Society Review* 13 (1979): 250, table 2.

14. Walker, *Popular Justice,* pp. 93–95.

15. Mennel, *Thorns and Thistles;* Steven L. Schlossman, *Love and the American*

Delinquent: The Theory and Practice of "Progressive" Juvenile Justice, 1825–1920 (Chicago: University of Chicago Press, 1977).

16. See David J. Rothman, *The Discovery of the Asylum: Social Order and Disorder in the New Republic* (Boston: Little, Brown, 1971); David J. Rothman, *Conscience and Convenience: The Asylum and Its Alternatives in Progressive America* (Boston: Little, Brown, 1980).

17. Clifford D. Shearing, "The Relation between Public and Private Policing," in Michael Tonry and Norval Morris, eds., *Crime and Justice: A Review of Research,* vol. 15 (Chicago: University of Chicago Press, 1992), pp. 403–408.

18. On the decline of citizens' power as jurors, see Ronald F. Wright, "Why Not Administrative Grand Juries?" *Administrative Law Review* 44 (1992): 481–500; Friedman, *Crime and Punishment,* p. 388.

19. See Allen Z. Gammage and Stanley L. Sachs, *Police Unions* (Springfield, Ill.: Charles C. Thomas, 1972), pp. 33–57; "Guards' Union Top Donor to State Lawmakers," *San Francisco Chronicle,* Sept. 8, 1999, p. A26.

20. Shearing, "Relation between Public and Private Policing"; Jennifer Susan Light, *Fortress America? Home Security Systems, Defensible Space, and Citizen-Police Relations, 1970–1998* Ph.D. diss., Harvard University, May 1999.

21. See David Garland, *The Culture of Control: Crime and Social Order in Contemporary Society* (Chicago: University of Chicago Press, 2001 pp. 11–12; Leslie Sebba, *Third Parties: Victims and the Criminal Justice System* (Columbus: Ohio State University Press, 1996), pp. 13–24; George P. Fletcher, *With Justice for Some: Victims' Rights in Criminal Trials* (Reading, Mass.: Addison Wesley, 1995), pp. 188–206.

22. See, e.g., Ahmed A. White, "Rule of Law and the Limits of Sovereignty: The Private Prison in Jurisprudential Perspective," *American Criminal Law Review* 38 (2001): 111–146.

23. See Robert J. Martin, "Symposium on Megan's Law: Introduction: Pursuing Public Protection through Mandatory Community Notification of Convicted Sex Offenders: The Trials and Tribulations of Megan's Law," *Boston University Public Interest Law Journal* 6 (1996): 29–56; Todd R. Clear and David R. Karp, *The Community Justice Ideal: Preventing Crime and Achieving Justice* (Boulder, Colo.: Westview, 1999); John Braithwaite, "Restorative Justice: Assessing Optimistic and Pessimistic Accounts," in Michael Tonry, ed., *Crime and Justice: A Review of Research,* vol. 25 (Chicago: University of Chicago Press, 1999), pp. 1–127, esp. pp. 18, 59, 65–67.

24. See Ahmed A. White, "Victims' Rights, Rule of Law, and the Threat to Liberal Jurisprudence," *Kentucky Law Journal* 85 (1999): 357–415.

25. Shearing, "Relation between Public and Private Policing," p. 427; Stanley Cohen, "Taking Decentralization Seriously: Values, Visions and Policies," in John

Lowman, Robert J. Menzies, and T. S. Palys, eds., *Transcarceration: Essays in the Sociology of Social Control* (Aldershot, Eng.: Gower, 1987), pp. 359–361; Clifford D. Shearing and Philip C. Stenning, "Private Security: Implications for Social Control," *Social Problems* 30 (1983): 504.

26. See President's Commission on Law Enforcement and Administration of Justice, *Task Force Report, Crime and Its Impact—An Assessment* (Washington, D.C.: GPO, 1967), p. 19.

27. Richard Maxwell Brown, *Strain of Violence: Historical Studies of American Violence and Vigilantism* (New York: Oxford University Press, 1975), p. 3.

28. Charles Loring Brace, *The Dangerous Classes of New York City,* 3d ed. (1880; Montclair, N.J.: Patterson Smith, 1967), p. 27.

29. Ibid.; National Commission on Law Observance and Enforcement, *Report on Crime and the Foreign Born* (Washington, D.C.: GPO, 1931), pp. 23–44. See also Charles E. Rosenberg, "Sexuality, Class and Role in Nineteenth-Century America," *American Quarterly* 25 (1973): 152–153; Friedman, *Crime and Punishment,* p. 174.

30. Ayers, *Vengeance and Justice,* pp. 238–244.

31. Kenneth O'Reilly, "A New Deal for the FBI: The Roosevelt Administration, Crime Control and National Security," *Journal of American History* 69, no. 3 (1982): 642.

32. Arthur C. Millspaugh, *Crime Control by the National Government* (Washington, D.C.: Brookings Institution, 1937), pp. 271–272.

33. Richard Gid Powers, *Secrecy and Power: The Life of J. Edgar Hoover* (New York: Free Press, 1987), p. 204. Hoover's public relations efforts were not without result; the FBI's budget more than doubled from 1933, when FDR first took office, to 1936. O'Reilly, "New Deal for the FBI," p. 645.

34. Walker, *Popular Justice,* pp. 157–160.

35. Quoted in Patricia Wald, "Keynote Address: A Retrospective on the Thirty-Year War against Crime," in OJP, *The Challenge of Crime in a Free Society: Looking Back, Looking Forward* (Washington, D.C.: OJP, 1998), p. 81.

36. See Roger Lane, "Urban Police and Crime in Nineteenth-Century America," in Tonry and Morris, *Crime and Justice: A Review of Research,* vol. 15, pp. 31–33; Ted Robert Gurr, ed., *Violence in America: The History of Crime,* vol. 1 (Newbury Park, Calif.: Sage, 1989); James Q. Wilson and Richard J. Herrnstein, *Crime and Human Nature* (New York: Simon & Schuster, 1985), pp. 408–410.

37. Louis Newton Robinson, *History and Organization of Criminal Statistics in the United States* (Boston: Houghton Mifflin, 1911), pp. 34, 104; Thorsten Sellin, "The Basis of a Crime Index," *Journal of Criminal Law and Criminology* 22 (1931): 336.

38. See the analysis of "lethal violence" in Franklin E. Zimring and Gordon

Hawkins, *Crime Is Not the Problem: Lethal Violence in America* (New York: Oxford University Press, 1998).

39. See Robert M. O'Brien, "Police Productivity and Crime Rates: 1973–1992," *Criminology* 34 (1996): 199. David Cantor and Lawrence E. Cohen, "Comparing Measures of Homicide Trends: Methodological and Substantive Differences in Vital Statistics and Uniform Crime Report Time Series (1933–1975)," *Social Science Research*, 9 (1980): 121–145.

40. The sharp upswing in the middle 1940s might be explained by the many young men who were returning to society after service in the armed forces.

41. See William Julius Wilson, *The Truly Disadvantaged: The Inner City, the Underclass, and Public Policy* (Chicago: University of Chicago Press, 1987), pp. 3, 20–26, 30–32; Roger Lane, *Murder in America: A History* (Columbus: Ohio State University Press, 1997), p. 321.

42. See Lane, *Murder in America*, pp. 341–353.

43. From data presented in Zimring and Hawkins, *Crime Is Not the Problem*, p. 8, fig. 1.3. The United States is by no means the leader among all nations in homicide victimization: based on United Nations data for 1991, Colombia held that distinction with a homicide rate more than five times the American rate. Reported homicides in Brazil and Ecuador were also slightly higher per capita than in the United States (p. 54, table 4.2).

44. See generally Zimring and Hawkins, *Crime Is Not the Problem*, chap. 1; BJS, *Crime and Justice in the United States and in England and Wales, 1981–96* (Washington, D.C: BJS, 1998), pp. 4, 14.

45. See Zimring and Hawkins, *Crime Is Not the Problem*, pp. 4–7.

46. Alfred Blumstein and Joel Wallman, eds., *The Crime Drop in America* (New York: Cambridge University Press, 2000).

47. See FBI, *Uniform Crime Reports. January–December 2001* (Washington, D.C.: FBI, 2002), p. 1; Sarah Kershaw, "Report Shows Serious Crime Rose in 2001," *New York Times*, June 24, 2002, p. A12; and BJS, *Criminal Victimization, 2001: Changes 2000–2001 with Trends 1993–2001* (Washington, D.C.: BJS, 2002), p. 3, table 1.

48. See Franklin E. Zimring and Gordon Hawkins, *The Scale of Imprisonment* (Chicago: University of Chicago Press 1991), pp. 121–124; Friedman, *Crime and Punishment*, p. 14.

49. Margaret Werner Cahalan, *Historical Corrections Statistics in the United States, 1850–1984* (Washington, D.C.: GPO, 1986), p. 28, table 3–1 (number of prisoners); U.S. Census Bureau, *Historical Statistics*, vol. 1, p. 38, ser. A 210–263 (number of states).

50. The average state prison population in 2000, across all fifty states, was approximately 25,000. BJS, *Prison and Jail Inmates at Midyear 2000* (Washington, D.C.: BJS, 2001), p. 3, table 2.

51. Cahalan, *Historical Corrections Statistics,* p. 29, table 3-2.

52. BJS, *Prison and Jail Inmates at Midyear 2000,* p. 1.

53. U.S. Census Bureau, *Historical Statistics,* vol. 1, p. 8 ser. A 6–8; U.S. Census Bureau, *Population . . . for the United States: 1990 and 2000,* PHC-T-1, table 1.

54. U.S. Census Bureau, *Historical Statistics,* vol. 1, p. 8 ser. A 6–8; U.S. Census Bureau, *Population . . . for the United States: 1990 and 2000,* PHC-T-1, table 1.

55. Figure 1.2 charts the absolute size of prison populations, not the imprisonment rate corrected for population change. According to the Justice Department, in the seven years from 1939 to 1946, including most dramatically the years of World War II (when many young men of crime-prone age were in military service), U.S. per capita imprisonment rates declined by 27 percent, and then turned slowly upward again until the early 1960s. See BJS, *Sourcebook of Criminal Justice Statistics, 1999* (Washington, D.C.: GPO, 2000), p. 503, table 6.26. According to Census data, the net result for the 1940s was a slight increase in the number of prison inmates, of 12,543. See Cahalan, *Historical Corrections Statistics,* pp. 29, table 3-2. There are competing Justice Department figures for the 1940s, however, that show a decline in prison populations of 7,583 during that decade. See BJS, *1999,* p. 503, table 6.26.

56. Margaret Cahalan was one of the first observers of U.S. punishment practices to notice the rapid increase in the use of incarceration from 1972 onward. See Cahalan, "Trends in Incarceration in the United States since 1880: A Summary of Reported Rates and the Distribution of Offenses," *Crime & Delinquency* 25 (1979): 10, 16.

57. See Cahalan, *Historical Corrections Statistics,* pp. 73–75; President's Commission on Law Enforcement and Administration of Justice, Task Force Report, "Crime and Its Impact—An Assessment" (Washington, D.C.: GPO, 1967), p. 131.

58. Cahalan, *Historical Corrections Statistics,* p. 75, p. 76, table 4-1; BJS, *Sourcebook of Criminal Justice Statistics, 2000* (Washington, D.C.: GPO, 2001), p. 502, table 6.21, and p. 507, table 6.27.

59. Cahalan, *Historical Corrections Statistics,* p. 34, table 3-6, and p. 77, table 4-2.

60. BJS, *Prison and Jail Inmates at Midyear 2000,* p. 1.

61. The Justice Department hypothesized that the lifetime risk of spending time in prison, based on 1991 incarceration statistics, was 5.1 percent for the average American. BJS, *Lifetime Likelihood of Going to State or Federal Prison* (Washington, D.C.: BJS, 1997), p. 1. The prisons, however, made up only 60 percent of total incarceration populations in 1991.

62. Even in the 1970s, before the full force of the incarceration explosion, America led the industrialized first-world nations in incarceration rates. Cahalan, "Trends in Incarceration," p. 21; Irving Waller and Janet Chan, "Prison Use: A

Canadian and International Comparison," *Criminal Law Quarterly* 17 (1974): 47–71; Eugene Doleschal, "Rate and Length of Imprisonment: How Does the U.S. Compare with the Netherlands, Denmark, and Sweden?" *Crime and Delinquency* 23 (Jan. 1977): 51–56.

63. BJS, *Prison and Jail Inmates at Midyear 2000*, p. 1.

64. The Russian incarceration rate in 2000 was down from 730 per 100,000 in 1999, as a result of a mass amnesty declared by the Russian Parliament to address overcrowding. The Sentencing Project, "U.S. Surpasses Russia as World Leader in Rate of Incarceration," visited at *www.sentencingproject.org* on Apr. 30, 2001.

65. See André Kuhn, "Incarceration Rates across the World," *Overcrowded Times* 10, no. 2 (1999): 1, 12–20.

66. Roy Walmsley, *World Prison Population List*, 2d ed. (London: Home Office Research, Development and Statistics Directorate, 2000).

67. Henry David Thoreau, *Walden* (Boston: Houghton Mifflin, ca. 1964), chap. 1.

68. BJS, *Sourcebook 2000*, p. 502, table 6.21, and p. 507, table 6.27; BJS, *Prison and Jail Inmates at Midyear 2000*, p. 1.

69. These numbers are derived from BJS, *Prison and Jail Inmates at Midyear 2000*, p. 2, table 1. The person-year total for an entire decade is estimated by cumulating the inmate counts for each year while assuming that each base population was present for the next full year. The resulting estimate does not take into account that inmate populations grew *during* each year between 1972 and 2000. Statistical adjustment for this fact does not alter the full-decade totals by very much, and the important thing is to apply a consistent method across all the decades that are examined and compared.

70. State prison growth across the country slowed to its slowest one-year pace since 1972, and the prison populations in twelve states actually declined from June 2000 to June 2001. BJS, *Prison and Jail Inmates at Midyear 2001* (Washington, D.C.: BJS, 2002), p. 1.

71. See John Augustus, *John Augustus: First Probation Officer* (1852; Montclair, N.J.: Patterson Smith, 1972).

72. Friedman, *Crime and Punishment*, p. 161.

73. See, e.g., Warner, "Survey of Criminal Statistics," p. 73.

74. BJS, *Probation and Parole in the United States, 2001* (Washington, D.C.: BJS, 2002), p. 1.

75. This rough estimate is based on the estimate of the 8.5 percent lifetime likelihood faced by the average American of serving a prison or jail sentence, multiplied by a factor of two reflecting the greater likelihood of serving a community sentence. See BJS, *Lifetime Likelihood*, p. 1.

76. President's Commission on Law Enforcement and Administration of Justice, Task Force Report, *Corrections* (Washington, D.C.: GPO, 1967), p. 202.

77. Law Enforcement Assistance Administration, *State and Local Probation and Parole Systems* (Washington, D.C.: GPO, 1978), p. 3.

78. The sources for these calculations are the same as those for Figure 1.4.

79. As of this writing, U.S. probation and parole numbers were still on the increase in the early 2000s. See BJS, *Probation and Parole in the United States, 2001,* p. 1.

80. See Petersilia, *Community Corrections;* Norval Morris and Michael Tonry, *Between Prison and Probation: Intermediate Punishments in a Rational Sentencing System* (New York: Oxford University Press, 1990).

81. BJS, *Correctional Populations in the United States, 1997* (Washington, D.C.: BJS, 2000), p. 81, table 5.10a; BJS, *Correctional Populations in the United States, 1995* (Washington, D.C.: BJS, 1997) p. 13, table 1.15.

82. BJS, *Correctional Populations in 1997,* p. 81, table 5.10a.

83. From 1977 to 1999, 482 of 599 executions were performed in the Southern states, accounting for 80 percent of executions nationwide. Texas alone executed 199 persons from 1977 to 1999, or one-third of the national total. BJS, *Capital Punishment, 1999* (Washington, D.C.: BJS, 2000), p. 6, table 5, and p. 10, table 10.

84. The 98 executions in 1999 were the highest number since 1951, and they occurred on average nearly twelve years after the defendants' convictions. Twelve years earlier, in 1987, there were a total of 20,100 homicides nationwide. Working with these figures to derive an estimate of the probabilities of execution, only 0.488 percent of all homicide offenders in 1987 would face execution, even in a high-execution year such as 1999. Compare BJS, *Capital Punishment, 1999,* p. 1; BJS, *Sourcebook of Criminal Justice Statistics, 2000* (Washington, D.C.: BJS, 2001), p. 278, table 3.120.

85. Harry A. Ploski and James Williams, *The Negro Almanac: A Reference Work on the Afro-American,* 4th ed. (New York: John Wiley & Sons, 1983), pp. 347–350, tables 1–3.

86. See Ayers, *Vengeance and Justice,* pp. 164, 240.

87. Cahalan, *Historical Corrections Statistics,* p. 19, table 2-8.

88. Ibid., p. 16, table 2-6.

89. Franklin E. Zimring and Gordon Hawkins, *Capital Punishment and the American Agenda* (Cambridge, Eng.: Cambridge University Press, 1986), pp. 26–33; BJS, *Capital Punishment, 1999,* p. 10.

90. *Furman v. Georgia,* 408 U.S. 238 (1972).

91. See American Law Institute, *Model Penal Code and Commentaries (Official Draft and Revised Comments), Part II, §§ 210.0 to 213.6* (Philadelphia: American Law Institute, 1980), § 210.6 and commentary.

92. *Gregg v. Georgia,* 428 U.S. 153 (1976).

93. BJS, *Sourcebook 1999,* p. 547, table 6.82; BJS, *Capital Punishment, 1999,* p. 7, fig. 1.

94. BJS, *Sourcebook 1999*, p. 553, table 6.89; BJS, *Capital Punishment, 1999*, p. 1.

95. BJS, *Capital Punishment, 2000* (Washington, D.C.: BJS, 2001), pp. 1, 12.

96. See *Report of the Governor's Commission on Capital Punishment, George H. Ryan Governor* (State of Illinois, 2002), available at *www.idoc.state.il.us/ccp/ ccp/reports/commission_report*, visited on Apr. 22, 2002; Dennis O'Brien and David Nitkin, "Glendening Halts Executions," *Baltimore Sun*, May 10, 2002, p. A1.

97. Cahalan, *Historical Corrections Statistics*, p. 11, table 2-2.

98. Ibid., pp. 10, table 2-1; p. 14, table 2-4; p. 15 table 2-5.

99. BJS, *Sourcebook of Criminal Justice Statistics, 1993* (Washington, D.C.: GPO, 1994), p. 676, table 6.120.

100. BJS, *Capital Punishment, 2000*, p. 11, table 11.

101. *McCleskey v. Kemp*, 481 U.S. 279 (1987); David C. Baldus, George G. Woodsworth, and Charles A. Pulaski, *Equal Justice and the Death Penalty* (Boston: Northeastern University Press, 1990); GAO, *Death Penalty Sentencing: Research Indicates Pattern of Racial Disparities* (Washington, D.C.: GPO, 1990), p. 5.

102. See *McCleskey*, 481 U.S. at 321 (Brennan, J., dissenting); Randall Kennedy, *Race, Crime, and the Law* (New York: Pantheon, 1997), chap. 2; Hans Zeisel, "Race Bias in the Administration of the Death Penalty: The Florida Experience," *Harvard Law Review* 95 (1981): 458.

103. See John Peter Altgeld, *Live Questions: Including Our Penal Machinery and Its Victims* (Chicago: Donohue and Henneberry, 1890), p. 163.

104. Cahalan, "Trends in Incarceration," p. 39.

105. Ayers, *Vengeance and Justice*, p. 75.

106. Hindus, *Prison and Plantation*; Ayers, *Vengeance and Justice*, pp. 135, 137.

107. Ayers, *Vengeance and Justice*, p. 197.

108. Ibid., pp. 197, 179. The incarceration of women inmates increased by a factor of seven, and nearly all female inmates were African American (p. 200).

109. See ibid., chap. 6. At some of the convict camps, annual death rates among laborers, virtually all of whom were black, exceeded 40 percent (p. 196).

110. Cahalan, *Historical Corrections Statistics*, p. 65, table 3-31. BJS, *Prisoners in 1998*, p. 9. For the years since 1998, the Justice Department has changed its method of counting black inmates—the more recent figures exclude blacks who are also Hispanic. See BJS, *Prisoners in 2001* (Washington, D.C.: BJS, 2002), p. 12, table 15 (46.3 percent of prisoners in 2001 were black, but black Hispanics are no longer included).

111. Cahalan, *Historical Corrections Statistics*, p. 91, table 4-15; BJS, *Prison and Jail Inmates at Midyear 2000*, p. 7.

112. BJS, *Lifetime Likelihood*.

113. Alfred Blumstein and Allen J. Beck, "Population Growth in U.S. Prisons, 1980–1996," in Michael Tonry and Joan Petersilia, eds., *Crime and Justice: A*

Review of Research, vol. 26 (Chicago: University of Chicago Press, 1999), pp. 22–23.

114. John Micklethwait, "The United States Survey: "Oh, Say, Can You See?" *Economist,* Mar. 11, 2000, after p. 60.

115. BJS, *American Indians and Crime* (Washington, D.C.: BJS, 1999), p. 1, p. 26, table 33.

116. See Michael Tonry, *Malign Neglect: Race, Crime, and Punishment in America* (New York: Oxford University Press, 1995) p. 50.

117. Criminologists have tested the validity of the racial breakdowns contained in arrest statistics, and have found that they hold up well when compared with the racial data collected in victims' surveys and offender self-report surveys, at least for serious crimes. See Michael J. Hindelang, "Race and Involvement in Common Law Personal Crimes," *American Sociological Review* 43 (1978): 93–109; Alfred Blumstein, "Racial Disproportionality of U.S. Prison Populations Revisited," *University of Colorado Law Review* 64 (1993): 748; Gary LaFree, *Losing Legitimacy: Street Crime and the Decline of Social Institutions in America* (Boulder, Colo.: Westview, 1998), pp. 37–39; Michael R. Gottfredson, "Substantive Contributions of Victimization Surveys," in Michael Tonry and Norval Morris, eds., *Crime and Justice: An Annual Review of Research* (Chicago: University of Chicago Press, 1986), vol. 7, p. 267.

118. This manner of display is borrowed from Zimring and Hawkins, *Crime Is Not the Problem,* p. 76, table 5.1.

119. Franklin E. Zimring, *American Youth Violence* (New York: Oxford University Press, 1998), p. 19.

120. FBI, *Crime in the United States, 1990: Uniform Crime Reports* (Washington, D.C.: FBI, 1991), p. 192, table 38.

121. See Zimring and Hawkins, *Crime Is Not the Problem,* p. 77, fig. 5.2 (similar finding using 1992 data).

122. BJS, *Violent Victimization and Race, 1993–98* (Washington, D.C.: BJS, 2001), p. 7, table 11; p. 10, table 14. The report defined "serious injury" as including gunshot wounds, knife wounds, broken bones, being knocked unconscious, and sustaining internal injuries (p. 7, table 11).

123. James Alan Fox, *Trends in Juvenile Violence: A Report to the Attorney General on Current and Future Rates of Juvenile Offending* (Washington, D.C.: BJS, 1996), 1997 update, p. 2, table 2; p. 3, table 4.

124. Calculated from FBI, *Crime in the United States, 1999: Uniform Crime Reports* (Washington, D.C.: GPO, 2000), p. 230, table 43.

125. LaFree, *Losing Legitimacy,* pp. 51–52. For example, LaFree's data show roughly a ten-to-one imbalance in black robberies of whites versus white robberies of blacks going back at least to the 1950s (p. 51, table 3.4).

126. Lane, *Murder in America,* p. 321. Lane does not believe that this pattern ex-

tended back into the nineteenth century, however. See Lane, "Urban Police and Crime," p. 44.

127. BJS, *Prison and Jail Inmates at Midyear 2000*, p. 9, table 13.

128. See Cassia Spohn and David Holleran, "The Imprisonment Penalty Paid by Young, Unemployed Black and Hispanic Male Offenders," *Criminology* 38 (2000): 281–306; Darrell Steffensmeier, Jeffery Ulmer, and John Kramer, "The Interaction of Race, Gender, and Age in Criminal Sentencing: The Punishment Cost of Being Young, Black, and Male," *Criminology* 36 (1998): 763–797; Jon A. Meyer and Paul Jesilow, "Research on Bias in Judicial Sentencing," *New Mexico Law Review* 26 (1996): 107–131; Steven Klein, Joan Petersilia, and Susan Turner, "Race and Imprisonment Decisions in California," *Science* 247 (1990): 812–816; William Wilbanks, *The Myth of a Racist Criminal Justice System* (Monterey, Calif.: Brooks/Cole, 1987); Patrick A. Langan, "Racism on Trial: New Evidence to Explain the Racial Composition of Prisons in the United States," *Journal of Criminal Law and Criminology*, 76 (1985): 666–683; Alfred Blumstein et al., eds., *Research on Sentencing: The Search for Reform*, 2 vols., Report of the National Academy of Sciences Panel on Sentencing Research (Washington, D.C.: National Academy Press, 1983); Gary Kleck, "Racial Discrimination and Criminal Sentencing: A Critical Evaluation of the Evidence with Additional Evidence on the Death Penalty," *American Sociological Review* 46 (1981): 783–805; and John Hagan, "Extra-Legal Attributes and Criminal Sentencing," *Law and Society Review* 8 (1974): 357–383.

129. Alfred Blumstein, "On the Racial Disproportionality of United States' Prison Populations," *Journal of Criminal Law and Criminology* 73 (1983): 1259–1281; Blumstein, "Racial Disproportionality Revisited."

130. See Blumstein, "Racial Disproportionality Revisited," pp. 748–749; Blumstein, "On Racial Disproportionality," pp. 1268–1270.

131. Baldus has called this phenomenon "victim discounting" in the death penalty context. David C. Baldus et al., "Comparative Review of Death Sentences: An Empirical Study of the Georgia Experience," *Journal of Criminal Law and Criminology* 74 (1983): 709.

132. Indeed, in his 1991 study, Blumstein found that fewer blacks were housed in U.S. prisons for homicide than one would expect based on the number of blacks arrested for homicide. Blumstein, "Racial Disproportionality Revisited," p. 751, table 2. This could be the result of victim discounting, given that the great majority of the victims of homicide by blacks are themselves black.

133. Blumstein, "Racial Disproportionality Revisited," p. 751, table 2; Blumstein, "On Racial Disproportionality," p. 1274.

134. Blumstein, "Racial Disproportionality Revisited," pp. 751–752; Blumstein, "On Racial Disproportionality," p. 1274.

135. Blumstein, "Racial Disproportionality Revisited," p. 752, fig. 3.

136. Robert J. Sampson and William Julius Wilson, "Toward a Theory of Race, Crime, and Urban Inequality," in John Hagan and Ruth D. Peterson, eds., *Crime and Inequality* (Stanford, Calif.: Stanford University Press, 1995), pp. 37–54; William Julius Wilson, *The Truly Disadvantaged: The Inner City, the Underclass, and Public Policy* (Chicago: University of Chicago Press, 1987), pp. 22–26; and Robert J. Sampson, "Neighborhood and Crime: The Structural Determinants of Personal Victimization," *Journal of Research in Crime and Delinquency,* 22 (1985): 7–40.

137. Research has documented that the "underclass" status of a community is associated with high crime rates among the people who live there, regardless of race and ethnicity. Lauren J. Krivo and Ruth D. Peterson, "Extremely Disadvantaged Neighborhoods and Urban Crime," *Social Forces* 75 (1996): 619–650; Faith Peeples and Rolf Loeber, "Do Individual Factors and Neighborhood Context Explain Ethnic Differences in Juvenile Delinquency?" *Journal of Quantitative Criminology* 10 (1994): 141–158.

138. Elijah Anderson, *Code of the Street: Decency, Violence, and the Moral Life of the Inner City* (New York: W. W. Norton, 1999). See also Elijah Anderson, *Street Wise: Race, Class, and Change in an Urban Community* (Chicago: University of Chicago Press, 1990).

139. Franklin Zimring, Keynote Speech, 2000 Law and Policy Symposium, "Reactions to Youth Violence: The Legacy of Columbine," University of Denver College of Law, Denver, Colo., Mar. 24, 2000; Darnell F. Hawkins, John H. Laub, and Janet H. Lauritsen, "Race, Ethnicity, and Serious Juvenile Offending," in Rolf Loeber and David P. Farrington, eds., *Serious and Violent Juvenile Offenders: Risk Factors and Successful Interventions* (Thousand Oaks, Calif.: Sage, 1998), p. 38.

140. BJS, *Homicide Trends in the U.S.: 1998 Update* (Washington, D.C.: BJS, 2000), pp. 1–3; BJS, *Violent Victimization and Race, 1993–98,* p. 10, table 14.

141. See Zimring and Hawkins, *Crime Is Not the Problem,* p. 87.

2. Knowledge and Assessment

1. Henry S. Ruth, Jr., "Promoting Consistent Policy in the Criminal Justice Process," *University of Virginia Law Review* 53 (1967): 1491–1492.

2. See Georg Rusche and Otto Kirchheimer, *Punishment and Social Structure* (New York: Columbia University Press, 1939), pp. 141–142; David Garland, *Punishment and Modern Society* (Chicago: University of Chicago Press, 1990), p. 7; Malcolm Feeley and Jonathan Simon, "Actuarial Justice: The Emerging New Criminal Law," in David Nelken, ed., *The Futures of Criminology* (Thousand Oaks, Calif.: Sage, 1994), pp. 173–201.

3. Deborah Stone, *Policy Paradox: The Art of Political Decision Making* (New

York: Norton, 1997); Charles E. Lindblom, *Inquiry and Change: The Troubled Attempt to Understand and Shape Society* (New Haven, Conn.: Yale University Press, 1990).

4. Michael D. Maltz, "Crime Statistics: A Historical Perspective," *Crime & Delinquency* 23 (1977): 33–37.

5. See National Commission on Law Observance and Enforcement, *Report on Criminal Statistics* (Washington, D.C.: GPO, 1931), pp. 12–17, 42–52.

6. Ibid., pp. 37–39; Samuel B. Warner, "Crimes Known to the Police—An Index of Crime," *Harvard Law Review* 45 (1931): 307–334.

7. See James D. Calder, *The Origins and Development of Federal Crime Control Policy: Herbert Hoover's Initiatives* (Westport, Conn.: Praeger, 1993), pp. 88–95; Janet Schmidt Sherman, Jon Christensen, and Joel Henderson, "Reorganized Crime: The Creation of the Uniform Crime Report," in Steven Spitzer and Rita J. Simon, eds., *Research in Law, Deviance, and Social Control* (Greenwich, Conn.: JAI Press, 1982), vol. 4, pp. 3–52.

8. Thorsten Sellin and Marvin E. Wolfgang, *The Measurement of Delinquency* (New York: John Wiley and Sons, 1964), p. 18.

9. See Albert D. Biderman and James P. Lynch, *Understanding Crime Incidence: Why the UCR Diverges from the NCS Statistics* (New York: Springer-Verlag, 1991), pp. 42–50; BJS, *Criminal Victimization, 2000: Changes 1999–2000 with Trends 1993–2000* (Washington, D.C.: BJS, 2001), p. 10.

10. See Gary F. Jensen and Maryaltani Karpos, "Managing Rape: Exploratory Research on the Behavior of Rape Statistics," *Criminology* 31 (1993): 363–385. Confounding factors have also come into play for larceny, burglary, and motor vehicle theft, as police reports have become a common prerequisite for insurance recovery. See President's Commission on Law Enforcement and Administration of Justice, Task Force Report, *Crime and Its Impact—An Assessment* (Washington, D.C.: GPO, 1967) [hereinafter "Assessment Task Force Report"], p. 24.

11. Michael D. Maltz, *Bridging Gaps in Police Crime Data: A Discussion Paper from the BJS Fellows Program* (Washington, D.C.: OJP, 1999), p. 1. Many states now mandate crime reporting by local agencies as a matter of state law, and such requirements have been encouraged by federal funding criteria. See Maltz, "Crime Statistics," p. 37.

12. Assessment Task Force Report, pp. 20, 129, and table 1.

13. Warner, "Crimes Known to the Police," pp. 311–316; Assessment Task Force Report, p. 27.

14. Maltz, "Crime Statistics," pp. 38–39; Institute of Public Administration, "Crime Records in Police Management," in Marvin E. Wolfgang, L. Savitz, and N. Johnson, eds., *The Sociology of Crime and Delinquency,* 2d ed. (New York: John Wiley, 1970).

15. Assessment Task Force Report, pp. 22–23.

16. Ibid., p. 22, fig. 7.

17. Christopher Jencks, "Is Violent Crime Increasing?" *The American Prospect* (Winter 1991): 101; Robert M. O'Brien, "Police Productivity and Crime Rates: 1973–1992," *Criminology* 34 (1996): 188, 204.

18. See generally Michael D. Maltz, "From Poisson to Present: Applying Operations Research to Problems of Crime and Justice," *Journal of Quantitative Criminology* 12 (1996): 47; Maltz, *Bridging Gaps,* pp. 5–9.

19. The cases of Philadelphia and Ventura County are discussed in the text. For news reports on the remaining jurisdictions, see Walter F. Roche, Jr. and Tim Craig, "Baltimore Police Underreported Serious Crimes in '99, Report Says: Department Deflated Almost 10,000 Incidents," *Baltimore Sun,* Mar. 15, 2000, p. B30; Associated Press, "Crime Statistics Falsified, Police Chief in Boca Quits," *Florida Times Union,* May 7, 1998, p. B3; Alexandra Navarro and Clifton Palm, "Altered Boca Police Stats Worse than First Reported," *Palm Beach Post,* Aug. 7, 1998; Lyda Longa, "Police Crime Statistics Dispute Roiling Ranks; Divisive Issue: Low Morale Is Plaguing Atlanta Police Rocked by Recent Accusations of Manipulating Crime Stats," *Atlanta Journal-Constitution,* June 27, 1998, p. F4; Michael Cooper, "Police Say Subway Crime Was Undercounted by 20 Percent," *New York Times,* Jan. 8, 1998, p. A3; David Kocieniewski, "Safir Is Said to Seek to Punish a Chief over False Crime Data," *New York Times,* Feb. 28, 1998, p. B1.

20. Mark Fazlollah, "Hidden Rapes: The Stories behind the Numbers," *Justice Research and Statistics Association Forum* 19, no. 1 (January 2001): 1, 13–14; Mark Fazlollah, Michael Matza, and Craig R. McCoy, "How to Cut the City's Crime Rate: Don't Report It," *Philadelphia Inquirer,* Nov. 1, 1998, p. A1.

21. Tribune News Service, "Philadelphia Crimes Higher than Reported," *Chicago Tribune,* Sept. 15, 2000, p. 10.

22. Associated Press, "Crime Recount May Lift Philadelphia to No. Two," *New York Times,* Sept. 15, 2000, p. A26; Fazlollah et al., "How to Cut the City's Crime Rate."

23. Daryl Kelley, "Ventura Police Counting Crime a New Way: Statistics Change in Methodology Brings Department into Line with FBI Regulations and Other Law Enforcement Agencies," *Los Angeles Times,* July 26, 2000, p. B1.

24. For methodological analyses of the NCVS, see Joseph G. Weis and Brian C. Wold, "Statistics: Reporting Systems and Methods," in Joshua Dressler, ed., *Encyclopedia of Crime and Justice,* 2d ed. (New York: Macmillan Reference, 2002), pp. 1523–1541; Michael R. Gottfredson, "Substantive Contributions of Victimization Surveys," in Michael Tonry and Norval Morris, eds., *Crime and Justice: An Annual Review of Research,* vol. 7 (Chicago: University of Chicago Press, 1986), vol. 7, pp. 251–287; Richard F. Sparks, "Surveys of Victimization—An Optimistic Assessment," in Michael Tonry and Norval Morris, eds.,

Crime and Justice: An Annual Review of Research, vol. 3 (Chicago: University of Chicago Press, 1981), pp. 1–60. One concern regarding the NCVS arises from changes in the survey methodology over time. For instance, the Census Bureau has increasingly used telephone interviews rather than face-to-face interviews since 1973, fostering concern that victims may be less forthcoming about certain experiences over the phone. See O'Brien, "Police Productivity," p. 198. Also, the survey questionnaire used in the NCVS was revised heavily in 1992, raising questions about the compatibility of data before and since. See BJS, *Effects of the Redesign on Victimization Estimates* (Washington, D.C.: BJS, 1997), p. 1.

25. President's Commission on Law Enforcement and Administration of Justice, *The Challenge of Crime in a Free Society* (Washington, D.C.: GPO, 1967), pp. 20–22, reporting results of the first national crime victims survey.

26. O'Brien, "Police Productivity"; Jencks, "Is Violent Crime Increasing?" p. 100.

27. See BJS, *Effects of NIBRS on Crime Statistics* (Washington, D.C.: BJS, 2000).

28. See Ruth, "Promoting Consistent Policy," pp. 1494–1495; James Q. Wilson, *Varieties of Police Behavior: The Management of Law and Order in Eight Communities* (Cambridge: Harvard University Press, 1968), p. 7; Kenneth Culp Davis, *Discretionary Justice: A Preliminary Inquiry* (Baton Rouge: Louisiana State University Press, 1969), pp. 88–90.

29. President's Commission on Law Enforcement and Administration of Justice, *The Challenge of Crime in a Free Society* (Washington, D.C.: GPO, 1967), p. 7; Lawrence M. Friedman, *Crime and Punishment in American History* (New York: Basic Books, 1993), p. 461.

30. See Assessment Task Force Report, p. 124.

31. Malcolm M. Feeley, *Court Reform on Trial: Why Simple Solutions Fail* (New York: Basic Books, 1983).

32. The most famous of these was the Cleveland Survey of Criminal Justice, *Criminal Justice in Cleveland* (Cleveland: Cleveland Foundation, 1922), discussed in Walker, *Popular Justice,* p. 152. Other prominent surveys included Missouri Association for Criminal Justice, *Missouri Crime Survey* (New York: Macmillan, 1926); Illinois Association for Criminal Justice, *The Illinois Crime Survey* (Chicago: Illinois Association for Criminal Justice, 1929); New York State Legislature, *Report of the Joint Committee on the Government of the City of New York* (New York: Hofstadter and Seabury Committee, 1932), 5 vols.

33. Cleveland Survey of Criminal Justice, *Criminal Justice,* pp. v–vi.

34. See the following works authored by the National Commission on Law Observance and Enforcement: *Report on Prosecution, Report on Penal Institutions, Probation and Parole, Report on Lawlessness in Law Enforcement, Report on the Cost of Crime, Report on the Causes of Crime,* and *Report on Police,* all published in Washington, D.C. by GPO, 1931.

35. National Commission on Law Observance and Enforcement, *Report on Criminal Statistics*, p. 3.

36. President's Commission, *The Challenge of Crime in a Free Society*, p. 273; Assessment Task Force Report, p. 123.

37. Assessment Task Force Report, p. 123.

38. Calder, *Origins and Development*, p. 100.

39. Henry S. Ruth, Jr., "To Dust Shall Ye Return?" *Notre Dame Lawyer* 43 (1968): 821.

40. For retrospectives, see Patricia Wald, "Keynote Address: A Retrospective on the Thirty-Year War against Crime," in OJP, *The Challenge of Crime in a Free Society, Looking Back Looking Forward* (Washington, D.C., OJP, 1998), pp. 81–92; John A. Conley, ed., *The 1967 President's Crime Commission Report: Its Impact Twenty-five Years Later* (Cincinnati: Anderson Publishing Company, 1994).

41. Michael Tonry, "Building Better Policies," in OJP, *The Challenge of Crime in a Free Society*, pp. 110, 111. See also Steven R. Donziger, ed., *The Real War on Crime: The Report of the National Criminal Justice Commission* (New York: Harper Perennial, 1996), p. xvi.

42. President's Commission, *The Challenge of Crime in a Free Society*, p. 273.

43. BJS, *Justice Expenditure and Employment in the United States* (Washington, D.C.: BJS, 2002), p. 1.

44. Alfred Blumstein and Joan Petersilia, "Investing in Criminal Justice Research," in James Q. Wilson and Joan Petersilia, eds., *Crime* (San Francisco: ICS Press, 1995), p. 468.

45. Alfred Blumstein, "Interaction of Criminological Research and Public Policy," *Journal of Quantitative Criminology* 12 (1997): 350–353.

46. Robert Martinson, "What Works?—Questions and Answers about Prison Reform," *Public Interest* 35 (1974); Lee Sechrest, Susan O. White, and Elizabeth D. Brown, eds., *The Rehabilitation of Criminal Offenders* (Washington, D.C.: National Academy of Sciences, 1979).

47. OJP, *Preventing Crime: What Works, What Doesn't, What's Promising* (Washington, D.C.: OJP, 1997).

48. Ibid., pp. 4–28, 8–33, 9–49.

49. Ibid., pp. 5–32 through 5–36; 9–52.

50. Ibid., p. 8–19; Anthony Petrosino, Carolyn Turpin-Petrosino, and James O. Finckenauer, "Well-Meaning Programs Can Have Harmful Effects! Lessons from Experiments of Programs Such as Scared Straight," *Crime & Delinquency* 46 (2000): 354–379.

51. Petrosino et al., "Well-Meaning Programs," pp. 362–366.

52. See David H. Bayley, ed., *What Works in Policing* (New York: Oxford University Press, 1998), p. 51.

53. Rosemary Chalk and Patricia A. King, eds., *Violence in Families: Assessing Prevention and Treatment Programs* (Washington, D.C.: National Academy Press, 1998), pp. 16, 66 (on the hostility of some program and victims' advocates to scientific evaluation of domestic violence interventions); pp. 174–178 (on mandatory arrest policies); and pp. 160–163 (on mandatory child-abuse reporting requirements).

54. On the potential of arrest policies to increase crime, see Lawrence W. Sherman, "Defiance, Deterrence, and Irrelevance: A Theory of the Criminal Sanction," *Journal of Research in Crime and Delinquency* 30 (1993): 445; Lawrence W. Sherman et al. "From Initial Deterrence to Long-Term Escalation: Short-Custody Arrest for Poverty Ghetto Domestic Violence," *Criminology,* 29 (1991): 821–850; Franklyn W. Dunford, "The Measurement of Recidivism in Cases of Spouse Assault," *Journal of Criminal Law and Criminology* 83 (1992): 120–136. On the absence of a link between response time and crime solution or reduction, see William Bieck and David A. Kessler, *Response Time Analysis* (Kansas City, Mo.: Board of Police Commissioners, 1977).

55. See generally George Mair, "Community Penalties and the Probation Service," in Mike Maguire, Rod Morgan, and Robert Reiner, eds., *Oxford Handbook of Criminology* (New York: Oxford University Press, 1994), p. 1223. For a focus on economic cost and benefit measures, see Franklin E. Zimring and Gordon Hawkins, *Incapacitation: Penal Confinement and the Restraint of Crime* (New York: Oxford University Press, 1995), pp. 137–153.

56. Andrew von Hirsch, *Censure and Sanction* (New York: Oxford University Press, 1993); Michael Moore, "The Moral Worth of Retribution," in Ferdinand Schoeman, ed., *Responsibility, Character, and the Emotions: New Essays in Moral Philosophy* (Cambridge, Eng.: Cambridge University Press, 1987), pp. 179–219.

57. William J. Stuntz, "Race, Class, and Drugs," *Columbia Law Review* 98 (1998): 1795–1842.

58. Leena Kurki, "Restorative and Community Justice in the United States," in Michael Tonry, ed., *Crime and Justice: A Review of Research,* vol. 27 (Chicago: University of Chicago Press, 2000), pp. 265–266.

59. See Andrew Ashworth and Andrew von Hirsch, "Desert and the Three R's," in Andrew von Hirsch and Andrew Ashworth, *Principled Sentencing: Readings on Theory and Policy* (Oxford: Hart, 1998), pp. 331–335; John Braithwaite, *Restorative Justice and Responsive Regulation* (New York: Oxford University Press, 2002), p. 46.

60. See, e.g., John Braithwaite, "Restorative Justice: Assessing Optimistic and Pessimistic Accounts" in Michael Tonry, ed., *Crime and Justice: A Review of Research,* vol. 25 (Chicago: University of Chicago Press, 1999), pp. 7, 55–56; Kurki, "Restorative and Community Justice," pp. 287–288.

61. Julian W. Mack, "The Juvenile Court," *Harvard Law Review* 23 (1909): 104.

62. See Braithwaite, "Optimistic and Pessimistic Accounts," pp. 8, 79.

63. The discussion that follows borrows and reorganizes materials from John Braithwaite, *Restorative Justice*, chap. 3; and Braithwaite, "Optimistic and Pessimistic Accounts," pp. 1–127.

64. See Leena Kurki, *Incorporating Restorative and Community Justice into American Sentencing and Corrections* (Washington, D.C.: NIJ, 1999).

65. In New Zealand, family group conferences are available for all crimes short of homicide. Kurki, "Restorative and Community Justice," p. 275. For an attempted application of restorative processes to a case of serious violent injury, see *The Queen v. Patrick Dale Clotworthy,* discussed in Braithwaite, "Optimistic and Pessimistic Accounts," pp. 87–88.

66. See Kurki, "Restorative and Community Justice," pp. 276–277.

67. See Heather Strang et al. *Experiments in Restorative Policing: A Progress Report on the Canberra Reintegrative Shaming Experiments (RISE)* (Canberra: Centre for Restorative Justice, Australian National University, 2000), pp. 51–57. Braithwaite collected reports of occasional conferences that are much larger (up to seventy-five people) or longer (up to five hours) than the averages from the Canberra study. See his "Optimistic and Pessimistic Accounts," p. 39.

68. See Kurki, "Restorative and Community Justice," p. 266.

69. Braithwaite, "Optimistic and Pessimistic Accounts," pp. 18–19.

70. See Andrew von Hirsch, Andrew Ashworth, and Clifford Shearing, "Can Meaningful Aims and Limits for Restorative Justice Be Specified? The Example of a 'Making Amends' Model" (forthcoming).

71. See Braithwaite, *Restorative Justice*, p. 55; Philip Pettit with John Braithwaite, "Republicanism in Sentencing: Recognition, Recompense, and Reassurance," in Andrew von Hirsch and Andrew Ashworth, *Principled Sentencing: Readings on Theory and Policy* (Oxford, Eng.: Hart, 1998), pp. 317–330.

72. Braithwaite, "Optimistic and Pessimistic Accounts," pp. 18, 59, 65–67.

73. This includes the presence of adequate sample sizes, a demonstrated temporal sequence of studied causes coming before studied effects, and the use of control groups that closely resemble the target population of the studied intervention. See OJP, *Preventing Crime*, pp. 2–15 to 2–19.

74. Lawrence W. Sherman, Heather Strang, and Daniel J. Woods, *Recidivism Patterns in the Canberra Reintegrative Shaming Experiments (RISE)* (Canberra: Centre for Restorative Justice, Australian National University, 2000). See also Braithwaite, *Restorative Justice*, pp. 55–62.

75. Braithwaite's allegiance to this position is not as consistent as we would like. Although Braithwaite in 1999 adopted a strong pro-evaluation stance (see "Optimistic and Pessimistic Accounts," pp. 8, 79), his 2002 book expressed reservations about whether controlled investigations of offender recidivism should be a continued priority. See Braithwaite, *Restorative Justice*, pp. 69–70.

76. Braithwaite, *Restorative Justice,* p. 52; Strang et al., *Experiments in Restorative Policing,* p. 125. For a restorative justice study sensitive to the need to follow up on victim attitudes, see Richard Young and Benjamin Goold, "Restorative Police Cautioning in Aylesbury," *Criminal Law Review* (1999): 136.

77. See, e.g., Wesley G. Skogan, "The Impact of Community Policing on Neighborhood Residents: A Cross-Site Analysis," in Dennis P. Rosenbaum, ed., *The Challenge of Community Policing: Testing the Promises* (Thousand Oaks, Calif.: Sage, 1994), pp. 167–181.

78. See R. A. Duff and David Garland, "Thinking about Punishment," in R. A. Duff and David Garland, eds., *A Reader on Punishment* (New York: Oxford University Press, 1997), p. 1.

79. See Braithwaite, *Restorative Justice,* p. 45.

80. Ibid., pp. 47–51. See also Strang et al., *Experiments in Restorative Policing,* pp. 126–127; Paul McCold and Benjamin Wachtel, *Restorative Policing Experiment: The Bethlehem Pennsylvania Police Family Group Conferencing Project* (Pipersville, Pa.: Community Service Foundation, 1998); Claudia Fercello and Mark Umbreit, *Client Evaluation of Family Group Conferencing in Twelve Sites in First Judicial District of Minnesota* (Minneapolis: University of Minnesota, Center for Restorative Justice & Mediation, 1998), p. 11.

81. Braithwaite, *Restorative Justice,* pp. 51–52. See also Jeff Latimer, Craig Dowden, and Danielle Muise, *The Effectiveness of Restorative Justice Practices: A Meta-Analysis* (Ottowa: Department of Justice, Canada, 2001); Strang et al., *Experiments in Restorative Policing,* p. 125; and McCold and Wachtel, *Restorative Policing Experiment.*

82. Braithwaite, *Restorative Justice,* pp. 54–55. See also McCold and Wachtel, *Restorative Policing Experiment,* pp. 59–61.

83. See Strang et al., *Experiments in Restorative Policing,* pp. 111–112. Lawrence Sherman has hypothesized that resentful and defiant offenders are more likely to be lawbreakers in the future. See Lawrence W. Sherman, "Defiance, Deterrence, and Irrelevance: A Theory of the Criminal Sanction," *Journal of Research in Crime and Delinquency* 30 (1993): 448–449.

84. See Michael Cavadino and James Dignan, "Reparation, Retribution, and Rights," *International Review of Victimology* 4 (1997): 233–253; Braithwaite, "Optimistic and Pessimistic Accounts," pp. 77, 89, 97.

85. For example, Braithwaite acknowledges that there are no present measures for some of his values such as "spirituality," "self-transcendence," and finding "meaning in life beyond one's self." Braithwaite, *Restorative Justice,* p. 53.

86. See Braithwaite, "Optimistic and Pessimistic Accounts," pp. 72–79.

87. See Andrew Ashworth, "Some Doubts about Restorative Justice," *Criminal Law Forum* 4 (1993): 277–299; von Hirsch, Ashworth, and Shearing, "Can Meaningful Aims and Limits for Restorative Justice Be Specified?"; Sharon Levant, Francis T. Cullen, and John F. Wozniak, "Reconsidering Restorative

Justice: The Corruption of Benevolence Revisited?" *Crime & Delinquency* 45 (1999): 3–27; Barry C. Feld, "Rehabilitation, Retribution, and Restorative Justice: Alternative Conceptions of Juvenile Justice," in Gordon Bazemore and Lode Walgrave, eds., *Restorative Juvenile Justice: Repairing the Harm of Youth Crime* (Monsey, N.Y.: Willow Tree, 1999), pp. 17–44.

88. Braithwaite, *Restorative Justice*, pp. 49–50, 54–55. See also Strang et al., *Experiments in Restorative Policing*, pp. 93, 126; Fercello and Umbreit, *Client Evaluation*, p. 9; McCold and Wachtel, *Restorative Policing Experiment*; Lily Trimboli, *An Evaluation of the NSW Youth Justice Conferencing Scheme* (Sydney: New South Wales Bureau of Crime Statistics and Research, 2000), pp. 34–54.

89. Braithwaite, "Optimistic and Pessimistic Accounts," p. 50.

90. Ibid., p. 103.

91. See von Hirsch, Ashworth, and Shearing, "Meaningful Aims."

3. The Current Era of Crime Response Policy

1. For an alternative summary, see David Garland, *The Culture of Control: Crime and Social Order in Contemporary Society* (Chicago: University of Chicago Press, 2001), chap. 1.

2. See Kevin R. Reitz, "Sentencing: Allocation of Authority," in Joshua Dressler, ed., *Encyclopedia of Crime and Justice*, 2d ed. (New York: Macmillan Reference, 2002), pp. 1400–1416.

3. See Christian Parenti, *Lockdown America: Police and Prisons in the Age of Crisis* (London: Verso, 1999), pp. 174–177; John Irwin and James Austin, *It's About Time: America's Imprisonment Binge* (Belmont, Calif.: Wadsworth, 1997), pp. 75–76.

4. *Prison Litigation Reform Act of 1995*, Pub. L. No. 104–134, 110 Stat. 1321 (1996), codified as amended at 11 U.S.C. §523, 18 U.S.C. §3624, 18 U.S.C. §3626, 28 U.S.C. §123, 28 U.S.C. §1346, 28 U.S.C. §1915, and 42 U.S.C. §1997. For a general discussion of the effects of the act, see Mark Tushnet and Larry Yackle, "Symbolic Statutes and Real Laws: The Pathologies of the Antiterrorism and Effective Death Penalty Act and the Prison Litigation Reform Act," *Duke Law Journal* 47 (1997): 1–86.

5. See, for example, *Illinois v. Gates*, 462 U.S. 213 (1983) (relaxing the legal standard for probable cause required before police can initiate search or make an arrest); *United States v. Leon*, 468 U.S. 897 (1984) (allowing evidence to be admitted at trial even though seized in violation of the Fourth Amendment, so long as police reasonably believed they had a valid search warrant); *United States v. White*, 401 U.S. 745 (1971) (police do not need probable cause or a search warrant to conduct electronic surveillance so long as one party to the electronic monitoring has consented to be surveilled); *California v. Green-*

wood, 486 U.S. 35 (1988) (police may search private citizen's trash placed on curbside without probable cause and without obtaining search warrant); *United States v. Watson*, 423 U.S. 411 (1976) (police are not required to procure arrest warrant before arresting suspect in a public place, so long as they have probable cause); *Whren v. United States*, 517 U.S. 806 (1996) (police may make pretextual stops of suspects; for example, they may stop someone's car for a minor traffic violation even if their true motivation is to search the car for drugs); *Illinois v. Rodriguez*, 497 U.S. 177 (1990) (police may search private residence after receiving permission to do so from person with no authority to give such permission, as long as police reasonably believed that such person had authority); *Michigan Department of State Police v. Sitz*, 496 U.S. 444 (1990) (police may stop drivers and ask questions at roadside sobriety checkpoints without warrants or probable cause); *United States v. Place*, 462 U.S. 696 (1983) (police may subject private luggage to dog sniff searches without probable cause or search warrant); *Moran v. Burbine*, 475 U.S. 412 (1986) (police may interrogate suspect who has not yet been charged with a crime even when suspect's attorney has demanded to see her client; police may mislead attorney and inform her incorrectly that suspect is not being interrogated); *New York v. Quarles*, 467 U.S. 649 (1984) (police are excused from complying with *Miranda* rules in fast-breaking emergency situations); *Illinois v. Wardlow*, 528 U.S. 119 (2000) (police may stop and frisk persons in high-crime neighborhoods when such persons run from police).

6. See Kenneth J. Peak, *Policing America: Methods, Issues, Challenges* (Upper Saddle River, N.J.: Prentice Hall, 1997), pp. 213–225.

7. *United States v. Salerno*, 481 U.S. 739 (1987).

8. *Bordenkircher v. Hayes*, 434 U.S. 357 (1978).

9. *Ross v. Moffitt*, 417 U.S. 600 (1974).

10. *Strickland v. Washington*, 466 U.S. 668 (1984).

11. *United States v. Williams*, 504 U.S. 36 (1992).

12. See, for example, *Wainwright v. Sykes*, 433 U.S. 72 (1977); *Stone v. Powell*, 428 U.S. 465 (1976); and *Teague v. Lane*, 489 U.S. 288 (1989). Congress added further limitations to state prisoners' statutory rights to seek federal habeas corpus relief in the Antiterrorism and Effective Death Penalty Act of 1996, Pub. L. No. 104–132, 106(b)(3)(E), 110 Stat. 1214, 1221 (1996), amending 28 U.S.C. §§2241–2266. For a discussion of the act's effects, see Tushnet and Yackle, "Symbolic Statutes and Real Laws"; "Rewriting the Great Writ: Standards of Review for Habeas Corpus under the New 28 U.S.C. §2254," *Harvard Law Review* 110 (1997): 1868–1885.

13. *Wainwright v. Witt*, 469 U.S. 412 (1985). Compare *Witherspoon v. Illinois*, 391 U.S. 510 (1968).

14. *McCleskey v. Kemp*, 481 U.S. 279 (1987).

15. *United States v. Watts,* 519 U.S. 148 (1997).

16. See Garland, *Culture of Control,* pp. 11–12; Leslie Sebba, *Third Parties: Victims and the Criminal Justice System* (Columbus: Ohio State University Press, 1996), pp. 13–24.

17. Garland, *Culture of Control,* p. 35.

18. See Michael Massing, *The Fix* (Berkeley: University of California Press, 1998).

19. See generally Marvin E. Frankel, *Criminal Sentences: Law without Order* (New York: Hill and Wang, 1973); Norval Morris, *The Future of Imprisonment* (Chicago: University of Chicago Press, 1974); Sheldon L. Messinger and Philip D. Johnson, "California's Determinate Sentencing Statute: History and Issues," in U.S. Department of Justice, Law Enforcement Assistance Administration, *Determinate Sentencing: Reform or Regression* (Washington, D.C.: GPO, 1979), pp. 13–58; David Boerner and Roxanne Lieb, "Sentencing Reform in the Other Washington," in Michael Tonry, ed., *Crime and Justice: A Review of Research,* vol. 28 (Chicago: University of Chicago Press, 2001), pp. 71–136.

20. See Steven R. Belenko, ed., *Drugs and Drug Policy in America: A Documentary History* (Westport, Conn.: Greenwood, 2000), pp. 287–299, 345–349; Ronald Bayer and Gerald M. Oppenheimer, eds., *Confronting Drug Policy: Illicit Drugs in a Free Society* (Cambridge, Eng.: Cambridge University Press, 1993), p. 19; James Q. Wilson, *Thinking about Crime* (New York: Basic Books, 1975), pp. 145–146.

21. *Mapp v. Ohio,* 367 U.S. 643 (1961).

22. *Miranda v. Arizona,* 384 U.S. 436 (1966).

23. *Gideon v. Wainwright,* 372 U.S. 335 (1963); *Douglas v. California,* 372 U.S. 353 (1963).

24. See, for example, *In re Gault,* 387 U.S. 1 (1967); *In re Winship,* 397 U.S. 358 (1970).

25. *Fay v. Noia,* 372 U.S. 391 (1963).

26. See, e.g., *Powell v. Alabama,* 297 U.S. 45 (1932); Dan T. Carter, *Scottsboro: A Tragedy of the American South* (Baton Rouge: Louisiana State University Press, 1979). See also Harper Lee, *To Kill a Mockingbird* (Philadelphia: Lippincott, 1960).

27. See Malcolm M. Feeley and Edward L. Rubin, *Judicial Policy Making and the Modern State: How the Courts Reformed America's Prisons* (Cambridge, Eng.: Cambridge University Press, 1999).

28. See Garland, *Culture of Control,* chap. 6; Kevin R. Reitz, "The Disassembly and Reassembly of U.S. Sentencing Practices," in Michael Tonry and Richard S. Frase, eds., *Sentencing and Sanctions in Western Countries* (New York: Oxford University Press, 2001), pp. 222–258.

29. See Garland, *Culture of Control,* p. 53.

30. See Katherine Beckett, *Making Crime Pay: Law and Order in Contemporary*

American Politics (New York: Oxford University Press, 1997), pp. 57–61; David C. Anderson, *Crime and the Politics of Hysteria: How the Willie Horton Story Changed American Justice* (New York: Times Books, 1995); See also Wendy Kaminer, *It's All the Rage: Crime and Culture* (Reading, Mass.: Addison-Wesley, 1995), pp. 195–198.

31. See generally Garland, *Culture of Control.* Other works that have posited sociological, cultural, and political explanations include Loïc Wacquant, "Deadly Symbiosis: When Ghetto and Prison Meet and Mesh," *Punishment & Society* 3 (2001): 95–134; Jonathan Simon, "Governing through Crime," in Lawrence M. Friedman and George Fisher, eds., *The Crime Conundrum: Essays on Criminal Justice* (Boulder, Colo.: Westview, 1997); Gary LaFree, *Losing Legitimacy: Street Crime and the Decline of Social Institutions in America* (Boulder, Colo.: Westview, 1998); Beckett, *Making Crime Pay.*

32. See, for example, William J. Chambliss, *Power, Politics, and Crime* (Boulder, Colo.: Westview, 2001), pp. 28, 141; Beckett, *Making Crime Pay,* pp. 28–29, 32–33, 107; Irwin and Austin, *It's About Time,* p. xvii; Steven R. Donziger, ed., *The Real War on Crime: The Report of the National Criminal Justice Commission* (New York: Harper Perennial, 1996), p. 2; Jerome G. Miller, *Search and Destroy: African-American Males in the Criminal Justice System* (Cambridge, Eng.: Cambridge University Press, 1996), pp. 1–2; Michael Tonry, *Malign Neglect: Race, Crime, and Punishment in America* (New York: Oxford University Press, 1995), pp. 41, 123, 190; Elliott Currie, *Confronting Crime: An American Challenge* (New York, Pantheon, 1985), p. 48; Ronald Bayer, "Crime, Punishment, and the Decline of Liberal Optimism," *Crime & Delinquency* 27 (1981): 177; American Friends Service Committee, *Struggle for Justice: A Report on Crime and Punishment in America* (New York: Hill & Wang, 1971), pp. 107, 121–122.

33. For similar analyses, see Robert M. O'Brien, "Police Productivity and Crime Rates: 1973–1992," *Criminology* 34, no. 2 (1996): 183–207; Donzinger, *Real War on Crime,* chap. 1; Christopher Jencks, "Is Violent Crime Increasing?" *The American Prospect* (Winter 1991): 98–109.

34. For UCR trends in the 1930s, 1940s, and 1950s, see President's Commission on Law Enforcement and Administration of Justice, Task Force Report, *Crime and Its Impact—An Assessment* (Washington, D.C.: GPO, 1967), pp. 19–20.

35. BJS, *Sourcebook of Criminal Justice Statistics, 1998* (Washington, D.C.: GPO, 1999), p. 260, table 3.114.

36. See O'Brien, "Police Productivity," p. 204 for a similar conclusion for the years 1973 to 1992.

37. We are hardly the first to suggest such a comparison. See Franklin E. Zimring, *American Youth Violence* (New York: Oxford University Press, 1998); O'Brien, "Police Productivity."

38. See BJS, *Criminal Victimization, 2000: Changes 1999–2000 with Trends 1993–2000* (Washington, D.C.: BJS, 2001), p. 2.

39. See Wilson, *Thinking about Crime* (1975), p. 4; Charles Murray, "Does Prison Work?" in Malcolm Davies, Andrew Rutherford, and Jock Young, eds., *Does Prison Work?* (London: Institute of Economic Affairs, 1997), pp. 1–28; John J. DiIulio, Jr., "Crime," in Henry J. Aaron and Charles L. Schultze, eds., *Setting Domestic Priorities: What Can Government Do?* (Washington, D.C.: Brookings Institution, 1992), p. 114.

40. See Miller, *Search and Destroy*, pp. 1–2; Chambliss, *Power, Politics, and Crime*, p. 28; Katherine Beckett and Theodore Sasson, *The Politics of Injustice: Crime and Punishment in America* (Thousand Oaks, Calif.: Pine Forge, 2000), pp. 10–11; and Anderson, *Crime and the Politics of Hysteria*.

41. FBI, *Uniform Crime Reports, 1950–99*, www.ojp.usdoj.gov/bjs/homicide/tables/totalstab.htm; FBI, *Crime in the United States, 2000: Uniform Crime Reports* (Washington, D.C.: GPO, 2001), p. 14.

42. See Garland, *Culture of Control*, pp. 65–68; Elliott Currie, "The New Criminology," *Crime and Social Justice* 2 (1974): 113; Tony Platt and Paul Takagi, "Intellectuals for Law and Order: A Critique of the New 'Realists,'" *Crime and Social Justice* 8 (1977): 16; Carl B. Klockars, "The Contemporary Crises of Marxist Criminology," *Criminology* (Feb. 1979): 477–515, 506; Richard F. Sparks, *A Critique of Marxist Criminology*, in Norval Morris and Michael Tonry, eds., *Crime and Justice: An Annual Review of Research*, vol. 2 (Chicago: University of Chicago Press, 1980), pp. 159–210.

43. Richard Bernstein, "A Thinker Attuned to Thinking: James Q. Wilson Has Insights, Like Those on Cutting Crime, That Tend to Prove Out," *New York Times*, Aug. 22, 1998, p. B7, quoting Ester Fuchs, professor of political science at Barnard College and Columbia University.

44. Wilson, *Thinking about Crime* (1975); James Q. Wilson, *Thinking About Crime*, revised ed. (New York: Basic Books, 1983).

45. President's Commission on Law Enforcement and Administration of Justice, *The Challenge of Crime in a Free Society* (Washington, D.C.: GPO, 1967), p. 6.

46. James Q. Wilson, "A Reader's Guide to the Crime Commission Reports," *Public Interest* (Fall 1967): 64–82.

47. See Wilson, *Thinking about Crime* (1975), pp. xiii–xv, 3–4, 206 (on the social environment as a cause of crime); pp. 169–170 (on the failure of rehabilitation); pp. 163–167, 208 (on the problems of individualized sentencing); and pp. 44, 55–63 (on the tendency of liberals to substitute personal ideology for scientific knowledge).

48. Ibid., pp. 175–176, 209.

49. Ibid., p. 209.

50. For Wilson's criticism of liberals on this score, see Wilson, *Thinking about Crime* (1975), pp. 4, 58. See also Francis A. Allen, *The Crimes of Politics: Politi-*

cal Dimensions of Criminal Justice (Cambridge: Harvard University Press, 1974), p. 14; Bayer, "Crime, Punishment," p. 176; Currie, *Confronting Crime,* p. 13.

51. See Wilson, *Thinking about Crime* (1975), p. 58 (stating that "scholars (properly) criticized the statistical and empirical weaknesses in these published rates [that is, crime rates as reported in the UCR]"); and p. 62 ("published crime rates are unreliable"). In contrast, for an example of Wilson's uncritical reference to the UCR crime series, see p. 4: "Crime soared [in the 1960s]. It did not just increase a little; it rose at a faster rate and to higher levels than at any time since the 1930s and, in some categories, to higher levels than any experienced in this century".

52. Wilson, *Thinking about Crime* (1975), pp. 53, 168–171; Robert Martinson, "What Works—Questions and Answers about Prison Reform," *Public Interest* 35 (1974): 22–54.

53. Kevin R. Reitz, "Sentencing," in Michael Tonry, ed., *The Handbook of Crime and Punishment* (New York: Oxford University Press, 1998), pp. 545–556.

54. See Bayer, "Crime, Punishment," p. 182; Francis T. Cullen and Karen E. Gilbert, *Reaffirming Rehabilitation* (Cincinnati: Anderson Publishing Company, 1982), pp. 247, 261; Ted Palmer, "Martinson Revisited," *Journal of Research in Crime and Delinquency* 12 (1975): 133–152; Ted Palmer, *Correctional Intervention and Research: Current Issues and Future Prospects* (Lexington, Mass.: Lexington Books, 1978).

55. See Currie, *Confronting Crime*, p. 14.

56. Francis A. Allen, *The Decline of the Rehabilitative Ideal: Penal Policy and Social Purpose* (New Haven, Conn.: Yale University Press, 1981).

57. Andrew von Hirsch, *Doing Justice: The Choice of Punishments* (New York: Hill and Wang, 1976); Herbert L. Packer, *The Limits of the Criminal Sanction* (Stanford, Calif.: Stanford University Press, 1968).

58. Marvin E. Frankel, *Criminal Sentences: Law without Order* (New York: Hill and Wang, 1973), pp. 98–100; Albert W. Alschuler, "Sentencing Reform and Prosecutorial Power: A Critique of Recent Proposals for 'Fixed' and 'Presumptive' Sentencing," *University of Pennsylvania Law Review* 126 (1978): 552.

59. See Garland, *Culture of Control*, pp. 65–68.

60. See Bayer, "Crime, Punishment," p. 171; Karl Menninger, *The Crime of Punishment* (New York: Viking, 1966), p. 28.

61. See Irwin and Austin, *It's About Time*, p. 162; Miller, *Search and Destroy,* pp. 137, 276–277;; Currie, *Confronting Crime*, p. 13; Menninger, *Crime of Punishment*, p. 218.

62. See Wilson, *Thinking about Crime* (1975), p. 203. The book's introductory materials prepared readers to accept this theme. See pp. xiii, 4.

63. See, for example, Charles A. Murray, *Losing Ground: American Social Policy,*

1950–1980 (New York: Basic Books, 1984), pp. 171–172; Ben J. Wattenberg, *Values Matter Most: How Republicans or Democrats or a Third Party Can Win and Renew the American Way of Life* (New York: Free Press, 1995), p. 155.

64. Wilson, *Thinking about Crime* (1975), p. 4.

65. Ibid., pp. 4, 203.

66. Ibid., pp. 3–20.

67. See Bayer, "Crime, Punishment," p. 175; Herbert L. Packer, "Revolving Door Millenium," *New Republic,* Nov. 15, 1969, pp. 24–26. For liberal arguments along such ambitious lines, see Elliott Currie, *Crime and Punishment in America* (New York: Metropolitan Books, 1998), pp. 110–161; Jeffrie Murphy, "Marxism and Retribution," *Philosophy and Public Affairs* 2 (1973): 242; Ramsey Clark, *Crime in America: Observations on Its Nature, Causes, Prevention and Control* (New York: Simon and Schuster, 1970), pp. 239–260.

68. For Wilson's charges see Wilson, *Thinking about Crime* (1975), pp. 53, 55. On the thinness of the literature prior to the 1970s, see Daniel Nagin, "General Deterrence: A Review of the Empirical Literature," in Alfred Blumstein, Jacqueline Cohen, and Daniel Nagin, eds., *Deterrence and Incapacitation: Estimating the Effects of Criminal Sanctions on Crime Rates* (Washington, D.C.: National Academy of Sciences, 1978), p. 95; Franklin E. Zimring and Gordon Hawkins, *Incapacitation: Penal Confinement and the Restraint of Crime* (New York: Oxford University Press, 1995), p. 18.

69. A similar charge could be leveled concerning Wilson's selective citation of deterrence research. Wilson made prominent use of Isaac Ehrlich's pro-deterrence work (see Wilson, *Thinking about Crime* [1975], pp. 174–175) without expressly endorsing Ehrlich's conclusions. In the end, Wilson's support for deterrence-based incarceration policy rested less on his ability to reconcile the conflicting research, and more on the bland claim that "informed persons [should be persuaded] to take [the deterrence studies] seriously" (p. 175).

70. Ibid., p. 173. Later in the same paragraph Wilson repeated that incapacitative prison policies "may produce major reductions in crime rates." By the end of the paragraph this has mutated into the incautious claim that "the gains to society from crimes not committed while they [repeat offenders] were in prison would be real and substantial" (p. 173). Over several sentences, all doubts about effectiveness had been resolved.

71. Ibid., p. 173.

72. Ibid., pp. 200–202.

73. For literature surveys, see Kevin R. Reitz, "The American Experiment: Crime Reduction through Prison Growth," *European Journal on Criminal Policy and Research* 4, no. 3 (1996): 74–91; Zimring and Hawkins, *Incapacitation,* chap. 2.

74. James Q. Wilson, "Crime and Public Policy," in James Q. Wilson and Joan Petersilia, eds., *Crime* (San Francisco: ICS Press, 1995), pp. 498–503.

4. Prisons and Jails

1. BJS, *Prison and Jail Inmates at Midyear 2001* (Washington, D.C.: BJS, 2002), p. 1.

2. Dina Rose and Todd Clear, "Incarceration, Social Capital, and Crime: Implications for Social Disorganization Theory," *Criminology* 36 (1998): 458, 465–466; John Hagan and Ronit Dinovitzer, "Collateral Consequences of Imprisonment for Children, Communities, and Prisoners," in Michael Tonry and Joan Petersilia, eds., *Crime and Justice: A Review of Research*, vol. 26 (Chicago: University of Chicago Press, 1999), pp. 121–162.

3. BJS, *Incarcerated Parents and Their Children* (Washington, D.C.: BJS, Aug. 2000), p. 1.

4. John J. Donohue III and Peter Siegelman, "Allocating Resources among Prisons and Social Programs in the Battle against Crime," *Journal of Legal Studies* 27 (1998): 5.

5. National Association of State Budget Officers, *State Expenditure Report, 2000* (Washington, D.C.: National Association of State Budget Officers, 2001), p. 17, table 3; Stan C. Proband, "Corrections Costs Lead State Budget Increases for 1995," *Overcrowded Times* 6, no. 2 (Apr. 1995): 1, 8–9.

6. BJS, *Justice Expenditure and Employment in the United States, 1999* (Washington, D.C.: BJS, 2002), p. 3, table 2.

7. Katherine Beckett, *Making Crime Pay: Law and Order in Contemporary American Politics* (New York: Oxford University Press, 1997), p. 106.

8. Marc Mauer and Tracy Huling, *Young Black Americans and the Criminal Justice System: Five Years Later* (Washington, D.C.: The Sentencing Project, 1995), p. 1.

9. BJS, *Prison and Jail Inmates at Midyear 2001*, p. 2, table 1; p. 3, table 2.

10. See Diane Jennings, "State Housing Fewer Inmates: Decline Comes after a Decade of Growth," *Dallas Morning News*, Mar. 6, 2001, p. A1; David Rohde, "After Long Climb, Prison Population Falls in New York," *New York Times*, Feb. 2, 2001, p. A1; Associated Press, "Tennessee Prison Population Swelled in '90s, Now Slowing," *Chattanooga Times*, Sept. 11, 2000, p. B5; James Rainey, "California and the West: Prison Population Drops for First Time in Years," *Los Angeles Times*, July 4, 2000, p. 3.

11. John J. DiIulio, Jr., "The Question of Black Crime," *Public Interest* 117 (Fall 1994): 15–16, 21.

12. See John J. DiIulio, Jr., "The Value of Prisons," *Wall Street Journal*, May 13, 1992, p. A14; John J. DiIulio, Jr., "Let 'Em Rot," *Wall Street Journal*, Jan. 26, 1994, p. A14. To be fair to DiIulio, the title of the "Let 'Em Rot" op-ed piece was created by the *Wall Street Journal* editors. See John J. DiIulio, Jr., "Your Ugly Sentiments, Not Mine," *Wall Street Journal*, Feb. 3, 1994.

13. William J. Bennett, John J. DiIulio, Jr., and John P. Walters, *Body Count: Moral Poverty . . . and How to Win America's War against Crime and Drugs* (New York: Simon & Schuster, 1996), p. 136.

14. Ibid., p. 17.

15. John J. DiIulio, Jr., "Two Million Prisoners Are Enough," *Wall Street Journal,* Mar. 12, 1999, p. A14.

16. Anne Morrison Piehl, Bert Useem, and John J. DiIulio, Jr., *Right-Sizing Justice: A Cost-Benefit Analysis of Imprisonment in Three States* (New York: Center for Civic Innovation at the Manhattan Institute, 1999), p. 9.

17. Ibid., pp. 11–13.

18. John J. DiIulio, Jr., "Zero Prison Growth: Thoughts on the Morality of Effective Crime Policy," *American Journal of Jurisprudence* 44 (1999): 70.

19. Michael Tonry, *Malign Neglect: Race, Crime, and Punishment in America* (New York: Oxford University Press, 1995), pp. 45, 205–207.

20. See Franklin E. Zimring and Gordon Hawkins, *Incapacitation: Penal Confinement and the Restraint of Crime* (New York: Oxford University Press, 1995), chap. 4.

21. See Franklin E. Zimring and Gordon Hawkins, *Crime Is Not the Problem: Lethal Violence in America* (New York: Oxford University Press, 1998).

22. The outline of the next three paragraphs borrows from Franklin E. Zimring, "Imprisonment Rates and the New Politics of Criminal Punishment," *Punishment & Society* 3, no. 1 (2001): 161–166 and from the plenary address delivered by Zimring at the Annual Conference of the American Society of Criminology, San Francisco, Nov. 17, 2000.

23. Alfred Blumstein and Allen J. Beck, "Population Growth in U.S. Prisons, 1980 to 1996," in Tonry and Petersilia, *Crime and Justice,* pp. 20–22.

24. Ibid., p. 45.

25. Allen J. Beck, "Understanding Growth in U.S. Prison and Parole Populations," paper presented at the Annual Conference on Criminal Justice Research and Evaluation: Enhancing Policy and Practice, Washington, D.C., July 21, 1999, p. 5, table 8.

26. This trend is analyzed in Blumstein and Beck, "Population Growth," pp. 36–39.

27. Ibid., p. 35.

28. Ibid., p. 36.

29. Beck, "Understanding Growth," p. 5, table 8.

30. Ibid.

31. Charles Murray, et al., *Does Prison Work?* (London: Institute of Economic Affairs, 1997); Gary S. Becker, "How the U.S. Handcuffed the Crime Rate," *Business Week,* Dec. 28, 1998, p. 28.

32. From 1972 to 1991, reported-recorded-transmitted robbery rates rose by 51

percent, aggravated assault rates by 130 percent, and rape rates by 88 percent. BJS, *Sourcebook of Criminal Justice Statistics, 2000* (Washington, D.C.: BJS, 2001), pp. 278–279, table 3.120.

33. Richard Rosenfeld, "Patterns in Adult Homicide, 1980–1995," in Alfred Blumstein and Joel Wallman, eds., *The Crime Drop in America* (Cambridge, Eng.: Cambridge University Press, 2000), p. 148, table 5.4.

34. The calculations are derived from data presented in ibid.

35. These findings resulted from averaging crime reduction estimates derived from four separate methodologies. See Zimring and Hawkins, *Incapacitation*, pp. 116–117.

36. Ibid., pp. 117–119.

37. This is considerably more than the homicide avoidance estimated by Rosenfeld, but Rosenfeld was attempting to measure only the incapacitative effects of prison growth, whereas the Zimring and Hawkins study assessed the crime-reduction effects of prison growth from all causes, including incapacitation as well as such things as general deterrence and rehabilitation of ex-offenders.

38. The California prisons grew by approximately 10,000 inmates per year through the 1980s.

39. BJS, *National Crime Victimization Survey Property Crime Trends, 1973–2000* (*www.ojp.usdoj.gov/bjs/glance/tables/proptrdtab.htm*), visited on Sept. 5, 2002. As with violent offending, the case for the crime-reductive efficacy of incarceration is weakened if one consults UCR statistics instead of the NCVS for crime trends over time. See BJS, *Sourcebook of Criminal Justice Statistics, 2000* (Washington, D.C.: BJS, 2001), pp. 278–279, table 3.120.

40. Jeremy Bentham, "An Introduction to the Principles of Morals and Legislation," excerpted in Sanford H. Kadish and Stephen J. Schulhofer, *Criminal Law and Its Processes: Cases and Materials,* 6th ed. (Boston: Little, Brown, 1995), pp. 110–111.

41. Alfred Blumstein, "Racial Disproportionality of U.S. Prison Populations Revisited," *University of Colorado Law Review* 64 (1993): 743–760; Tonry, *Malign Neglect,* pp. 49–50, 63–80; John J. DiIulio, Jr., "The Question of Black Crime," *Public Interest* 117 (Fall 1994): 4–7; Zimring and Hawkins, *Crime Is Not the Problem,* chap. 5; William Julius Wilson, *The Truly Disadvantaged: The Inner City, the Underclass, and Public Policy* (Chicago: University of Chicago Press, 1987), pp. 22–26.

42. See BJS, *Hispanic Victims of Violent Crime, 1993–2000* (Washington, D.C.: BJS, 2002), pp. 1–3; J. F. Kraus, S. B. Sorenson, and P. D. Juarez, eds., *Proceedings of Research Conference on Violence and Homicide in Hispanic Communities* (Los Angeles: University of California, 1988); BJS, *Violent Victimization and Race, 1993–98* (Washington, D.C.: BJS, 2001), p. 3, table 2.

43. Wilson, *The Truly Disadvantaged*, pp. 21–22.

44. See David Cole, *No Equal Justice: Race and Class in the American Justice System* (New York: The New Press, 1999), p. 5; Eileen Poe-Yamagata and Michael A. Jones, *And Justice for Some: Differential Treatment of Minority Youth in the Justice System* (Washington, D.C.: Building Blocks for Youth, 2000), p. 6; Jerome G. Miller, *Search and Destroy: African-American Males in the Criminal Justice System* (Cambridge, Eng.: Cambridge University Press, 1996), pp. 1–2; William J. Chambliss, *Power, Politics, and Crime* (Boulder, Colo.: Westview, 2001).

45. Randall Kennedy, *Race, Crime, and the Law* (New York: Pantheon, 1997), pp. 69–75.

46. BJS, *Criminal Victimization in the United States, 1995* (Washington, D.C.: BJS, 2000), p. 49, table 42.

47. James Alan Fox, *Trends in Juvenile Homicide: A Report to the United States Attorney General on Current and Future Rates of Juvenile Offending, 1997 Update* (Washington, D.C.: BJS, 1997), p. 3, tables 3 and 4.

48. See Zimring and Hawkins, *Crime Is Not the Problem*, p. 84, fig. 5.4; and p. 87.

49. See Kennedy's *Race, Crime, and the Law*, chap. 2.

50. Zimring and Hawkins, *Crime Is Not the Problem*, pp. 83–86.

51. See Michael R. Gottfredson and Travis Hirschi, *A General Theory of Crime* (Stanford, Calif.: Stanford University Press, 1990), p. 91.

52. Statement of John Steer, Vice Chair, U.S. Sentencing Commission, Before the House Governmental Reform Subcommittee on Criminal Justice, Drug Policy and Human Resources, May 11, 2000, p. 14.

53. Piehl et al., *Right-Sizing Justice*, p. 12; Daniel S. Nagin, "Criminal Deterrence Research at the Outset of the Twenty-First Century," in Michael Tonry, ed., *Crime and Justice: A Review of Research* (Chicago: University of Chicago Press, 1998), p. 29.

54. We base this conjecture on John DiIulio's prediction that a prison policy of renewed emphasis on violent crimes, but with heavy deemphasis on drug crimes, would result in stasis, or even in slight growth, of present prison populations. See John J. DiIulio, Jr., "Zero Prison Growth: Thoughts on the Morality of Effective Crime Policy," *American Journal of Jurisprudence* 44 (1999): 67–74; John J. DiIulio, Jr., "Federal Crime Policy: Declare a Moratorium," in Henry J. Aaron and Robert D. Reischauer, eds., *Setting National Priorities: The 2000 Election and Beyond* (Washington, D.C.: Brookings Institution, 1999).

55. See, e.g., William Spelman, "The Limited Importance of Prison Expansion," in Alfred Blumstein and Joel Wallman, eds., *The Crime Drop in America* (Cambridge, Eng.: Cambridge University Press, 2000), pp. 111–112; Zimring and Hawkins, *Incapacitation*, pp. 50–51; James Q. Wilson, "Crime and Public

Policy," in James Q. Wilson and Joan Petersilia, eds., *Crime* (San Francisco: ICS Press, 1995), p. 501.

56. See Henry J. Steadman, "From Dangerousness to Risk Assessment of Community Violence: Taking Stock at the Turn of the Century," *Journal of the American Academy of Psychiatry and the Law* 28, no. 3 (2000): 265–271.

57. See Peter W. Greenwood and Susan Turner, *Selective Incapacitation Revisited: Why the High-Rate Offenders Are Hard to Predict* (Santa Monica, Calif.: RAND Corporation, 1987).

58. For a personalized and qualitative study of "false positives" who successfully turned away from crime, see Shadd Maruna, *Making Good: How Ex-Convicts Reform and Rebuild Their Lives* (Washington, D.C.: American Psychological Association, 2001).

59. For another reluctant defense of such a policy, see Norval Morris and Marc Miller, "Predictions of Dangerousness," in Michael Tonry and Norval Morris, eds., *Crime and Justice: An Annual Review of Research,* vol. 6 (Chicago: University of Chicago Press, 1985), pp. 1–50. Less hesitant, perhaps, is Nigel Walker, *Why Punish? Theories of Punishment Reassessed* (New York: Oxford University Press, 1991), pp. 57–58.

60. The institution of the sentencing commission was first suggested by Federal Judge Marvin E. Frankel, in his classic work *Criminal Sentences: Law without Order* (New York: Hill and Wang, 1973). Recent surveys of the sentencing reform "movement" include Tonry, *Sentencing Matters;* Richard S. Frase, "Sentencing Guidelines . . . A Twenty-Year Retrospective," *Federal Sentencing Reporter* 12, no. 2 (1999): 69–82; Kevin R. Reitz, "Sentencing Guidelines," in Joshua Dressler, ed., *The Encyclopedia of Crime and Justice* (New York: MacMillan, 2002).

61. See Ronald F. Wright, "Counting the Cost of Sentencing in North Carolina, 1980–2000," in Michael Tonry, ed., *Crime and Justice: A Review of Research,* vol. 29 (Chicago: University of Chicago Press, 2002); Kim Hunt, "Sentencing Commissions as Centers for Policy Analysis and Research: Illustrations from the Budget Process," *Law & Policy* 20 (1998): 465–489; and U.S. Sentencing Commission, *The Federal Sentencing Guidelines: A Report on the Operation of the Guidelines System and Short-Term Impacts on Disparity in Sentencing, Use of Incarceration, and Prosecutorial Discretion and Plea Bargaining* (Washington, D.C.: U.S. Sentencing Commission, 1991).

62. See Kate Stith and José A. Cabranes, *Fear of Judging: Sentencing Guidelines in the Federal Courts* (Chicago: University of Chicago Press, 1998), pp. 195–197, nn. 12 and 13.

63. See Tonry, *Sentencing Matters,* p. 71. See also Richard S. Frase, "Is Guided Discretion Sufficient? Overview of State Sentencing Guidelines," *Saint Louis University Law Journal* 44 (2000): 443–445; Kevin R. Reitz, "The Status of Sen-

tencing Guideline Reforms in the U.S.," *Overcrowded Times* 10 (Dec. 1999): 1–14; Wright, "Counting the Cost of Sentencing"; and American Bar Association, *Standards for Criminal Justice, Sentencing,* 3d ed. (Chicago: ABA Press, 1994), pp. xxi–xxvii.

64. See Kay A. Knapp, "What Sentencing Reform in Minnesota Has and Has Not Accomplished," *Judicature,* 68 (1984): 185; David Boerner, "The Role of the Legislature in Guidelines Sentencing in 'The Other Washington,'" *Wake Forest Law Review* 28, no. 2 (1993): 381–420; David J. Gottlieb, "Kansas Adopts Sentencing Guidelines," *Federal Sentencing Reporter* 6, no. 3 (1993): 158–161; and John Kramer and Cynthia Kempinen, "The Reassessment and Remaking of Pennsylvania's Sentencing Guidelines," *Federal Sentencing Reporter* 8, no. 2 (1995): 75; Ronald F. Wright, *Managing Prison Growth in North Carolina through Structured Sentencing* (Washington, D.C.: National Institute of Justice, 1998); Richard Kern, "Sentencing Reform in Virginia," *Federal Sentencing Reporter* 8, no. 2 (1995): 84–88.

65. Reitz, "Status of Sentencing Guideline Reforms;" Thomas B. Marvell, "Sentencing Guidelines and Prison Population Growth," *Journal of Criminal Law and Criminology* 85 (1995): 696–707; Jon Sorenson and Jon Stemen, "The Effect of State Sentencing Policies on Incarceration Rates," *Crime & Delinquency* 48 (2002): 456.

66. Both the U.S. Sentencing Commission and the Pennsylvania Sentencing Commission were originally charged with drafting sentencing guidelines to increase the severity of prison sentences in their respective jurisdictions. Both commissions were able to do so with demonstrable success. See Reitz, "Status of Sentencing Guideline Reforms," pp. 12–13.

67. Michael Tonry, "The Success of Judge Frankel's Sentencing Commission," *University of Colorado Law Review* 64 (1993): 713–722.

68. See Marvell, "Sentencing Guidelines and Prison Population Growth," p. 707.

69. American Bar Association, *Sentencing Standards,* 3d ed., standard 18–1.3.

70. See American Law Institute, *Model Penal Code: Sentencing, Plan for Revision* (Philadelphia: American Law Institute, 2002), One of the authors of the present book serves as reporter for the Model Penal Code project.

71. See DiIulio, "Zero Prison Growth"; James Q. Wilson, Letter to the Editor, *Washington Post,* Feb. 8, 2001, p. A22; Tonry, *Malign Neglect.*

72. BJS, *Prison and Jail Inmates at Midyear 2000* (Washington, D.C.: BJS, 2000), p. 2, table 1; BJS, *Sourcebook of Criminal Justice Statistics, 1999,* p. 498, table 6.21; p. 503, table 6.26; Margaret Werner Cahalan, *Historical Corrections Statistics in the United States, 1850–1984* (Washington, D.C.: GPO, 1986), p. 76, table 4-1.

73. See Jan M. Chaiken and Marcia R. Chaiken, *Varieties of Criminal Behavior* (Santa Monica, Calif.: RAND Corporation, 1982); M. Peterson et al., *Survey*

of Prison and Jail Inmates: Background and Methods (Santa Monica, Calif.: RAND Corporation, 1982); Alfred C. Miranne and Michael R. Geerken, "The New Orleans Inmate Survey: A Test of Greenwood's Predictive Scale," *Criminology* 29, (1991): 497–518; Kim English and Mary Mande, *Measuring Crime Rates of Prisoners* (Denver: Colorado Department of Public Safety, Division of Criminal Justice, Office of Research and Statistics, 1992).

74. See BJS, *Correctional Populations in the United States, 1997* (Washington, D.C.: BJS, 2000), p. 50, table 4.3.

75. The estimates for 1998, which are the most recent produced by the U.S. Justice Department, were based on the 1997 survey of state correctional facilities, as reported in BJS, *Prisoners in 1999* (Washington, D.C.: BJS, 2000), p. 10, table 15.

76. See, for example, Alfred Blumstein and Joan Petersilia, "Investing in Criminal Justice Research," in James Q. Wilson and Joan Petersilia, eds., *Crime* (San Francisco, Calif.: ICS Press, 1995), pp. 472–475; Zimring and Hawkins, *Incapacitation*, pp. 44–47; David P. Farrington, "A Criminological Research Agenda for the Next Millenium," *International Journal of Offender Therapy and Comparative Criminology* 43 (1999): 154–157; Delbert S. Elliott, "Serious Violent Offenders: Onset, Developmental Course, and Termination—The American Society of Criminology 1993 Presidential Address," *Criminology* 32 (1994): 1–21.

77. Piehl et al., *Right-Sizing Justice*, p. 16.

78. Ibid.

79. See Maruna, *Making Good*, pp. 111–115; Dan A. Lewis and Shadd Maruna, "Person-Centered Policy Analysis," *Research in Public Policy Analysis and Management* 9 (1998): 213–230.

80. See David Garland, *The Culture of Control: Crime and Social Order in Contemporary Society* (Chicago: University of Chicago Press, 2001), p. 133.

81. The long history of failed rehabilitative programs is recounted in David J. Rothman's books *The Discovery of the Asylum: Social Order and Disorder in the New Republic* (Boston: Little, Brown, 1971) and *Conscience and Convenience: The Asylum and Its Alternatives in Progressive America* (Boston: Little, Brown, 1980). For a contemporary review of the weak evidence of the effectiveness of in-prison rehabilitative programming, see Gerald G. Gaes et al., "Adult Correctional Treatment," in Tonry and Petersilia, *Crime and Justice*, pp. 361–426.

82. See Gordon Hawkins, "Prison Labor and Prison Industries," in Michael Tonry and Norval Morris, eds., *Crime and Justice: An Annual Review of Research*, vol. 5 (Chicago: University of Chicago Press, 1983), pp. 85–128.

83. M. Douglas Anglin and Yih-Ing Hser, "Treatment of Drug Abuse," in Michael Tonry and James Q. Wilson eds., *Crime and Justice: A Review of Research*, vol.

13 (Chicago: University of Chicago Press, 1990), pp. 393–460; OJP, *Preventing Crime: What Works, What Doesn't, and What's Promising* (Washington, D.C.: OJP, 1997), pp. 9–41 to 9–43.

84. See, e.g., Norval Morris, *The Future of Imprisonment* (Chicago: University of Chicago Press, 1974), p. 96.

85. Joan Petersilia, "A Crime Control Rationale for Reinvesting in Community Corrections," *Prison Journal* 75, no. 3 (1995): 479–504.

86. See Norval Morris and Michael Tonry, *Between Prison and Probation: Intermediate Punishments in a Rational Sentencing System* (New York: Oxford University Press, 1990); James M. Byrne, Arthur J. Lurigio, and Joan Petersilia, *Smart Sentencing: The Emergence of Intermediate Sanctions* (Newbury Park, Calif.: Sage, 1992).

87. See Tonry, *Sentencing Matters*, chap. 4.

88. Michael Tonry and Kathleen Hatlestad, eds., *Sentencing Reform in Overcrowded Times: A Comparative Perspective* (New York: Oxford University Press, 1997).

89. Reitz, "Status of Sentencing Guideline Reforms."

90. Allen J. Beck, "State and Federal Prisoners Returning to the Community: Findings from the Bureau of Justice Statistics," paper presented at the First Reentry Courts Initiative Cluster Meeting, Washington, D.C., Apr. 13, 2000.

91. Jeremy Travis, *But They All Come Back: Rethinking Prisoner Reentry* (Washington, D.C.: NIJ, 2000), p. 3.

92. See, e.g., David Farabee et al., "Barriers to Implementing Effective Correctional Treatment Programs," *Prison Journal* 157 (1999).

93. Joan Petersilia, "Parole and Prisoner Reentry in the United States," in Tonry and Petersilia, *Crime and Justice*, pp. 479–529; Shadd Maruna and Thomas P. LeBel, "Revisiting Ex-Prisoner Re-Entry: A Buzzword in Search of a Narrative," in Michael Tonry and Susan Rex, eds., *Reform and Punishment: The Future of Sentencing* (Devon, Eng.: Willan, 2002).

94. Lawrence W. Sherman, "Reducing Incarceration Rates: The Promise of Experimental Criminology," *Crime & Delinquency* 46, no. 3 (2000): 299–314.

95. FBI, *Crime in the United States, 1999* (Washington D.C.: GPO, 2000), p. 229, table 42.

96. BJS, *Prison and Jail Inmates at Midyear 1999* (Washington, D.C.: BJS, 2000), p. 10, table 12.

97. See U.S. Department of Justice, *Incarcerated Inmates and Their Children* (Washington, D.C.: BJS, 2000), p. 1.

98. Blumstein and Beck, "Population Growth," p. 22.

99. See BJS, *Prison and Jail Inmates at Midyear 1999* (Washington, D.C.: BJS, 2000), p. 10, table 12.

100. Blumstein and Beck, "Population Growth," p. 26.

101. GAO, *State and Federal Prisoners: Profiles of Inmate Characteristics in 1991 and 1997* (Washington, D.C.: GAO, 2000), p. 72, table VI.1. As the women's prisons have grown in the 1990s, the percentage of women prisoners convicted of violent crimes has dropped (p. 75, table VI.2).

102. BJS, *Prison and Jail Inmates at Midyear 1999*, p. 10, table 12.

103. See American Bar Association, *Sentencing Standards*, Standard 18–2.3; Wright, "Counting the Cost of Sentencing"; U.S Department of Justice, Bureau of Justice Assistance, *National Assessment of Structured Sentencing* (Washington, D.C.: Bureau of Justice Assistance, 1996), pp. 44–45, table 4-3.

104. Kevin R. Reitz, "Sentencing," in Michael Tonry, ed., *The Handbook of Crime and Punishment* (New York: Oxford University Press, 1998), p. 549.

105. Tonry, *Malign Neglect*, p. 104.

5. Public and Private Paths to Security from Crime

1. William Cunningham and Todd Taylor, "The Growing Role of Private Security," Research in Brief, NIJ, Oct. 1984, p. 3.

2. Ibid., pp. 2, 4.

3. William Cunningham, John Strauch, and Clifford Van Meter, *Private Security Trends, 1970 to 2000—The Hallcrest Report II* (Stoneham, Mass.: Butterworth-Heinemann, 1990), p. 294.

4. Albert Reiss, "Private Employment of Public Police," Research in Brief, NIJ, Dec. 1988.

5. U.S. House of Representatives Committee on the Judiciary, *Private Security Officer Quality Assurance Act of 1997*, 105th Congress, 1st sess., H.R. Rept. 105–161, pp. 2–7; Cunningham, Strauchs, and Van Meter, *Hallcrest Report II*, p. 176.

6. Cunningham, Strauchs, and Van Meter, *Hallcrest Report II*, p. 127.

7. Ibid., pp. 163–172.

8. Ibid., p. 175.

9. Office of National Drug Control Policy, *National Drug Control Strategy* (Washington, D.C.: GPO, 1999), p. 51.

10. Cunningham, Strauchs, and Van Meter, *Hallcrest Report II*, pp. 56–59.

11. Ibid., p. 74.

12. Marcel Niglii, "Rational Choice and the Legal Model of the Criminal," in Graeme Newman, Ronald Clarke, and Giora Shoham, eds., *Rational Choice and Situational Crime Prevention* (Aldershot, Eng.: Dartmouth and Ashgate, 1997), pp. 25–45.

13. Ibid.

14. John Eck, "Preventing Crime at Places," in Lawrence Sherman et al., eds., *Evidence-Based Crime Prevention* (London: Routledge, 2002).

15. Ibid.

16. Ibid.

17. Ibid.

18. "New York City Notes a Plunge in Auto Theft," *New York Times*, Jan. 22, 2000, p. A13.

19. Robert Barr and Ken Pease, "Crime Placement, Displacement, and Deflection," in Michael Tonry and Norval Morris, eds., *Crime and Justice: A Review of Research*, vol. 12 (Chicago: University of Chicago Press, 1990): 277–318; Eck, "Preventing Crime" (2002).

20. Marcus Felson, *Crime and Everyday Life: Insight and Implications for Society* (Thousand Oaks, Calif.: Pine Forge, 1994), pp. 119–122.

21. Ibid., p. 118.

22. Ibid., pp. 125–128. For several other examples of situational prevention, see R. V. Clarke, *Situational Crime Prevention: Successful Case Studies* (Albany, N.Y.: Harrow and Heston, 1992).

23. Eck, "Preventing Crime" (2002).

24. Ralph Taylor, "Physical Environment, Crime, Fear, and Resident-Based Control," in James Wilson and Joan Petersilia, eds., *Crime: Public Policies for Crime Control* (Oakland, Calif.: ICS Press, 2002), pp. 413–434.

25. Barry Poyner, *Design against Crime—Beyond Defensible Space* (London: Butterworths, 1983), pp. 106–108.

26. Mary Smith, "Crime Prevention through Environmental Design in Parking Facilities," Research in Brief, NIJ, Apr. 1996.

27. Corey Gordon and William Brill, "The Expanding Role of Crime Prevention through Environmental Design in Premises Liability," Research in Brief, NIJ, Apr. 1996.

28. Edward Blakely and Mary Snyder, *Fortress America: Gated Communities in the United States* (Washington, D.C.: Brookings Institution Press, with Lincoln Institute of Land Policy, 1997), pp. 6–7, 180.

29. Ibid., p. 126.

30. Ibid., pp. 126–129, 99–122.

31. Ibid., pp. 149–160.

32. Jonathan Rubinstein, *City Police* (New York: Farrar, Straus and Giroux, 1973), p. 127.

33. Ibid.

34. Egon Bittner, *The Functions of the Police in a Modern Society: A Review of Background Factors, Current Practices and Possible Role Models* (Rockville, Md.: National Institute of Mental Health, p. 46.

35. National Commission on Law Observance and Enforcement (Wickersham Commission), *Report on Police* (Washington, D.C.: GPO, 1931), p. 1.

36. Wickersham Commission, *Report on Lawlessness in Law Enforcement* (Washington, D.C.: GPO, 1931), p. 153.

37. See Lloyd Ohlin, "Surveying Discretion by Criminal Justice Decision Makers," in Lloyd Ohlin and Frank Remington, eds., *Discretion in Criminal Justice: The Tension between Individualization and Uniformity* (Albany: State University of New York Press, 1993), pp. 1–22.

38. President's Commission on Law Enforcement and Administration of Justice, *The Challenge of Crime in a Free Society* (Washington, D.C.: GPO, 1967), pp. 13, 273, 277.

39. President's Commission, *Task Force Report: Crime and Its Impact: An Assessment* (Washington, D.C.: GPO, 1967), pp. 17–19.

40. President's Commission, *Challenge of Crime in a Free Society,* pp. 250–255.

41. George Kelling, et al., *The Kansas City Preventive Patrol Experiment: A Technical Report* (Washington, D.C.: Police Foundation, 1974); Kansas City Police Department, *Response Time Analysis: Volume II–Part I Crime Analysis* (Washington, D.C.: GPO, 1980); Peter Greenwood, Joan Petersilia and Jan Chaiken, *The Criminal Investigation Process* (Lexington, Mass.: Heath, 1977); Albert Reiss, Jr., *The Police and the Public* (New Haven, Conn.: Yale University Press, 1971), pp. 102–109.

42. For examples, see Robert Fogelson, *Big-City Police* (Cambridge: Harvard University Press, 1977), pp. 141–166, 219–242.

43. For the Los Angeles experience, see Gerald Woods, *The Police in Los Angeles: Reform and Professionalization* (New York: Garland, 1993), pp. 223–246.

44. President's Commission, *Task Force Report: The Police* (Washington, D.C.: GPO, 1967), pp. 51–53, 144–207, 221–228.

45. George Kelling and Catherine Coles, *Fixing Broken Windows: Restoring Order and Reducing Crime in Our Communities,* paperback ed. (New York: Touchstone, Simon & Schuster, 1997), pp. 89–91.

46. Michael Farmer, ed., *Differential Police Response Strategies* (Washington, D.C.: Police Executive Research Forum, 1981), pp. 8–9, 13–38.

47. William Bratton, *Turnaround: How America's Top Cop Reversed the Crime Epidemic* (New York: Random House, 1998), p. 93.

48. Farmer, *Differential Police Response Strategies,* exhibit 3, p. 49.

49. Antony Pate and Edwin Hamilton, *The Big Six: Policing America's Largest Cities* (Washington, D.C.: The Police Foundation, 1991), pp. 34, 111–112, 114.

50. Brian Reaves and Andrew Goldberg, *Law Enforcement Management and Administrative Statistics, 1997: Data for Individual State and Local Agencies with 100 or More Officers* (Washington, D.C.: BJS, 1999), NCJ171681, tables 1a, 9a.

51. Herman Goldstein, *Problem-Oriented Policing* (New York: McGraw-Hill, 1990), pp. 151–152.

52. David Bayley, *Police for the Future,* paperback ed. (New York: Oxford University Press, 1994), p. 43.

53. Lawrence Sherman, "Attacking Crime: Policing and Crime Control," in Mi-

chael Tonry and Norval Morris, eds., *Modern Policing* (Chicago: University of Chicago Press, 1992), pp. 176–183.

54. Ibid., p. 176.

55. Eck, "Preventing Crime" (2002).

56. John Eck, "Preventing Crime at Places," in University of Maryland Department of Criminology and Criminal Justice, *Preventing Crime: What Works, What Doesn't, What's Promising* OJP, NCJ165366 (1997), p. 7–1.

57. William Spelman and John Eck, "Sitting Ducks, Ravenous Wolves and Helping Hands: New Approaches to Urban Policing," *LBJ School of Public Affairs Comment* 35, no. 2 (1989): 3.

58. Lawrence Sherman, "Fair and Effective Policing," in Wilson and Petersilia, *Crime: Public Policies for Crime Control,* pp. 383, 386–398; Lawrence Sherman, "Hot Spots of Predatory Crime: Routine Activities and the Criminology of Place," in *Criminology* 27, no. 1 (1989): 27–55; Lawrence Sherman, "Police Crackdowns: Initial and Residual Deterrence," in Tonry and Morris, *Crime and Justice,* pp. 1–48.

59. Lawrence Sherman, "Attacking Crime," in Tonry and Morris, *Modern Policing,* pp. 185–186; Lawrence Sherman, "Policing for Crime Prevention," in University of Maryland, *What Works,* pp. 8–20 to 8–21; William Spelman, *Repeat Offender Programs for Law Enforcement* (Washington, D.C.: Police Executive Research Forum, 1990).

60. John Eck and Edward Maguire, "Have Changes in Policing Reduced Violent Crime?—An Assessment of the Evidence," in Alfred Blumstein and Joel Wallman, eds., *The Crime Drop in America* (Cambridge, Eng.: Cambridge University Press, 2000), pp. 235–238.

61. Ibid., pp. 238–243.

62. Robert Barr and Ken Pease, "Crime Placement, Displacement, and Deflection," in Tonry and Morris, *Crime and Justice,* pp. 277–318; John Eck, "Preventing Crime" (2002).

63. John Eck, "Preventing Crime at Places," in University of Maryland, *What Works,* pp. 7–41; John Eck, "Preventing Crime" (2002).

64. Lawrence Sherman, *Policing Domestic Violence: Experiments and Dilemmas* (New York: Free Press, 1992), pp. 75–91.

65. Ibid., pp. 104–111.

66. Ibid., p. 247; Lawrence Sherman, "Evidence-Based Policing," one of the pamphlet series on "Ideas in American Policing" (Washington, D.C.: Police Foundation, July 1998), pp. 7–12; Lawrence Sherman, "Fair and Effective Policing," in Wilson and Petersilia, *Crime: Public Policies for Crime Control,* pp. 383, 391–392.

67. John Eck and Edward Maguire, "Changes in Policing," in Blumstein and Wallman, *Crime Drop,* p. 249; Ana Joanes, "Does the New York City Police

Department Deserve Credit for the Decline in New York City's Homicide Rates?—A Cross-City Comparison of Policing Strategies and Homicide Rates," in *Columbia Journal of Law and Social Problems* 33 (2000): 265–311; Peter Manning, "Theorizing Police: The Drama and Myth of Crime Control in the NYPD," *Theoretical Criminology* 5, no. 3 (2001): 315–344.

68. Lawrence Sherman, "The Police," in James Wilson and Joan Petersilia, eds., *Crime* (San Francisco: ICS Press, 1995), pp. 331–334, 339–341; John Eck and Edward Maguire, "Changes in Policing," in Blumstein and Wallman, *Crime Drop*, pp. 245–251.

69. Eli Silverman, *NYPD Battles Crime: Innovative Strategies in Policing* (Boston: Northeastern University Press, 1999), pp. 147–177, esp. pp. 175–177.

70. Reaves and Goldberg, *Law Enforcement Statistics, 1997*, pp. 1–10, table 1a.

71. Ibid., pp. 2, 7; Ann Pastore and Kathleen Maguire, eds., *Sourcebook of Criminal Justice Statistics, 1999*, BJS, (Washington, D.C.: GPO, 2000), p. 288, table 3.128.

72. Lawrence Sherman, "The Police," in Wilson and Petersilia, *Crime*, pp. 328–329.

73. John Eck and Edward Maguire, "Changes in Policing," in Blumstein and Wallman, *Crime Drop*, pp. 208–224.

74. Pastore and Maguire, *Sourcebook 1999*, p. 339, table 4.2.

75. Ibid., p. 266, table 3.120.

76. Ibid., p. 339, table 4.2.

77. Ibid., p. 339, table 4.2, and p. 266, table 3.120.

78. FBI, *Crime in the United States, 2000* (Washington, D.C.: GPO, 2001), p. 222, table 34.

79. Ibid.

80. Ibid., p. 66, table 1; BJS, "Criminal Victimization, 2000: Changes 1999–2000 with Trends 1993–2000," National Crime Victimization Survey, June 2001, NCJ187007.

81. James Wilson, *Varieties of Police Behavior: The Management of Law and Order in Eight Communities*, paperback ed. (New York: Atheneum, 1974), pp. 16–34.

82. Community Policing Consortium, "Understanding Community Policing: A Framework for Action," Monograph, Bureau of Justice Assistance, Washington, D.C., August 1994.

83. Ibid., pp. 44–45.

84. Ibid., pp. 15–22.

85. Mark Moore, "Problem-Solving and Community Policing," in Tonry and Morris, *Modern Policing*, pp. 99–158.

86. Wesley Skogan and Susan Hartnett, *Community Policing, Chicago Style* (New York: Oxford University Press, 1997).

87. Ibid., pp. 236–246.

88. Edward Maguire, et al. "Patterns of Community Policing in Nonurban America," in *Journal of Research in Crime and Delinquency* 34 (1997): 368–394.

89. Office of Community Oriented Policing Services, "COPS Accomplishments," in *COPS Fact Sheet* (Washington, D.C.: U.S. Dept. of Justice, Sept. 3, 1999). Local police departments reported that they had included 91,000 community policing officers or their equivalent in 1999, up from 16,000 such officers in 1997. BJS, *Community Policing in Local Police Departments, 1997 and 1999* (Washington, D.C.: U.S. Dept. of Justice, Feb. 2001), p. 2.

90. Herman Goldstein, *Problem-Oriented Policing* (New York: McGraw-Hill, 1990); John Eck and William Spelman, *Problem-Solving: Problem-Oriented Policing in Newport News* (Washington, D.C.: Police Executive Research Forum and NIJ, 1987), pp. 1–9.

91. Presentations at Tenth International Conference on Problem-Oriented Policing, San Diego, Nov. 1999; Eck and Spelman, *Problem-Solving in Newport News*, pp. 66–72; John Eck and William Spelman, "Who Ya Gonna Call?—The Police as Problem-Busters," *Crime and Delinquency* 33 (Jan. 1987): 31–52; Ronald Clarke and Gisela Bichler-Robertson, "Place Managers, Slumlords and Crime in Low Rent Apartment Buildings," *Security Journal* 11 (1998): 11–19.

92. Community Policing Consortium, "Understanding Community Policing," p. 47.

93. James Q. Wilson and George Kelling, "Broken Windows: The Police and Neighborhood Safety," *Atlantic Monthly*, Mar. 1982, pp. 29–38.

94. George Kelling, "Acquiring a Taste for Order: The Community and Police," *Crime & Delinquency* 33 (Jan. 1987): 93.

95. Jack Maple, *The Crime Fighters: Putting the Bad Guys Out of Business* (New York: Doubleday, 1999), pp. 154–155.

96. Ibid., p. 131.

97. Ibid., pp. 155–175.

98. Jeffrey Roth and Joseph Ryan, "The COPS Program after Four Years–National Evaluation," Research in Brief, NIJ, Aug. 2000, NCJ183644, p. 18. Indeed, the "broken windows" co-author, James Q. Wilson, endorsed New York City's zero tolerance for all misdemeanors and suggested arrests of "guilty people" for having a brake light out, jaywalking, and not having a driver's license. James Q. Wilson, "Six Things Police Leaders Can Do about Juvenile Crime," in *Subject to Debate* (Police Executive Research Forum Newsletter), vol. 11, nos. 9/10, 1997, p. 9.

99. David Bayley et al., "Remarks on Zero Tolerance by Conference Participants," *Criminal Law Bulletin* 35 (1999): 369–387.

100. In New York City, Mayor Bloomberg's police commissioner, Raymond Kelly, disbanded the citywide street crime unit that had stressed aggressive tactics

and caused tension and hostility in several parts of the city. See "Commissioner Will Disband a Controversial Police Unit," *New York Times,* Apr. 10, 2002, p. A23. Zero-tolerance practices have sometimes led to intolerable school discipline, e.g., punishing students for giving mints to classmates, possessing nail clippers, or unknowingly leaving a grandmother's bread knife in the bed of a truck after the student and his father had spent part of the weekend taking some of her belongings to a thrift shop ("High School Expels Junior after Guard Finds Knife in Truck," *New York Times,* Mar. 21, 2002).

101. "Keeping Tabs on the People Keeping Tabs," *New York Times,* Jan. 15, 2002, p. A20.

102. Eli Silverman, "Below Zero Tolerance: The New York Experience," in Roger Burke, ed., *Zero Tolerance Policing* (Leicester, Eng.; Perpetuity Press, 1998), pp. 39–48.

103. Wesley Skogan et al., "Problem Solving in Practice: Implementing Community Policing in Chicago," Research Report, NIJ NCJ179556, (Apr. 2000), pp. 3–4.

104. Jeffrey Roth and Joseph Ryan (coprincipal investigators) et al., "National Evaluation of the COPS Program—Title I of the 1994 Crime Act," Research Report, NIJ, NCJ183643, (Aug. 2000), pp. 179–240.

105. Ibid., pp. 21–23.

106. New York City Police Department, "COMPSTAT: Leadership in Action," an undated twenty-page brochure, probably issued in 1998; Silverman, *NYPD Battles Crime,* pp. 97–124, 182–204.

107. Silverman, *NYPD Battles Crime,* pp. 101–103.

108. Christopher Swope, "The COMSTAT [sic] Craze," in *Governing* (Sept. 1999): 40–43.

109. "Heads of Two Precincts Demoted," *New York Times,* Jan. 8, 2000.

110. James Clarke, *The Lineaments of Wrath: Race, Violent Crime, and American Culture* (New Brunswick, N.J.: Transaction, 1998).

111. FBI, *Crime, 2000,* p. 15.

112. Ibid., p. 234, table 43.

113. Lawrence Sherman, "Fair and Effective Policing," in Wilson and Petersilia, *Crime: Public Policies for Crime Control* pp. 383, 402–403.

114. Alton White, "Ragtime, My Time," *The Nation,* Oct. 11, 1999, pp. 11–12.

115. "Four Officers in Diallo Shooting Are Acquitted of All Charges," *New York Times,* Feb. 26, 2000, p. A1; "Department Rejects Penalty for Officers in Diallo Shooting," *New York Times,* Apr. 27, 2001, p. A1.

116. FBI, *Crime, 2000,* p. 234, table 43.

117. Office of National Drug Control Policy, *National Drug Control Strategy* (Washington, D.C.: GPO, 2001), p. 146, table 7.

118. Ibid., p. 151, table 12.

119. FBI, *Crime in the United States: Uniform Crime Reports, 1999* (Washington, D.C.: GPO, 2000), p. 231, table 43.

120. Bigotry in drug enforcement can extend to any minority. In January 2002, the Dallas district attorney dismissed 39 drug defendants after defense lawyers established that all of the cocaine allegedly seized by Dallas police was in fact ground-up wallboard material apparently provided as evidence by an often-used police informant. All of the defendants were blue-collar Mexican immigrants who spoke little or no English. "'Sheetrock Scandal' Hits Dallas Police," *Washington Post,* Jan. 18, 2002, p. A12.

121. John Lamberth, Ph.D., Report to the Court, *Wilkins v. Maryland State Police,* C.A. no. CCB-93–483 (1997).

122. *Whren v. United States,* 517 U.S. 806 (1996); *Atwater v. City of Lago Vista,* 532 U.S. 318 (2001).

123. David Harris, "'Driving While Black' and All Other Traffic Offenses: The Supreme Court and Pretextual Traffic Stops," *Journal of Criminal Law & Criminology* 87 (1997): 544, 561–563.

124. Ibid., pp. 568–569.

125. David Cole, *No Equal Justice: Race and Class in the American Criminal Justice System,* (New York: New Press, 1999), pp. 16–22.

126. "U.S. Will Monitor New Jersey Police on Race Profiling," *New York Times,* Dec. 23, 1999, p. A1.

127. Office of the Attorney General, *The New York City Police Department's "Stop and Frisk" Practices: A Report,* New York, Dec. 1, 1999, pp. 94–110.

128. Ibid., pp. xi, 126–128. A separate analysis of New York City street stops concluded that they were not based on "broken windows" or "quality-of-life" policing, but rather reflected police selection of poor people in their neighborhoods. Jeffrey Fagan and Garth Davies, "Street Stops and Broken Windows: *Terry,* Race and Disorder in New York City," in *Fordham Urban Law Journal* 28 (2000): 457–504.

129. "Most in U.S. Believe Cops Use Racial Profiling, Poll Says," *Arizona Daily Star,* Dec. 11, 1999, p. A18.

130. Marshall Miller, "Police Brutality," *Yale Law & Policy Review* 17 (1998): 149–200. The federal statute is 42 U.S. Code, sec. 14141.

131. Consent Decree, *United States v. City of Pittsburgh et al.,* U.S. District Court for the Western District of Pennsylvania, Apr. 16, 1997, *www.pittsburghpolice.com/condec.htm;* "Policing the Police Is a Dicey Business," *U.S. News & World Report,* Apr. 30, 2001, p. 28.

132. Gerald Woods, *The Police in Los Angeles: Reform and Professionalization* (New York: Garland, 1993), p. 259 and n. 128.

133. Los Angeles Police Dept. Board of Inquiry, Public Report, *Ramparts Area Corruption Incident,* Mar. 1, 2000, p. 55.

134. Ibid., preface through p. 330; Lou Cannon, "One Bad Cop," *New York Times Magazine,* Oct. 1, 2000, beginning p. 32.

135. Los Angeles Board of Inquiry Public Report, p. 331.

136. "CRASH in Los Angeles," *Los Angeles Times,* Mar. 4, 2000; "Chief of Police Disbands Antigang Units," *New York Times,* Mar. 4, 2000.

137. Cole, *No Equal Justice,* pp. 45–46.

138. Kathleen Maguire and Ann Pastore, eds., *Sourcebook of Criminal Justice Statistics, 2000,* BJS (Washington, D.C.: GPO, 2001), p. 297, table 3.129; "New York City Murder Rate Rising, Despite Police Effort," *New York Times,* Apr. 5, 2000, p. A21.

139. Los Angeles Board of Inquiry Public Report, p. 354.

140. Commission to Investigate Allegations of Police Corruption and the City's Anti-Corruption Procedures, *Commission Report,* Dec. 26, 1972, p. 61.

141. Ibid., p. 13.

142. Commission to Investigate Allegations of Police Corruption and the Anti-Corruption Procedures of the Police Department, *Commission Report,* July 7, 1994, p. 10.

143. Ibid., pp. 1–2.

144. "Holiday Arrests Low," *Arizona Daily Star,* Jan. 2, 2001, p. A4.

145. Compare Frank Remington and Herman Goldstein, "Law Enforcement Policy: The Police Role," chap. 2, in President's Commission, *Task Force Report: The Police,* pp. 13–41, with George Kelling, *"Broken Windows" and Police Discretion* (Washington, D.C.: NIJ, 1999), NCJ178259. See also Herman Goldstein, *Policing a Free Society,* paperback ed. (Madison: University of Wisconsin, 1990), pp. 93–130; Debra Livingston, "Police Discretion and the Quality of Life in Public Places: Courts, Communities, and the New Policing," in *Columbia Law Review* 97 (1997): 551–672.

146. Kelling, *"Broken Windows,"* pp. 49–57. For a summary of the present extent and nature of internal police administrative regulations, see Matthew Hickman and Brian Reaves, "Local Police Departments 1999," BJS (May 2001), NCJ186478.

147. "Chicago Makes Another Effort to Disrupt Gangs," *New York Times,* Aug. 3, 2000, p. A14.

148. *City of Chicago v. Morales,* 527 U.S. 41 (1999).

149. Municipal Code of Chicago, sec. 8-4-015, 8-4-017 (Feb. 16, 2000).

150. Chicago Police Department General Order 00-02, effective Apr. 15, 2000.

151. Telephone conversations in January 2000 with an attorney for the Lawyer's Committee for Civil Rights under Law, with a social worker from the Coalition for the Homeless, and with a lawyer in the San Francisco City Attorney's Office.

152. E-mail from Herman Goldstein to authors in January 2000.

153. New York Police Commissioner Kerik termed this "the worst kind of dysfunctional thinking in government." "Kerik Asks That the FBI Share Terror Information," *New York Times,* Dec. 12, 2001, p. A18.

154. Each federal effort against business crime (so-called white-collar crime) is so specialized, so time-intensive, so costly, and therefore so distant from street crime enforcement that it requires a discussion and analysis apart from this book. See David Weisburd et al., *Crimes of The Middle Class: White Collar Offenders in the Federal Courts* (New Haven, Conn.: Yale University Press, 1991); James Stewart, *The Prosecutors: Inside the Offices of the Government's Most Powerful* Lawyers (New York: Simon & Schuster, 1987).

155. James Strazzella, Task Force Reporter, *The Federalization of Criminal Law* (Washington, D.C.: American Bar Association Criminal Justice Section, 1998), pp. 7–12.

156. Ibid., pp. 9–12, 91–94.

157. Commission on the Advancement of Federal Law Enforcement, *Law Enforcement in a New Century and a Changing World: Improving the Administration of Federal Law Enforcement* (Washington, D.C.: GPO, 2000), pp. 33–38, 168–171. See also Brian Reaves and Timothy Hart, "Federal Law Enforcement Officers," BJS, July 2001, NCJ187231.

158. David Burnham and Susan Long, "The Clinton Era by the Numbers," *The Nation,* Jan. 29, 2001, p. 20.

159. Strazzella, *Federalization of Criminal Law,* pp. 19–21. Even the new concentration on counterterrorism by the U.S. Department of Justice involves only 10 percent of that agency's annual $25 billion budget. "Ashcroft Plans to Reorganize Justice, Curtail Programs," *Washington Post,* Nov. 9, 2001, p. A17.

160. Chitra Ragavan, "FBI Inc.," *U.S. News & World Report,* June 18, 2001, pp. 13–21.

161. Strazzella, *Federalization of Criminal Law,* p. 30, chart 7.

162. BJS, *Federal Criminal Case Processing, 1999—With Trends 1982–99* U.S. Dept. of Justice NCJ186180, (Feb. 2001), p. 11.

163. Strazzella, *Federalization of Criminal Law,* p. 20, n. 38.

164. Ibid., pp. 17–45; Commission on Federal Law Enforcement, *Improving Federal Law Enforcement,* pp. 87–94.

165. Commission on Federal Law Enforcement, *Improving Federal Law Enforcement,* pp. 123–125.

166. Ibid., pp. 91–94.

167. See, e.g., Clifford Shearing, "The Relation between Public and Private Policing," in Tonry and Morris, *Modern Policing,* pp. 399–434; David Sklansky, "The Private Police," *UCLA Law Review* 46 (1999): 1165–1287.

168. David Bayley and Clifford Shearing, "The New Structure of Policing: Description, Conceptualization, and Research Agenda," Research Report, NIJ, NCJ187083 (July 2001).

169. Eck and Maguire, "Changes in Policing," in Blumstein and Wallman, *Crime Drop*, p. 253, n. 24.

170. "Cities Reduce Crime and Conflict without New York-Style Hardball," *New York Times*, Mar. 4, 2000, p. A1.

171. Bernard Harcourt, "After the 'Social Meaning Turn': Implications for Research Design and Methods of Proof in Contemporary Criminal Law Policy Analysis," in *Law & Society Review* 34 (2000): 179–211. Narrower efforts trying to "prove" that crime reduction occurred because the "broken windows" theory had been implemented by aggressive order maintenance have been severely challenged. See D. W. Miller, "Poking Holes in the Theory of 'Broken Windows,'" in *Chronicle of Higher Education* (Feb. 9, 2001); Bernard Harcourt, *Illusion of Order: The False Promise of Broken Windows Policing* (Cambridge: Harvard University Press, 2001), pp. 57–89.

172. Professor Waldeck suggests just such a partnership between police and other public agencies, joining with the community in programs to uphold social norms. Sarah Waldeck, "Cops, Community Policing, and the Social Norms Approach to Crime Control: Should One Make Us More Comfortable with the Others?" *Georgia Law Review* 34 (2000): 1253, 1299–1310.

173. David Kennedy et al., "Reducing Gun Violence: The Boston Gun Project's Operation Ceasefire," Research Report, NIJ, NCJ188741, (Sept. 2001); David Kennedy, "Pulling Levers: Getting Deterrence Right," in *National Institute of Justice Journal* (July 1998): 2–8.

174. Telephone conversations with Herman Goldstein, a participant in that effort.

175. Roth and Ryan, "The COPS Program after Four Years," pp. 17–18.

176. David Weisburd and Tom McEwen, *Crime Mapping and Crime Prevention*, Crime Prevention Studies, vol. 8 (Monsey, N.Y.: Criminal Justice Press, 1998); Nancy La Vigne, "Computerized Mapping as a Tool for Problem-Oriented Policing," in *Crime Mapping News* (Winter 1999): 1–3; Thomas Rich, "Mapping the Path to Problem Solving," in *National Institute of Justice Journal* (Oct. 1999): 2–9.

177. Matthew Hickman and Brian Reaves, "Local Police Departments 1999," BJS, NCJ186478, (May 2001); Reaves and Goldberg, *Law Enforcement Statistics, 1997*, pp. 81–90, table 9a; pp. 151–180, tables 16a–18a.

178. Roth and Ryan, "National Evaluation of the COPS Program," pp. 12–16, 143–148.

6. Guns, Crime, and Crime Gun Regulation

1. FBI, *Crime in the United States: Uniform Crime Reports, 2000*, (Washington, D.C.: GPO, 2001), pp. 11–12.

2. Ibid., pp. 18–22.

3. Ibid., pp. 31, 35.

4. Callie Rennison, *Criminal Victimization, 2000: Changes 1999–2000 with Trends 1993–2000* (Washington, D.C.: BJS, June 2001), NCJ187007, pp. 3, 8–9; Ann Pastore and Kathleen Maguire, eds., *Sourcebook of Criminal Justice Statistics, 1999* (Washington, D.C.: GPO, 2000), NCJ183727, p. 186, tables 3.14, 3.15.

5. Pastore and Maguire, *Sourcebook 1999,* p. 141, table 2.71; "Touched by Guns," *Washington Post Weekly,* May 22, 2000, p. 34.

6. Pastore and Maguire, *Sourcebook 1999,* table 3.136, p. 295.

7. Ibid., table 3.156, p. 310; FBI, *Crime in the United States: Uniform Crime Reports, 1999* (Washington, D.C.: GPO, 2000), p. 29.

8. Pastore and Maguire, *Sourcebook 1999,* table 3.159, p. 312; FBI, *Crime in the United States, 1999,* p. 33.

9. Alfred Blumstein, "Violence Certainly Is the Problem–And Especially with Handguns, *University of Colorado Law Review* 69 (1998): 945, 960–965.

10. Jeffrey Roth, *Firearms and Violence,* Research in Brief (Washington, D.C.: OJP, 1994), NCJ145533.

11. Phillip Cook and Jens Ludwig, *Gun Violence: The Real Costs* (New York: Oxford University Press, 2000), pp. 21–22.

12. Garen Wintemute, "Guns and Gun Violence," in Alfred Blumstein and Joel Wallman, eds., *The Crime Drop in America* (New York: Cambridge University Press, 2000), pp. 45, 52.

13. James Fox, "Homicide Trends in the United States: 1998 Update," Crime Data Brief (Washington, D.C.: OJP, 2000), NCJ179767.

14. Philip Cook, Mark Moore, and Anthony Braga, "Gun Control," in James Wilson and Joan Petersilia, eds., *Crime: Public Policies for Crime Control* (Oakland, Calif.: ICS Press, 2002), pp. 291, 302.

15. Howard Snyder and Melissa Sickmund, *Juvenile Offenders and Victims: 1999 National Report,* OJJDP (Washington, D.C.: GPO, 1999), pp. 19–20.

16. Criminal Justice Statistics Center, *Report on Juvenile Felony Arrests in California, 1998* (Sacramento: California Department of Justice, 2000), pp. 14–16, 22.

17. Snyder and Sickmund, *Juvenile Offenders and Victims,* p. 19.

18. U.S. Census Bureau, *Statistical Abstract of the United States: 1998* (Washington, D.C.: GPO, 1998), p. 110, table 152; FBI, *Crime, 1999,* p. 14.

19. "Law Enforcement Officers Killed," *Arizona Daily Star,* May 16, 2000.

20. Marianne Zawitz and Kevin Strom, "Firearm Injury and Death from Crime, 1993–97" (Washington, D.C.: OJP, 2000).

21. Ibid.

22. Glenn Pierce, LeBaron Briggs, and David Carlson, *The Identification of Patterns in Firearms Trafficking: Implications for Focused Enforcement Strategy* (Washington, D.C.: ATF, 1995).

23. Roth, *Firearms and Violence*, p. 4.

24. Philip Cook, Mark Moore, and Anthony Braga summarize the research findings about user motivation and instrumentality effect in their chapter, "Gun Control," in Wilson and Petersilia *Crime: Public Policies for Crime Control*, pp. 192, 296–302.

25. FBI, *Crime in the United States: Uniform Crime Reports, 1998* (Washington, D.C.: GPO, 1999), pp. 29, 32; FBI, *Crime, 1999*, pp. 28–29, 33.

26. Roth, *Firearms and Violence*, p. 4.

27. Pastore and Maguire, *Sourcebook 1999*, p. 186, table 3.15.

28. The gun self-defense data are described and analyzed in Jens Ludwig, "Gun Self-Defense and Deterrence," in Michael Tonry, ed., *Crime and Justice: A Review of Research*, vol. 27 (Chicago: University of Chicago Press, 2000), pp. 363–417; Cook and Ludwig, *Gun Violence*, pp. 36–39; Philip Cook and Jens Ludwig, *Guns in America* (Washington, D.C.: Police Foundation, 1996), pp 57–76; and Pastore and Maguire, *Sourcebook 1999*, p. 141, table 2.71.

29. Marianne Zawitz, *Guns Used in Crime*, (Washington, D.C.: OJP, 1995), p. 3.

30. James Wright and Peter Rossi, *The Armed Criminal in America: A Survey of Incarcerated Felons* (Washington, D.C.: GPO, 1985), pp. 37–39.

31. Ibid.

32. Scott Decker, Susan Pennell, and Ami Caldwell, *Illegal Firearms: Access and Use by Arrestees*, Research in Brief (Washington, D.C.: OJP, 1997), pp. 1–3.

33. Joseph Sheley and James Wright, *Gun Acquisition and Possession in Selected Juvenile Samples*, Research in Brief (Washington, D.C.: OJP, 1994), pp. 1–7; Cook and Ludwig, *Guns in America*, pp. 29–30.

34. ATF, *The Youth Crime Gun Interdiction Initiative—Crime Gun Trace Analysis Report: The Illegal Youth Firearms Markets in Twenty-seven Communities* (Washington, D.C.: Department of the Treasury, 1999), pt. 1, pp. 7–19.

35. National Commission on the Causes and Prevention of Violence, *To Establish Justice, To Insure Domestic Tranquility* (Washington, D.C.: GPO, 1969), pp. 170–171.

36. Cook and Ludwig, *Guns in America*, pp. 9–15, 33.

37. Ibid.

38. ATF response, dated Aug. 1, 2000, to our Freedom of Information Act Request.

39. Ibid.; Pastore and Maguire, *Sourcebook 1999*, tables 3.120, 3.136.

40. "Handgun Sales in State Sink to Twenty-five-year Low," *Los Angeles Times*, Oct. 4, 1998, p. 1.

41. Pastore and Maguire, *Sourcebook 1999*, tables 2.66 through 2.70.

42. Jens Ludwig, Philip Cook, and Tom Smith, "The Gender Gap in Reporting Household Gun Ownership," *American Journal of Public Health* 88 (1998): 1715–1717.

43. Kathleen Maguire and Ann Pastore, eds., *Sourcebook of Criminal Justice Statistics, 2000* (Washington, D.C.: BJS, 2001), p. 198, table 3.19.

44. Cook and Ludwig, *Guns in America,* pp. 33, 39.

45. GAO, *Gun Sales: Implementation of the National Instant Criminal Background Check System* (Washington, D.C.: GAO, 2000), pp. 34–35.

46. Departments of Treasury and Justice, *Gun Shows: Brady Checks and Crime Gun Traces* (Washington, D.C., January 1999), pp. 1–9.

47. Cook and Ludwig, *Guns in America,* p. 35.

48. FBI, *Crime, 1999,* p. 212.

49. Sheley and Wright, *Gun Acquisition and Possession;* and Decker, Pennell, and Caldwell, *Illegal Firearms.*

50. ATF, *Youth Crime Gun Interdiction Initiative,* pp. 7–19.

51. Office of National Drug Control Policy, *National Drug Control Strategy: 2001 Annual Report* (Washington, D.C.: GPO, 2001), p. 141, table 2.

52. U.S. Census Bureau, *Statistical Abstract of the United States: 2000* (Washington, D.C.: GPO, 2000), p. 97, table 135.

53. "Accidental Deaths on Rise as the Population Ages," *New York Times,* Apr. 26, 2000, p. A18

54. "Gun Deaths Lowest since Mid-1960s, Report Says," *Arizona Daily Star,* Apr. 13, 2001, p. A1.

55. Statement of ATF Director John Magaw before the House Appropriations Subcommittee on Treasury, Postal Service, and General Government, Mar. 6, 1996.

56. Commission on the Advancement of Law Enforcement, *Law Enforcement in a New Century and a Changing World: Improving the Administration of Federal Law Enforcement* (Washington, D.C.: GPO, 2000), pp. 112–113.

57. William Vizzard, *In the Cross Fire* (Boulder, Colo.: Lynne Rienner, 1997), p. x.

58. Title 18, U.S. Code, sec. 921(a)(21)(C).

59. Title 18, U.S. Code, sec. 926(a).

60. Title 18, U.S. Code, sec. 923(g)(1)(B).

61. Title 18, U.S. Code, sec. 923(g)(3)(B).

62. Title 18, U.S. Code, sec. 925(b).

63. Title 18, U.S. Code, sec. 922 (p), (v), and (w) and repeal notes and historical and statutory notes (sunset provision); also sec. 921(a)(30), (31) repeal note.

64. These provisions exist primarily in Title 18, U.S. Code, sec. 921 through 929 and in vol. 27, Code of Federal Regulations, pts. 47, 178, 179.

65. Michael Bowling et al., *Background Checks for Firearms Transfers, 2000,* Bulletin, BJS, NCJ187985 (July 2001).

66. Jens Ludwig and Philip Cook, "Homicide and Suicide Rates Associated with Implementation of the Brady Handgun Violence Prevention Act," *Journal of*

the *American Medical Association* 284 (2000): 585–591; Wintemute, "Guns and Gun Violence," pp. 45, 77.

67. GAO, *Gun Control: Implementation of the National Instant Criminal Background Check System* (Washington, D.C.: GAO, 2000), GAO/GGD/AIMD-00-64, app. 3.

68. ATF, *National Integrated Ballistics Information Network* (Washington, D.C.: ATF, 1999); ATF-FBI Joint Press Release, *The Future of Ballistics Imaging Is Now*, Dec. 23, 1999.

69. ATF, *Youth Crime Gun Interdiction Initiative*, pp. 16–18.

70. ATF Press Release, *Gun Trafficking Actions*, Feb. 4, 2000.

71. Gary Kleck, "BATF Gun Trace Data and the Role of Organized Gun Trafficking in Supplying Guns to Criminals," *St. Louis University Public Law Review* 18 (1999): 23–45.

72. "Recycled District of Columbia Police Guns Tied to Crimes," *Washington Post*, Nov. 12, 1999, p. A1.

73. John Eck and Edward Maguire, "Have Changes in Policing Reduced Violent Crime? An Assessment of the Evidence," in Blumstein and Wallman, *Crime Drop*, pp. 207, 235–238; Wintemute, "Guns and Gun Violence," pp. 45, 70–73; Lawrence Sherman, "Fair and Effective Policing," in Wilson and Petersilia, *Crime: Public Policies for Crime Control*, pp. 392–393.

74. Lawrence Sherman, James Shaw, and Dennis Rogan, *The Kansas City Gun Experiment*, Research in Brief (Washington, D.C.: NIJ, 1995).

75. David Kennedy et al., *Reducing Gun Violence: The Boston Gun Project's Operation Ceasefire* (Washington, D.C.: OJP, 2001), NCJ188741.

76. Remarks of Andrew Vita, ATF, at Joint Hearing before the Subcommittees on Youth Violence and on Criminal Justice Oversight, of the U.S. Senate Committee on the Judiciary, on "Review of DOJ Firearms Prosecutions," Mar. 22, 1999. Even with Exile, opposition to the more intense tactics soon arose. See "Ready, Aim, Misfire," in *U.S. News & World Report*, May 21, 2001, pp. 16–18.

77. FBI, *Crime, 1999*, p. 216, table 32.

78. Transactional Records Access Clearinghouse, *Federal Prosecutions Resulting from ATF Criminal Referrals: 1992–1998*, http://trac.syr.edu.

79. ATF response, dated Aug. 1, 2000, to our Freedom of Information Act Request.

80. GAO, *Gun Control: Implementation of the National Instant Criminal Background Check* (Washington, D.C.: GAO, 2000), p. 83.

81. Vanessa O'Connell and Paul Barrett, "In the Market for Guns: The Customers Aren't Coming Back for More," *Wall Street Journal*, Oct. 26, 1999, p. A1.

82. "Straight Shooters Soaring: Women's Participation Primary Reason for Sporting Growth," *Denver Post*, June 11, 2000, p. 1C.

83. Wintemute, "Guns and Gun Violence," pp. 45, 78–80.

84. Maguire and Pastore, *Sourcebook 2000,* table 1.101.
85. "Heavy Use of Gun Seizure Law Stuns Backers," *New York Times,* Dec. 6, 1999.
86. A summary chart of these laws, state by state, can be found in Maguire and Pastore, *Sourcebook 2000,* table 1.101.
87. The Center to Prevent Handgun Violence commenced a campaign in March 2001 to convince twenty states to follow this Massachusetts example. See "Gun Control Advocates Signal a Retreat," *Washington Post National Weekly Edition,* Apr. 2–8, 2001, p. 13.
88. The polls cited here can be found in Pastore and Maguire, *Sourcebook 1999,* tables 2.73, 2.80; Kathleen Maguire and Ann Pastore, eds., *Sourcebook of Criminal Justice Statistics, 1998* (Washington, D.C.: GPO, 1999), NCJ176356, table 2.67.
89. "The Gun War Comes Home," *Newsweek,* Aug. 23, 1999, pp. 23–42.
90. *Sourcebook 1998,* p. 141, table 2.67.
91. John Lott, Jr., *More Guns, Less Crime: Understanding Crime and Gun Control Laws,* 2d ed. (Chicago; University of Chicago Press, 2000), pp. 197–202.
92. A detailed description of Lott's analyses, as well as a new analysis responding to Lott are found in Jens Ludwig, "Gun Self-Defense and Deterrence," in Michael Tonry, ed., *Crime and Justice: A Review of Research,* vol. 27 (Chicago: University of Chicago Press, 2000), pp. 363, 397–408. Among other analyses are Mark Duggan, "More Guns, More Crime," *Journal of Political Economy* 109 (2001): 1086–1114; Dan Black and Daniel Nagin, "Do 'Right to Carry' Laws Reduce Violent Crime?" *Journal of Legal Studies* 27 (1998): 209–219; Franklin Zimring and Gordon Hawkins, "Concealed Handguns: The Counterfeit Deterrent," *Responsive Community* 7 (Spring 1997): 46–60.
93. Title 10, U.S. Code, sec. 311–312, 331–333.
94. Title 10, U.S. Code, sec. 4307–4313; Stephen Halbrook, "Second-Class Citizenship and the Second Amendment in the District of Columbia," *George Mason University Civil Rights Law Journal* 5 (1995): 105, 155–157.
95. In *United States v. Miller,* 307 U.S. 174, 178 (1939), the Supreme Court overruled a lower court's dismissal, on Second Amendment grounds, of a federal criminal indictment that charged an individual with transporting an unregistered shotgun in interstate commerce. The Supreme Court remanded the case to the trial court to take evidence about the nature, purpose, and capability of the firearm at issue. The Court's ruling holds that any right to bear arms might apply only if the weapon at issue is "any part of the ordinary military equipment *or* that its use could contribute to the common defense" (emphasis ours). The background history of the Second Amendment and the militia is recounted in the *Miller* opinion and, most recently, in *United States v. Timothy Joe Emerson,* 2001 USApp LEXIS 22386 (Fifth Cir.), revised opinion of Nov. 2, 2001. The academic debate about the Second Amendment's purpose, meaning and history again heated up in the 1990s. "Dueling Scholars Fray

over a Constitutional Challenge to Gun Control Laws," *New York Times,* Sept. 21, 2000, p. A22.

96. Cesare Beccaria, "False Ideas of Utility," in Richard Bellamy, ed., *On Crimes and Punishments and Other Writings,* trans. Richard Davies with Virginia Cox and Bellamy (Cambridge, Eng.: Cambridge University Press, 1995), p. 101.

97. "*Rolling Stone* Interview—President Clinton," *Rolling Stone,* Dec. 28, 2000–Jan. 4, 2001, p. 97.

98. Pastore and Maguire, *Sourcebook 1999,* table 3.199.

99. Departments of Justice and the Treasury, and ATF, *Gun Shows: Brady Checks and Crime Gun Traces* (Washington, D.C.: ATF, Jan. 1999), pp. 1–12.

100. "U.S. to Develop a System for 'Fingerprinting' Guns," *New York Times,* Dec. 20, 1999, p. A17.

101. "Justice Department Bars FBI from Records on Detainees' Gun Buying," *New York Times,* Dec. 6, 2001, p. A1.

102. "Suit against Gun Makers Gains Ground in Illinois," *New York Times,* Jan. 3, 2002, p. A14; David Kairys, "The Origin and Development of the Governmental Handgun Cases," *Connecticut Law Review* 32 (2000): 1163–1174; Kairys, "The Governmental Handgun Cases and the Elements and Underlying Policies of Public Nuisance Law," *Connecticut Law Review* 32 (2000): 1175–1187; Elliot Zaret, "The Battle to Come: *District of Columbia v. Beretta USA Corp.,*" in *Washington Lawyer* (Sept. 2000): 22–28; "Citing Public Nuisance, New York Will Be First State to Sue Gun Maker," *New York Times,* June 26, 2000, p. A16.

103. The agreement, along with the manufacturer's "Clarification" of its terms, was reproduced on Apr. 6, 2001 at *www.smith-wesson.com/misc/agreement .html.*

104. "Hawaii's Xerox-Office Shooting Throws into Relief State's Effective Gun Laws," *Wall Street Journal,* Nov. 8, 1999.

105. Maguire and Pastore, *Sourcebook 2000,* table 3.125, p. 291.

106. FBI, *Crime, 2000,* p. 74, table 4.

7. Crime, Alcohol, and Illegal Drugs

1. David Musto, "The American Experience with Stimulants and Opiates," in *Perspectives on Crime and Justice: 1997–1998 Lecture Series* (Washington, D.C.: NIJ, 1998), NCJ172851, pp. 51–55.

2. *United States v. Doremus,* 249 U.S. 86 (1919); *Webb v. United States,* 249 U.S. 96 (1919).

3. Mike Gray, *Drug Crazy: How We Got into This Mess and How We Can Get Out* (New York: Random House, 1998), pp. 72–91.

4. The events in this and the preceding paragraph are depicted in original docu-

ments and media reporting displayed at the Drug Enforcement Administration's (DEA) Museum in Arlington, Va., in the exhibit "Illegal Drugs in America: A Modern History"; see particularly Robert MacCoun and Peter Reuter, *Drug War Heresies: Learning from Other Vices, Times, and Places* (New York: Cambridge University Press, 2001), pp. 183–204; David Musto, *The American Disease: Origins of Narcotic Control* (New York: Oxford University Press, 1987).

5. DEA Museum, depicting a *New York Times* article of June 21, 1970.

6. Statement of John R. Steer, vice chair, U.S. Sentencing Commission, Before the House Governmental Reform Subcommittee on Criminal Justice, Drug Policy and Human Resources, May 11, 2000, pp. 4–7.

7. For a detailed summary of the evolution of federal responses to the drug problem, see John Carnevale and Patrick Murphy, "Matching Rhetoric to Dollars: Twenty-Five Years of Federal Drug Strategies and Budgets," *Journal of Drug Issues* 29, no. 2 (1999): 299–322.

8. ONDCP, *National Drug Control Strategy* (Washington, D.C.: GPO, 2001), p. 7.

9. Ibid., p. 9.

10. 21 U.S. Code, sec. 802(6), 812(b) and (c). For a good, brief description of each major drug's types of use and effects, see Elliott Currie, *Reckoning: Drugs, the Cities, and the American Future* (New York: Hill and Wang, 1993), app. pp. 333–343.

11. 21 U.S. Code, sec. 802(6).

12. FBI, *Crime in the United States, 2000* (Washington, D.C.: GPO, 2001), p. 220, table 32.

13. Ibid.

14. Ibid., p. 216, table 4.1.

15. ONDCP, *National Drug Control Strategy* (Washington, D.C.: GPO, 2002), p. 76, table 28.

16. Kathleen Maguire and Ann Pastore, eds., *Sourcebook of Criminal Justice Statistics, 2000* (Washington, D.C.: BJS, 2001), NCJ190251, p. 392, table 4.28.

17. Laura Maruschak, *DWI Offenders under Correctional Supervision,* Special Report (Washington, D.C.: BJS, June 1999), NCJ172212, p. 4, table 4.

18. FBI, *Crime in the United States: Uniform Crime Reports, 2000* (Washington, D.C.: GPO, 2001), pp. 220, 222, tables 32, 34.

19. Ann Pastore and Kathleen Maguire, eds., *Sourcebook of Criminal Justice Statistics, 1999* (Washington, D.C.: BJS, 2000), NCJ183727, p. 263, table 3.117; Maruschak, *DWI Offenders,* pp. 1–4.

20. "A Shot in the Dark about Drug Use?" *Washington Post Weekly,* Jan. 12, 1998, pp. 32–33.

21. For a complete discussion of drug survey accuracy problems and issues, see John Pepper, "How Do Response Problems Affect Survey Measurement of

Trends in Drug Use?" in National Research Council, *Informing America's Policy on Illegal Drugs: What We Don't Know Keeps Hurting Us* (Washington, D.C.: National Academy Press, 2001), pp. D-1 through D-30.

22. U.S. Census Bureau, *Statistical Abstract of the United States: 2000* (Washington, D.C.: GPO, 2000), p. 148, table 238.

23. Ibid., p. 142, table 226.

24. ONDCP, *National Drug Control Strategy* (2002), p. 58, table 2.

25. Dept. of Health and Human Services–Substance Abuse and Mental Health Services Administration, *Summary of Findings from the 1999 National Household Survey on Drug Abuse (www.samhsa.gov./OAS/NHSDA/1999/TitlePage/htm)*, chap. 4, pp. 5–7, table 4.1 (2000).

26. Ibid., chap. 4, p. 4.

27. Peter Reuter, "Drug Use Measures: What Are They Really Telling Us?" *National Institute of Justice Journal*, Apr. 1999, pp. 12–19.

28. Ibid.

29. ONDCP, *National Drug Control Strategy* (2001), p. 10.

30. Ibid., pp. 23–24.

31. E.g., ONDCP, *Pulse Check: Trends in Drug Abuse* (Washington, D.C.: GPO, November 2001), NCJ191248.

32. U.S. Census Bureau, *Statistical Abstract: 2000*, p. 100, tables 141, 142.; ONDCP, *National Drug Control Strategy* (2002), p. 71, table 20.

33. Dept. of Health and Human Services, *Summary of 1999 Household Survey on Drug Abuse*, p. 5.

34. ONDCP, *National Drug Control Strategy* (2002), pp. 13–14.

35. Maguire and Pastore, *Sourcebook 2000*, p. 269, table 3.107.

36. Mark Kleiman, *Against Excess: Drug Policy for Results*, paperback ed. (New York: Basic Books, 1993), p. 213.

37. Paul Goldstein et al., "Crack and Homicide in New York City: A Case Study in the Epidemiology of Violence," in Craig Reinarman and Harry Levine, eds., *Crack in America: Demon Drugs and Social Justice* (Berkeley: University of California Press, 1997), p. 115.

38. ONDCP, *The National Drug Control Strategy* (Washington, D.C.: GPO, 1997), pp. 19–20.

39. ONDCP, *The National Drug Control Strategy, 1998: A Ten-Year Plan* (Washington, D.C.: GPO, 1998), p. 17.

40. Maguire and Pastore, *Sourcebook 2000*, p. 278, table 3.120.

41. ONDCP, *National Drug Control Strategy* (2002), p. 74, table 26.

42. Alfred Blumstein, "Disaggregating the Violence Trends," in Alfred Blumstein and Joel Wallman, eds., *The Crime Drop in America* (New York: Cambridge University Press, 2000), pp. 13–44.

43. Goldstein et al, "Crack and Homicide," pp. 113–130.

44. Franklin Zimring and Gordon Hawkins, *Crime Is Not the Problem: Lethal Violence in America* (New York: Oxford University Press, 1997), pp. 138–155.

45. Jan Chaiken and Marcia Chaiken, "Drugs and Predatory Crime," in Michael Tonry and James Wilson, eds., *Drugs and Crime* (Chicago: University of Chicago Press, 1990), p. 210.

46. Ibid., p. 235.

47. Ibid., pp. 212–213.

48. Christopher Mumola, *Substance Abuse and Treatment, State and Federal Prisoners, 1997,* Special Report (Washington, D.C.: BJS, 1999), NCJ172871.

49. Chaiken and Chaiken, "Drugs and Predatory Crime," p. 235.

50. Elijah Anderson, *Code of the Street: Decency, Violence and the Moral Life of the Inner City* (New York: W. W. Norton, 1999).

51. Willam Bennett, John DiIulio, and John Walters, *Body Count: Moral Poverty and How to Win America's War against Crime and Drugs* (New York: Simon & Schuster, 1996).

52. Ibid., p. 193.

53. Bruce Taylor et al., *ADAM Preliminary 2000 Findings on Drug Use and Drug Markets—Adult Male Arrestees* (Washington, D.C.: OJP, Dec. 2001), NCJ189101; Arrestee Drug Abuse Monitoring Program, *1998 Annual Report on Drug Use among Adult and Juvenile Arrestees* (Washington, D.C.: NIJ, 1999), NCJ175656, pp. 5–16.

54. Arrestee Drug Abuse Monitoring Program, *1998 Annual Report,* pp. 1–4, 18–103.

55. Taylor et al., *ADAM Preliminary 2000 Findings,* pp. 15–19, tables 7, 8.

56. ONDCP, *National Drug Control Strategy* (2000), p. 5.

57. ONDCP, *National Drug Control Strategy* (2001), p. 3.

58. ONDCP, *National Drug Control Strategy* (1998), p. 5.

59. James Q. Wilson discusses these detriments to criminalizing drugs in his "Drugs and Crime," in Tonry and Wilson, *Drugs and Crime,* p. 521.

60. ONDCP, *National Drug Control Strategy: Performance Measures of Effectiveness* (Washington, D.C.: GPO, 2000), pp. E-41 to E-45.

61. Marla Schlaffer, *Fact Sheet: Drug-Related Crime* (Rockville, Md.: Drug Policy Information Clearinghouse, 1997), NCJ163928, p. 3.

62. ONDCP, *National Drug Control Strategy* (2001), p. 5.

63. Bridget Grant, "Estimates of U.S. Children Exposed to Alcohol Abuse and Dependence in the Family," *American Journal of Public Health* 90 (2000): 112–115.

64. Lawrence Greenfeld, *Alcohol and Crime* (Washington, D.C.: BJS, 1998), NCJ168632, p. 1.

65. Thomas Greenfield, Lorraine Medanik, and John Rogers, "A Ten-Year Na-

tional Trend Study of Alcohol Consumption, 1984–1995: Is the Period of Declining Drinking Over?" *American Journal of Public Health* 90 (2000): 47–52.

66. Greenfeld, *Alcohol and Crime,* p. 1.

67. Ibid., pp. 1–2.

68. Ibid., pp. 2–3.

69. Ibid., p. 4.

70. Ibid., p. 21.

71. U.S. Census Bureau, *Statistical Abstract: 2000,* p. 637, table 1042; Greenfeld, *Alcohol and Crime,* pp. 11–12.

72. For descriptions and summaries of this research, see Robert Parker and Randi Cartmill, "Alcohol and Homicide in the United States, 1934–1995—Or One Reason Why U.S. Rates of Violence May Be Going Down," *Journal of Criminal Law and Criminology* 88 (1998): 1369–1398; "Special Focus: Alcohol, Aggression, and Injury," *Alcohol Health & Research World* 17 (1993): 91–172; National Institute on Alcohol Abuse and Alcoholism, *Alcohol Alert* 38 (Oct. 1997); and Daniel Yalisove, "A Review of the Research on the Relationship between Alcohol Consumption and Aggressive Behavior . . . ," *Security Journal* 11 (1998): 237–241.

73. Yalisove, "Review of Research," pp. 237–241.

74. Peter Annin, "Prohibition Revisited?" *Newsweek,* Dec. 7, 1998, p. 68.

75. David Boyum and Mark Kleiman, "Substance Abuse Policy from a Crime-Control Perspective," in James Wilson and Joan Petersilia, eds., *Crime: Public Policies for Crime Control* (Oakland, Calif.: ICS Press, 2002), pp. 348–350.

76. Yalisove, "Review of Research," p. 240.

77. ONDCP, *National Drug Control Strategy: FY 2003 Budget Summary* (Washington, D.C.: GPO, 2002), pp. 6, 8, 158.

78. Carnevale and Murphy, "Matching Rhetoric to Dollars," pp. 306–307, table 1.

79. ONDCP, *National Drug Control Strategy: FY 2001 Budget Summary* (Washington, D.C.: GPO, 2000), p. 13; Statement of Jess Ford, Associate Director, International Relations and Trade Issues, GAO, before the Subcommittee on Criminal Justice, Drug Policy and Human Resources, House Committee on Government Reform, Jan. 27, 2000 (Washington, D.C., GAO/T-NSIAD-00–77).

80. ONDCP, *National Drug Control Strategy: FY 2003 Budget Summary,* pp. 16–23; ONDCP, *National Drug Control Strategy* (2002), app. B, pp. 33–34.

81. ONDCP, *National Drug Control Strategy* (2002), pp. 7–26.

82. National Research Council, *Informing America's Policy,* p. 9–7.

83. ONDCP, *National Drug Control Strategy* (2001), pp. 174–175, tables 49, 51.

84. National Research Council, *Informing America's Policy,* pp. 5–16 through 5–24.

85. Carnevale and Murphy, "Matching Rhetoric to Dollars, pp. 306–307, table 1.

86. ONDCP, *National Drug Control Strategy* (2002), pp. 3–5.

87. Ibid., pp. 1–2.

88. National Research Council, *Informing America's Policy,* first page of preface.

89. Brian Reaves and Andrew Goldberg, *Law Enforcement Management and Administrative Statistics, 1997* (Washington, D.C.: BJS, 1999), NCJ171681, p. xvi, table C; and p. 107.

90. FBI, *Crime, 2000,* p. 216, table 29.

91. Matthew Durose, David Levin, and Patrick Langan, *Felony Sentences in State Courts, 1998,* BJS, NCJ190103 (Oct. 2001).

92. Peter D. Hart Research Associates, *Drugs and Crime across America: Police Chiefs Speak Out* (Washington, D.C.: Police Foundation, 1996), p. 17.

93. Commission on the Advancement of Federal Law Enforcement, *Law Enforcement in a New Century and a Changing World: Improving the Administration of Federal Law Enforcement* (Washington, D.C.: GPO, 2000), p. 85.

94. Ibid., pp. 90–91.

95. Transactional Records Access Clearinghouse, Syracuse University, *trac.syr .edu/tracfbi/findings/national,* checked Aug. 30, 2000.

96. Ibid.

97. David Burnham and Susan Long, "The Clinton Era by the Numbers," *The Nation,* Jan. 29, 2001, p. 21. Updated statistics in a different form are also provided by the BJS. See BJS, *Federal Drug Offenders, 1999, with Trends 1984–99,* NCJ187285 (Aug. 2001); BJS, *Federal Criminal Case Processing, 2000, with Trends 1982–2000,* Special Report, reconciled data, NCJ189737 (Jan. 2002).

98. John Eck and Edward Maguire, "Have Changes in Policing Reduced Violent Crime? An Assessment of the Evidence," in Blumstein and Wallman, *Crime Drop,* pp. 207, 240.

99. *Problem-Oriented Drug Enforcement: A Community-Based Approach for Effective Policing,* monograph (Washington, D.C.: BJS, 1993), NCJ143710.

100. John Eck and Julie Wartell, "Improving the Management of Rental Properties with Drug Problems: A Randomized Experiment," in Lorraine Mazerolle and Jan Roehl, eds., *Civil Remedies and Crime Prevention: Crime Prevention Studies* (Monsey, N.Y.: Criminal Justice Press, 1998), vol. 9, pp. 161–186.

101. Bruce Johnson, Andrew Golub, and Eloise Dunlap, "The Rise and Decline of Hard Drugs, Drug Markets, and Violence in Inner-City New York," in Blumstein and Wallman, *Crime Drop,* pp. 164–206.

102. Ibid., pp. 185–196.

103. Ibid., p. 185.

104. Ibid. pp. 188–189; "City Police Arrest Record Number in Marijuana Crackdown," *New York Times,* Nov. 17, 1998.

105. "Violent Crimes Undercut Marijuana's Mellow Image," in *New York Times*, May 19, 2001, p. A1.

106. Andrew Golub and Bruce Johnson, "Crack's Decline: Some Surprises across U.S. Cities," Research in Brief (Washington, D.C. NIJ, 1997), NCJ165707.

107. ONDCP, *National Drug Control Strategy* (2002), p. 75, table 27. (The percentage of total drug abuse arrests attributed to heroin/cocaine sales appears to be misstated in this table.)

108. "Drug Agency Looks Again at an Informer's Career," *New York Times*, June 28, 2000, p. A14.

109. Laura Sager, "State-Based Organizing," in *Drug Policy Letter* (July–Aug. 2000): 11–13.

110. Bennett, DiIulio, and Walters, *Body Count*, pp. 160–162.

111. ONDCP, *National Drug Control Strategy* (2001), p. 141, table 2.

112. Ibid., p. 167, table 38; FBI, *Crime, 2000*, p. 234, table 43.

113. Human Rights Watch, *Punishment and Prejudice: Racial Disparities in the War on Drugs*, www.hrw.org./reports/2000/usa/rcedrg00.htm, p. 1.

114. Ibid.

115. U.S. Sentencing Commission (USSC), *1999 Sourcebook of Federal Sentencing Statistics* (Washington, D.C.: GPO, 2000), p. 69, table 34.

116. Substance Abuse and Mental Health Services Administration (SAMHSA), *Summary of Findings from the 1999 National Household Survey on Drug Abuse*, www.samhsa.gov/OAS/NHSDA/1999/TitlePage.htm, checked Sept. 1, 2000, p. 2.

117. ONDCP, *National Drug Control Strategy* (2001), p. 27; FBI, *Crime, 2000*, p. 66, table 1.

118. BJS, *Federal Criminal Case Processing, 2000*, p. 1.

119. USSC, *1999 Federal Sentencing Statistics*, p. 29, table 13.

120. Federal Sentencing Guidelines, sec. 2D1.1(c).

121. USSC, *1999 Federal Sentencing Statistics*, p. 81, fig. 3.

122. Federal Sentencing Guidelines, chap. 4, pt. A; Title 18 U.S. Code, sec. 3553(f).

123. USSC, *1999 Federal Sentencing Statistics*, p. 79, table 44.

124. ONDCP, *Drug Strategy FY 2003 Budget Summary*, p. 6, table 2.

125. GAO, *Drug Control: U.S. Assistance to Colombia Will Take Years to Produce Results* (Washington, D.C.: GAO, 2000); "More Drugs Flow into U.S. Than Estimated," *Los Angeles Times*, Nov. 14, 1999, p. 1.

126. "A Drug Plan Fraught with Risk," *New York Times*, Aug. 31, 2000, p. A11.

127. "Colombia's Coca Up, U.S. Says," *New York Times*, Mar. 9, 2002, p. A5.

128. "Mexico Imprisons Two Generals, Longtime Suspects in Drug Cases," *New York Times*, Sept. 2, 2000, p. A14; "McCaffrey Visits Dutch after Blasting Drug Policy," *Denver Post*, July 17, 1998, p. A23.

129. "Fungus Considered as a Tool To Kill Coca In Columbia," *New York Times,* July 6, 2000, p. A1; "No Crops Spared in Columbia's Coca War," *New York Times,* Jan. 31, 2001, p. A1; "Colombia's War on Coca: Mass Spraying Damages Farmers' Livelihoods Along with the Illegal Drug Crop," *Washington Post* (national weekly ed.), Jan. 15–21, 2001, p. 16.

130. "A Drug-Policy Dilemma," *Washington Post* (national weekly ed.), Jan. 15–21, 2001, p. 16.

131. ONDCP, *National Drug Control Strategy* (2001), p. 171, table 45.

132. Henry Ruth was a member of the group representing New York City Mayor John Lindsay's administration in 1973 when the state legislature was debating the drug bill in Albany, N.Y.

133. "A War We May Never Win," *Washington Post* (national weekly ed.), Mar. 26–Apr. 1, 2001, p. 34.

134. Jann Wenner, "The *Rolling Stone* Interview," *Rolling Stone,* Dec. 28, 2000–Jan. 4, 2001, pp. 84, 98; "A Drug Warrior Who Would Rather Treat Than Fight," *New York Times,* Jan. 8, 2001.

135. "For an Office with a Heart, a Man with a Change of One," *New York Times,* Feb. 9, 2001.

136. U.S. Census Bureau, *Sourcebook 2000,* pp. 158–160, tables 2.83, 2.84, and 2.85.

137. For a good example of the kind of legalization discussion needed on a drug-by-drug basis, see MacCoun and Reuter, *Drug War Heresies;* Boyum and Kleiman, "Substance Abuse Policy," pp. 342–348.

138. ONDCP, *National Drug Control Strategy* (2002), p. 2.

139. "For Users of Heroin, Decades of Despair," *New York Times,* May 22, 2001, p. D5.

140. Drug Court Clearinghouse and Technical Assistance Program, *Looking at a Decade of Drug Courts* (Washington, D.C.: Office of Justice Programs, rev. 1999); ONDCP, *Drug Control Strategy: FY 2003 Budget Summary,* p. 130. Evaluations of drug treatment in the criminal justice system have so many different approaches and flaws as to render overall judgments quite tentative. See the full discussion by Jeanette Covington, "Linking Treatment to Punishment: An Evaluation of Drug Treatment in the Criminal Justice System," in National Research Council, *Informing America's Policy,* app. E, pp. E–1 through E–29.

141. ONDCP, *National Drug Control Strategy* (2001), p. 79; ONDCP, *National Drug Control Strategy* (2000), p. 66.

142. "New York to Offer Addicts Treatment Instead of Prison," *New York Times,* June 23, 2000, p. A1.

143. "California Gets Set to Shift on Sentencing Drug Users," *New York Times,* Nov. 10, 2000, p. A18.

144. Boyum and Kleiman, "Substance Abuse Policy," pp. 378–381.

145. Christy Visher and David Weisburd, "Identifying What Works: Recent Trends

in Crime Prevention Strategies," in *Crime, Law & Social Change* 28 (1998): 223, 231–233; ONDCP, *National Drug Control Strategy* (2001), pp. 75–76.

146. Christopher Mumola, *Substance Abuse and Treatment, State and Federal Prisoners, 1997* (Washington, D.C.: BJS, 1999), NCJ172871, p. 10.

147. Joseph Califano, "A New Prescription," in *Washington Monthly,* Oct. 1998, p. 9.

148. "Nation's Top Drug Official Proposes Shift in Policy," *New York Times,* Dec. 9, 1999.

149. ONDCP, *National Drug Control Strategy* (2000), p. 59.

150. National Center on Addiction and Substance Abuse at Columbia University, *Shoveling Up: The Impact of Substance Abuse on State Budgets* (New York: National Center, 2001), p. 2.

151. John DiIulio, Jr., "Two Million Prisoners Are Enough," *Wall Street Journal,* Mar. 12, 1999.

152. See statement of John Steer, May 11, 2000.

153. ONDCP, *National Drug Control Strategy* (2001), p. 91; ONDCP, *National Drug Control Strategy* (2000), p. 74.

154. Lynn Zimmer and John Morgan, *Marijuana Myths, Marijuana Facts* (New York: Lindesmith Center, 1997), pp. 151–163.

155. Janet Joy, Stanley Watson, Jr., and John Benson, Jr., eds., *Marijuana and Medicine: Assessing the Science Base* (Washington, D.C.: National Academy Press, 1999), pp. 5–7.

156. Ibid., p. 6.

157. "DEA Raids Medical Pot Club," *Arizona Daily Star,* Feb. 13, 2002; David Broder, "The DEA's Marijuana Madness," *Washington Post* (national weekly ed.), Nov. 19–25, 2001.

158. Alan Lesher, "Addiction Is a Brain Disease–and It Matters," *National Institute of Justice Journal* (Oct. 1998): 1–6; "Seeing Drugs as a Choice or as a Brain Anomaly," *New York Times,* June 24, 2000, p. A17.

159. National Research Council, *Informing America's Policy,* pp. 7–13, 7–20. The prevention research issues as a whole are discussed pp. 7–1 through 7–31.

160. "Study Finds Teenagers Smoking Less; Campaign Is Cited," in *New York Times,* Dec. 20, 2001, p. A18.

161. "New Ads Target Indians' Drug Abuse," *Arizona Daily Star,* Sept. 7, 2000, p. A5; Conversation with Associated Press reporter Matt Kelley, Sept. 8, 2000.

162. National Research Council, *Informing America's Policy.*

8. Juvenile Crime

1. See John R. Sutton, *Stubborn Children: Controlling Delinquency in the United States, 1640–1981* (Berkeley: University of California Press, 1988), p. 1; Barry

C. Feld, "Justice by Geography: Urban, Suburban, and Rural Variations in Juvenile Justice Administration," *Journal of Criminal Law and Criminology* 82 (1991): 156–210; Mark L. Moore and Stewart Wakeling, "Juvenile Justice: Shoring up the Foundations," in Michael Tonry, ed., *Crime and Justice: A Review of Research,* vol. 22 (Chicago: University of Chicago Press, 1997), pp. 253–301.

2. OJJDP, *Juvenile Offenders and Victims: 1999 National Report* (Washington, D.C.: OJJDP, 1999) [hereinafter *"1999 National Report"*], p. 93.

3. *1999 National Report,* p. 99.

4. See David J. Rothman, *Conscience and Convenience: The Asylum and Its Alternatives in Progressive America* (Boston: Little, Brown, 1980), chap. 6.

5. See generally Franklin E. Zimring, "The Common Thread: Diversion in Juvenile Justice," *California Law Review* 88 (2000): 2477–2495; Robert M. Mennel, *Thorns and Thistles: Juvenile Delinquents in the United States, 1825–1940* (Hanover, N.H.: University Press of New England, 1973).

6. See Steven L. Schlossman, *Love and the American Delinquent: The Theory and Practice of "Progressive" Juvenile Justice, 1825–1920* (Chicago: University of Chicago Press, 1977), pp. 167–168, 188–192; Ellen Ryerson, *The Best Laid Plans: America's Juvenile Court Experiment* (New York: Hill and Wang, 1978), pp. 82–86.

7. See Rothman, *Conscience and Convenience,* pp. 243–248.

8. *In re* Gault, 387 U.S. 1 (1967), p. 28; *Kent v. United States,* 383 U.S. 541 (1966), p. 566.

9. Barry C. Feld, "A Comparative Analysis of Organizational Structure and Inmate Subcultures in Institutions for Juvenile Offenders," *Crime & Delinquency* 27 (1988): 336–363.

10. Barry Feld, for example, would abolish the juvenile court entirely. Barry C. Feld, *Bad Kids: Race and the Transformation of the Juvenile Court* (New York: Oxford University Press, 1999), chap. 8. See also Janet E. Ainsworth, "Reimagining Childhood and Re-constructing the Legal Order: The Case for Abolishing the Juvenile Court," *North Carolina Law Review* 69 (1991): 1083–1133; "Will the Juvenile Court System Survive?" *Annals of the American Academy of Political and Social Science* 564 (1999): 1–213. Stephen Morse, in "Immaturity and Irresponsibility," *Journal of Criminal Law and Criminology* 8 (1997): 61–67, has argued that current distinctions in punishment based solely on age should be abolished in favor of a system in which an individual's ability to accept responsibility for his or her actions is assessed regardless of age. And Travis Hirschi and Michael Gottfredson would prefer to see adult crime response reconfigured along the lines of the traditional juvenile system. See Travis Hirschi and Michael Gottfredson, "Rethinking the Juvenile Justice System," *Crime & Delinquency* 39 (1993): 262–271.

11. See, for example, Feld, *Bad Kids*, pp. 331–332; Jeffrey A. Butts and Ojmarrh Mitchell, "Brick by Brick: Dismantling the Border between Juvenile and Adult Justice," in U.S. Department of Justice, *Criminal Justice 2000* (Washington, D.C.: NIJ, 2000), vol. 2, p. 167; and Christopher Slobogin, Mark R. Fondacaro, and Jennifer Woolard, "A Prevention Model of Juvenile Justice: The Promise of *Kansas v. Hendricks* for Children," *Wisconsin Law Review* (1999): 188.

12. Eileen Poe-Yamagata and Michael A. Jones, *And Justice for Some: Differential Treatment of Minority Youth in the Justice System* (Washington, D.C.: Building Blocks for Youth, 2000); Mike Males and Dan Macallair, *The Color of Justice: An Analysis of Juvenile Adult Court Transfers in California* (Washington, D.C.: Building Blocks for Youth, 2000); Kimberly Kempf Leonard, Carl E. Pope, and William H. Feyerherm, eds., *Minorities in Juvenile Justice* (Thousand Oaks, Calif.: Sage, 1995); Amnesty International, *Betraying the Young: Human Rights Violations against Children in the U.S. Justice System* (New York: Amnesty International, 1998); D. Hamparian and M. Leiber, *Disproportionate Confinement of Minority Juveniles in Secure Facilities* (Champaign, Ill.: Community Research Associates, 1997).

13. See DeNeen L. Brown, "Guns and Children: A Deadly Environment; Six-Year-Old Killer's World Had No Place for Toys," *Washington Post*, Mar. 21, 2000, p. A1; Lisa Belkin, "Parents Blaming Parents," *New York Times*, Oct. 31, 1999, p. 61 (discussing numerous school shootings); Sue Anne Pressley, "Preadolescent on Trial in Toddler's Death: Austin Girl, 12, Joins Swelling Roster of Children Accused of Killing Children," *Washington Post*, Aug. 6, 1996, p. A3.

14. Franklin Zimring, keynote speech, 2000 Law and Policy Symposium, *Reactions to Youth Violence: The Legacy of Columbine*, University of Denver College of Law, Denver, Colo., Mar. 24, 2000.

15. See Herb Whitney, "Changed Forever," *Arizona Republic*, June 11, 1999, p. 1; George Hunter and Janet Naylor, "School's in, So Is Security: Cameras, More Cops Watch over Students," *Detroit News*, Aug. 23, 1999, p. A1; Sandra Barbier, "Threats Plague Local Schools: Colorado Violence Has System Edgy," *Times-Picayune*, May 1, 1999, p. A1.

16. *1999 National Report*, p. 63.

17. See Franklin E. Zimring, *American Youth Violence* (New York: Oxford University Press, 1998), pp. 29–30.

18. See Michael R. Gottfredson and Travis Hirschi, *A General Theory of Crime* (Stanford, Calif.: Stanford University Press, 1990), pp. 124–126.

19. Delbert S. Elliott, "Serious Violent Offenders: Onset, Developmental Course, and Termination—The American Society of Criminology 1993 Presidential Address," *Criminology* 32 (1994): 19.

20. Franklin E. Zimring and Jeffrey Fagan, "Two Patterns of Age Progression in Adolescent Criminality," unpublished ms.

21. OJJDP, *Juvenile Offenders and Victims: 1997 Update on Violence* (Washington, D.C.: OJJDP, 1997), p. 36.

22. Zimring, *American Youth Violence*, pp. 20–21, 27–28.

23. Peter W. Greenwood, "Juvenile Crime and Juvenile Justice," in James Q. Wilson and Joan Petersilia, eds., *Crime* (San Francisco: ICS Press, 1995), p. 103.

24. Our calculations are based on homicide statistics in the OJJDP's *1999 National Report* (p. 53), including the OJJDP's estimates of how many homicides involved adult and / or juvenile offenders. We rest our calculations on the OJJDP's estimates of the true level of juvenile involvement in homicide, not the lower number of homicides where juveniles are "known" to have been involved.

25. Elliott, "Serious Violent Offenders," pp. 11–12, 14–15.

26. See Philip J. Cook and John H. Laub, "After the Epidemic: Recent Trends in Youth Violence in the United States," in Michael Tonry, ed., *Crime and Justice: A Review of Research*, vol. 29 (Chicago: University of Chicago Press, 2002), p. 121.

27. John J. DiIulio, Jr., "The Coming of the Super-Predators," *Weekly Standard*, Nov. 27, 1995, p. 23, reprinted as John J. DiIulio, Jr., "Moral Poverty: The Coming of the Super-Predators Should Scare Us into Wanting to Get to the Root Causes of Crime a Lot Faster," *Chicago Tribune*, Dec. 15, 1995, p. 31.

28. James Q. Wilson, "Crime and Public Policy," in Wilson and Petersilia, *Crime*, p. 507.

29. Quoted in Richard Zoglin, Sam Allis, and Ratu Kamlani, "Now for the Bad News: A Teenage Time Bomb," *Time*, Jan. 15, 1996, p. 52.

30. James Alan Fox, *Trends in Juvenile Violence: A Report to the Attorney General on Current and Future Rates of Juvenile Offending* (Washington, D.C.: BJS, 1996), p. 15, fig. 15.

31. See Carol Kreck, "Lock 'em Up or Rehabilitate? Programs Vary in Five States," *Denver Post*, Nov. 1, 1994, p. E1; Laura Mansnerus, "Treating Teen-Agers as Adults in Court: A Trend Born of Revulsion," *New York Times*, Dec. 3, 1993, p. B7.

32. Zimring, "Common Thread"; Jonathan Simon, "Power without Parents: Juvenile Justice in a Postmodern Society," *Cardozo Law Review* 16 (1995): 1363–1426; Simon I. Singer, *Recriminalizing Delinquency: Violent Juvenile Crime and Juvenile Justice Reform* (New York: Cambridge University Press, 1996).

33. *1999 National Report*, p. 54. See also Alfred Blumstein, "Disaggregating the Violence Trends," in Alfred Blumstein and Joel Wallman, eds., *The Crime Drop in America* (New York: Cambridge University Press, 2000), pp. 29–35; Zimring, *American Youth Violence*, pp. 35–38; Cook and Laub, "After the Epidemic," p. 142.

34. See Franklin E. Zimring and Gordon Hawkins, *Crime Is Not the Problem: Lethal Violence in America* (New York: Oxford University Press, 1998), pp. 122–123.

35. See Blumstein, "Disaggregating the Violence Trends"; Daniel Cork, "Examining Space-Time Interaction in City-Level Homicide Data: Crack Markets and the Diffusion of Guns among Youth," *Journal of Quantitative Criminology* 15 (1999): 379–406. For an analysis skeptical of this theory, see Cook and Laub, "After the Epidemic."

36. Zimring, *American Youth Violence*, p. 35.

37. *1999 National Report*, p. 54.

38. Fox, *Trends in Juvenile Violence*, p. 5, table 3.

39. For black males aged fourteen to seventeen, the risk of homicide victimization increased by 46 deaths per 100,000 in the general population. For white males in the same age group, the victimization rate increased by only 3.5 deaths per 100,000. For black males aged eighteen to twenty-four, the homicide victimization rate increased by 79 deaths per 100,000, while the white risk grew by only 1.2 fatalities per 100,000. For blacks and whites aged twenty-five and above, homicide risks actually decreased substantially from 1980 to 1994, largely because the victims of the juvenile homicide spike were almost all juveniles and young adults. See James Alan Fox, *Trends in Juvenile Violence: 1997 Update* (Washington, D.C.: BJS, 1997), p. 3, table 3.

40. *1999 National Report*, p. 55.

41. The ratio of serious assaults to homicides used in the text is a rough estimate, but it is probably not ridiculously inaccurate. Zimring's research in the 1960s and 1970s found that the ratio between nonfatal gunshot wounds and fatalities was approximately seven to one, but the ratio of knife wounds to fatalities was roughly thirty-five to one. See Franklin E. Zimring, "The Medium Is the Message: Firearms Caliber as a Determinant of the Death Rate from Assault," *Journal of Legal Studies* 1 (1972): 98; Franklin E. Zimring, "Is Gun Control Likely to Reduce Violent Killings?" *University of Chicago Law Review* 35 (1968): 728.

42. Elliott, "Serious Violent Offenders," p. 9.

43. See *1999 National Report*, p. 115; Lewis Yablonsky, *Juvenile Delinquency: Into the Twenty-first Century* (Belmont, Calif.: Wadsworth/Thompson Learning, 2000), pp. 562–566.

44. Butts and Mitchell, "Brick by Brick," p. 178; OJJDP, *Juvenile Transfers to Criminal Court in the 1990s: Lessons Learned from Four Studies* (Washington, D.C.: OJJDP, 2000).

45. *1999 National Report*, p. 87. See also Craig Hemmens, Eric J. Fritsch, and Tory J. Caeti, "The Rhetoric of Juvenile Justice Reform," *Quinnipiac Law Review* 18 (1999): 661–685.

46. Hemmens et al., "Rhetoric of Juvenile Justice Reform," pp. 683–684, table 1;

Barry C. Feld, "Juvenile and Criminal Justice Systems' Responses to Youth Violence," in Michael Tonry and Mark H. Moore, eds., *Crime and Justice: A Review of Research,* vol. 24 (Chicago: University of Chicago Press, 1998), p. 222.

47. See Feld, "Juvenile and Criminal Justice Systems' Responses," p. 224; *1999 National Report,* p. 108.

48. *1999 National Report,* p. 93.

49. Ibid., p. 101. See also BJS, *Privacy and Juvenile Justice Records: A Mid-Decade Status Report* (Washington, D.C.: BJS, 1997); John B. Sanborn, Jr., "Second-Class Justice, First-Class Punishment: The Use of Juvenile Records in Sentencing Adults," *Judicature* 81, no. 5 (1998): 206–213.

50. *Thompson v. Oklahoma,* 487 U.S. 815 (1988); *Stanford v. Kentucky,* 492 U.S. 361 (1989).

51. *1999 National Report,* p. 211.

52. BJS, *Capital Punishment in 1999* (Washington, D.C.: BJS, 2000), p. 9, table 8.

53. Kari Haskell, "One Step Farther from Death," *New York Times,* Aug. 27, 2000, Week in Review, p. 3.

54. Amnesty International, *Facts and Figures on the Death Penalty* (Dec. 18, 1999) at *www.amnesty.org/alib/intcam/dp/dpfacts.htm,* visited Aug. 29, 2000 (ten executions of juvenile offenders from 1990 through 1999); Haskell, "One Step Farther from Death," p. 3 (four executions of juvenile offenders in 2000).

55. Compare Feld, *Bad Kids;* Janet E. Ainsworth, "Re-imagining Childhood and Re-constructing the Legal Order: The Case for Abolishing the Juvenile Court," *North Carolina Law Review* 69 (1991): 1083–1133; Ainsworth, "Youth Justice in a Unified Court: Response to Critics of Juvenile Court Abolition," *Boston College Law Review* 36 (1995): 949–950; Hirschi and Gottfredson, "Rethinking the Juvenile Justice System."

56. See American Bar Association, *Standards Relating to Adjudication* (Cambridge, Eng.: Ballinger, 1980), p. 2; Slobogin et al., "A Prevention Model of Juvenile Justice"; Gary B. Melton, "Taking Gault Seriously: Toward a New Juvenile Court," *Nebraska Law Review* 68 (1989): 146–181.

57. See, e.g., Butts and Mitchell, "Brick by Brick," pp. 178–192; Jeffrey Fagan, "Punishment or Treatment for Adolescent Offenders: Therapeutic Integrity and the Paradoxical Effects of Punishment," *Quinnipiac Law Review* 18 (1999): 386–389; Jonathan Simon, "On Their Own: Delinquency without Society," *Kansas Law Review* 47 (1999): 1001–1002; Feld, *Bad Kids,* pp. 208–241; Amnesty International, *Betraying the Young: Children in the U.S. Justice System* (New York: Amnesty International, 1998).

58. See *Kent v. United States,* 383 U.S. 541 (1966).

59. Butts and Mitchell, "Brick by Brick," p. 179; Charles M. Puzzanchera, *Delinquency Cases Waived to Criminal Court, 1988–1997* (Washington, D.C.: OJJDP, 2000), p. 1. The growth in numbers of juvenile filings for violence

through the 1990s was probably also an important cause. See *1999 National Report*, p. 171. Much of this growth was in assault—and may have been linked to the increased likelihood of police to arrest for assault. See Zimring, *American Youth Violence*, pp. 38–45; *1999 National Report*, pp. 131–132.

60. Puzzanchera, *Delinquency Cases Waived*, p. 1.

61. *1999 National Report*, p. 171.

62. Puzzanchera, *Delinquency Cases Waived*, p. 1.

63. The research is summarized in OJJDP, *Juvenile Transfers to Criminal Court in the 1990s*.

64. *1999 National Report*, pp. 170, 173. The criminal court data are based on reports from the criminal courts of the nation's 75 largest counties in the years 1990, 1992, and 1994.

65. Ibid., p. 174.

66. The research is summarized in Butts and Mitchell, "Brick by Brick," pp. 194–196. At least one researcher, based on evidence from California, has questioned whether juveniles found guilty of violent crimes in the juvenile courts receive less severe sentences than their counterparts in adult courts. See Greenwood, "Juvenile Crime and Juvenile Justice," pp. 103–105.

67. See *1999 National Report*, p. 53.

68. Ibid., p. 186.

69. BJS, *Prison and Jail Inmates at Midyear 1997* (Washington, D.C.: BJS, 1998), p. 1.

70. While many juvenile custody facilities are prison-like in environment, some are not. Bradford Smith, "Children in Custody: Twenty-Year Trends in Juvenile Detention, Correctional, and Shelter Facilities," *Crime & Delinquency* 44 (1998): 531, fig. 3. All told, about 45 percent of institutionalized juveniles in 1995 did not live under lock-and-key arrangements like those used for adults.

71. FBI, *Crime in the United States, 1997: Uniform Crime Reports* (Washington, D.C.: GPO, 1998), p. 232, table 38.

72. *1999 National Report*, p. 116.

73. FBI, *Crime, 1997*, p. 232, table 38.

74. BJS, *Prison and Jail Inmates at Midyear 1997*, p. 1; BJS, *Sourcebook of Criminal Justice Statistics, 1999* (Washington, D.C.: BJS, 2000), p. 503, table 6.26 (for 1975 prisoner count); Margaret Werner Cahalan, *Historical Corrections Statistics in the United States, 1850–1984* (Washington, D.C.: GPO, 1986), p. 76, table 4-1 (basis for 1975 estimate of U.S. jail population).

75. BJS, *Children in Custody, 1975–85* (Washington, D.C.: BJS, 1989), p. 2; *1999 National Report*, p. 186.

76. The slow growth in juvenile custody as compared with adult confinement has also drawn comment from Franklin Zimring, "Common Thread," pp. 2491–2494. Zimring states, "These data suggest that the diversionary objective of

the juvenile justice system insulated delinquents from the brunt of a high magnitude expansion in incarceration in the criminal justice system" (p. 2493).

77. Smith, "Children in Custody," p. 531.

78. BJS, *Profile of State Prisoners under Age 18, 1985–1997* (Washington, D.C.: BJS, 2000), pp. 1, 3; BJS, *Prison and Jail Inmates at Midyear 2001* (Washington, D.C.: BJS, 2002), p. 6, table 6.

79. Of prison admittees who were under the age of eighteen, 74 percent were seventeen years old when admitted; only 1 percent of admittees under eighteen were fourteen years old or younger. BJS, *Profile of State Prisoners under Age 18, 1985–1997*, p. 6, table 6.

80. See Department of Health and Human Services (DHHS), *Youth Violence: A Report of the Surgeon General* (Washington, D.C.: GPO, 2001), p. 118 ("Results from a series of reports indicate that young people placed in adult criminal institutions, compared to those placed in institutions designed for youths, are eight times as likely to commit suicide, five times as likely to be sexually assaulted, twice as likely to be beaten by staff, and 50 percent as likely to be attacked with a weapon").

81. *1999 National Report*, pp. 192, 195, 197; BJS, *Profile of State Prisoners under Age 18, 1985–1997*, p. 3.

82. *1999 National Report*, pp. 195, 197; BJS, *Profile of State Prisoners under Age 18, 1985–1997*, p. 8, table 9.

83. Joan McCord, Cathy Spatz Widom, and Nancy A. Crowel, eds., *Juvenile Crime, Juvenile Justice: Panel on Juvenile Crime; Prevention, Treatment and Control* (Washington, D.C.: National Academy Press, 2001), p. 230.

84. *1999 National Report*, p. 197.

85. BJS, *Profile of State Prisoners under Age 18, 1985–1997*, p. 3.

86. These calculations are based on data presented in BJS, *Children in Custody, 1975–85*, p. 39, table 31, and *1999 National Report*, p. 196.

87. Poe-Yamagata and Jones, *And Justice for Some*, p. 21.

88. See ibid., pp. 28–29; Amnesty International, *Betraying the Young*, pp. 13–14.

89. See Michael Tonry, *Malign Neglect: Race, Crime, and Punishment in America* (New York: Oxford University Press, 1995), p. viii.

90. See, for example, Poe-Yamagata and Jones, *And Justice for Some*; Amnesty International, *Betraying the Young*; Erin Texeira, "Justice Is Not Color Blind, Studies Find," *Los Angeles Times*, May 22, 2000, p. B1; Carol Kreck, "Youth Justice Deemed Unfair: Minorities in Study Detained More Often," *Denver Post*, Apr. 26, 2000, p. A1; Michael Finley and Marc Schindler, "Punitive Juvenile Justice Policies and the Impact on Minority Youth," *Federal Probation* 63 (1999): 11–14; Paul Wellstone and David Cole, "Balance Check: We Need to Track the Jailing of Young Minorities," *Washington Post*, June 14, 1999, p. A21; McCord et al., eds., *Juvenile Crime, Juvenile Justice*, p. 229.

91. *1999 National Report*, p. 55.

92. The black rate was 11.2 times the white rate in 1993, and 10.1 times the white rate in 1994. Fox, *Trends in Juvenile Violence, 1997 Update*, p. 3, table 4.

93. See *1999 National Report*, p. 55; FBI, *Crime in the United States, 1997*, p. 241, table 43; *1999 National Report*, pp. 195, 197.

94. Darnell F. Hawkins, John H. Laub, and Janet L. Lauritsen, "Race, Ethnicity, and Serious Juvenile Offending," in Rolf Loeber and David P. Farrington, eds., *Serious and Violent Juvenile Offenders: Risk Factors and Successful Interventions* (Thousand Oaks, Calif.: Sage, 1998), pp. 35–36.

95. Based on FBI, *Crime in the United States, 1997*, p. 241, table 43.

96. The racial disproportionalities in juvenile crime commission that are reflected in official arrest records are also found in victims surveys. See Hawkins et al., "Race, Ethnicity, and Serious Juvenile Offending," p. 39; Carl E. Pope and Howard N. Snyder, "Investigation into Racial Bias in Juvenile Arrest," paper presented at the annual meeting of the American Society of Criminology, San Francisco, Nov. 2000.

97. Poe-Yamagata and Jones, *And Justice for Some*, pp. 8–15.

98. BJS, *Prisoners in 1999* (Washington, D.C.: BJS, 2000), p. 9, table 13.

99. Smith, "Children in Custody," p. 536; Poe-Yamagata and Jones, *And Justice for Some*, p. 18.

100. Peter W. Greenwood et al., *Diverting Children from a Life of Crime: Measuring Costs and Benefits* (Santa Monica, Calif.: RAND, 1998), p. xi.

101. Delbert S. Elliott, "Editor's Introduction," in *Blueprints for Violence Prevention, Book One: Multisystemic Therapy* (Boulder, Colo.: Center for the Study and Prevention of Violence, 1998), pp. xxvii–xxx.

102. Some critics might charge that early prevention programs intrude upon the privacy and autonomy of families and the child-rearing process. It does not help matters that early prevention programs tend to be targeted at poor urban minority populations. See John J. Donohue III and Peter Siegelman, "Allocating Resources among Prisons and Social Programs in the Battle against Crime," *Journal of Legal Studies* 27 (1998): 41.

103. Greenwood et al., *Diverting Children*, p. 26; pp. 28–29, n. 14.

104. This is our own calculation, based on RAND estimates presented in Greenwood et al., *Diverting Children*, p. 26; pp. 28–29, n. 14; and p. 29, table 4.

105. See ibid., p. 3.

106. See Patricia Wald, "Keynote Address: A Retrospective on the Thirty-Year War against Crime," in OJP, *The Challenge of Crime in a Free Society: Looking Back, Looking Forward* (Washington, D.C., OJP, 1998), pp. 84–85.

107. Wilson, "Crime and Public Policy," p. 504.

108. See also William J. Bennett, John J. DiIulio, Jr., and John P. Walters, *Body Count: Moral Poverty . . . and How to Win America's War against Crime and*

Drugs (New York: Simon & Schuster, 1996), pp. 57–64; John J. DiIulio, Jr., "Broken Streets, Broken Lives," *Public Interest* (Spring 2000): 109.

109. See Weston Kosova, "Where's the Pork?" *New Republic*, Sept. 5, 1994, p. 10; Gwen Ifill, "Spending in the Crime Bill: Prevention or Just Pork?" *New York Times*, Aug. 16, 1994, p. B7.

110. The research is collected in OJP, *Preventing Crime: What Works, What Doesn't, What's Promising* (Washington, D.C.: OJP, 1997), pp. 5–32 to 5–36.

111. See Joseph B. Sanborn, Jr., "Second-Class Justice, First-Class Punishment: The Use of Juvenile Records in the Sentencing of Adults," *Judicature* 81 (1998): 206–213; BJS, *Privacy and Juvenile Justice Records: A Mid-Decade Status Report* (Washington, D.C.: BJS, 1997); NIJ, *State Laws on Prosecutors' and Judges' Use of Juvenile Records* (Washington, D.C.: NIJ, 1995).

112. Zimring, *American Youth Violence*, pp. 81–83; Franklin E. Zimring, *The Changing World of Legal Adolescence* (New York: Free Press, 1982), pp. 90–93.

113. See Rothman, *Conscience and Convenience*, pp. 213–214.

114. Robert Martinson, "What Works?—Questions and Answers about Prison Reform," *Public Interest* 35 (1974): 22–54.

115. See Robert Martinson, "New Findings, New Views: A Note of Caution Regarding Sentencing Reform," *Hofstra Law Review* 7 (1979): 243.

116. Mark W. Lipsey and David B. Wilson, "Effective Intervention for Serious Juvenile Offenders: A Synthesis of Research," in Rolf Loeber and David P. Farrington, eds., *Serious and Violent Juvenile Offenders: Risk Factors and Successful Interventions* (Thousand Oaks, Calif.: Sage, 1998). On the stature of Lipsey's meta-analysis in the broader scientific community, see Department of Health and Human Services, *Youth Violence*, pp. 115–116; Greenwood, "Juvenile Crime and Juvenile Justice," pp. 111–112.

117. A "meta-analysis" considers many items of preexisting research and subjects them to new statistical manipulation. Often, because the original studies gathered in the meta-analysis used small sample sizes, or were attempting to discern small changes in behavior, the statistical significance of their collective results can be enhanced by the grouping of many studies together.

118. In addition, Lipsey included only studies in which most or all of the juveniles had been adjudicated delinquents, and most or all had records of prior offending. See Lipsey and Wilson, "Effective Intervention," p. 315.

119. See Elliott, "Editor's Introduction."

120. Mark W. Lipsey, "Can Intervention Rehabilitate Serious Delinquents?" *Annals of the American Academy of Political and Social Science* 564 (1999): 146.

121. Ibid., pp. 150–151, 160–161.

122. See Peter W. Greenwood and Susan Turner, "Evaluation of the Paint Creek Youth Center: A Residential Program for Serious Delinquents," *Criminology* 31 (1993): 263–279.

123. See DHHS, *Youth Violence*, p. 101.

124. Ibid., p. 102. See also Elliott, "Editor's Introduction," p. xi.
125. DHHS, *Youth Violence*, p. 102.
126. Such programs are described in M. J. Chandler, "Egocentrism and Antisocial Behavior: The Assessment and Training of Social Perspective-Taking Skills," *Developmental Psychology* 9 (1993): 326–332. The high marks for specific interventions of this kind are consistent with more general findings in the meta-analyses conducted by Lipsey and Andrews. See DHHS, *Youth Violence*, p. 115; Lipsey, "Can Intervention Rehabilitate?"; D. A. Andrews et al., "Does Correctional Treatment Work? A Clinically Relevant and Psychologically Informed Meta-Analysis," *Criminology* 28 (1990): 369–404.
127. These included three interventions that the Surgeon General's report was willing to endorse as "model" programs: functional family therapy, multisystemic therapy, and multidimensional treatment foster care. DHHS, *Youth Violence*, pp. 115–117. These programs are discussed in depth in Delbert S. Elliott, ed., *Blueprints for Violence Prevention, Book Three: Functional Family Therapy* (Boulder, Colo.: Center for the Study and Prevention of Violence, 1998); Richard A. Mendel, *Less Hype, More Help: Reducing Juvenile Crime, What Works—What Doesn't* (Washington, D.C.: American Youth Policy Forum, 2000); Delbert S. Elliott, ed., *Blueprints for Violence Prevention, Book Six: Multisystemic Therapy* (Boulder, Colo.: Center for the Study and Prevention of Violence, 1998); Elliott, ed., *Blueprints for Violence Prevention, Book Eight: Multidimensional Treatment Foster Care* (Boulder, Colo.: Center for the Study and Prevention of Violence, 1998); and T. N. Thornton et al., *Best Practices of Youth Violence Prevention: A Sourcebook for Community Action* (Atlanta, Ga.: Centers for Disease Control and Prevention, 2000).
128. For more information, see OJP, *Preventing Crime;* Center for the Study and Prevention of Violence, *CSPV Blueprints Promising Fact Sheet: Intensive Protective Supervision Project* (Boulder, Colo.: Center for the Study and Prevention of Violence, 1999).
129. DHHS, *Youth Violence*, p. 131.
130. See Elliott, "Editor's Introduction," p. xiv.
131. Ibid.
132. Greenwood et al., *Diverting Children*, p. xiii.
133. See Elliott, "Editor's Introduction," p. xvi.
134. One theory extant in the social science literature is that high-risk clients subjected to rehabilitative programming are more likely to benefit from treatment, and to benefit more, than lower-risk clients. There is limited empirical support for this proposition, however. See Gerald G. Gaes et al., "Adult Correctional Treatment," in Michael Tonry and Joan Petersilia, eds., *Crime and Justice: A Review of Research*, vol. 26 (Chicago: University of Chicago Press, 1999), p. 364.
135. See Norval Morris and Marc Miller, "Predictions of Dangerousness," in Mi-

chael Tonry and Norval Morris, eds., *Crime and Justice: An Annual Review of Research*, vol. 6 (Chicago: University of Chicago Press, 1985), pp. 1–50.

136. Mark W. Lipsey and James H. Derzon, "Predictors of Violent or Serious Delinquency in Adolescence and Early Adulthood: A Synthesis of Longitudinal Research," in Loeber and Farrington, *Serious and Violent Juvenile Offenders*, pp. 86–105.

137. See Nigel Walker, *Why Punish? Theories of Punishment Reassessed* (New York: Oxford University Press, 1991), pp. 57–58.

138. Schlossman, *Love and the American Delinquent*, pp. 67–69.

139. Zimring, "Common Thread."

140. See Zimring, *American Youth Violence*, pp. 74–81; Morse, "Immaturity and Irresponsibility."

141. See Steven D. Levitt, *Juvenile Crime and Punishment* (Chicago: American Bar Foundation, 1997).

142. See Michael Tonry, "Rethinking Unthinkable Punishment Policies in America," *U.C.L.A. Law Review* 46 (1999): 1759–1763.

Index

ADAM. *See* Arrestee Drug Abuse
Monitoring Program
African Americans: attitudes toward police/
courts among, 7, 55; lynching of, 13–14,
26, 28; poverty among, 17, 37, 218–219;
state-authorized death sentences for, 28,
69; as victims of crime, 28–29, 34, 35–36,
37, 103–104, 146–147, 168, 170, 257–258,
300n125, 301n132, 353n39; juvenile
offenders among, 93, 215–216, 218–219,
257–258, 266–269, 286; and drug crimes,
208–209, 215–216, 218–219, 222, 233–
235; street culture among, 219, 221. *See
also* Racial and ethnic disparities
Aggressive order maintenance, 3, 137, 140–
143, 145–146, 149, 156–157, 164, 287,
335n171
AIDS, 246
Alcoholics Anonymous (AA), 214
Alcohol treatment programs, 207, 214, 217,
223–224, 226, 248
Alcohol use, 6, 64, 223–226; drunk driving,
59, 181, 207, 211–212, 225; public
drunkenness, 71, 157, 207, 292n5; deaths
related to, 181, 213, 214, 224–225;
Prohibition, 182, 206, 207, 210–211, 241;
vs. tobacco use, 206, 210, 214; vs. drug
use, 206, 210–214, 216, 224–225, 228,
238, 240–241, 245, 246, 247–248, 249,
285; relationship to crime, 206, 211–212,
223–226; government regulation of, 207;
minimum age for, 207, 210; education
programs regarding, 207, 213–214, 226,
248; treatment programs for, 207, 214,

217, 223–224, 226, 248; and
incarceration, 211–212, 225; alcohol
dependence, 214; level of, 214, 223–224
Allen, Francis, 84
Alschuler, Albert, 84–85
American Bar Association, 108, 126, 159
American Indians, 32, 93, 266
American Law Institute, 108
Amphetamines, 210
Andean Counterdrug Initiative, 226
Anderson, Elijah, 37, 218, 219, 221
Anslinger, Harry, 208
Antiterrorism and Effective Death Penalty
Act of 1996, 311n12
Appeals, criminal, 9, 69
Arizona, 95, 110–111
Arlington, Tex., 122
Arrestee Drug Abuse Monitoring Program
(ADAM), 219–220, 224, 231–232
Ashworth, Andrew, 62–63
Asians, 266
Assault, aggravated, 7, 17, 42, 109–110;
definition of, 33, 97; blacks vs. whites
regarding commission of, 33–34, 35,
267–268; increase in, 74, 75, 99, 136, 195;
relationship to homicide, 75–76, 259,
353n41; involving guns, 168, 169, 171–
172, 179, 180, 199–200, 255; relationship
to drug use, 221, 223; and alcohol use,
224; by juveniles, 254, 255, 257, 264
Assault, simple, 97, 109–110, 224
ATF. *See* Bureau of Alcohol, Tobacco, and
Firearms
Atlanta, 42

361

Harvard University Press is a member of Green Press Initiative
(greenpressinitiative.org), a nonprofit organization working to
help publishers and printers increase their use of recycled paper
and decrease their use of fiber derived from endangered forests.
This book was printed on recycled paper containing 30%
post-consumer waste and processed chlorine free.